THE
TOURIST
BUSINESS

2005

THE TOURIST BUSINESS

SIXTH EDITION

DONALD E. LUNDBERG, PH.D.

**DEAN, SCHOOL OF HOSPITALITY MANAGEMENT
UNITED STATES INTERNATIONAL UNIVERSITY
SAN DIEGO, CALIFORNIA, AND BUSHEY, ENGLAND**

VNR VAN NOSTRAND REINHOLD
————————— New York

Library of Congress Catalog Card Number   89-31189
ISBN 0-442-23376-0

Printed in the United States of America

Production supervision by
Editorial Services of New England, Inc.

Van Nostrand Reinhold
115 Fifth Avenue
New York, New York 10003

Van Nostrand Reinhold International Company Limited
11 New Fetter Lane
London EC4P 4EE, England

Van Nostrand Reinhold
480 La Trobe Street
Melbourne, Victoria 3000, Australia

Nelson Canada
1120 Birchmount Road
Scarborough, Ontario M1K 5G4, Canada

16 15 14 13 12 11 10 9 8 7 6 5 4 3 2 1

Library of Congress Cataloging in Publication Data

Lundberg, Donald E., 1916–
    The tourist business / Donald E. Lundberg — 6th ed.
        p.   cm.
    Bibliography: p.
    Includes index.
    ISBN 0-442-23376-0
    1. Tourist trade.   I. Title.
    G155.A1LB   1990
    380.1'459104 — dc20   89-31189
                                                         CIP

CONTENTS

PREFACE

This book is intended to be an interesting and informative overview of a developing, dynamic field serving the business and pleasure traveler. The tourist business is a loosely defined field, adjunctive and allied to the hotel/restaurant business, with both fields interfacing and complementary. There are two audiences: those who are directly interested in a travel career as a travel agent, airline person, tour operator, car rental person, or related travel marketer; and hotel/restaurant students who need to know the travel business as adjunctive to and part of the hospitality field.

Travel/tourism is being aggressively defined to include areas already claimed by other businesses. So be it. The definition will probably continue to expand. Witness the claims that travel/tourism is or soon will be the world's largest business, exceeding even the defense industry, manufacturing, the oil industry, and agriculture. The inclusive travel/tourism definition does serve a useful purpose: it announces that many seemingly separate businesses in reality have a common purpose: better serving the traveling public to make the total travel experience more pleasant, more convenient, less expensive, and safer. If, along the way, travel reduces animosities, overcomes cultural differences, and encourages cooperation, then so much the better. "World peace and understanding through education and travel" creates a win-win exchange between host and visitor.

This book builds on the fifth edition of *The Tourist Business*, updates information, briefly traces travel/tourism historically, and adds a chapter—Travel and Cultural Geography—that has been requested by students.

ACKNOWLEDGMENTS

My appreciation goes to the faculty and staff of the School of Travel Industry Management, University of Hawaii, where as a visiting professor I was encouraged to write a tourism textbook, and to the hundreds of students taking my travel management courses, who have made valuable suggestions for text material.

Government travel offices, particularly the Hawaiian Visitors Bureau and Travel Canada, have been very responsive to requests for information. Current travel/tourism statistics have been made readily available by Somerset Waters in his annual publication, *Travel Industry World Yearbook*. Guest lecturers and others have been generous in providing information and insights.

I am grateful to Jane Libby, the developmental editor of this book. Finally, my gratitude goes to all others who have made this book possible.

ONE

INTRODUCTION

WHAT IS TOURISM/TRAVEL?

Definitions

Who are the travelers and the tourists? Webster's New Collegiate Dictionary defines a tourist as "one that makes a tour for pleasure or culture." A nineteenth-century dictionary had a more interesting definition: "people who travel for the pleasure of traveling, out of curiosity, and because they have nothing better to do," and even, "for the joy of boasting about it afterwards."[1]

Nineteenth-century novelist Henry James, on the other hand, described tourists as "vulgar, vulgar, vulgar," a sentiment that seems to be echoed in the change from "tourist class" to "Economy class" on airlines. Tourism, says a National Tourism Policy Report, is synonymous with travel.[2] The term *tourism* now includes business travel as well as travel for pleasure. For more precise definitions, see Figure 1-1, Classification of Travelers.

---

1. Gilbert Sigaux, "The History of Tourism," *Dictionnaire Universel du XIXe Siècle*. Geneva, Switzerland: Edito Service Ltd., 1876. The definition undoubtedly still applies to some tourists.
2. *National Tourism Policy Study Final Report*, United States Government Printing Office, Washington, D.C.: 1978.

Travel Statistics

Imprecise definitions result in imprecise statistics. Border crossings are not to be confused with *bona fide* tourist visits. Some 23 million border crossings occur each year at places between San Ysidro, near San Diego, and Tijuana, Mexico, yet the number of visitors to all of Mexico who are classified as tourists is under 6 million. Some governments, the State of Hawaii for example, try to avoid some of the problems of definition by substituting the word *visitor* for *tourist*.

The terms *international*, *overseas*, and *going abroad* need precise definition, and travel researchers are careful to spell out what is meant when they are used. Presently an international traveler may be anyone who crosses a national border—or it may be a tourist who sleeps at least 24 hours in a foreign country. To go abroad, a traveler must cross an ocean.

The air traveler, of course, differs widely around the world. In less developed areas, travelers on airplanes include pigs and chickens as well as men, women, and children. American Airlines identifies its United States passengers as typically being business people between the ages of thirty-five and fifty. They are likely to be well educated and married, with two or more children between the ages of two and fifteen.

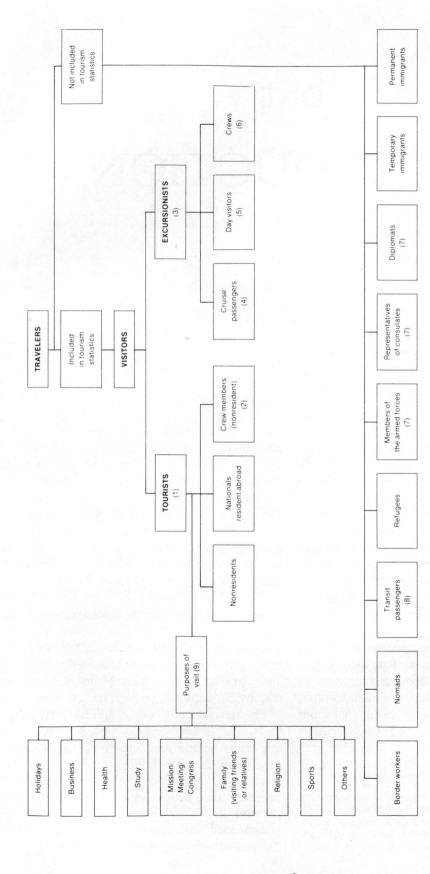

Notes:
(1) Visitors who spend at least one night in the country visited.
(2) Foreign air or ship crews docked or in layover and who used the accommodation establishments of the country visited.
(3) Visitors who do not spend at least one night in the country visited although they may visit the country during one day or more and return to their ship or train to sleep.
(4) Normally included in excursionists. Separate classification of these visitors is nevertheless preferable.
(5) Visitors who come and leave the same day.
(6) Crews who are not residents of the country visited and who stay in the country for the day.
(7) When they travel from their country of origin to the duty station and vice-versa.
(8) Who do not leave the transit area of the airport or the port. In certain countries, transit may involve a stay of one day or more. In this case, they should be included in the visitor statistics.
(9) Main purposes of visit as defined by the Rome Conference (1963).

SOURCE: Bernard Ascher: "Obstacles to International Travel and Tourism." *Journal of Travel Research,* Winter 1984, p. 13.

1-1. Classification of travelers.

INTRODUCTION

A 1987 survey found the split between business travelers and leisure travelers within the United States to be almost equal: 52 percent leisure travelers, 48 percent business travelers.[3]

IMPORTANCE OF TOURISM

Who Spends? Who Receives?

Figure 1-2 shows the world's top tourism earners and spenders in 1986 in terms of money received from visitors and money spent by citizens on travel/tourism outside the country. Spain was the clear winner with over $12 billion intake and only $1.513 billion outgo. Italy ranked second in travel winnings. France, the United Kingdom, Austria, Switzerland, Mexico, Singapore, Greece, Portugal, Korea, Brazil, and Thailand also took in more from visitors than their nationals spent outside the country. Travel deficits were experienced by the United States, Canada, Belgium, the Netherlands, Denmark, Sweden, and Japan. The largest deficit by far was experienced by Germany, a nation of travelers who are seen as tourists around the world.

In 1987 over 40 million U.S. citizens went to foreign destinations, creating a travel deficit of $9.9 billion despite the fact the United States earns more from foreign visitors than any other country.

Travel/tourism in the United States is the top source of employment in fifteen states: Alaska, Arizona, Colorado, Florida, Hawaii, Idaho, Maine, Nevada, New Hampshire, New Jersey, New Mexico, Utah, Vermont, Virginia, and Wyoming. In cities such as Paris, London, or New York, tourism supplements and supports other industries, while it is the principal source of income in places such as the Bahamas, Barbados, the Dominican Republic, the Cayman Islands, and Bermuda. In many other places—for example, Mexico and Spain—tourism may not be the number-one

industry, but it is certainly a necessary and important number-two source of foreign exchange.

Tourism in its broadest sense generates spending exceeding $300 billion within the United States, an amount that is about 10 percent of the U.S. national product. Surprisingly, with less than 5 percent of the world's population, the United States accounts for roughly 25 percent of world spending for domestic and international travel.[4] Some thirteen million jobs are generated, either directly or indirectly, by tourism in this country.

Government Promotion

Tourism has received increasing attention from local, state, and federal government officials as a spur to a sluggish economy or as financial icing on the income cake. An array of government entities promote travel. On the national level are the national tourist offices (NTOs). In the United States the NTO is the U.S. Travel and Tourism Administration (USTA), which is part of the Department of Commerce. All states have state travel offices, which go under different titles. Many cities advertise travel or help fund travel promotion efforts. Government money is usually a big part of the budgets of convention and visitor bureaus, whose main function is to attract groups to the area served by the bureau.

The federal government sees tourism as a possible means for developing the economies of such states as Kentucky and West Virginia. The Economic Development Administration, a federal agency, has underwritten millions of dollars worth of resort developments for parks in those states and has set aside other millions to foster tourism on Indian lands. States such as Nevada, Colorado, Wyoming, Arizona, and Florida, where tourism is the major industry, are well aware of the value of the tourist dollar.

Many areas turn to tourism as the only realistic way of raising themselves from the poverty level. The tourist dollar, it is maintained, is more valuable to a local economy than the dollar generated

---

3. Gallup Organization for the Air Transport Association, 1987.

4. Somerset R. Waters, *Travel Industry World Yearbook. The Big Picture—1988.* New York: Child and Waters, 1988.

1-2. World's top tourism earners and spenders, 1986

Country	International Tourism Records (Million US $)	Rank	International Tourist Arrivals (Thousands)	Rank	International Tourism Expenditures (Million US $)	Rank	Percentage Change (1980–1986) Receipts	Percentage Change (1980–1986) Arrivals	Percentage Change (1980–1986) Expenditures	Share of the World (in percent) Receipts	Share of the World (in percent) Arrivals
United States	12,927	1	22,004	4	17,789	2	28.5	-2.2	-71.3	10.1	6.5
Spain	12,058	2	29,910	2	1,513	17	73.0	27.8	23.1	9.4	8.9
Italy	9,855	3	24,672	3	2,758	12	20.0	11.7	44.6	7.7	7.3
France	9,704	4	36,080	1	6,504	5	17.6	19.9	7.9	7.6	10.7
United Kingdom	7,921	5	13,776	7	8,686	3	14.9	10.9	-9.3	6.2	4.1
Germany (F.R.)	7,826	6	12,217	8	20,663	1	19.2	9.9	0.3	6.1	3.6
Austria	6,076	7	15,096	6	3,257	9	-5.7	8.8	14.4	4.8	4.5
Switzerland	4,227	8	11,400	9	3,368	8	34.2	3.2	42.9	3.3	3.4
Canada	3,860	9	15,660	5	4,294	7	69.0	21.6	37.6	3.0	4.6
Mexico	2,984	10	4,625	16	2,132	14	-19.9	11.6	104.2	2.3	1.4
Belgium	2,271	11	7,000	14	2,889	10	25.5	4.5	-11.7	1.8	2.1
Hong Kong	2,211	12	3,733	18	—	—	32.1	113.0	—	1.7	1.1
Netherlands	1,900	13	3,142	19	4,427	6	13.9	19.6	-5.1	1.5	0.9
Singapore	1,842	14	2,902	21	652	22	28.5	13.3	102.5	1.4	0.9
Greece	1,834	15	7,025	13	494	25	5.8	46.5	160.0	1.4	2.1
Denmark	1,759	16	4,423	17	2,119	15	31.6	25.2	35.8	1.4	1.3
Portugal	1,574	17	5,409	15	332	28	37.2	98.1	14.5	1.2	1.6
Korea (Rep. of)	1,550	18	1,659	29	613	23	320.0	70.0	75.7	1.2	0.5
Sweden	1,540	19	824	38	2,811	11	60.0	32.0	25.8	1.2	0.2
China	1,530	20	9,000	11	—	—	175.7	294.6	—	1.2	2.7
Brazil	1,527	21	1,934	26	1,464	18	-14.9	52.2	26.2	1.2	0.6
Japan	1,463	22	1,842	28	7,229	4	114.1	127.2	57.4	1.1	0.5
Thailand	1,421	23	2,818	22	296	30	63.9	52.6	21.3	1.1	0.8

Source: World Travel Organization.

4

and spent within the economy. Much of the tourist dollar goes to pay for services by people who are involved both in constructing and operating vacation facilities. Tourist money is brought in fresh; it is money from outside the economy that triggers several rounds of additional spending.

Interconnecting Businesses

Travel/tourism is a complex of interrelated businesses that serve the traveling public in one way or another. Obvious travel businesses are travel retailers such as travel agents and tour operators. The airlines are directly involved. So are rental car companies, railroads, bus lines, and hotels and restaurants. As a group they are called the hospitality business. Among related businesses are financial institutions that make loans for hospitality business construction and provide credit cards for travelers.

The growth and complexity of the travel business encourages specialization. Reception services, for example, are businesses that make all arrangements—travel, accommodations, entertainment—primarily for incentive travel (groups awarded travel as a reward for sales or other accomplishment).

Figure 1-3 suggests some of the many businesses and activities that together spell travel/tourism. This book is especially interested in

1-3. The travel and tourism mix.

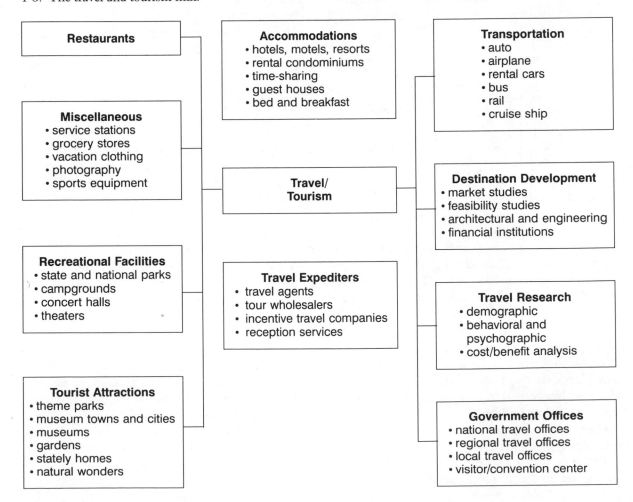

what is called the hospitality business—hotels, restaurants, travel expediters such as travel agents and tour wholesalers, and the airlines and other public carriers.

Travel marketing and destination development are closely related. Much of the hotel and restaurant business has a symbiotic relationship with airlines serving the area. The relationship is obvious for destinations such as Hawaii, Tahiti, and Fiji. The relationship is less obvious for hotels such as the Bonaventure and Biltmore in downtown Los Angeles; yet it becomes apparent when Pacific air fares are reduced and hotel occupancy in Los Angeles rises sharply. Sales volume for name restaurants near such hotels also reflects changing air fares.

Figure 1-4 can be applied to many hotels and restaurants. It shows the interdependence of three parties—travel expediters, carriers, and food and lodging vendors.

1-4. Symbiotic relationships in the travel equation		
Travel Expediters	**Public Carriers**	**Food and Lodging**
Travel agents Incentive travel agents Tour bookers Tour operators	Air Rail Bus Ship	Hotels/motels Rental condominiums Restaurants

A similar connection exists for most rental car agencies, sight-seeing services, ski resorts, and other travel-related businesses. Fare changes reflect this interdependence. A reduced air fare between New York City and Denver increases the number of skiers at Steamboat Springs and Aspen. Conversely, an increased air fare between the continental United States and Hawaii reduces the attendance at the Polynesian Village on Oahu, the number of cars rented, and the number of condominiums and hotel rooms sold. Similarly, air fares between Japan and Los Angeles affect the attendance at Disneyland.

Other factors, of course, also affect the players in the travel game: promotion and advertising, government policy, general economic conditions, the value of a particular currency, the relations between the governments of two countries, the appeal of competing destinations, the safety of a destination, and its general reputation.

Restaurant operators often overlook the relationship between tourism and eating out, but consider just expenditures by foreign visitors: In 1987 approximately 28.5 million foreigners visited our country. Excluding air fare, these foreign tourists spent more money on food than on any other travel expense.

Business Travel

Business trips accounted for about one quarter of all U.S. trips in 1987, up by more than an estimated 50 percent between 1982–87. (U.S. Travel Data Centers, Seacaucus, NJ).

Airlines, hotels/restaurants, and car rental companies court business travelers, and for good reasons. There are a lot of them, and the number grows.

Business travel is tax deductible and considered a necessary expense of doing business. The business traveler often travels on short notice and cannot take advantage of advance-purchase or discounted airline fares. Many business travelers are "frequent fliers" and are especially sought after by the airlines. Most in-city hotels are especially built and operated to cater to business travelers, who may comprise 80 percent or more of the guests Monday through Friday.

While no one can be sure how total travel breaks down into travel for business purposes as compared to travel for pleasure, a 1987 study reports that 35 million people took 158 million business trips in the U.S. and spent 820 million nights away from home (Hyatt Travel Futures Project, Research and Forecasts, Inc., New York, 1988). One third of these trips involved an element of leisure. In addition, the report says that 29 million business travelers— 83 percent of the total—stayed in hotels. Another study estimates that business travelers spent $75 billion on their trips (U.S. Travel Data Center, Seacaucus, NJ). More than half of that $75 billion was spent with airlines; 21 percent was spent for hotels; and the remainder was evenly divided between meals/entertainment and expenditure for auto travel.

Business trips can be stressful because of traffic jams, delays at airports, long lines at hotel check-in, canceled meetings, and "dead time," unavoidable waiting. There were also feelings of anonymity and aloneness. The Hyatt study, however, also found that business travel can create positive feelings of purpose and excitement as well as feelings of power and accomplishment. Many travelers were ambivalent toward travel indicating a love-hate relationship for the travel experience. They enjoyed the break from routine and the exposure to new people and places.

WHERE DO AMERICANS TRAVEL?

U.S. Vacation Spots

We tend to think of vacation spots as beaches, mountains, and forests, yet the greatest number of vacations take place in our major cities. *U.S. News and World Report* projected that for the year 1988, 31 percent of vacations would be spent in cities, 26 percent at the oceanside, 5 percent at lakes, 6 percent in national parks, 10 percent in the mountains, and 22 percent in a small rural town.[5] The same magazine collected estimates of the number of visitors reported by tourist bureaus of the large cities. California cities reported the most visitors, followed by Atlantic City, Washington, D.C., and New York City. Figure 1-5 gives the numbers for 23 cities.

Travel within the United States—that is, domestic travel—increases year after year. Over 592 million trips were taken in 1986 according to the U.S. Travel Data Center. More trips are taken to visit friends and relatives than for other purposes. Pleasure trips are next in number, followed by trips for business or conventions. As Figure 1-6 shows, autos or trucks and recreation vehicles carried the bulk of travelers. Travel by air, however, continues to grow.

5. *U.S. News & World Report*, June 13, 1988, p. 71.

Travel Abroad

Mass travel/tourism, as we know it today, did not begin until after World War II when superhighways, the commercial jet, and disposable income

1-5. Number of visitors to cities in the United States	
Los Angeles	49.3 Mil.
Anaheim-Orange County	35.3 Mil.
San Diego	32.0 Mil.
Atlantic City	31.8 Mil.
Washington, D.C.	19.0 Mil.
New York City	17.8 Mil.
Las Vegas	16.2 Mil.
San Francisco	12.8 Mil.
Atlanta	12.5 Mil.
Dallas	12.0 Mil.
Minneapolis–St. Paul	11.0 Mil.
Niagara Falls	10.0 Mil.
Orlando	10.0 Mil.
Boston	8.6 Mil.
Philadelphia	7.5 Mil.
Baltimore	7.3 Mil.
Nashville	7.1 Mil.
Chicago	7.0 Mil.
Houston	6.9 Mil.
Reno	6.8 Mil.
Miami	6.7 Mil.
St. Louis	6.5 Mil.
New Orleans	6 Mil.

SOURCE: *U.S. News and World Report*, June 13, 1988, p. 71.

1-6. Number of U.S. resident's trips and person-trips by major trip characteristics (to places 100 miles or more from home), 1986		
Trip Characteristics	Trips (millions)	Person-Trips (millions)
All trips	592.3	1,121.5
Purpose of trip	214.9	442.5
Visit friends or relatives		
Other Pleasure	200.3	418.9
Business/convention	140.0	189.0
Mode of transport	405.6	832.1
Auto/truck/RV		
Air	143.4	231.0
Vacation trip	354.3	752.4
Weekend trip	252.0	513.5
Type of lodging	464.3	483.2
Hotel/motel		

SOURCE: U.S. Travel Data Center.

made it possible for tens of millions of people in this country and other industrialized nations to hit the road and take to the skies. Figure 1-7 shows the amazing growth of international travel between 1950 and 1987. From a little over 25 million international tourists in 1950 the number shot up to some 355 million in 1987.

Nearly half the Americans who go overseas visit Western Europe (49 percent); 21 percent travel to the Caribbean region; 18 percent to the Far East. The United Kingdom is the most popular European destination, followed by France and West Germany. Armed forces personnel undoubtedly contribute to the large numbers visiting West Germany. Figure 1-9 shows what many American travelers have seen when traveling overseas: New York is the origin of 13 percent of U.S. residents traveling overseas. Los Angeles, the origin of 5 percent of overseas travelers, is a distant second. The average overseas traveler was on a trip for almost three weeks and spent about $1000 while overseas.

In 1987 some 40 million U.S. residents traveled abroad, more than half of them to Canada and Mexico, as shown in Figure 1-10.

VISITORS TO THE UNITED STATES

Figure 1-11 shows the countries of origin of foreign arrivals in 1987. Sharing our northern border, Canada is number one in providing visitors who spend one or more nights in the United States. Our southern neighbor, Mexico, is number two.

Travel flows change continuously and are dependent upon such things as exchange rates, political factors, and business conditions. The most dramatic changes in travel flows have resulted from the affluence and business power of the Japanese. Until about 1980 their travel propensity was low. In 1987, the Japanese became number one in overseas foreign arrivals to the United States, edging out visitors from the United Kingdom. Their favorite destination: Hawaii.

PROSPECTS FOR FUTURE TRAVEL

Trends That Favor Travel

Positive factors that favor the acceleration of travel include the following:

1. *Rising disposable incomes (money that can be spent for other than necessities)*. Overall, more money means more travel. More than half of the women over the age of eighteen in the United States are working outside the home; the two-income family is widespread and growing. In coming years between 25 and 50 percent of all business travel will be done by women. Moreover, the world

1-7. World tourism growth, 1950–1987		
Years	International Tourist Arrivals (thousands)	International Tourism Receipts[1] (million US$)
1950	25,282	2,100
1960	69,296	6,867
1961	75,281	7,284
1962	81,329	8,029
1963	89,999	8,887
1964	104,506	10,073
1965	112,729	11,604
1966	119,797	13,340
1967	129,529	14,458
1968	130,899	14,990
1969	143,140	16,800
1970	159,690	17,900
1971	172,239	20,850
1972	181,851	24,621
1973	190,622	31,054
1974	197,117	33,822
1975	214,357	40,702
1976	220,719	44,436
1977	239,122	55,631
1978	257,366	68,837
1979	273,999	83,332
1980	284,841	102,363(r)
1981	285,058	101,684(r)
1982	286,727(r)	98,420(r)
1983	292,441(r)	98,155(r)
1984	319,035(r)	102,811(r)
1985	332,941(r)	108,110(r)
1986	341,534(r)	129,182(r)
1987	355,000(p)	150,000(p)

[1]Excluding international fare receipts
(r) Revised figures
(p) Preliminary
SOURCE: World Travel Organization.

1-8. South Island in New Zealand rivals Switzerland in majestic beauty. Mitre Peak on Milford sound is one of New Zealand's major tourist attractions.

is experiencing a redistribution of income. Countries such as Norway suddenly find themselves rich from oil and gas. Segments of the population in the Arab oil-producing nations receive incredible incomes, making them the world's biggest spenders. The World Bank pours billions into less developed countries, and much of the money finds its way to people who can then travel at will.

2. *Increased numbers of retired persons.* They have the wherewithal, the desire, and the energy to travel. In the United States, persons over sixty-five constitute more than 11 percent of the population. Life expectancy continues to rise, albeit slowly. Fewer deaths occur from heart diseases and strokes as concern for diet and health grows. More people engage in planned exercise—cycling, jogging, tennis, snow and water skiing, exercise classes, and the like.

Transportation discounts for senior citizens are widespread in Europe and are growing in the United States as Americans get progressively grayer. The median age in 1981 was thirty years. In the year 2000 it will be thirty-five. (Compare this figure to several of the less developed countries, where more than half the population is under fifteen.)

3. *Greater mobility.* People become accustomed to making moves required by their careers and to traveling in general.

4. *Greater discretionary time.* In the future people will enjoy shorter work weeks and longer vacations. The work week has shrunk considerably since the turn of the century, from fifty or sixty hours to less than forty hours. Flextime programs permit a three- or four-day work week. Some European governments mandate paid vacations for all workers.

5. *Smaller families and changing roles.* American and European birthrates have declined sharply, giving the adults more free time away from family responsibilities. Sexual equality and shifts in household roles and composition favor more travel.

1-9. Profile of U.S. residents to overseas destinations, 1986

Category	Percent of Total Overseas Visitors	Category	Percent of Total Overseas Visitors
Residence		**Sex and age of visitors**	
New York	18	Children under 18	4
New York City	13	Male adults	57
California	15	Female adults	38
Los Angeles	5	Avg. age of male adults (years)	44.5
San Francisco	3	Avg. age of female adults (years)	42.5
Texas	6	**Occupation of visitors**	
New Jersey	6	Manager, executive	28
Illinois	5	Professional, technical	33
Florida	5	Clerical, sales	6
Connecticut	4	Craftsman, mechanic	3
Pennsylvania	3	Government military	4
Massachusetts	3	Homemaker	10
Minnesota	3	Student	5
Washington	3	Retired	9
Purpose of trip[1]		Airline employee	2
Business	34	Other	1
Attend convention	5	**Annual family income**	
Vacation, holiday	57	Average	$55,519
Visit friends	10	Median	$57,496
Visit relatives	20	**Types of accommodations[1]**	
Study	2	Hotel, motel	77
Other	2	Private home	34
Foreign trip expense		Other	9
First-time visitors	9	**Number of countries visited**	
Repeat visitors	91	One country	68
Means of booking air trip		Two countries	18
Travel agent	73	Three or more countries	14
Self	13	Average (countries)	1.6
Company travel department	9	Median (countries)	1.0
Travel club	2	**Main overseas destinations visited**	
Other	4	Western Europe	49
Information sources[1]		France	12
Airline	21	Germany, West	12
Travel agency	64	Italy	7
U.S. government	7	Switzerland	5
Company travel dept.	11	United Kingdom	24
Friends, relatives	26	Eastern Europe	1
Newspapers, magazines	11	Caribbean	21
Published sources	16	Bermuda	4
Other	2	Dominican Republic	3
Type of airline ticket		South America	6
First class	8	Central America	3
Executive business	15	Oceania	5
Economy, tourist	74	Australia	3
Other	4	Far East	18
Use of prepaid package/inclusive tour		Hong Kong	7
Yes	23	Japan	2
No (independent)	77	Africa	2
Type and size of traveling party		**Nights outside the U.S.**	
Traveling alone	36	Average (nights)	20.6
Family group	44	Median	12.0
Business group	9	**Average non-U.S. expenditures**	
Mixed bus., family, other	12	Per traveler	$ 1,022
Avg. party size (persons)	1.6	Per traveler per day	$ 49
Median party size (persons)	1.0		

[1]Multiple responses tabulated.

Source: U.S. Dept. of Commerce—USTTA.

1-10. U.S. citizen departures, 1987[1]

Destination	Departures
Canada	13,245
Mexico	13,500
Overseas	13,800
Europe	6,200
South America	780
Central America	470
Caribbean	3,850
Asia/Middle East	1,960
Africa	40
Total	**40,545**

[1]Estimate
SOURCE: U.S. Travel and Tourism Administration.

6. *A high divorce rate and many singles*. People living alone have more discretionary time than couples, and many want to socialize via travel.
7. *Smaller living space*. Higher costs of homebuilding increase apartment and condominium living. Smaller living spaces stimulate the need to "get away from it all."

1-11. Foreign arrivals in U.S., 1987[1]

Origin	Arrivals (in thousands)
Canada	12,410
Mexico	5,935
Overseas	10,505
Europe	4,705
U.K.	1,365
Germany	970
France	555
Italy	330
Switzerland	240
Netherlands	205
South America	940
Central America	330
Caribbean	920
Asia	2,765
Japan	2,160
Middle East	305
Africa	125
Oceania	415
Australia	270
Total	**28,850**

[1]Estimates
SOURCE: U.S. Travel and Tourism Administration.

8. *Growth of multinational businesses*. Worldwide business interests increase both the need and habit of travel.
9. *Greater credit availability*. Charge cards and bank loans provide credit for tourists. "Travel now, pay later" stimulates travel.
10. *Growth in government security programs*. Disability plans, pensions, and social security make people less concerned with saving for the future. In Holland, 15 percent of the working-age group receive disability payments equal to 80 percent of what they would earn if working.
11. *Increased education*. As millions more attend colleges and universities, they tend to think more in global terms and become interested in foreign cultures. Moreover, if the forecast is true that millions of "overeducated" college graduates will be forced to take blue-collar jobs, some of their ambitions and talents may be underutilized. Travel could become an outlet for their frustrated lifestyles.
12. *Growth of cities*. At the beginning of the century only 15 percent of the world's population lived in cities. In 1980 that percentage had risen to 41 percent. Most cities are growing. In 1950 the world's giant cities of 5 million-plus population were home for 47 million. By 1980 that figure had leaped to 252 million. The United Nations projects a jump to 650 million by the year 2000.

San Francisco, New York, Paris, London, and Vienna have been tourist centers for a long time. Other large cities have far less visitor appeal. Mexico City, for example, is a city where congestion and pollution tend to override cultural and entertainment appeal. That city, with an estimated population of 20 million, is said to have 6,000 tons of gas and soot strangling it daily. Breathing the air is like smoking two packs of cigarettes a day, and average traffic speed is only half of that in London or Paris.

Business travel to the megalopolises will probably increase but pleasure travel may decrease. What is important is that urban dwellers travel more than do people living in rural areas. Figure 1-12 is a United Nations projection of populations of the world's largest cities for the year 2000.
13. *Travel simplification—the package tour*. Travel packaging has been significant in the industry since Thomas Cook shepherded his tour groups around England and later around much of Europe

1-12. United Nations projection of megalopolis populations for the year 2000			
Mexico City	31 million	Beijing (Peking)	20 million
São Paulo	26 million		
Tokyo/ Yokohama	24 million	Rio de Janeiro	19 million
Shanghai	23 million	Jakarta	17 million
New York/ New Jersey	23 million	Calcutta	17 million

and the Middle East. Package tours cover the travel spectrum, from the around-the-world tour to the overnight gambling junket from New York to Atlantic City. Tour packages in which everything is planned, arranged, and included in one price—are usually more important to the older traveler, the new, inexperienced traveler, and the less sophisticated traveler.

What would you like in a package trip? A scuba-diving package to the Cayman Islands; a golf package to Oceania; a fishing package to Ireland; a gaming package to Reno; an island hopper package to the South Pacific; a honeymoon package from Tokyo to Honolulu? All these package trips and more are available.

14. *Shift in values.* Social scientists say that a shift in values is taking place. Possession of such things as expensive cars, houses, clothes, and jewels has less appeal than it had in the past. For many people, doing something, "being there," taking part in something has assumed more importance than the material possessions they have. Millionaires may live in relatively modest condos, wear blue jeans, and drive older cars. The luster of travel, however, shines ever brighter. "Conspicuous culture" may be part of the motivation for travel. The widely traveled person may be showing off his or her travel experiences.

15. *Interest in new places.* Television and movies enlarge the travel perspective. The world comes into the living room via television: romance in Vienna, international intrigue in Paris, a documentary of a distant land such as the Galápagos or Antarctica can create interest in places never before considered as travel destinations.

Trends That Inhibit Travel

This rosy scenario of future travel may not come true. Travel inhibitors are also at work. Economic uncertainty, recession, political unrest, and excessive labor costs in public transportation are obvious inhibitors over which travel managers have no control. Also real income may not increase much as we pay for the excesses of the past.

Negative factors that the tourist business does have some control over relate to such "travel hassles" as baggage problems, delays, overbooking, and jammed airport terminals. Lack of security in public places, hotels, and travel centers may cause people to prefer remaining in the security of neighborhood and home. Areas may acquire the reputation of being dangerous and thus become less desirable travel destinations, as has happened in Honolulu, the Caribbean, and parts of Spain, Mexico, and Italy, where there have been sharp increases in the number of robberies and assaults.

Terrorism could become a huge travel inhibitor. Instant communication may also inhibit travel. Teleconferencing partially eliminates the need for business travel. Video phoning, when it comes, will bring people face to face by video screen without the need for them to leave their homes or offices.

Predictions

Even if the forecasters are only partially right, employment opportunities in the travel and tourism field will burgeon. Direct employment in the hotel and restaurant business in the United States numbers in the millions. Entry-level jobs are plentiful; supervisory and management jobs less so. The air transportation industry employs about 450,000 persons. Travel agencies promise to grow. The best advice for anyone interested in a travel career is to pursue it diligently, in academic preparation and in gaining practical experience at even low-paying entry-level positions. Overall the future of the industry, and of the people employed in the industry, appears bright.

INTRODUCTION

DISCUSSION QUESTIONS

1. Why are the terms *tourism* and *travel business* considered umbrella concepts?
2. Why are so many travel statistics suspect?
3. Take a position for or against this statement: "Travel and tourism should be set up as a separate discipline of study on the university level."
4. Why should persons in the hotel and restaurant business be well informed about what is happening in the travel and tourism of their area?
5. The word *tourist* is often used pejoratively. Is there any valid basis for this? Explain.
6. If you had to select three of the factors that will influence the amount of pleasure travel in the future, what would they be?
7. In what way would anthropology be useful to the study of travel and tourism?
8. The number of guest rooms in the world is estimated at between ten and eighteen million. Why is it so difficult to produce a firm figure?
9. In what ways are major theme parks such as Disneyland related to the hotel business?
10. The large majority of international travel takes place within and between North America and Western Europe. What are some factors that account for this phenomenon?
11. Americans spend by far the most on travel of any national group, yet they do not travel internationally as much as northern Europeans. What accounts for this situation?
12. What two countries receive the largest number of visitors from the United States?
13. In general, where do U.S. residents travel overseas?
14. Just what is meant by "conspicuous culture" as related to travel?
15. Give at least five reasons why travel may continue to grow domestically and worldwide.
16. Give three reasons why travel may not grow domestically and worldwide.
17. As more cities pass the million mark in population, how will travel be affected?

TWO

TRAVEL AND TOURISM HISTORY

"No sooner do you set foot upon American ground than you are stunned by a kind of tumult. Everything is in motion," stated French author Alexis de Tocqueville in 1835. Over a century has passed, yet de Tocqueville's comment is still valid. The advanced industrial nations require and thrive on mobility; business and commuter travel is required, and pleasure travel is common. Originally, tourism referred to a rather limited style of travel by people on tours and to the supporting businesses. Today the term, which has subsumed business and pleasure travel, by some definitions includes even commuter travel.

By any definition travel/tourism is a megabusiness. According to one expert, global expenditures for trips exceeding twenty-five miles from home reached $2.3 trillion in 1987, 12 percent of the world's economy. The United States accounts for roughly 25 percent of that total.[1]

Government travel estimates are much lower because they do not include commuter statistics. The multiplier effect—the effect of re-spending of current dollars in a local economy—may also be excluded. Whatever the definition, travel/tourism is among the top three industries in many econ-

omies, and it is growing. Details of the economic importance of tourism will be discussed later in this book.

The history of travel/tourism is inextricably tied to economic, technological, and social history. Technology sets the pace of travel. Each advance not only changes the speed, comfort, and cost of travel but has repercussions throughout society, changing time–space relations, economics, and relations between peoples. Figure 2-1 is a time-chart showing the major technological advances in travel mode, from stagecoach to the modern jet. Each advance has changed the way we see ourselves and the world around us.

The technology of travel determines the number and location of public accommodations. The first taverns in this country were located in port towns or on rivers connected to the Atlantic Ocean to serve people traveling by ship. With the coming of the stagecoach, taverns were built along principal roads. The railroads brought a need for hotels located near rail depots. The automobile and highway system called for tourist camps and motels. Air travel has resulted in huge complexes of hotels close by and in airports and has set the stage for a new business, that of the rental car. Destination resorts were made viable in such formerly remote areas as Canada, the Caribbean,

---

1. Somerset R. Waters, *Travel Industry Yearbook. The Big Picture—1988* (New York: Child and Waters, 1988), p. 4.

15

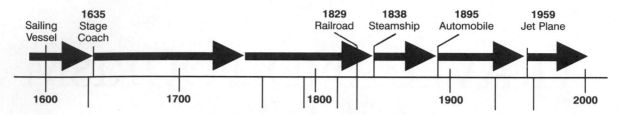

2-1. Travel is thousands of years old.

Hawaii, and the Mediterranean. The airplane makes it relatively easy for shoppers to reach London, Paris, or Dubai, or for international conferences to be held in Stockholm, Moscow, or Iceland.

People in many third world countries travel by bicycle, not by choice, but from necessity. A first impression of Beijing is of people slowly pedaling on tens of thousands of black bicycles. In Taipei, capital of Taiwan, people move on hordes of noisy motorbikes. The Dutch and Danes ride bikes from choice. Passenger traffic in much of Africa is by old trucks.

Travel as we know it today is a distinctly twentieth-century phenomenon. It has been largely shaped by the automobile and the jet plane. To be sure, travel for trade, conquest, and religious purposes dates back to antiquity. Caravans moved through the Middle East, and the early Phoenicians toured the Mediterranean as traders. Pilgrimages to sacred sites were often undertaken. War forced travel upon soldier and noncombatant alike. Nomads moved in search of pasture for their animals. Travel for pleasure was occasionally undertaken as well.

TRAVEL BEFORE MODERN TIMES

Travel is thousands of years old. As early as 3000 B.C. the ancient Egyptians were sailing up and down the Nile, carrying huge rocks with which to build pyramids as tombs for their leaders. The early Phoenicians sailed the Mediterranean from what are now the shores of Lebanon and Syria, setting up colonies and trading. About 500 B.C. the Greek city-states sailed and rowed to battle and to trade.

The Traveling Romans

By about 200 B.C. the Romans were expanding beyond Italy; over the next few hundred years they conquered much of the known world, including Britain. They traveled by ship, on horse, by chariot, and on foot. Their road system seems incredible given the level of technology at the time. By employing relays of horses, distances of 100 miles or more could be covered in a day. With paved roads, the Roman legions of 3,000 to 6,000 men and an equal number of animals could cover thirty miles a day, moving quickly to anywhere they were needed in an empire stretching from Egypt to Britain. The portion of a military road map of the Roman empire in the time of Theodosius is a kind of tour guide of the time (Figure 2-2).

Well-to-do Romans traveled to Egypt and Greece, to baths, shrines, and seaside resorts.[2] Testimony to their vacation habits are the excavated towns of Herculaneum and Pompeii, buried for centuries by lava, mud, and volcanic ash from the eruptions of nearby Mt. Vesuvius. Tabernas, snack bars and restaurants still stand partly intact for the tourist of today to view.

Roman tourists were interested in history and religion, making the rounds of Greek temples, trekking to where Alexander the Great slept, where Socrates lived, where Ajax committed suicide, where Achilles was buried. Believe it or not, they visited Egypt to see the Pyramids, the Sphinx, and the Valley of the Kings — just as modern tourists do. They flocked to tourist attractions, too.

2. Lickorish and Kershaw, *Travel Trade* (London: Practical Press, 1958), p. 21, and "A Short History of Tourism," *Travel and Tourism Encyclopedia* (London: Travel World, 1959), p. 29.

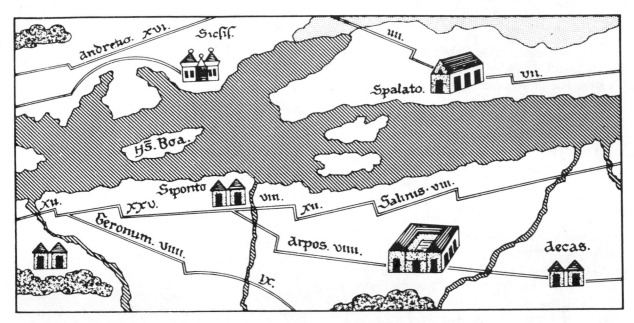

A segment of a military road map of the Roman Empire in the time of Emperor Theodosius Magnus (347–395 A.D.). The symbols on the map indicate types of accommodation:

 1. the simplest roadside accommodations suitable only for rest

 2. better accommodations than the places uninhabited

 3. better quarters for larger units but no service (no live-in slaves or local vassals)

 4. good shelter, a place for longer rest, recuperation, and refurbishing of supplies.

2-2 Artist's rendering of a military road map of the Roman Empire in the time of Emperor Theodosius Magnus (347–395 A.D.). The symbols on the map indicate types of accommodation.

SOURCE: Map privately printed in Vienna in 1753. Used here courtesy of Chef Louis Szathmary, The Bakery, Chicago, Illinois.

Up in the hills some priests had taught their sacred crocodiles to come when called and, on command, to open their jaws and show their teeth to the crowd.[3] The tourists then, like those today, also griped about the inns and the guides and scratched their names on statues.

Those who could afford to travel before the time of Christ had the Seven Wonders of the ancient world to see. A Greek guidebook from before the time of Christ listed them as the following:

1. The Great Pyramid of Khufu, the largest of the Pharaohs' tombs in Egypt, built about 2600 B.C.
2. The Hanging Gardens at Babylon, built about the same time by King Nebuchadnezzar for his bride
3. The statue of Zeus at Olympia, a 40-foot statue of the king of gods on the site of the original Olympic Games in Greece
4. The Temple of Artemis at Ephesus on the coast of what is now Turkey
5. The Mausoleum at Halicarnassus, from which we get the word *mausoleum* today
6. The Colossus at Rhodes, built in 280 B.C. at the harbor entrance of that island city in the Aegean Sea
7. A lighthouse outside of Alexandria known as the Pharos, built about 240 B.C.

---

3. Lionel Casson, "After 2000 Years Tours Have Changed But Tourists Have Not," *Smithsonian*, September 1971.

Medieval Travel

During the medieval period, travel was almost at a standstill. Travel, derived from the same Latin root as *travail*, was indeed burdensome, unpredictably dangerous, and demanding. Most of society was bound to the soil, immobile and parochial. Travel for pleasure was inconceivable for most.

Yet there was religious travel, particularly pilgrimages. Religious persuasion motivated millions to travel to shrines—Moslems to Mecca, Christians to Jerusalem and Rome, other millions to other shrines. Chaucer's *Canterbury Tales* describes a group of pilgrims traveling to the Cathedral of Canterbury in the fourteenth century. Fear and guilt motivated much of such travel; however, the sense of excitement and adventure and the desire to escape everyday routines colored the religious feelings with mundane sentiments.

The medieval church came to be the dominant medieval institution and the only authority recognized from one country to another. Monasteries and other religious houses took in travelers (and welcomed donations). Hospices, a form of inn, were operated by religious orders; guest houses were also maintained by some of these orders.

One such religious order, the Knights of St. John of Jerusalem, was founded in 1048 when a hospital was erected in Jerusalem to care for pilgrims there. Later, it became a military and religious order of considerable power and the Pope gave it the responsibility of protecting pilgrims on their way to and from Jerusalem.

Many cathedrals and monasteries made guests welcome, the rich and noble sitting with the head prelate, the poor being housed in separate quarters. There were no room rates. Often the monastery porter, whose primary function was that of gatekeeper, also managed the guest house. It might be said that the church operated the first hotel chain.

Revival of Trade and Towns

The Crusades, which began in 1095 and lasted over the next 200 years, brought about a mass movement of people. Tens of thousands of Euro-peans became familiar with the Middle East and its cultures. Although often irrational and the cause of massive suffering and death, the Crusades were also responsible for stimulating cultural exchange. The result was a great social revolution and the revival of trade that led to the rise of a middle class. Indirectly, these changes also revived innkeeping and travel.

Northern Italy was the first to feel the effects of the Renaissance that followed the Crusades. By controlling the trade between Europe and the East, the northern Italian cities made vast profits. Innkeeping there became a solid business, and guilds of innkeepers flourished, making regulations for themselves and for their guests.

In Florence, for example, there were enough innkeepers by 1282 to form a guild, a mutual-benefit society. The guild innkeepers of Florence controlled business to the extent that all strangers to the city were interviewed at the gates by city officials, who directed them to officers of the guild. These guild members then assigned foreigners to designated inns; natives of Tuscany, the local province, were assigned to other hostelries.

Travel for Education

With the Renaissance, a few prestigious universities developed, and "travel for education" was introduced, largely by the British. A few scholars went off to Oxford, Paris, Salamanca, or Bologna. Travel for education became popular in the sixteenth century. The young aristocracy, as well as members of the rising middle class, journeyed to the continent to round out their education, and perhaps to sin a little. By 1670, what was known as the Grand Tour was no light undertaking; it sometimes lasted as long as three years. Its snob appeal must have been great.

Inns and Travel by Coach

Without intending to do so, Henry VIII fostered the growth of innkeeping in England when he suppressed the monasteries in 1539. They had played a major role in travel, maintaining the

2-3. The Swan, Lavenham, England. This half-timbered inn grew from three houses built in 1425. In its early day, it had stabling for fifty horses. Here, traveling apothecaries invited sufferers of diverse diseases to come to the Inn to be cured. In 1607, John Girling, the innkeeper, issued a trader's token—a sure sign of a good reputation.
SOURCE: Courtesy of Trust House, Limited.

principal roads for pilgrims to the larger cathedrals. At hostels established adjacent to an abbey or monastery pilgrims could stay for two days, accommodated and fed according to their rank. When the church lands were given away or sold, the church's function as host to the traveler disappeared.

Another factor that favored the development of inns was the fact that, long before a national postal system was established, selected innkeepers were forced to retain stables and horses to meet the demands of the royal post.

Early stagecoaches in England, first mentioned in 1635, were huge, lumbering vehicles that crashed over the ruts of the poor roads. The trip was joyless for the riders, especially since travel began early in the morning, usually before sun-up, and lasted until late at night. Later stagecoaches were improved models with springs and seats for four travelers inside and eight or ten on top. Outside passengers were treated as a "superior race of Spartans," while the interior seats were left for "anemic spinsters and querulous invalids."

English common law early declared the inn to be a public house and made the innkeeper responsible for the well-being of travelers. The innkeeper was required to receive all travelers who presented themselves in reasonable condition and were willing to pay a reasonable price for accommodations.

2-4. The Black Swan Hotel, Helmsley, North of York, England. This inn has been added to and renovated many times in its four hundred years. The rough stone walls are more than two feet thick. For many years the Earl of Feversham held his annual Rent Dinner here, entertaining over seventy tenants. Venison from the Earl's deer park has been served here at least once a week in season.
SOURCE: Courtesy of Trust House, Limited.

Some 200 of the old coaching and posting inns in England and Wales, together with some hotels, still operate today as part of the Trust House Forte (Figures 2-3 and 2-4). Some of these inns date back more than 400 years.

The image most people are likely to have of the old English inn is that of the coaching inn, which flourished during the eighteenth and early nineteenth centuries. The coaching era in Great Britain began in earnest in 1784 when Parliament commissioned government mail delivery by coach. Until then, mail had been carried by postboys riding horseback over the poor roads of the time.

Mail coaches were easily identified by their scarlet wheels and underbody and black upper parts. At one time England and Wales had fifty-nine of the large mail coaches, each pulled by four horses; Scotland had sixteen more; and Ireland, twenty-nine. The size of the operation was indicated by the more than 30,000 men and 150,000 horses employed primarily in moving the mail.

The mail coaches carried a maximum of seven passengers: four inside and three up in front with the coachman; only the guard rode in the rear. At the height of the coaching era, seventeen mail coaches assembled each evening at the General Post Office in London. Nine others left inns in Piccadilly and the West End of London each day of the week.

The traveler paid a little more for riding in the mail coach with its security and its limitations on the number of passengers. Private stagecoach companies had their own coaches and took as many passengers as could be squeezed inside or on top of the coach. Sometimes as many as thirteen people rode in and on a coach, four inside, four up front, and five in back, with luggage piled on the roof.

A traveler with the money and the desire for prestige and privacy could ride a post chaise. This was drawn by two horses, one of which was ridden by a youngster called a postboy. Although costs for such elegant travel were twice as much as for the usual coach, many people used the post chaises. A nation-wide posting system was established, with many inns used exclusively as posting inns.

Speeding the Stagecoach

Speed was the challenge, and the coach company that could cut travel time got the business. The mail coaches averaged about ten miles an hour, and the stages or inns where the horses were changed were ten miles apart. Competition to decrease travel time was fierce. One way was to cut the time required to change horses, which was finally reduced to forty-five seconds. In 1830, the Birmingham Independent Tallyho averaged 14.5 miles per hour on the trip from London to Birmingham.

The coachmen were the athletic heroes of the day, many of them driving four horses and averaging sixty miles a day, three stages out and three stages back. Young gentlemen often bribed the coachmen to let them take the reins. So intense was the interest in driving that a few noblemen set up their own stagecoach companies to ensure their participation in the sport of driving.

The country inns were largely dependent upon the travel habits of their customers, and a large part of their business came from providing horses for the coaches. Several inns maintained as many as 50 horses; the Bow and Mouth in London kept 400 horses. Travel was still slow, however, and it required some 34 stages and 42 hours to cover 400 miles.

When the railroad appeared in England in 1825, most people were unaware of its implications for innkeeping; the innkeepers were no exception. The steam locomotive reduced travel time from London to Bath, a distance of 110 miles, from the 11 hours required by coach to only 2.5 hours. The choice of travel was obvious.

In 1838, when Parliament permitted mail to be carried by railroad, the coaching era was over. It was not until the 1900s, when the country inns were rediscovered by cyclists and later by motorists, that the beautiful inns of the countryside of England, Wales, and Scotland returned to their former prominence.

Coaching Inns in America

Coaching inns were also popular in the American colonies. The first regular stagecoach inn was established in 1760, between New York City and Philadelphia.

The Blue Anchor, on the Delaware, in what is now Philadelphia, was where William Penn first stopped on his arrival in the New World. In Colonial Williamsburg some thirty inns, taverns, and ordinaries welcomed guests. The King's Arms in Williamsburg offered a meal of some fifteen courses. Now four well-known taverns of the period have been reconstructed on their original foundations and reopened as distinctive colonial-style eating places: Christina Campbell's Tavern, the King's Arms Tavern, Chownings, and The Raleigh Tavern.

As in Britain, travel was generally rugged. Travelers were called at 3:00 a.m. and rode until 10:00 p.m. One pair of horses usually pulled the stage twelve to eighteen miles. In time as many as forty coaches were on the road between Boston and Providence at one time.

Populous sections such as Pennsylvania, where the 66-mile Lancaster Turnpike was located, had sixty taverns of varying social acceptability. Wagon drivers slept on bags of hay and oats on the taproom floor. Cattle drovers stopped at drover stands, taverns that had lots into which the livestock could be turned and fed. These taverns were also known by their signboards, which were often imaginative: "The Jolly Tar," "A Man Free of Trouble."

The word turnpike came from the practice of placing a pike or staff across the toll road. One side was embedded with spikes. When the toll was paid, the pike was turned, spikes down, so the traveler could pass. The first turnpike was built between Philadelphia and Lancaster in 1792. By 1838 Pennsylvania had 2,500 miles of turnpike.

American Taverns and Hotels

Accommodations follow travel. In the late 1820s, the state of Pennsylvania began the development of what eventually became 1,200 miles of canals. Canal taverns sprang up every ten or twelve miles.

New York State also developed a fairly extensive canal system with taverns, and later hotels, edging the canals.

Many New England villages and towns today contain taverns that date to Colonial times. Most of these old taverns were constructed as large homes to be used by the tavernkeeper and his family as well as guests. The early furnishings and equipment of some old taverns have been preserved. For example, in Old Deerfield, Massachusetts, the Hall Tavern has a long table for guests set with *treen*, the name for wooden dishes, hornspoons, and cups. The barroom stands ready to serve the traveler. One can almost hear the tavernkeeper calling out, "Mind your p's and q's (pints and quarts)!" to permit another round of drinks before closing time.

The Tremont House in Boston, opened in 1829, is generally credited with being the first hotel designed from cellar to eaves as a hotel, complete with hotel clerk, bellboys, room keys for guests, and inside water closets. It set the design for American hotels for many years. City hotels built to serve the railroads were usually located near the railway station. The railroads also spurred the resort business, and resort properties were built in Vermont, New Hampshire, and Maine. Henry Morrison Flagler, who had been treasurer of Rockefeller's Standard Oil Company, built the first luxury hotel in Florida, the Ponce de Leon, in St. Augustine in 1887. Way out west, on Coronado Island across the bay from San Diego, the Hotel Del Coronado was built in 1888; it is still a leading resort property.

Nearly every community of any size had to have at least one hotel as a matter of economic growth and civic pride. In Europe luxury hotel-keeping is associated with Caesar Ritz who from about 1870 to 1907 created the Ritz Hotels, most of which were licensed to operate under the Ritz name. Ellsworth Statler was the first American hotel tycoon. By 1907 this small dynamo of a man had recognized the value of the mass travel market, at that time the traveling businessman and salesman. The Statler Hotels changed hotel-keeping. The Buffalo Statler provided "a room and a bath at a dollar and a half." The modern hotel chain was born. By the 1930s the Sheraton and Hilton chains had laid the basis for hotel chain operation, which today controls 80 percent of the hotel rooms of the country. During the 1930s the big names in hotel-keeping were Conrad Hilton (the Hilton Hotels) and Ernest Henderson (the Sheraton Hotels). Later, motels were built by the thousands. The current hotel/motel scene is discussed in Chapter 5.

Health Resorts Attract Tourists

Travel for health became important about the end of the seventeenth century. At first, only those with *bona fide* illness went to the spas, named after a small Belgian village, to drink or bathe in the horrible smelling waters. By the 1750s, "taking the waters" (really, in many cases to "dry out") became a social necessity.

Tunbridge Wells in Kent (not far from London) gained importance as a spa in the 1660s. King Charles II transferred his court there from time to time. During the reign of Queen Anne, ladies and gentlemen were carried to the baths in sedan chairs and with the greatest of decorum immersed themselves in the so-called healing waters.[4]

After entertainment was added, dozens of watering spots became, in effect, resort hotels. Bath in England, Baden Baden in Germany, Baden in Austria, Baines-les-Baines in France, Lucca in Italy, Karlsbad and Marienbad in Bohemia, and dozens of other springs were fashionable in the eighteenth and nineteenth centuries. The *Twentieth Century Health and Pleasure Resort Guide*, published in about 1900, briefly described some 750 resorts in and near Europe! In the United States, White Sulphur Springs, French Lick Springs, and Saratoga Springs were resorts of renown, built around the idea of drinking or bathing in mineral waters for their alleged medical benefit. Packaged laxatives are more convenient today.

The spas are not dead; they live on today in Russia and in Europe. Nowhere is the "health vacation" more widely practiced or taken more

4. James Laver, *The Age of Illusion* (New York: David McKay Co., 1972), pp. 48–49.

seriously than in the Soviet Union. There are special spas for heart conditions and others for tuberculosis, but most are designed to revitalize the work weary. Upon the recommendation of a doctor, the worker is assigned to a resort where he or she embarks upon a therapeutic program of mineral baths, mud packs, daily walks, and body building. Switzerland, Germany, and France have a number of spas. Switzerland, for example, has 109 spa hotels and high altitude sanitoria with almost 10,000 beds. West Germany has more than 500,000 beds in health–tourist resorts. In many countries, the government pays part or all of the cost.

Changes in Vacationing

An indication of how quickly fashions in vacationing can change came early, even before the word *tourist* was coined. About 1750, the En- glish spas lost their favored position when sea water suddenly became popular and "medicinal." Scarborough and Margate changed into seaside resorts. First the sick came to be healed; pleasure seekers followed. Brighton, a small fishing village in England, became the most famous resort of all. How and why? Where the elite go, the masses follow.

The Duke of Gloucester came to Brighton in 1765. In 1783, the Prince of Wales began his famous pavilion, a Chinese pleasure house, there. By 1800, Brighton was the most fashionable resort in Europe. Today the Prince's Pavilion is open to the public, but few royalty or other elite are to be seen. They have long since deserted Brighton for other, more exclusive spots.

The Railroad Revolution

Travel by rail made possible the travel rev olution — mass travel for everyone. Railroads made long distance travel cheap and fast. The story of the rise and decline of railways as the favored means of travel in the United States is fascinating.

Figure 2-5 shows the amazing increase in U.S. railroad mileage between 1830 and 1916, when the number of miles of track reached its maximum.

Railroads and Changes in Accommodations

The railroad offered cheap transportation and rapid travel as compared to the horse and ship. Vast rail networks across North America and Europe made the railroad station a central part of nearly every community. When the railroad replaced the stagecoach, it also replaced the tavern with what by 1790 was being called the *hotel*, a French word meaning a town mansion or public building. Hotels quite naturally were built conveniently close to railroad stations. Prime examples are those complexes around Grand Central Station and Pennsylvania Station in New York. Thousands of hotel rooms surround and sit upon Grand Central Station. The Pennsylvania Statler (now the Penta), the largest hotel when it was built in 1919, was financed by the Pennsylvania Railroad and was joined to the station by an underground walkway (now closed). Nearly every sizable town in North America and England had at least one hotel adjacent to its depot.

The flesh-and-blood horse, the primary mode of travel before the 1830s, was no match for the iron horse in cost per passenger mile or in speed. The success of the railroad was immediate and pervasive. By 1842, twenty million people were using the railroads in Britain. In the coaching days of 1837, the average Englishman traveled thirteen miles per year at nine miles per hour at a cost of 5 cents a mile. Fifty years later, the cost of travel by train was 1.25 cents per mile at speeds of twenty-five to thirty miles an hour. (Express trains at that time averaged forty-two miles per hour.)

With the coming of the railroad, the tranquillity of stage and canal travel vanished. The steam and noise of the locomotive roared across the United States to become a symbol of America's energy and restlessness. Railroad words entered our vocabulary: *whistle stop*, *highballing*, *gandy dancer*, *jerkwater town*, *tank town*, *cowcatcher*. The railroad depot, which ranged from a little sod hut in the prairies to the magnificent Grand Central and Pennsylvania stations in New York, became a permanent part of the national architecture.

The railroads set the pattern for mobility and permitted contact between the distant parts of the country. Railroading soon became the largest business after agriculture. At the end of the nineteenth century, 59 percent more capital was invested in U.S. railroads than all other manufacturing enterprises combined. Railroads were the vehicle for the huge growth of our modern economy. Without them, western expansion would have been delayed for decades.

Oddly enough, the railway operated for several years before anyone thought to offer passage to people. The English are credited with starting modern tourism, and it was they who first used a locomotive to transport passengers from Stockton to Darlington, ten miles away. A railroad between Liverpool and Manchester, completed in 1830, cut the time between the two cities by three fourths and cut the fare by two thirds. Between 1830 and 1850, 12,000 miles of track were built in England and in the principal European countries.

The railroad had no less an impact in the United States. In 1831 the first railroad in the United States pulled two "pleasure cars" filled with about a hundred invited guests between Charleston and Hamburg, South Carolina. Suitably enough for such a momentous occasion, one of the cars carried a detachment of military, who loaded and fired a field piece borrowed for the event.

Early rail travel had its dangers, however, as was learned a few months later. The fireman of a locomotive, annoyed by the rush of steam escaping from the safety valve, sat on the lever that controlled it: The boiler burst. When a new engine arrived, the railroad officials took no chance of injury to the passengers. The first car behind the locomotive was piled high with baled cotton.

In the United States, resorts and seaside areas that were some distance from population centers were now made accessible by train. Mountain resorts were the first to feel the impact of tourist travel by rail. The mountains had long been used as a summer retreat from the heat, even though travel by carriage was tiring and time-consuming. The railroad made many mountain areas convenient to the population centers on the East Coast. In the early 1870s, men in deerstalker hats and women in bonnets rode the open platform cars of

2-5. Miles of railroad track in the United States			
Year		**Year**	
1830	23	1900	193,346
1840	2,808	1916	254,037
1850	5,021	1920	240,293
1860	30,626	1940	233,370
1870	52,922	1960	217,552
1880	93,267	1980	178,955
1890	163,597		

SOURCE: John F. Stover, *American Railroads* (Chicago: University of Chicago Press, 1976), and the U.S. Department of Commerce.

the New Haven Railroad to the White Mountains of New Hampshire. One of the thrills there was the ascent of Mount Washington by cogwheel railroad, an attraction still enjoyed today.

In the 1880s and 1890s, resort hotels became fashionable up and down the East Coast. Numbers of sprawling white hotels were built in New England, in the mountains and at the seacoast. A few, close to cities, still survive.

Railroads enabled people to go places hitherto beyond their means and endurance. Railroad companies built hotels in Europe, Canada, and the United States. The Canadian Pacific and the Canadian National railroads still operate a sizable number of hotels and resorts. The Union Pacific built the Glacier Park Hotel and the resort at Sun Valley.

The train also made it possible, for those with the means, to escape from cold winters in the north by traveling to Florida, Arizona, and California. By the 1890s the flight to the sun was well under way. Henry M. Flagler, who had been treasurer of Standard Oil and had managed to sequester some $50 million on his own, went to St. Augustine on a second honeymoon and was so enchanted with Florida that he decided to make it into a grand resort area. For each mile of railroad that Flagler built, he was given acres of land by the

State of Florida. As the railroad traveled down through Florida, hotels were built along the way, two at St. Augustine, the Ormond at Ormond Beach, the Royal Poinciana and the Breakers at Palm Beach, and the Royal Palm at Miami. Later, Flagler pushed the railroad all the way to Key West. The Florida East Coast Railway transported millionaires and would-be millionaires to Florida during the winter season. Henry Plant, who made his millions in railroads, pushed a railroad down the west coast of Florida to Tampa, building a series of resort hotels along the way.

Riding to Florida in one's private railroad car was the apogee of luxury. Dozens of private railway cars could be seen parked at resorts on both coasts of Florida during the height of the winter season at the turn of the century and on into the 1920s. Today, however, only a few of the famous resorts of the dozens that operated in the early 1900s are left, among them the Homestead at Hot Springs, Virginia, and the Greenbrier in West Virginia (Figure 2-6).

Luxuries of Rail Travel

The railroads made travel possible for the masses, but special arrangements and luxury cars were available to the rich. A few of the best-known trains had barbershops and manicurists. Some of the cars contained paintings; there were fully fitted bathrooms and libraries with red and gold brocaded chairs.

One of the great pleasures of early rail travel was the excellent food and service found on many of the long-distance trains. In 1868 the Chicago and Alton introduced the Delmonico diner. Ten years later, dining cars ran on all mainline railroads. Many of the dining cars were generously stocked with fine wines, and the menus offered by some were elaborate. They included oysters, turtle, trout, mutton, buffalo tongue, chicken, turkey, beef, pheasant larded with truffles, pâté de foie gras, sweetbreads, antelope, woodcock, prairie chicken, snipe, and a dozen or so desserts.

2-6. Possibly the best-known mountain resort in the world, the Greenbrier in White Sulphur Springs, West Virginia.

One writer who traveled from Chicago to Omaha in 1872 commented, "It is now the custome to charge a dollar per meal on these cars, and as the cooking is admirable, the service excellent, and the food various and abundant, this is not too much. You may have your choice in the wilderness, eating, at the rate of twenty-two miles an hour, off buffalo, elk, antelope, beef-steak, mutton chops, and grouse. Breakfast wines are claret and sauterne; Champagne wines, Heidsieck and Krug."

George Pullman built the Pullman car in 1836. It attracted so much publicity that Mary Todd Lincoln insisted on riding in it as part of the funeral train for her husband. She was not deterred by the fact that the Chicago and Alton Railroad had to add two feet to the clearance of every bridge, depot, and platform along its entire right of way to accommodate the special car.

By 1939 the Twentieth Century Limited gave everyone the red-carpet treatment. A real red carpet, nearly a quarter of a mile long, was laid out in the station for departures in Chicago and New York. In Germany the Flying Hamburger hurtled between Hamburg and Berlin at eighty miles per hour. The British, proud of their Coronation Scot, sent it on a tour of the United States. Several of today's passenger train systems in Europe and Japan are viewed with envy by North Americans, but these tourists do not realize the cost to the governments involved. Japanese railway subsidies in 1985 totaled more than $90 billion a year. Germany subsidized its lines with $5 billion; France, $3.5 billion, and Britain, $1.2 billion.

Decline of Rail Travel

The number of rail passengers per year reached a peak of 1,269,913 in 1920, but has declined since. In 1980 only 281,503 people traveled by rail, and between 1940 and 1980 the number of rail employees was halved, dropping from about a million to fewer than 460,000.[5]

What caused the decline in rail travel? By the 1920s bus routes were operating, and the private automobile began siphoning off much of the passenger travel on the railroads. The Great Depression of the 1930s did little to increase the number of railroad passengers, even though the new streamliners introduced in the mid-1930s were well received.

World War II put extreme demands on the railroads and brought a tremendous surge in the number of passengers. Old passenger cars were brought out of retirement, and rail traffic soared to a record 95.6 billion passenger miles. People were seldom traveling for pleasure, however. At the close of the war, passenger service held for a while, but by 1950 it had slipped to 31.8 billion passenger miles. Since then, with the exception of two routes, the mileage has dropped even more.

Following the war, automobiles were again available, and people had the money to buy them. Also, by 1960 air travel took over much long-distance travel. The railroads wanted to end passenger service, which was steadily losing money. The Interstate Commerce Commission, however, forced them to continue service. In response the railroads purposely made rail service unattractive and in many instances intolerable. Train windows went unwashed, and upholstery unrepaired; ticket service was intolerable. Railroad stations were uncleaned and deteriorating. The public took the hint, and passenger traffic plunged.

Despite the decline in rail travel, the story is not over. In fact, in Europe and parts of Asia, travel by rail has steadily increased in recent years. In time, trains on some rail lines will offer frequent service at speeds up to 200 miles per hour. At these speeds they will challenge the commercial airlines and may pull some travelers from their private automobiles. Yesterday's iron horse will become the aluminum or alloy horse floating a fraction of an inch above its rails, lifted and propelled by the effects of magnetism. Travel agents will ticket rail passengers by computer. Nevertheless, mass intercity and long distance travel by rail will probably be restricted to special situations and along highly populated corridors.

5. John F. Stover, *American Railroads* (Chicago: University of Chicago Press, 1976), and the U.S. Department of Commerce.

Rise of Motels

The automobile led to new kinds of accommodations for travelers—tourist camps and minimal accommodations, built alongside major roads. During the Great Depression of the 1930s enterprising homeowners hung a sign outside their homes, "Tourist Rooms." The price, one dollar, was hard to beat. The motel, a word coined in 1927, became an industry unto itself.

For many years little love was lost between hotel operators and motel owners. As one wit put it, "the motel was sired by the tourist camp and damned by the hotel." The first motels were small affairs, a row of rooms each lit by a single light bulb. A sign saying "modern" meant indoor plumbing. But motel owners were quick to modernize and in the 1940s began adding amenities, including swimming pools. Large motels changed character to become motor hotels. The larger ones are virtually hotels in everything but name, a fact that led the American Hotel Association to change its name to The American Hotel and Motel Association. Still, many small motel operators see themselves as being in a business separate from that of hotels. If there is a distinction between hotels and motels, it is that motels are built and located to serve the motoring public. Public space and services are limited, and many motels do not include restaurants.

Rails Give Way to Roads

A transition period between rail and auto travel saw the steam-driven coach, an ungainly contraption that the British saw fit to restrict to a speed of four miles per hour. The Locomotives on Highways Act of 1865 also required every vehicle to carry a crew of three, one of whom walked 60 yards in front, waving a red flag.

The internal combustion-engine automobile, invented in Germany, became America's obsession. In 1895 there were about 300 horseless carriages of one kind or another in the United States—gasoline buggies, electric cars, and steam cars. In 1914 there were some 2 million. By the 1930s the total had risen to over 25 million. Even

during the Great Depression, about two-thirds of American families had automobiles. Henry Ford's development of the assembly line and the building of good roads such as the Pennsylvania Turnpike helped make the automobile the symbol of American life that it is today.

The auto changed the American way of life, especially in the leisure area. It created and satisfied the urge to travel and made the commute commonplace.

The automobile has also become a kind of monster, polluting the air, taking thousands of lives each year, and adding to already great urban congestion. In the downtown business district of Detroit, for example, 62 percent of all land is devoted to the automobile in the form of roads, parking lots, and garages.

The automobile has also proved to be a dangerous weapon, killing more people than all of our wars. Even with better roads and safer cars, about 40,000 Americans die in auto accidents each year; half of the accidents involve alcohol.

Still, for the average person not living in a congested downtown area, the automobile remains the most convenient and rapid form of transportation for short and medium distances. Without question, it has made Americans the most mobile people in history and has given them options not otherwise possible. It is fairly common for an individual to drive 20,000 miles a year. The family car has given way to the family cars.

Road Systems

The Sumerians invented the wheel; the Romans gave it something smooth to roll over by making a base of stone blocks with flint gravel for topdressing. The Romans also came up with a "fast lane," the *cursus rapidi*, a lane straight down the middle of the road, with one-way lines on both sides. Their freeways had descriptive names: Appian Way, Cassian Way, Valerian Way.

The Romans built more than 50,000 roads in their empire; some of them are still in use. The system began in 312 B.C., when Roman legions and slaves paved a road from Rome to Capua. Eventually the network of Roman roads crossed the Alps, reached Britain, and circled the Mediterranean from North Africa to Syria, with major routes linking ports. The phrase "all roads lead to Rome" was very nearly a fact.

European roads deteriorated during the Middle Ages, but by the thirteenth century there were some improvements. Certain main roads in England were higher than the surrounding ground as earth was thrown from the side ditches toward the center. Because they were higher, they were called *highways*. In colonial America, inland roads were often merely trails marked by piles of stone at intervals and by blazed trees. In South America, on the other hand, in the fifteenth and sixteenth centuries the Incas had completed a road network of 10,000 miles that connected the cities in their empire of perhaps eight million people.

The first concrete road in the United States was laid in Detroit in 1908. In 1916 Congress passed an act that directed the federal government to match state appropriations for new roads dollar for dollar. By 1925, when more than half of all American families either owned a car or were about to buy one on the installment plan, appropriations for hard-top roads began to pour freely from the state legislatures. Road building continued even during the years of deepest depression. The interstate system was made possible by legislation passed by Congress in 1956.

The U.S. road system today is one of the wonders of the world. Some 2.8 million miles in state and local roads, plus interstate superhighways, allow us to travel hither and yon, faster than we should probably go. The interstate system offers gas savings, rapid transportation, and increased driving safety.

PARKS AND CAMPING

Getting away to forests, mountains, and the seaside was accelerated by the Romantic movement of the 1800s, which brought a new appreciation for the beauties of nature. "Go to the mountains," said a brochure of the times, for "deep reflections, leading to wisdom and happiness." The Catskills, romanticized by Washington Irving as Rip Van

Winkle country, and nature paintings by Winslow Homer and Thomas Cole helped heighten the aura of desirability for a return to nature.

John James Audubon, the famous ornithologist, created interest in wildlife generally through his paintings of birds in their natural settings. Ralph Waldo Emerson preached the universality of man and nature. The British discovered the beauties of Switzerland in the 1850s and 1860s and popularized walking and mountain climbing. As railroads expanded, getting back to nature became easier. When roads and the automobile came along, the Great Outdoors became an adventure for millions. Parks provided destinations and amenities.

Visitors to Parks

In Europe parks were mostly the private property of royalty and aristocrats, used to set off stately homes and palaces or as hunting reserves. At one time England's Duke of Somerset could travel all the way from southern England to London without leaving his own property. The Duke of Sutherland could move across Scotland, sea to sea, on his own land. The Duke of Devonshire moved an entire village so that his estate, Chatsworth, could have a proper view. Many of the estate parklands today are owned by England's National Trust or by Scotland's Trust and are open to the public.

In 1872 the U.S. government began what was to become a grand-scale park system by establishing Yellowstone as a National Park. Yellowstone was the first national park in what today includes 49 national parks covering more than 125,000 square miles. Even larger are the national forests, covering 286,000 square miles, many of which are used for recreational purposes, welcome visitors, and provide camping and hotel facilities.

The Great Smoky Mountains National Park is the nation's most popular because of its 250 miles of roads winding among forests and low mountains, which are often shrouded by gray, smoke-colored mists. Great Smoky has 500,000 acres of wooded wilderness, 900 miles of hiking trails, and some 1,000 campsites. Other parks, such as Grand

TRAVEL AND TOURISM HISTORY

Canyon, Denali, Yellowstone, and Glacier, offer more spectacular scenery but are more remote.

National parks are so popular that much thought is being given as to how to restrict or control the vast numbers of visitors. In 1985 nearly 16 million people stayed overnight, about 3.5 million of them in hotels. State parks attracted an additional 30 million; national forests, 12 million.

Government-owned parks in the United States attract more than 360 million people each year. The National Forest Service, part of the Department of Agriculture, estimates that 233 million people visited the nation's forests in 1985. Almost 3,000 state parks attract additional millions. Illustrating the enormous numbers of park visitors is Figure 2-7, which names the national parks, gives their size in acres, and tells the number of visitors in 1987.

The park systems call for accommodations nearby—hotels, motels, cabins—and food services. Many of these facilities are government built; others are built by concessionaires, private persons, or companies. All plans and specifications for new construction must be approved in advance by the Park Service. The government controls accommodation and other rates, including food prices. Advertising and items for sale are also government controlled. Standards covering public health, sanitation, and visitor comfort and convenience are set and maintained under government supervision. Government control even extends to concession wages, hours of work, and conditions of employment, safety, and sanitation.

The concessionaire is given certain assurances. Once granted a contract to build and operate, he or she may hold a contract for up to thirty years. In some people's eyes, the arrangement is the best of two worlds: the government is ensured that facilities are available for the public, and the concessionaire is motivated by a desire for profit. In many state tourist facilities, however, the state itself builds and operates the facilities.

The Forest Service supervises campgrounds, picnic grounds, hotels and lodges, swimming sites, boating areas, winter sport and skiing centers, major observation sites, and visitor centers.

2-7. Visitors to United States parks		
	Visits	Acres
Great Smoky Mountains, Tenn.–N.C.	10,209,800	520,269
Acadia, Maine	4,288,154	41,357
Grand Canyon, Ariz.	3,513,030	1,218,375
Yosemite, Calif.	3,152,275	761,170
Olympic, Wash.	2,822,850	921,935
Yellowstone, Wyo.–Mont.–Idaho	2,573,194	2,219,785
Rocky Mountain, Colo.	2,531,864	265,200
Zion, Utah	1,777,619	146,598
Shenandoah, Va.	1,767,727	195,382
Glacier, Mont.	1,660,737	1,013,572
Mammoth Cave, Ky.	1,636,300	52,428
Grand Teton, Wyo.	1,450,800	310,521
Haleakala, Hawaii	1,333,900	28,655
Mount Rainier, Wash.	1,292,027	235,404
Badlands, S.D.	1,174,398	243,302
Sequoia, Calif.	1,139,389	402,482
Hot Springs, Ark.	1,101,242	5,839
Kings Canyon, Calif.	1,081,172	461,901
Hawaii Volcanoes, Hawaii	1,006,058	229,117
Everglades, Fla.	787,493	1,398,938
Virgin Islands, V.I.	785,354	14,689
Carlsbad Caverns, N.M.	781,300	46,755
Petrified Forest, Ariz.	758,082	93,532
Mesa Verde, Colo.	728,566	52,085
Bryce Canyon, Utah	718,342	35,835
North Cascades, Wash.	651,606	504,781
Redwood, Calif.	610,897	110,178
Biscayne, Fla.	607,968	173,039
Denali, Alaska	575,013	4,716,726
Wind Cave, S.D.	563,720	28,292
Lassen Volcanic, Calif.	472,431	106,372
Arches, Utah	468,916	73,379
Crater Lake, Oreg.	460,550	183,224
Capitol Reef, Utah	428,808	241,904
Theodore Roosevelt, N.D.	424,846	70,416
Big Bend, Tex.	227,921	735,416
Voyageurs, Minn.	201,727	218,056
Channel Islands, Calif.	174,607	249,354
Canyonlands, Utah	172,384	357,570
Guadalupe Mountains, Tex.	156,344	76,293
Glacier Bay, Alaska	130,926	3,225,284
Great Basin, Nev.	63,532	77,109
Kenai Fjords, Alaska	60,428	669,541
Katmai, Alaska	38,212	3,716,000
Isle Royale, Mich.	31,760	571,790
Wrangell-Saint Elias, Alaska	29,191	8,331,604
Lake Clark, Alaska	16,418	2,636,839
Gates of the Arctic, Alaska	1,060	7,523,888
Kobuk Valley, Alaska	230	1,750,421

Note: Figures are for 1987.

SOURCE: Basic data—National Park Service.

Hundreds of resorts operate on national forest land; most of them are owned and operated by concessionaires.

The State of Kentucky, for example, has an elaborate state-operated resort system. These resort facilities are among the most modern and attractive in the country. Eight state resort parks are open year-round, offering package vacations that can be charged on any interbank credit card. Reservations can be made toll-free from within the state and from adjoining states. Sixteen Kentucky resort parks have hotel rooms, motel rooms, and various-sized cottages. Some of the facilities also offer rental cars and houseboats, golf, ski lifts, regattas, and planned recreation programs. One park has constructed trails for minibikes. The state has involved itself in tourism by offering facilities for state residents, as well as by attracting visitors from out of state to bolster the economy.

Several other states also operate tourist facilities in state parks. State recreation land systems cover millions of acres. Michigan and Washington, for example, have more than four million acres each for such purposes. Minnesota, New York, and Pennsylvania have an excess of three million acres each. Louisiana, Illinois, Hawaii, and Mississippi each have over one million acres for such purposes.

Camping

Camping out—whether it be in recreational vehicles, tents, or sleeping bags—is sometimes overlooked as part of travel/tourism. The Grand Tour was for the rich. The Great Outdoors is for anyone with a car, some discretionary time, and gasoline money. The Great Outdoors is a break from urban routine, fun for the family, and an excuse to see new places and perhaps use the camper and the campsite, "roughing it" in a modern cabin or a hotel room with a view. Travel to the Great Outdoors is a multibillion dollar business, very much a part of tourism/travel. In a sense camping is competitive with the hotel/motel and restaurant business. Campers travel millions of miles a year in the United States, Canada, and Europe, carry-ing their "motel rooms" with them. Statistics in dollars and numbers of campers show camping to be an enormous business with vast expenditures for RV's and other camping equipment. In 1981 over six million RV's were estimated to be in operation, and the number of nights they were used each year was estimated at 138 million.[6]

Campers cut across demographic and economic lines but are concentrated among families and the semiretired or retired. The first group may spend a month each year in camping; the older group may cruise for weeks, camping in different locations. Campers seem to prefer government-owned parks and national forests. Franchised campgrounds such as KOA (Kampgrounds of America) and Yogi Bear are likely to appear near well-traveled roads.

Canada has some excellent historic parks that are visitor highlights. Such parks, which evoke people, events, and lifestyles of the past, add another dimension to the travel experience. In Nova Scotia, for example, are Louisbourg and the Alexander Graham Bell National Historic Park. Louisbourg is a reconstruction of the French fortress that secured the area for the catching and processing of cod to be sent back to France as a mainstay in the diet of the eighteenth century. Park employees play the roles of people who actually lived in the fortress in 1744—fishermen, shopkeepers, restaurant operators, and soldiers. Each of the employees is costumed for the role, acts out an assigned part, and is conversant with the facts of the period. Visitors virtually see and hear the life of the fortress as it was in the eighteenth century.

Besides its exquisite location overlooking part of the Brac d'Or Lakes, the Bell Historic Park elucidates the accomplishments of Alexander Graham Bell, idealist, genius, inventor of the telephone, and scientist who researched the hydrofoil and airplane as well as ameliorating the lives of the hearing impaired.

---

6. Tom Powers, *Introduction to Management in the Hospitality Industry* (John Wiles, 1988), p. 344.

TRAVEL EXPEDITERS

Thomas Cook and Son

Persons with knowledge about travel have been arranging trips for others for centuries, but Thomas Cook is credited with being the first professional travel agent, a travel expediter appointed by public carriers to act in their behalf, for a commission (Figure 2-8).

A wood-turner by trade, Cook was a deeply religious person and a temperance enthusiast. In 1841 he chartered a train to carry 540 people to a temperance convention. Cook arranged the round trip from Leicester to Loughborough, a distance of twenty-two miles, at a shilling a person. Although Cook made no profit for himself, he did realize the potential in arranging travel for other people. From the outset he saw that the travel business was more than a business—it was also an opportunity for education and enlightenment.

In 1845 Cook became a full-time excursion organizer. Because the 5 percent commission he consequently received from Midland Counties

2-8. This picture of Thomas Cook (1808–93), pioneer in developing the business of pleasure travel, is seen on all of Cook's Traveler's Cheques.

Railroad was not enough to maintain a solvent business, he became a tour operator and, later, a retailer of tours as well. Dedicated to making tours as convenient and interesting as possible, Cook had printed a "handbook of the trip" for an 1845 tour from Leicester to Liverpool. Soon after, he produced coupons that could be used to cover hotel expenses. In 1846 Cook took 350 people by steamer and train on a tour of Scotland. A specially designed touring guide, the first of its kind, was prepared for the trip. In 1851 at least 165,000 people used Cook's lodging and transportation plans to visit London for the first World Exhibition at the Crystal Palace.

After Cook moved his offices to London, he began conjuring up all sorts of imaginative trips. Soon he was arranging "grand circular tours of Europe" with itineraries that included four different countries. He helped popularize Switzerland as a touring center by taking a group through the country in 1863. Soon after the American Civil War, his son John M. Cook traveled with a group to America and visited New York, Washington, D.C., and some of the Civil War battlefields.

In 1872 Cook achieved another first—an around-the-world trip. Cook's impressions were recorded in thoughtful letters to the London *Times*. (The trip was said to have inspired Jules Verne to write his novel *Around the World in Eighty Days*.) The ten-member group circled the globe in 222 days. Today, the same trip can be taken over a weekend.

Throughout the latter half of the nineteenth century, "The Cook's Tour" meant an escorted group tour, most often conducted by Thomas or one of his sons. After Thomas became blind, members of his family took over the business. John Cook became manager of the firm in 1878. He arranged trips into Yellowstone Park soon after it opened. In 1875 Cook tours were arranged in Norway. In collaboration with the P and O Steamship Line, travel to India became luxurious. Upon arriving in Bombay, the traveler was escorted to spacious compartments on Indian trains and served complete meals while en route to the Taj Mahal. The Cook's traveler could visit the Himalayas or Mount Everest or travel to Kashmir.

In 1884 John Cook arranged for the entire British Expeditionary Force of 18,000 men to be transported up the Nile for the attempted relief of General Charles George Gordon at Khartoum. The relief "tour" unfortunately arrived late; General Gordon had already been killed and Khartoum had fallen.

In the 1890s the Cooks ran pioneering trips across Europe to Asia via the Trans-Siberian Railroad. Cook often undertook the difficult — a trip to Jerusalem in 1890 required armed guards, mules, horses, cooks, tents, and a great deal of bargaining with local sheiks and pashas to permit travel through their domains.

Cook's company was successful at least partly because he made travel convenient and relatively simple. Another reason was Thomas's enthusiasm for travel as an enlightening venture not just for the upper classes, but for any who could afford the much lower prices engineered by Cook. He can be credited with making world travel possible for the middle class.

The Cooks were well aware of the elasticity of demand for travel. If the cost of travel was reduced, more people would travel. The more people travel by a particular mode of transportation, the more likely it is that the cost of that transportation can be reduced. By chartering whole trains and steamers and by booking large blocks of rooms, Cook was able to reduce travel expenses considerably. The cost of operating a train, steamship, or airplane that is 100 percent full is only a little more than operating one that is 25 percent full, and the cost per seat at 100 percent capacity is substantially less.

Many people, most notably Mark Twain, were enthusiastic about the group tour and felt that one traveled with a ready-made group of friends. But from the outset tours came in for their share of snide comments. A nineteenth-century snob had this to say:

It seems some enterprising and unscrupulous man had devised the project of conducting some forty or fifty persons from London to Naples and back for a fixed sum [referring to Thomas Cook]. He contracts to carry, feed, lodge, and amuse them.... You see them, forty in number, pouring along the street with a director — now in front, now at the rear — circling them like a sheep dog. Europe, in their eyes, is a great spectacle, like a showpiece at Covent Gardens; and it is theirs to criticize the performance and laugh at the performers at will.

When foreigners first inquired of me what this strange invasion might mean, I bethought myself to take aside the most gossip-loving of my acquaintances and tell him that our Australian colonies had made such a rumpus of late about being made convict settlements that we had adopted the cheap expedient of sending our rogues abroad to the Continent, apparently as tourists. The knaves, after a few weeks, take themselves off in various directions as tastes or inclinations suggest. Then that fussy little bald man that took such trouble about them will return to England.[7]

Although the Cooks were highly sensitive to criticism, they went about their business improvising, promoting, and being their ingenious selves. On an Italian tour featuring Holy Week in Rome, the reserved hotel reneged on reservations for Cook's party of fifty. Cook promptly hired a prince's palace for $2,500 and arranged meals at neighboring restaurants for the period of ten days. The trip produced a deficit, which led the tour members to volunteer a contribution of $1,000, probably the first and last such contribution. On a trip to New York, John — ever the improviser — hired a wagon to haul his and his group's luggage to the hotel at a fraction of the cost charged by the horse cabbies.

Travel Conglomerates Emerge

The Cooks also pioneered the travel conglomerate (one company engaging in a number of travel-related enterprises) long before the term was ever used. Before 1875 the firm had acquired the exclusive right to carry the mails, as well as special travelers and government officials, between Assiont and Assonan on the Nile. The company also operated ships and a ship repair service in Egypt.

---

7. K.C. Tessendorf, "Prophet of Mass Marketing" in *The Travel Agent*, October 16, 1972.

On Thomas Cook's death in 1893, ownership and management of the firm passed to his three sons. The business by that time had grown to include three divisions: tourists, banking, and shipping.

The modern around-the-world-tour was introduced by a Cook-chartered Cunard liner in 1923. In 1927 the company arranged for a special plane flight from New York to Chicago for fans attending the Dempsey-Tunney world championship prizefight; box lunches were supplied by Louis Sherry, the fashionable New York caterer. In 1931 Thomas Cook and Son merged with the Wagon-Lits Company, operators of the sleeping-car and express trains in Europe and a large travel agency as well.

The Cooks continued to do everything possible to make the trip easy for the traveler. Cook's agents often met planes with a car. They waited at the entrance to customs to whisk travelers directly to a reception or anywhere else they wanted to go. The all-inclusive price for a tour made it much easier for people to plan vacations and to budget their time and money.

Following World War II, the British government acquired the principal interest in Thos. Cook and Son, and policy was determined by the British government through the Transport Holding Company. In 1972 the British government sold the company for $858.5 million. Trust Houses Forte, the largest British hospitality company, and the Automobile Association of Britain are part of the owning consortium. The company today has over 625 offices and 10,000 employees around the world and is composed of five relatively independent divisions. Considered to be the largest of its kind, the company today has manifold interests other than in sale of travel as such.

Wagon-Lits (literally *coach-beds*, pronounced vah-gawn-lee) was the grande dame of European travel. A Franco-Belgian company with about 800 agencies and a tour company, it owns or operates 183 hotels in 32 countries. A cooperative agreement with Thomas Cook gives clients access to about 1,500 agencies in 136 countries and is the basis for Cook's claim to being the largest travel agency in the world.

U.S. Travel Agencies

Travel agencies as separate businesses started in the 1880s in the United States. The first travel agents sold steamship and rail tickets and some arranged tours. Hotel porters also acted as travel expediters and were called upon by hotel guests to go to the railroad station to get a train ticket, for which service the porter received a tip. With the advent of commercial flights the airlines offered the porters a five percent commission on airline tickets. Once the airlines hired their own sales personnel, however, commissions to porters were discontinued.

Ask Mr. Foster

"Ask Mr. Foster," the oldest U.S. travel agency, began in 1888 when Ward Grenelle Foster opened a "travel information office" in St. Augustine, Florida. When the town's residents and visitors had travel questions, they were directed to Foster's gift shop to "Ask Mr. Foster," a phrase that was adopted by Foster as his business slogan and the name for his travel business. In the 1890s, Ask Mr. Foster offices were opened in other Florida cities, and later, in New York City and other major U.S. cities and large resort centers.

The offices were usually located in large buildings such as hotels and department stores with heavy foot traffic. The company provided free information and reservations, and their brochure promised to "plan your trips, secure your ticket, make your reservations for hotels, steamers, autos, schools, railroads, anywhere in the world." Foster preferred women as agents, saying that "The work calls for a particular personality. It's not only the information that is given, it's the way it's given. I find that women are courteous, interested, patient, conscientious and above all, enthusiastic in helping people."[8] The women Foster hired and trained were called "Foster Girls." (Perhaps he recalled hearing of the Harvey Girls hired and trained by Fred Harvey for his restaurants serving the Santa Fe Railway.)

8. *Ask Mr. Foster*, Centennial calendar, 1988.

Foster sold the business in 1928, and it changed hands several times before being bought in 1979 by the Carlson Companies, the hospitality conglomerate based in Minneapolis. In 1988 the company had more than 750 offices in 46 states, and its total sales exceeded that of American Express travel agency sales. Also owned by the company are TGI Friday and Country Kitchen restaurants and Radison Hotels and Colony Resorts.

American Express

American Express is another worldwide travel agency. It grew out of the old Wells-Fargo Company of Pony Express and Wild West fame. The American Express Travelers Cheque was introduced in 1891 and is still the most popular of such checks. By 1968 Amexco had diversified and became a travel and financial conglomerate. Much of its earnings now come from casualty, life, and property insurance. It also owns one of the largest stock brokerages, Shearson Lehman/American Express. The company is a major factor in international currency transactions, buying and selling millions in foreign currency for corporations and individual customers each working day. American Express may best be described as a travel-oriented bank. The company integrates travel services in that it not only arranges tours but also sells traveler's checks, publishes *Travel & Leisure* magazine, offers the American Express credit card, and owns foreign-language teaching services.

Another major travel agency is the American Automobile Association, whose travel sales are in excess of $1.3 billion a year. A federation of automobile associations, it is headquartered near Washington, D.C. The total membership exceeds twenty million.

Growth of Travel Agencies

With the arrival of scheduled airlines, the travel agency business began to change. In the 1930s Pan American World Airways, so small that they could not afford a ticket office, borrowed three feet of counter space from Thomas Cook and Son in New York. Following World War II, the travel urge broke loose, and numbers of people set themselves up in business as travel agents. Teachers, clerks, and housewives worked out of their homes part-time as travel agents. Such an arrangement would be almost impossible today.

The idea of opening a travel agency has natural appeal to many people, who probably think that the business requires only limited capital and a minimum of travel information and will satisfy their desire to meet people and see the world themselves. In a later chapter it will become clear that being a travel agent is more complicated and expensive than it may seem.

Within the United States and Canada, some 30,000 retailers of travel are in operation; they include clubs, banks, department stores, airlines, and hotels. Each year over 1,000 new agencies are started, and every year several hundred are closed.

We have seen that until the nineteenth century, discretionary travel was limited to a very small percentage of the people. This changed dramatically as the industrial revolution gave millions of people in North America and Europe some discretional income. More important, the railroad made travel comparatively cheap and convenient. In response to travel demand, entrepreneurs such as Thomas Cook, and, later, travel expediters, helped promote and make travel arrangements easier.

Given discretionary income and relative convenience in travel, we have yet to ask why people travel, a question discussed in the next chapter.

DISCUSSION QUESTIONS

1. Why do North Americans travel so much more than other national groups?
2. If you were asked to define the word *tourist,* would you include commuters in the definition? Why or why not?
3. The ancient Romans were known for their roads and extensive road system. Who built these roads?
4. Can you name one of the seven wonders of the ancient world?
5. The first extensive system of accommodating travelers overnight was connected with what religious organization?
6. In what ways did the seven crusades to the Holy Lands stimulate tourism?
7. What is the origin of the word *stagecoach*?
8. Most newer resorts in this country contain health and fitness facilities. How are these related to the spas of eighteenth-century Europe?
9. Suppose fusion energy becomes a cheap and ubiquitous source of energy. What effects would this have on tourism? Will automobiles be powered by battery? Can we build huge resorts completely covered by domes with summerlike temperatures maintained year round?

THREE

WHY TOURISTS TRAVEL

The eighteenth-century author, Dr. Samuel Johnson, stated that the "use of traveling is to regulate imagination by reality, and instead of thinking how things may be, to see them as they are." Those legendary little green people in UFOs looking down on earth may be bewildered by the ceaseless movement of vehicles tracking across the land and the airships shooting hither and yon. The aliens may be hard put to understand what is happening—airships moving east and west across the oceans, wheeled vehicles going in every possible direction. Earthlings too have difficulty explaining.

Considering costs in time, energy, stress, and money, why is there so much travel for pleasure, travel not required by necessity?[1] Why do Canadians and Mexicans travel to the United States, Americans to Europe, Europeans to America, Swedes to Cyprus, Japanese to Guam and Hawaii, Australians to Manila and Singapore, New Yorkers to Israel and Puerto Rico?

The prospective traveler's selection of a destination is sometimes likened to a trip to a travel supermarket, where the shopper walks in and selects the destination from any one of thousands of choices. Although it is true that there are hundreds of thousands of possible destinations, the perspective of the traveler is usually circumscribed by a number of factors. Attitude, finances, sense of adventure or lack of it, energy level, and value system immediately serve to focus the choices to a relative few—whether a weekend in the mountains, a trip to a fun city, a visit to relatives, or a jaunt to a convention. The first trip abroad is overwhelmingly likely to be to Canada or Europe, to the Caribbean perhaps, and if the traveler lives on the West Coast, possibly to Hawaii, Mexico, or Alaska. Only after the first trip abroad is consideration usually given to the Orient and Russia and later to South America or to Africa.

Veteran travelers continually expand their range of choices. The mindset of some travelers, however, completely rules out large sections of the globe as too dull, too dangerous, too expensive, or noncompetitive in appeal. Such travelers find themselves rerouting a trip through Scandinavia; meandering through England, Scotland, and Wales; or revisiting London, Paris, Vienna, or Rome.

---

1. I wish to express special appreciation to Dr. Charles Metelka, travel sociologist, for several suggestions and the use of several of his ideas in this chapter.

THE TOURIST BUSINESS

SHOPPING FOR VALUE IN THE TRAVEL SUPERMARKET

Travel bargains are available in the travel supermarket just as they are in the food supermarket. Cost plays a large part in determining if and where pleasure travel takes place. Travel prices change more rapidly than food prices — some destinations rapidly become expensive; others, relatively inexpensive, depending on government policy, the shifting value of the American dollar against other currency around the world, and a number of other factors, such as relative labor costs in a country. From time to time a nation devalues its currency or the political situation in a country becomes unstable — factors that bring down tourist prices. For example, the revolution in Portugal in 1974–1976 was responsible for a large decrease in tourism to that country. Tourist-related activities, accommodations, and meals were slashed sharply, and a "Silver Platter" program offered discounts on rooms, meals, attractions, and rental cars to encourage visitors. The Mexican government's sudden devaluation of the peso in the early 1980s sharply reduced tourism prices there. The unexpected strength of the American dollar in the mid-1980s had a decided impact on international travel patterns, as more Americans traveled abroad.

A government that wants to encourage tourism can do a number of things to create travel bargains, such as placing ceilings on room and meal prices, as has been done in Spain and several communist countries. The government can set an artificially high or low rate of exchange for foreign currencies that acts either as a brake or an accelerator on tourism.

The traveler who is not restricted by time can look about the travel supermarket and pick up the trip that offers the best value. The situation anywhere in the world will almost certainly change within a few years, so that a destination once prohibitive in cost may become cheaper in the future. The wise traveler with no time restraints will order trips that take advantage of conditions existing at the moment.

For example, travel to London and England was relatively expensive until the British government devalued the pound, which made the country relatively inexpensive. Then the dollar dropped in value, and London became expensive, almost doubling in travel cost. Any large city that has a shortage of guest rooms is likely to have an artificially high room cost. When other hotels are built, the rates will be reduced, especially during off-season.

For persons living in high-cost areas, travel and vacationing in low-cost countries can indeed save money. It is possible for an English couple to rent their home in London for about $900 a month and live in Spain or Portugal for little more than the rental income. Tourists are forever seeking out those places that are inexpensive — they shop not only on the trip but for a particular trip as well. Following World War II, Austria was a low-cost vacation spot in Europe. Popularity and supply and demand raised the prices somewhat, and the budget-conscious switched to Spain and Portugal.

Within the same country, costs may vary widely, and the true bargain hunter soon becomes informed of the differences. Dublin hotels are about as expensive as hotels in New York, but a room with breakfast in an Irish farmhouse costs only fifteen dollars. Hotel tariffs in Puerto Rico and the Bahamas are high, while they are relatively inexpensive on some of the other islands and in Costa Rica and Colombia. Acquiring such knowledge is part of the travel game and is fun in itself.

Reduced Fares as a Factor

The cost of transportation, of course, looms large in the decision of whether and where to travel, especially when long distances are involved. The deregulation of airlines has played a large part in the travel upsurge since 1984. Eighty percent or more of air passengers fly at discounted fares. The increase in passengers only proved once more the sizable consideration that the cost of transportation plays in the travel decision. As costs of travel come down, more people decide to take that trip to London, Paris, or Timbuktu.

MOTIVATIONS FOR TRAVEL

Over the course of history, the motivations for most travel have been fairly obvious: religious conviction, economic gain, war, escape, migration. It would seem that motives for what is left—travel for pleasure—would be straightfoward and plainly understandable. This, however, is not the case.

Unfortunately, little research has been undertaken that reveals the reasons why people travel and vacation. Because research and an established motivation theory are lacking, the comments included here are necessarily impressionistic and are made principally to stimulate investigation.

Some surprising findings show up in consumer research. A 1987 study asked consumers which of twenty-two items they associated with success and accomplishment. The leading choice was "travel for pleasure."[2]

As psychologist Abraham Maslow theorized, at the very top of the hierarchy of human needs seem to be those for self-actualization or self-realization. This desire reflects the fundamental need to develop one's own potential, to gain aesthetic stimulation, to create or build one's own personality and character.

Certainly there are tremendous variations in what individuals need at the self-actualization level. Millions of people prefer not to travel or vacation because they are more comfortable in their present circumstances or are afraid to leave them or to take the chance of being injured or victimized while traveling or visiting a strange destination. Other people seem to thrive on the change brought by travel. Some need the letdown of a quiet vacation; others seek the same pitch of excitement that exists in their workaday world.

If we hypothesize the need for change, for diversion, for new scenery, for new experiences, then travel and vacationing take their place somewhere near the top of the list of means for meeting these needs. In fact, some psychotherapists posit a basic need for fun and freedom. Pleasure travel is certainly a rich source for fulfilling this need.

Tourism and Prostitution

Reliable statistics for the number of people who travel for sex are not available and probably never will be. The thought of meeting a desirable sex partner on a trip probably figures in much of the youth travel to and around Europe.

In some societies fantasies of sharing a bed with a relative stranger are displaced by the certain knowledge of pleasure with a prostitute. According to University of Copenhagen sociologist Susan Thorbeck, some 300,000 prostitutes are available, girls who are said in Danish and West German travel agency ads "to create heaven on earth for a man."[3] The cost for such pleasures in 1982 was $25 a day or $70 a week. Nothing is said of the cost of treating the social diseases that could result from spending a week in such a "heaven."

Sex in large part brought 1.3 million tourists, nearly all male, to Thailand in 1981 and helped make tourism the country's second largest foreign currency earner. Compared to the capital needed to develop most tourist attractions, that of sex tourism is relatively modest. The growing epidemic of AIDS, however, has cooled many travelers' desire for sex with unknown partners.

Different Places for Different People

Obviously, travelers select destinations for different reasons—climate, history or culture, sports, entertainment, shopping facilities, and so forth. The major appeal of England for Americans seems to be history and culture. American Express surveyed people going to several destinations—Florida, California, Mexico, Hawaii, the Bahamas, Jamaica, Puerto Rico, the Virgin Islands, and Barbados. The respondents represented a group almost half of whom were professionals, generally middle-aged, and well educated. Many of them were wealthy travelers taking frequent vacations outside the United States. These respondents ranked the appeals of travel in descending order of importance:[4]

2. Quoted in *The New York Times*, January 10, 1988, p. 13.

3. *Los Angeles Times*, November 22, 1981, p. 9.
4. Jonathan N. Goodrich, "Benefit Bundle Analysis: An Empirical Study of International Travelers," *Journal of Travel Research*, Fall 1977.

- scenic beauty
- pleasant attitudes of local people
- suitable accommodations
- rest and relaxation
- air fare cost
- historical and cultural interests
- cuisine
- water sports
- entertainment (e.g., nightlife)
- shopping facilities
- sports (golfing and tennis)

Four basic considerations emerged as factors influencing travel: entertainment, purchase opportunities, climate for comfort, and cost.

Even within a group, of course, different factors apply. One individual may select a destination primarily because of opportunities for challenging golf or tennis, another because of the friendly local people, and another because the place offers rest and relaxation. Most of the group would, however, be influenced by air fare costs.

Expectation and Reality

Satisfaction or dissatisfaction with the travel experience, of course, depends on how it is viewed by the traveler. A glorious sunset and majestic mountain may be seen as a great bore if an individual is highly gregarious and alone on the trip. The best service in a restaurant with the finest food and decor is meaningless if the person is dyspeptic at the moment.

One traveler loves the rain; another despises it. Mountains are one person's delight; heights make another person dizzy. The anthropologist revels in the remote village; the city-dwelling swinger finds the same place dull. So much depends upon what the person expects of the experience and how he or she actually experiences it.

Travel is an experience, not a tangible object. It results in psychic reward or punishment. It creates pleasant anticipation or aversion; excitement and challenge, or fatigue and disappointment. The anticipation, the experience, and the memory occur in the mind, leaving no tangible evidence as to why travel was undertaken and why the same

trip is experienced in so many different ways by different people.

Travel literature and films often falsify reality or are shot so selectively that the actual environment is not recognizable by the visitor. The phony shot that makes the pool look longer than it is, the colors that never exist in nature, the lavish buffet that was rigged especially for the photograph, the glorious sunset that occurs once a year—all of this creates expectations that cannot be realized and leads to disappointment.

Vacation Attitude Survey

In the late sixties, Travel Research International conducted a vacation travel attitude survey, the general results of which probably hold true today. The survey was based on 1,005 structured personal interviews of a nationwide sample of heads of households. It showed that an important factor in determining where Americans go on their vacations is the desire—or obligation—to visit friends and relatives. Another important reason for choosing a vacation destination was what the report labeled "the nostalgia/habit factor." In other words, vacationers were likely to go where they had been before.

Some marketing studies have attempted to discover the reasons why travelers, and especially vacationers, select a particular destination area. One such study, done by John S. Kay for a large land-holding company in Hawaii, conducted extensive research into the question through in-depth interviews and a questionnaire given to consumers and members of the travel industry.[5] The researchers soon found that most people viewed a vacation as a real extension of their personality and were reluctant, or unable, to verbalize directly their attitudes about vacations. The in-depth interview helped to circumvent this barrier.

According to the study, there seemed to be four principal determinants of vacation plans:

---

5. John S. Kay, "Land Development Plan and Program for C. Brewer and Co., Ltd., 1969–1982" (Honolulu, 1968).

1. *Financial*. Vacation trips are shaped or curbed by the amount of money the person has or wants to spend on a vacation.
2. *Obligation to visit*. The determination of a large number of vacation destinations was based on the need to visit relatives in the vacation area or during a stopover.
3. *Advertising*. Travel advertising affected the choice of a vacation spot when the cost was not so high as to exclude it from consideration.
4. *Family status*. The more people in the family, the more it was necessary to consider the cost of travel and the opinions of the children. It appeared that, within financial limits, the children chose the trip.

The Kay study supported the view that vacationers tend to idealize the vacation area. If the area lives up to the expectations of travelers, they are well satisfied; if not, they are dissatisfied. Should this theory be true, then much travel is motivated by the creation of an image or an ideal in the traveler's mind. The image may take form over a short period of time or over a number of years, formed, for example, by movies, books, TV, and the comments of others.

Even though a destination area may not remotely resemble the expectations of the traveler, those expectations provide the basic stimulus for the trip. The promise of balmy breezes, friendly people, and gorgeous scenery is what counts, at least for the first trip.

A Push/Pull Model

An interesting way of modeling travel motivations is to divide them into factors that pull, that is, attractions, and those that push, that is, personal needs. Arlin Epperson, a travel consultant, proposes the push/pull model.[6]

He lists push factors as the intangible desires that are generated from within the person. Examples include the following:

- escape
- self-discovery

---

6. Arlin Epperson, "Why People Travel," *Leisure Today*, April 1983, p. 54.

- rest, relaxation
- prestige
- challenge
- adventure

Pull factors are external travel stimulators, such as

- scenic beauty
- historical areas
- cultural events
- sporting events

Disney World attracts those motivated by a pull factor. A relaxing week on a Caribbean beach is probably inspired by a push factor. Much travel is likely motivated to some degree by both push and pull factors; for example, a vacation in an isolated mountain cabin would allow for escape, self-discovery, and rest, while at the same time providing scenic beauty.

Business Travel

Half or more of all airline travel is undertaken by business travelers. A Pan American Airlines study shows that the business–pleasure mix varies widely according to destination area.

Over 90 percent of the travel between the United States and the Caribbean is for pleasure. The figure for U.S. mainland–Hawaii pleasure travel is over 80 percent; for United States–trans-Atlantic flights, a little less than 80 percent; and for United States–Latin America flights, about 70 percent. Pleasure is the dominant reason for slightly over 60 percent of the passengers flying between the United States and the trans-Pacific area.

About 60 to 70 percent of the guests who check into Sheraton hotels around the world are traveling for business reasons. Much business travel is hard work, whether it is travel in one's own automobile or in the luxury of a first-class seat aboard an airline. A good portion of business travel is, however, mixed with pleasure.

It is difficult to say where business begins or pleasure ends when the business traveler is attending a convention in Las Vegas or Florida, where as much as half of his or her time may be spent gambling or gamboling. The trip to Europe may involve contacting potential customers, but it also may allow for sight-seeing or an evening at the Folies Bergère.

TRAVEL FOR PLEASURE

Pleasure is a state of mind where one person's meat may be another's poison. Pleasure depends partly upon prior conditions or the anticipation of good things to come. Pleasure may come from the relief of pain, respite from boredom, or escape from the routine of life. It may be the feelings that come with sensuous gratification—a warm bath, basking in the sun, eating, drinking, sex or even the thought of it. Change in itself may bring pleasure. Play is generally thought to be exciting and associated with pleasure.

Changing Views of Pleasure

What is pleasurable changes with time and culture. Most of the present older generation has been programmed into believing that work in itself is one of the highest goods; sensuous gratification has not been of overriding importance. Adherence to the so-called Puritan ethic, however, is fading; sensuous gratification is back in favor. Life can be fun. Work has become fused or interwoven with pleasure.

Vacationing for pleasure has changed and will continue to do so. In the 1890s travel to the mountain resort in the summer was viewed as highly pleasurable. The table and the rocking chair on the resort porch offered an escape from the hot city, gratification for the stomach, rest and rustication, and a chance to be with one's peers, or hopefully one's betters. The railroad took one there in some style.

Until the 1940s travel abroad was necessarily by ship. Shipboard activities proved exciting for some, relentlessly banal to others. During the five- or six-day trip from New York to England or France, there was a plethora of food and a round of activities planned by the cruise director. Trans-Atlantic travelers could sit in deck chairs, wrapped in blankets, shivering against the cold Atlantic winds. If they found no pleasure in this, at least they could think about how much better off they were than their friends and neighbors back home. Seasickness was best forgotten.

Today travel may involve a jet flight to Las Vegas for gambling, Hawaii for surfing, Florida for the beaches, Greece for the Parthenon, or London for the theater. Movies at 40,000 feet may even distract the passengers' attention from their small seats.

What is pleasurable in travel and vacation varies within a family and also changes for an individual as time passes. Surf riding is one of the most exciting sports imaginable, but only for the conditioned athlete and the young. A trip to Paris may mean the Lido and showgirls for some, but a tour of Notre Dame Cathedral or dinner at the Tour d'Argent restaurant for others. The college student in Bermuda may enjoy the mating game and the motorbike. Later in life Bermuda can provide a place for relaxation and an opportunity to view nature.

The Need for Change

The basic needs that drive our lives are overlaid with a need for stimulation that can be fulfilled by change. Once the basic needs such as food and shelter have been met, the mind seeks stimulation and titillation. Travel and vacationing can provide diversity, removing one from present, familiar surroundings to something that is new and, because it is new, pleasantly exciting.

Humans apparently need stimulation, and travel can stimulate. Sensory deprivation studies show that when the brain is deprived of adequate stimulation, it ceases to function in a normal way. Hallucinations and other aberrations become normal.

Aldous Huxley and others have noted an overriding boredom that overtakes humankind—a sense of universal futility that arouses a complementary desire to get away from where one is at the moment. Variety may be more than the spice of life; it may be a necessity.

Marketing research director Russ Johnston put it more simply: "The greatest reason for travel

WHY TOURISTS TRAVEL

can be summed up in one word, 'escape.' Escape from the dull daily routine. Escape from the familiar, the commonplace, the ordinary. Escape from the job, the boss, the customers, the commuting, the house, the lawn, the leaky faucets."[7]

Everyone, according to Johnston, is searching for change even though some do it actively, others passively. The "actives" are people who like to go to explore, and to experience new things. The "passives" are those who like to hide and lie on the beach.

For many people *any* change is a welcome change. The physician who, with his or her spouse, travels twenty miles from home to stay overnight is traveling to get away from the routines and demands of family and profession. The retired carpenter who regularly travels to Reno to gamble is seeking a change from dull routine. The secretary in Chicago who goes to San Juan or Miami Beach for a week is experiencing a whole new world. The buses that carry tens of thousands of retirees to Atlantic City are taking these people out of the daily humdrum to "a day on the town."

Humans are so plastic, so adaptable, so able to be conditioned to surroundings, that it is difficult to say what evokes pleasure in any particular person. There must be wide individual differences in the amount of change that is experienced as pleasurable. Some people learn to be comfortable only in the office, the coal mine, the classroom, or in the hurly-burly of downtown. Sometimes prisoners even become conditioned to their cells.

Frequent exposure to any stimuli tends to become pleasurable, or at least comfortable, to a person. We like the foods eaten in our childhood home, the music of our own particular culture, and the architectural style of our own society and time. Even so, most of us welcome change if it is not too drastic or demanding and all the creature comforts are supplied. Travel and vacationing can provide such a change.

---

7. Russ Johnston, "Motivation in a Changing Environment," *Operations Bulletin*, American Hotel and Motel Association, September 1970.

The Need for the Familiar

Evidence that North American travelers want change, but not too much, is seen in the hotels most of them select when abroad. Do they stay at an old established hotel in Madrid, Istanbul, or Rome? No; they are likely to have reserved a room at the new Hilton. The rooms at any Hilton are pretty much alike, the food is safe, and familiar hamburgers are served.

Returning to their rooms at the end of a day of sight-seeing, tourists welcome the Hilton rooms, which feel safe and familiar. They will sally forth each morning to see strange people, smell new smells, and hear exotic sounds, but at night they want security. Let the room have a few lamps and pictures reflecting the local color. But the bed must be large and American. The lobby decor can contain whatever symbolizes the locale; the dining room too. But the menu must be American. Most Americans do not play around with their stomachs.

It has been pointed out that balconies on hotels are popular because insecure travelers can sit on them, safe and secure, while participating vicariously in a strange environment. One Kenyan hotel carries the balcony idea a step further—the guest rooms are built in trees overlooking an area where wild animals congregate.

Increased Leisure Time

Leisure, great massive chunks of leisure, is scheduled to become available for millions in the affluent nations in the upcoming years. The length of the work week is expected to decline, and the number of days for vacation is forecast to increase.

Leisure time can be used for good or ill. At least people will have more opportunity for the happy life and less necessity to compete for their daily bread. Philosophers such as Bertrand Russell posit that if people are given the opportunity for a happy life, they will become more kindly and less suspicious of each other. The taste for war will die out, partly for this reason and partly because war involves unending hard work for all who engage in it. Other commentators foresee leisure resulting in a vast restiveness that bodes ill for all.

No matter what the viewpoint, it seems clear that there will be more money, more time, and a greater inclination for travel and vacationing.

TRAVEL FOR HEALTH

Travel and vacationing appeal to basic instincts. The search for health and longevity has fostered the spa, bathing in the sea, and more recently, the flight to the sun. Sun worship comes easily to those who live in the temperate zone, whereas the tropic dweller may welcome the cool and changing climate of the temperate zone. Spa vacations have long been popular in Europe, and the new resort hotels are likely to include a spa and a wide range of facilities related to wellness and health improvement.

The compulsion to acquire and display a vacation tan may be seated in snobbery, but basking in the sun is pleasant to most vacationers. Overdone, it can cause skin cancer, but, with the use of sunscreens, the resulting vitamin D and relaxation of muscles is beneficial for most. To the newly arrived tourist at a sun resort, sun and sand connote purity. The beach or the pool is almost a place of worship and healing.

Vacationing is often considered as an investment in health, a matter that lends itself to cost-benefit analysis. Many physicians urge not one all-out vacation per year but a series of vacations as a means of recouping one's energies, interest, and enthusiasm for the job. Schedule your health, say the health counselors, just as you schedule work activities.

Three one-week vacations are likely to be more healthful than one three-week vacation. Persons highly tuned to an achievement drive often become bored with a vacation after a few days. Spacing vacations over summer, fall, and winter can be more satisfying to the vacationer, and to the tour operator as well, for the peaks and valleys of the business are leveled out.

TRAVEL FOR ENLIGHTENMENT

The urge to learn is probably innate and can blossom into a persistent search for knowledge, truth, and understanding. Travel and vacationing offer an opportunity to satisfy the urge to learn. School-teachers have long constituted a sizable part of the crowd of Americans in Europe each summer. College students are also seen in sizable numbers, both on their own and as part of study groups sponsored by universities. Many American universities have arrangements with European universities that offer summer session courses for American students. Students may combine travel with learning and receive academic credit for doing so. Twelve million persons visit the Smithsonian Institution in Washington, D.C., each year. Why? To learn. Thousands of people tour the stately homes of England. Long lines of tourists file through room after room, viewing furnishings of another epoch and innumerable portraits of the former owners.

Once an interest becomes rooted in a person, the person is likely to enjoy pursuing it. Interest reinforces interest. The interest can be in almost anything—people, language, history, geography, old churches, Roman ruins, travel itself. The urge to meld oneself with the past, to understand it, to relive it runs strong in millions of people. The sense of history is quickened by a tour of Westminster Abbey or the ancient village church. Historic buildings, battlefields, and shrines are a means of communicating with the past, of feeling at one with those who came before.

Europe has a particular appeal to North Americans; their ancestors probably came from there, and their history classes were full of it. In Europe they can learn about a culture by viewing the cities and visiting the cathedrals and castles. More than that, travelers may gain the feeling of becoming part of the culture by attending a London theater or drinking at the local pub. In Spain they merge with the bullfight crowd; in France they bet on the races; in Munich they join the beer drinkers at Fasching-time.

A British Tourist Authority study of Canadians and Americans in Great Britain found that the aspects most enjoyed were the friendly and hospitable people and the historical places and buildings. Some 400 stately homes are open to the public in Britain, and more than 500,000 people a year visit some of them. Longleat, the Tudor mansion of the Marquis of Bath, has been visited by hundreds of thousands of tourists. Woburn Abbey, home of the Duke and Duchess of Bedford; Blenheim Palace, the Duke of Marlborough's mansion; Chatsworth, the ducal residence of the Duke of Devonshire—all are educational experiences, as well as being architecturally interesting.

Once an interest has been developed in a destination area, the interest grows as knowledge increases. Advertising, of course, sparks interest in a destination, but much more persuasive and compelling is the impact created by a good book, movie, or television program. James Michener's *Hawaii* undoubtedly caused thousands of readers to want to visit the islands. His *Iberia* is worth tens of thousands of dollars to Spain in tourist receipts.

Some books obviously create interest in an area; others are thought to dampen any such interest. Charles Dickens's books create interest in London, but that London seems rather grim, not necessarily the kind of place that stimulates a desire to visit the city. Some thought the book and movie of Richard Llewellyn's *How Green Was My Valley* presented Wales as a sad, depressing place, whereas in reality the natural beauty is inspiring.

The effects of such inputs are difficult to calculate; they may work on a subliminal level of awareness for the reader or viewer. Over the years, a person reads a book about a locale, sees a television program with that place as backdrop, hears a radio program from that locale, and suddenly discovers a desperate desire to go there.

This is not to say that every traveler learns. Many are mere spectators on their journeys. Humans learn from an environment only to the extent that they respond to it. The traveler can be overwhelmed by the squalor of a destination or by the frustrations suffered while getting there. Nevertheless, travel is an enriching experience for many.

TRAVEL FOR BEAUTY OR BELIEFS

Travel can give one a sense of power and freedom that is lacking in one's workaday life. Merely sitting behind the wheel of an automobile and driving across a state presents not only a series of visual impressions but also a sense of mastery and control. Soaring through the sky may not be a conquest of space, but it can provide a sense of awe, a time for philosophizing on one's insignificance in relation to nature.

Natural beauty—a sunset, the mountains, fall foliage, a valley, trees—is usually pleasurable to the viewer. Most people are inspired, or at least awed, by the grand sweeps of nature. The mass exodus from the city and suburbs to the country on weekends is evidence of the human need to see trees, grass, streams, and the open sky.

Travel for religious purposes also motivates millions to journey to Rome, Mecca, Jerusalem, Lourdes, and hundreds of churches, cathedrals, temples, and shrines. For some it is a duty. The haj, a pilgrimage to Mecca made during the holy month of Ramadan, is an objective in the religious life of all Muslims. Millions of Japanese travel to the Shinto temples and shrines of Kyoto.

TRAVEL AS INDULGENCE

Travel presents the opportunity for many to indulge themselves in the sensuous with the possibility of ego enhancement. Travel to a poor country may give the traveler a feeling of superiority. To be escorted personally to one's room by an assistant manager in a hotel where there are three employees for each guest, merely to clap one's hands to receive service, is ego enhancing, to say the least.

Much of the pleasure of the old-fashioned resort centered on the table. For many people, food still plays an important part in vacationing. A principal reason for visiting France is to experience its culinary tradition. The old-fashioned New England mountain resort was primarily a place of respite and good food. Today's fishing lodge and beach cottage, although somewhat rugged, are probably thought of by vacationers as a chance to take it easy and relax.

TRAVEL FOR SPORTS

Much travel has a sporting event as its *raison d'être*. Millions attend a variety of games—basketball, football, or baseball in the United States, soccer and other games in Europe and Latin America. The Olympic Games occasion the movement of millions.

Interest in sports, either as a participant or spectator, is absorbing for large segments of the population. Joffre Dumazedier, a French social scientist, interprets much of this interest in "play life" as accepting a "secondary reality." Sports represent a common denominator for millions of people, a kind of separate life divorced from the workaday world, a life in which identification with a team or a sports hero sometimes overrides logic. People from many walks of life suddenly become united in their feeling of ownership and identification with a sports team or super athlete.

THE URGE TO SHOP

Could the urge to shop, to gather, and to collect be instinctual, relating to the nesting behavior seen in many animals and, perhaps, humans? To be able to peruse, to examine, to feel, and to think of the joys derived from purchasing certain merchandise is indeed pleasurable to millions of people. For them, it may even be the major reason for travel. Hordes of cruise passengers descending upon Jamaica, St. Thomas, Curaçao, Hong Kong, Freeport, the Bahamas, Singapore, and other tax-free ports give witness to the strength of the shopping drive. Nearly everyone likes a bargain; nearly everyone likes to buy; nearly everyone likes to have a reason for going some place different to do so.

The tourist who has just spent $1,000 vacationing in St. Thomas gleefully totes five fifths of rum at considerable effort to the plane, through customs, and finally home—saving twenty to thirty dollars in the process. The tailor-made suit purchased in Hong Kong is a kind of prize to be exhibited for years to come. The bizarre straw hat acquired in Jamaica labels the owner as a true traveler. What better evidence of a trip to Hawaii than an aloha shirt? A sombrero and serape have got to mean that the owner has been to Mexico. The gift of fine French perfume to a friend takes on added glamor when purchased in an exotic port.

Bargain hunting can be an end in itself. Go to Portugal for a fisherman's sweater; Chile has bargains in copper; blankets are cheap in Ireland, and everybody knows about those hand-tailored suits in Bangkok. Buy your reading glasses in Germany, your tweeds in Scotland, and your leather goods in Mexico. Being able to get special merchandise at low cost adds purpose to the trip.

Shopping in a native bazaar has its own allure; the sounds, sights, and smells are different. Somehow, the fruit purchased from the floating market in Bangkok or in Singapore is more romantic than that bought at the local supermarket.

VAGABONDAGE

Vagabondage means bondage to travel. The peregrinations of the aristocrat, the pilgrim's progress, and the widow's wanderings may have elements in common with the basic need of the aborigine to "walk about." Instinct seems the compelling force of the walkabout. Our ancestors were hunters who necessarily moved with the herds or moved on when the game was depleted. The urge to walk about may still be deep-seated in many members of *Homo sapiens*. Vagabondage may explain something about travel in general.

Except for a few (the favored classes, gypsies, and those who had dropped out of society) the social climate did not encourage vagabondage in the past. The major suppressants to travel—the need to work and the work ethic—are fading, however. Northern Europeans, Scandinavians, and West Germans particularly evidence this phenomenon. West Germans flow over the borders into Austria, Italy, Yugoslavia, and Spain by the hundreds of thousands. In Austria 80 percent of the visitors are West Germans. Although travel by Britons is largely limited by economics, the urge itself appears to be endemic. The United States has always had its vagabonds. In the past they were hobos, schoolteachers on vacation, and the rich. Education seems to spread the vagabondage virus so that, given half a chance, a large percentage of college students are ready to take off for hither and yon. They crisscross the country and fan out across the world, with places such as Amsterdam, Rome, and Paris as gathering spots.

The onset and duration of vagabondage can be observed in Japan where, in the space of a few years, travel has mushroomed. True vagabondage as seen in the form of the FIT (foreign independent tour) is growing. Group travel for the Japanese led by the guide waving a flag has given way to small groups traveling on their own. Vagabondage cannot be far away.

The good vagabond rather enjoys the unexpected and the stress of travel. Sleep on a packed charter plane, riding a crowded bus or a train, restores the vagabond but depletes those who need routine. The good vagabond rolls with the punches and is not overly disturbed by rudeness or insult. The vagabond must be prepared to be victimized periodically, which he or she stoically accepts, recalling with enthusiasm the kindness and generosity of other residents of an area. The vagabond accepts the fact that many countries are interested only in the affluent visitor and view the traveler of modest means as an affliction. Vagabonds, rich or poor, who arrive in Budapest in the high season and without a reservation may be disappointed by their reception, while the conventional traveler is shocked by some of the discourtesies displayed by cab drivers and reception personnel. On the other hand, the mechanical parrotlike guide on some of the Budapest city tours is amusing to the good vagabond but incomprehensible and disturbing to the conventional traveler.

In bondage to travel, vagabonds are forever planning the next trip, recounting or recalling the last one, or recouping their energy and fortune while reading up on a trip behind the Iron Curtain, to West Africa, or to Katmandu. Travel can be an obsession—a way of life—which is what it is all about.

The inveterate traveler becomes a collector of countries, a fancier of distant places, a connoisseur of exotic spots, people, and things. Like an investor keeping a portfolio of stocks, the "professional" traveler keeps a portfolio of travel experiences and memories, adding to them each year. Off-season for such a person is the period not traveling, the time to husband resources for the next trip, the time to read, to plan, to relish the anticipation of sallying forth for the next experience. This person collects countries as others might collect rare stamps, coins, or lovers.

Travel for travel's sake is a self-perpetuating phenomenon: "We just got into our car and drove." The idea of movement, of making good time, of being on the highway or in a plane, can be and is pleasurable to millions of people. The highways of Britain are dotted with weekend picnickers sitting beside their cars alongside a road as other picnickers whiz by. Much of travel has no real excuse other than the pleasure of travel itself.

THE FUN OF THE TRIP

Travel en route to a destination can be great fun or a great bore. Shipboard travel is supposed to be one long gala, with champagne, bon voyage parties, captain's parties, and games galore. In between resting or drinking, there is the groaning table to be attacked. A certain glamor is added to new friendships made aboard ship. Friendships can be made that might last over several years, at least by correspondence.

Travel by plane in the 1950s and earlier partook of some of the same glamor, especially when en route to far-off places for vacations. Conversations between socially acceptable seat mates and the strangeness of air travel added luster to acquaintances made in flight. That luster has been tarnished by the nature of air travel nowadays. All social classes travel, and seat mates in the same row may include a company president, a serviceman, and a young wife with a small baby. The commonality of interest is limited; so too is the conversation.

The shuttle planes between Boston, New York, and Washington on the East Coast, and between San Francisco and Los Angeles on the West Coast are likely to be filled with business persons or sales personnel who have taken planes so often that the trip is little different from riding a subway. As pointed out by sociologists, little conversation occurs between passengers. When the plane lands, the passengers are galvanized in one direction, getting off the plane as fast as possible. In spite of admonitions from the flight attendants to remain in their seats until the plane has reached the terminal and the engines have been stopped, many passengers scramble up, frantically reaching for coats and hats, poised for the dash to the exit door.

On flights to obvious vacation destinations, such as the Virgin Islands, where the dress and behavior of the passengers identify them clearly, there is a certain camaraderie reminiscent of shipboard travel. Where extended meals are served in flight, along with "complimentary champagne," the atmosphere becomes noticeably more relaxed as the flight progresses. In such cases, getting there may be half the fun.

Tourists traveling first class often begin to experience the pleasures of their destination as soon as they step aboard the transporting vehicle. A flight to Japan via Japan Airlines is promoted as a Japanese experience. The trip, an extension of Japanese culture, includes kimonoed stewardesses and Japanese food, drink, decor, and music. One of the Chinese airlines presented itself as "the world's first flying Chinese restaurant." The Aloha flights to Hawaii are of the same nature, the first-class passengers being plied with goodies representative of the islands. The idea is not new. In the 1930s some of the supertrains between New York and Florida were giving the "Florida experience" to their first-class passengers.

The experience en route may be more exciting to some passengers than the actual destination. Shipboard passengers may remember the fun and games and the good life aboard ship as much or more than they do the ports of call. Several shipping lines have presented their accommodations not as transport but as "floating hotels" or as resort hotels, which in effect they are, especially if they are cruising Mediterranean or Caribbean waters. The shipboard experience can be as exciting, as novel, and as pleasurable as time spent at a vacation destination.

For many people, the vacation begins at the port or airport, continues to the destination, and only ends when the person arrives back at the starting point. The chartered bus full of sports enthusiasts going to a game may be as much a part of the total experience as the game itself. Travel can indeed be something more than an empty experience or one of waiting to get someplace. It need not be a void, a hiatus between home and destination.

Pleasures of Pre- and Post-Travel

According to Charles Metelka, the pleasures of travel can be divided into three phases: ante-trip, trip, and post-trip. Each can bring its own distinctive pleasures. Planning a trip is half the fun. Studies have shown that people often plan and arrange for an extended trip six months or even a year in advance.

Talking about the trip and learning about the destination can be an extensive and elaborate procedure, partaking of the nature of a ritual that involves reading books, going to dinner parties with people who have already been to the destination, even attempting to learn the language of the destination's people.

Many people plan for a trip, take the trip, and—even before the current trip is completed—begin planning the next one. For them, travel becomes a way of life. Indeed, for many people of the middle class who are over forty-five, travel and the thought of travel become a major interest. Children are grown and away from home, financial security is assured; career goals have lost their potency. One trip opens the way for others and presents the opportunity to become known as an expert on that little South Seas island or that tiny village in Spain.

Sales managers are well aware of the magic appeal of travel. The prizes awarded for winning sales contests are often a trip to the Bahamas, Puerto Rico, Greece, or some other spot viewed as romantic. Such prizes radiate an allure not attributed to an automobile, a color television set, or a swimming pool. The contestants may already have these.

VACATION HOMES SPUR TRAVEL

While not a primary urge to travel, ownership of a vacation cottage or second home reinforces the need to travel and to take vacations. The fishing lodge, the hunting camp, or the seaside cottage have long played a part in the vacationing behavior of thousands of North Americans.

Part of being well-to-do includes having more than one domicile—an apartment in Manhattan, a winter home in Palm Beach, a place in Cannes. At the turn of the century, it was a "cottage" (mansion) at Newport, Rhode Island. With the upper middle class, it might be a home on Kezar Lake in Maine or a small frame cottage on Lake George in New York. The fishing camp in Minnesota or in Canada appeals to the Midwesterner and involves only an automobile trip.

The middle-class American can also own a home or a condominium in the Caribbean. The Connecticut restaurant operator has a summer home in Barbados; the Kansas professor owns a condominium in Maui. When not using the house or apartment, the owner can have it rented by an agent, and the rental payments may cover the cost of the mortgage payment and maintenance fee. A condominium in Honolulu gives the owner a very good reason for spending vacations there. It may also be an excellent investment because of inflation and the growth of tourism in the islands.

Thousands of apartments in Florida are owned by New Yorkers and Midwesterners who spend winters there and rent the apartments for the rest of the year. The cost of the trip to Florida is taken as a business expense for income tax purposes. As affluence grows, the building of hundreds of thousands of vacation homes or apartments can be expected in the Caribbean, Central America, the Mediterranean, and other subtropical and tropical areas around the world—all of them inducing travel that combines business and pleasure. Owning a time-share at a resort almost assures an annual visit to the resort. The cost of the time-share remains whether or not the owner uses the room or apartment set aside in the time-share contract.

TRAVEL TO GAMBLE

The urge to gamble, to take a risk, is found in nearly every culture from the most simple to the most complex. Gambling can provide an excitement not found in the safe confines of suburbia. For the poor, it offers a chance to get a lot for a little. For some, it develops into an addiction as strong as that for drugs.

Travel for the purpose of gambling is growing in importance. Millions of people go to the remote desert town of Las Vegas each year for the opportunity to lose their money in nice, clean surroundings. Other millions go to Atlantic City, London, Reno, Monaco, the Bahamas, and other destinations where various games of chance are legal. Gambling on horses was a major appeal of Saratoga Springs in its heyday. The dog track at Hialeah and jai-alai courts are a major appeal of south Florida.

Places like Atlantic City offer a break in the sameness of life, a place for gamblers to enjoy a little risk, an inexpensive buffet meal, maybe even a risqué show. Thousands of buses arrive each month carrying passengers who then stand glued to the hundreds of slot machines, waiting for the three cherries to show and bring the glad clatter of nickels pouring into the winner trays. They may also feel some excitement in watching the high rollers win (and lose) thousands of dollars.

Las Vegas attracts about 14 million visitors a year. The visitor cuts free—for a few days. At the major shows the adrenaline is jump started by off-color jokes, scantily clad long-legged beauties, and a revved-up sound system that sends decibels careening through the nervous system. Get something for nothing: craps for the sophisticates, slots for the sluggish, keno for the bingo fans. The food is wonderful and inexpensive.

But, as one writer puts it, this goes on "for only three days. On the fourth morning the dreaded Vegas burnout usually sets in. Too much of most things, and too little of the rest. The central nervous system edges toward critical overload, the brain sags and sticks like last week's spaghetti found in the back of the refrigerator. The victim starts to yearn for home, limp and happily wasted. Vegas has done its job on you."[8]

Everyone wins? Not everyone, especially the addicted gambler who can't quit. In the end the house always wins.

TRAVEL AS A CHALLENGE

Travel appeals to the competitive instinct in people, especially travel to remote places involving ingenuity or hardship on the part of the traveler. To travel the length of the Pan American Highway is no easy task. Several thousand Americans visit Katmandu, capital of Nepal, each year. They may not be particularly happy with what they find, but the trip represents a challenge to be overcome.

Travel still can involve a number of risks—tropical diseases, food poisoning, immense frustrations over delays and inconveniences. Anyone who has "stacked up" for hours in a plane over Kennedy, O'Hare, or other large airport wonders why he or she did not stay home. A large number who go to Acapulco report the "Mexican two-step," a traveler's diarrhea resulting from the food. The travelers certainly did not enjoy feeling weak or nauseated, but perhaps they considered it a sign of courage, a merit badge for doing something relatively dangerous.

Some commentators deplore the conveniences and lack of problems presented by modern-day travel. Apparently, they would like us all to undertake travel only for the work and hardship that it can offer. Such inducements to travel are not widely welcomed, particularly since fear of air travel, of experiencing sickness while traveling, of being alone in a strange hotel, and other problems associated with being away from home are still major deterrents to travel.

To some people, however, travel is a chance to prove oneself. Whole families pack themselves into Volkswagen buses and take off cross-country. "We made 700 miles today driving" is meant partly as a commentary on one's stamina. To climb the Matterhorn is remembered as a thrilling accomplishment. Skiing is a constant challenge to life and limb, especially since most enthusiasts attempt the more difficult slopes.

How about the diver who travels to Australia for a chance to see a great white shark face to face through the bars of a safety cage? All it takes is $10,000 and a letter from your doctor saying you will probably not die from excitement.

Who would travel for the purpose of jumping out of a plane at 10,000 feet? Sky divers, that's who. Forget the fact that the chute may not open or the possibility of broken legs or ankles upon landing.

Perhaps every person has a touch of the "Ulysses factor," a label for the exploring instinct. According to writer J. R. L. Anderson, such an instinct is genetically rooted in some heroic types. Anderson says that the great explorers run to a type patterned after the Homeric hero Ulysses. Such heroes pit themselves against the unknown and glory in their own endurance and self-sufficiency. Driven by curiosity and imagination, they dare to seek out adventure and challenge.

THE SOCIAL NATURE OF TRAVEL

Much travel grows out of people's social nature. Humans, as social animals, feel comfortable in a tour group. Because they are with others of their kind who are predictable, a camaraderie often develops.

If a tour is for a special-interest group, the traveler may develop friendships that last for years. Some tour groups have reunions years after the tour took place. The Christmas greeting contains a reference to "the time Nellie Smith fell in the pool with her clothes on" or "I'll never forget Jack in that hula skirt."

In some subcultures, such as are found in a university faculty, travel is the accepted way of spending one's vacation. Just about every university faculty member has visited a foreign country and has a set of color slides ready to prove it. Sabbaticals and the foreign assignments possible for university teachers encourage travel and the development of a passion for it.

---

8. "His Las Vegas Is Decadent But Clean-Cut," *Los Angeles Times*, June 21, 1981.

According to Charles Metelka, travel increases the "sociability resources" of individuals. It makes us more interesting to ourselves and to others. Instead of name dropping, travelers "trip drop." They have a ready supply of stories of what happened in London, Tijuana, or Cape Cod.

THE TRAVEL SNOB

Travel can be a socially acceptable, almost limitless source of reward for those with the time, the money, and the energy to undertake it. For many, it is almost a necessity if one is to maintain status with one's neighbors. Undoubtedly, much travel is done merely for the sake of keeping up with the Joneses and being able to appear knowledgeable about foreign places. Travel snobbery can be just as gratifying as money snobbery, education snobbery, or family snobbery. It takes a certain amount of wealth, ingenuity, and energy to travel widely.

The travel snobs like to be able to tell about the places they have seen, the hotels where they have stayed, the restaurants that they have patronized—places that they hope their listener has not encountered.

Travel snobbery has its own rewards. Among large groups of people, the main reason for taking a trip is to be able to tell the folks back home about it. Moreover, being well traveled has a status similar to being well educated. The recent trip to Yucatan enriches the traveler and adds glamor to his or her personality. Travel talk is popular, especially if it is about travel to an out-of-the-ordinary destination.

Travel snobs exploit their trips while traveling, upon return home, and for years thereafter. On the trip there are postcards from Paris and souvenirs from Hong Kong to be sent to the right people. As Metelka points out, during the post-trip, the traveler has the opportunity of making points with the right stories. The story need not be only of that magnificent Chinese food; it can be a horror tale of being stacked up over London, lost baggage, or the stolen $300 camera. The recount value of travel and vacationing is part of their appeal, a part of the total travel package. Post-travel benefits extend over a lifetime.

VACATIONING AS A CULTURAL NORM

Travel is in part culturally determined. Where to go, when to go, and how often to go are influenced by where we grew up, what our social class is, where we live, and to what we aspire. Culture, anthropologists say, is custom, habit, and tradition. It is the way a person is programmed.

In the United States, lower-income families are much more likely to stay with friends and with relatives when away from home. Upper-income families fly more often and take more trips for sight-seeing and entertainment.

Travel and vacationing have become a cultural norm in many countries. In 1936 France decreed that twelve days of paid vacation were mandatory. A Holiday With Pay Act was passed in Britain in 1938. Such statutes established vacationing as a norm.

Seventy-five percent of the Swedish people take at least one annual trip lasting three to four days. The reasons seem plain enough. The Swedes have one of the highest per capita incomes; their long winters induce sun worship and send them flying off to Spain, Portugal, Greece, and St. Barts in search of beaches and warmth.

In England the figure is more than 50 percent. The holiday in England is a must, superseding all else, the subject of conversation year-round. Plans for the holiday are made months or even years in advance, and when the time comes, nothing is allowed to get in its way.

Where vacationing is a culture norm, not to vacation is an aberration. Approximately half of the French people take vacations away from home. In the month of August, when a large percentage of the residents go on holiday, business in Paris comes almost to a standstill. With their relatively new affluence, West Germans have also become big vacationers, spending more abroad than Americans do. The Japanese are also becoming travel conscious.

TRAVEL CAN SHARPEN PERSPECTIVE

Travel can awaken the senses and heighten awareness of one's own milieu. A trip to a foreign country is likely to provide a new perspective, greater appreciation of one's own community, and, better yet, a forceful reexamination of one's self. Many see travel as a means to gain international understanding and world peace. Travel exposures and experiences can alert one to new standards, new art forms, and even new systems of belief. By viewing a range and diversity of societies, people are likely to develop a greater tolerance for cultures other than their own. Being removed from their own culture often sharpens their perceptions and enlarges their personal data bank.

Dedicated travelers say they have a need for travel. Says Stephen F. Forsyth, a travel publisher, "Under the stimulation, excitement and self-esteem that travel brings to me, I think with a clarity seldom experienced at home. I am able to see the bigger picture, plan and dream about the future in a whole set of different mental rooms.

Knowledge and understanding seek out voids within me and solutions cascade from me. I come home eager to work and launch projects, refreshed and happy."[9]

A different view may come from the traveler to a poor country, who, seeing great poverty of a kind never before imagined, becomes grateful for his or her own conditions, or becomes ridden with anxiety, or merely feels more superior.

Why do people travel? The answers are psychological and sociological; they depend upon the individual and his or her cultural conditioning. What travelers cite as their motivations for traveling may be only reflections of deeper needs, needs that they themselves neither understand nor wish to articulate.

---

9. Forsyth Travel Library Newsletter, Fall/Winter 1987/88, Shawnee Mission, Kansas.

DISCUSSION QUESTIONS

1. Suppose you have been asked to speak on the subject "What makes people want to travel?" Give six reasons for pleasure travel.
2. If you were the minister of tourism and wanted to increase travel to your country, what recommendations would you make to your government?
3. Motivation for travel varies widely with the destination. What would you say is the basic motivation for travel to Hawaii compared with travel to Chicago?
4. Under what circumstances can travel become a social necessity?
5. Why will the average middle-class American business person traveling abroad stay at an American-affiliated hotel?
6. This textbook gives the term *vagabondage* a particular meaning as related to travel. Explain that meaning.
7. Explain the Ulysses factor as it relates to travel. Is it universal? Explain.
8. What kind of person is likely to prefer the tour group to independent foreign travel?
9. Describe the travel snob.
10. Las Vegas and Atlantic City attract millions of people each year. Other than the urge to gamble, what are the motives for going to these cities?
11. Mountain climbers, when asked why they climb a particular mountain, reply, "Because it's there." How does such a statement apply to travel?

FOUR

TRANSPORTATION

Part A: Air-Travel – Planes and Airports

The horse as a symbol of travel has persisted in the language since people walked (used shank's mare), rode horseback, or rode in horse-drawn carriages. Then came the iron horse, rail travel. Later, horsepower was placed under the hood of an automobile. Finally, it was the winged horse, the airplane, that became the symbol of travel.

Since about 1935, in the short space of fifty years, air travel has laced the world together, brought millions of strangers face to face, made possible great resorts on remote islands, fostered multinational enterprises, and broadened the horizons of hundreds of millions of people. In 1987 some 447 million passenger trips were taken on scheduled airline flights in the United States, amounting to almost 40 percent of the world's commercial air traffic. That number promises to grow, perhaps doubling by the year 2000.[1]

Amazingly, all of those tens of millions of air travelers in the United States are carried by only about 3,000 commercial jet planes, operated by about 100 U.S. airlines. Worldwide, the total number of commercial jets is only about 7,000.

This chapter discusses air travel and the airports that serve 80 percent of U.S. air passengers.

The next chapter discusses the airlines and the people who service and fly the planes and serve the public; it also looks briefly at the future of air travel.

DEVELOPMENT OF AIR TRAVEL

The DC-3, introduced in 1935, became the hero of aircraft design both for commercial flying and for military use during World War II. Built to carry twenty-one passengers, it enabled commercial airlines to make a profit without needing government subsidies for carrying mail. One of the safest planes ever constructed, the DC-3 can cross the Rocky Mountains using only one of its two engines. More than 10,000 planes were built, the last in 1946; by 1985, fifty years after being introduced, some 1,000 DC-3s were still carrying cargo and passengers. Flying at something less than 175 m.p.h. and below 10,000 feet, the planes—when properly maintained—have proved virtually indestructible.

By 1939 Pan American had scheduled a regular trans-Atlantic flight using a seaplane, the Dixie Clipper. It stopped in the Azores, Lisbon, and Marseilles. Today, some 100 jetliners are making trans-Atlantic flights at any given time.

---

1. Somerset R.Waters, *Travel Industry World Yearbook, The Big Picture – 1988*. New York: Child and Waters, 1988, p. 138.

During World War II every available plane was pressed into military service. The war familiarized thousands of service personnel with air travel. Thousands of pilots were trained, hundreds of airports were built, and great advances were made in aircraft design.

During the war, Boeing, Lockheed, and Douglas had huge staffs and developed large facilities. Following the war, in 1946, Douglas produced the DC-6, which carried fifty passengers at 300 miles per hour. Later changes raised passenger capacity to 102 and speed to 375 miles per hour. By the 1980s Boeing had outstripped its competitors.

From Propeller to Jet Engine

The giant step in the growth of the commercial aircraft industry was in the development of the jet plane by the Germans during the closing months of World War II. Imagine the surprise of Allied pilots, who saw a new German fighter plane that had no propeller, flew with a deep roar, and flashed through the air with a speed of more than 500 miles per hour. It was a jet-propelled Messerschmitt, the ME-262.

Figure 4-1 compares the simple propeller engine with the turboprop, the turbojet, and the turbofan jet engines.

The piston engine (which has pistons as in an automobile engine, only mounted radially) turns the propeller, which "bites" the air and shoots it to the rear and under the wings, both lifting the plane and propelling it forward.

The turboprop engine uses a gas turbine to spin the propeller in the same manner, which provides smoother power than that given by pistons. Both engines depend upon relatively dense air, which means the plane is limited to lower altitudes and speeds.

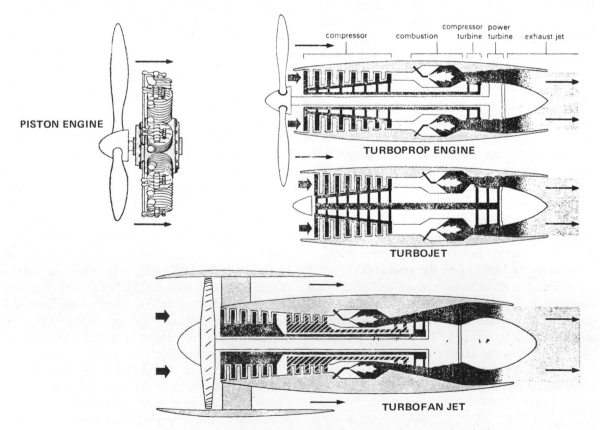

4-1. Four types of airplane engines: the piston, turboprop, turbojet, and turbofan jet.

The "pure" jet engine sends a column of super-heated thrust straight out the back, which pushes the plane forward. In the fan jet, part of the thrust is used to turn gears that operate a second fan in front of the original one, the front fan being a kind of propeller whirling inside a cowling. Some of the thrust created by the front fan is sent down vents alongside the engine. Ordinary air and super-heated air are intermingled and expanded and shot out the back. The forward, cowled fan acts as a propeller that pulls the plane, while the original jet engine creates its own thrust that pushes the plane. At speeds below 600 miles per hour, the fan jet is quieter and more efficient than the pure jet.

Commercial Jet Planes

The British took the lead in producing the commercial jetliner, but with tragic results. The Comet, built by Dehavilland, appeared in 1952 in the fleet of British Overseas Airways Corporation (now merged with British European Airways as part of British Air). For two years these jets flew BOAC routes to South Africa, Ceylon (now Sri Lanka), and the Far East. Then one day over Rome a Comet disintegrated, causing thirty-five deaths. A few months later a similar accident occurred over the Mediterranean. Altogether, three Comets were damaged on runways, and three exploded in the air. Intensive investigation revealed that after 9,000 flying hours metal fatigue caused the skin of the plane to crack. It was deduced that pressure stress created a small crack in a window frame; as the plane flew along at 450 miles per hour, the crack became a rip, and the plane was torn apart.

Jetliners are divided into the short- to medium-range types, which can fly about 3,500 miles without refueling, and the long-range planes that can fly 5,000 or more miles without refueling. To maximize their efficiency, these planes are kept in the air as many as eighteen out of every twenty-four hours.

Until the 1980s American manufacturers of jet planes virtually monopolized the field, because of the U.S. lead in military aircraft built for World War II. The catalog of U.S. jetliners is quite small. Nearly all are built by Boeing, headquartered in Seattle, Washington; McDonnell Douglas in Long Beach, California; or Lockheed of Burbank, California. In Europe, the A-300, the Airbus, is built by a consortium of European countries — Britain, France, Spain, and West Germany.

The Boeing 707 jet first appeared in 1954. On October 26, 1958, Pan American Airways inaugurated trans-Atlantic flights with a 707-120, carrying 111 passengers from New York to Paris. It became the standard aircraft for a number of airlines. With a cruising speed of 600 miles per hour, it has a range of about 6,000 miles. That same year, Douglas came out with its jet, the DC-8, today capable of 6,700 miles nonstop and of carrying up to 251 passengers.

The short- and medium-distance Boeing 727 is the most successful jetliner ever built. Adaptable to most domestic routes because of its seating capacity and because of the availability of a stretch version. The Boeing 737, brought out in 1968, is primarily a short-haul jet seating up to 140 passengers.

The Boeing 747, the jumbo jet that shook the airways when it appeared in 1969, is the major long-haul plane. The 747 was and is a remarkable plane. The tail stands sixty-three feet, five inches tall, about the same as a five-story building. The plane weighs 775,000 pounds and cruises at 625 miles per hour. Some models have a range of 6,210 miles without refueling. Its service ceiling is 40,000 feet, and it can carry up to 490 passengers. The 747 passenger jet carries as much cargo in its belly as any predecessor jet freighter does in the entire plane. The 747 is said to be safer and to give a smoother ride because its huge size lessens its reaction to air turbulence.

Each 747 costs approximately $120 million, depending on spare parts and extras ordered. Pan Am calls the ship "a highly leveraged machine." When loaded, or nearly so, it produces large profits. With few passengers, losses are great. Pan Am finds the "break-even load factor" to be about 46 percent, or 170 passengers, depending on fares, distance of flight, and other factors.

In 1976 Pan Am began flying the Boeing 747-SP — Special Performance — in nonstop service between New York and Tokyo. Westbound, it can

4-2. Planes Currently in Wide Use in the United States

Plane	Year Introduced	Number of Jets	Number of Seats (appr.)	Cruising Speed (mph)	Prominent Users	Comments
Boeing 707	1959	4	180	580	TWA, Pan Am, foreign carriers	One of the first transcontinental and intercontinental jets. Not considered fuel-efficient by today's standards and gradually being replaced.
Boeing 727	1964	3	145 (in 727-200 series "stretch" version)	600	Almost all U.S. domestic carriers	More 727s are flying today than any other commercial aircraft type. Known as the "workhorse" of the U.S. domestic fleet because of its adaptability to all kinds of routes. All engines are rear-mounted.
Boeing 737	1968	2	115 (737-200 series)	570	Used by regional carriers	Frequently flown in an all-coach (Y) configuration, the 737 is primarily a short-haul jet; it is economical to operate and currently in high demand. The new 737-300 series accommodates up to 140 passengers.
Boeing 747	1970	4	400–500	600	TWA, Pan Am, United, American, Northwest, most major foreign carriers	The terms wide-body and jumbo were coined to describe the 747. Mostly used on international routes. The 747-SP (a slightly smaller version) has a range of 8,000 miles. The new 747-400 extends the range to 8,800 miles.
McDonnell Douglas DC-8	1962 (Series 50)	4	260 (in Series 60 "stretch" version)	600	United, Delta	An early rival of the Boeing 707, the DC-8 is now being fitted with new engines to produce a fuel-efficient Series 70.
McDonnell Douglas DC-9	1965	2	120 (in Series 40 "stretch" version)	560	USAir, Eastern, New York Air, Republic, American, PSA	Popular in the short-haul market. The DC-9 has been stretched several times. The latest versions, the Series 50 and Series 80, carry up to 180 passengers.

Aircraft	Year	Engines	Seats	Speed	Carriers	Description
McDonnell Douglas DC-10	1971	3	280	560	American, United, Western, Continental, Pan Am, Northwest, and many foreign carriers	The DC-10 is the wide-body of the Douglas fleet, with 3 rear-mounted engines. The over-the-water version (Series 20 & Series 30) regularly flies transcontinental and international routes.
McDonnell Douglas MD-80	1983	2	150	500		Designed for short- to medium-range flights.
Lockheed L1011	1972	3	256	575	Delta, Eastern, Pan Am, TWA, and several foreign carriers	A rival to the DC-10 and similar in design, the L1011 is often known as the Tristar. The 500 Series known as the Dash is slightly smaller and does not operate intercontinentally as its big sister does.
Airbus Industrie A-300	1974	2	260	580	Eastern	Produced by a consortium of European countries, the A-300 is a wide body used around the world. The Airbus concept envisages a large aircraft which is still economical on short-haul routes.
Boeing 757	1982	2	175	n/a	Delta, Eastern	Designed to be an economical successor to the 727. A single-aisle, 180-seat plane.
Boeing 767	1982	2	210	590	United, American, Delta, TWA	A wide-body twin jet designed to be capable, like the A-300, of efficient operation both short-haul and long-haul. Both the 757 and 767 will not be permitted under current FAA regulations to fly over large bodies of water because they have only 2 engines.
Airbus Industrie A-310 & A-320						The A-310 and A-320 represent modifications of the A-300. The A-310 is similar in size to the Boeing 767. The 150-seat A-320 will be developed if the market looks promising. So far no U.S. airline has indicated willingness to purchase either the A-310 or A-320.

Source: Christopher Hoosen and Nona Starr, *Travel Career Development* (Wellesley, MA: Institute of Certified Travel Agents, 1983), pp. 4–5.

4-3. The Boeing 707, first of the Boeing jet series; some models carry as many as 189 passengers 1,600 miles at 600 miles per hour. Note the four fanjet engines mounted under the wing.

carry 203 passengers plus 2,000 pounds of cargo, twelve cabin crew, and five flight crew. Eastbound, it can carry 280 passengers. The plane, which can fly at a higher altitude and over a longer distance than the standard 747, reduces the flight time between New York and Tokyo by about three hours, covering the 6,930 miles in about thirteen and one-half hours.

Food service on the large planes is speeded by the use of modules, similar to cargo modules, which are snapped into place on a lower level in the aircraft. The galley modules contain prepared foods that are heated in flight by convection and microwave ovens located adjacent to the module storage area. Elevators raise the food to the passenger deck when ready.

Some airlines are hooking up their passenger seats to computers so that passengers can call for a display that gives current flight information — the date, local time, elapsed flight time, air and ground speed, and distance remaining. Pop-up video screens give passengers a choice of four channels — movies, news, sports, and weather.

The Boeing 757, which became available in 1982, was intended as the successor to the popular Boeing 727.

The latest Boeing entry is the smaller, two-engined 767, which carries a flight crew of only two, is transcontinental in range, and — best of all — is fuel efficient.

McDonnell Douglas has a similar plane, the MD-80. Designed for short- to medium-range flights, it is a 150-seat modified and stretched version of the older DC-9 that first appeared in 1980. A new version, the MD-83, will have a range of 2,900 miles, made possible by the addition of two fuel tanks. The MD planes cruise at a little over 500 miles per hour, are powered by two engines, and need only two persons in the cockpit.

The silhouettes of the major American commercial planes (Figure 4-11) include some of the planes in use today. The placement of the engines — in the wings, as in the Boeing 707; on the tail, as in the Boeing 727; and in the tail and wings, as in the DC-10 and L-1011 — is a primary

4-4. The Boeing 727 Trijet has three turbofan engines grouped at the rear and can accommodate as many as 178 passengers. Cruising speed is 600 miles per hour, range is 1,750 miles, and ceiling is 42,000 feet.

4-5. The Boeing 737 Twinjet, smallest of the Boeing line, can seat 130 passengers and can cruise at 575 miles per hour. Note that the plane is powered by two underwing jet engines.

4-6. The Boeing 747 jumbo jet, first of the wide bodies, is distinguishable by the hump on the nose that houses the flight crew and an upper lounge for the first-class passengers. It can carry 500 passengers and, with a normal load of 374 passengers, can go 5,800 miles without refueling.

4-7. The Boeing 757.

4-8. The Boeing 767.

4-9. The McDonnell-Douglas DC-10.

4-10. The McDonnell-Douglas MD-80 two-engine jetliner is the first of the new-technology twin jets. A quiet, fuel-efficient aircraft, the MD-80 is a direct descendent of the McDonnell-Douglas DC-9. It seats about 150 passengers and is used for relatively short flights.

factor in recognizing a plane. The jumbo jet B-747 is identified by the hump in the forward top of the fuselage.

McDonnell Douglas and Lockheed both tried and withdrew, at least temporarily, from the wide-bodied plane race. McDonnell Douglas (the DC-10) and Lockheed (L-1011) lost millions in developing their wide bodies before bowing out. Lockheed's Tristar costs soared to $2.5 billion and almost bankrupted the company.[2]

A consortium of English, French, West German, and Spanish manufacturers called Airbus Industrie built another wide-bodied plane, the A-300 series. A truly international project, the fuselage is built in Germany, the tail in Spain, and the wings in Britain. The plane is assembled in France. It seats 260 passengers and flies at speeds up to 660 miles per hour for distances up to 1,400 miles.

2. *Wall Street Journal*, December 1, 1986, p. 29.

The nations that own Airbus Industrie are its best customers. (If strict accounting procedures were used, however, the owner-nations are actually subsidizing the company.) Airbus A-320, a wide body, has the virtue of only two engines, an advantage shared by the Boeing 767. Though smaller than other wide bodies, both it and all other wide bodies are considered too difficult to maneuver in and out of metropolitan Washington's National Airport and were banned from operating there by the Federal Aviation Authority.

Because of the tremendous cost of commercial jets, the airlines have turned to leasing them as a way of controlling debt load and charging the planes off as an operating expense. Up to a third of the commercial jets flying in 1986 were leased from such companies as Chrysler, General Motors, IBM, and, yes, Greyhound. Buying planes and leasing them is a form of tax shelter for the

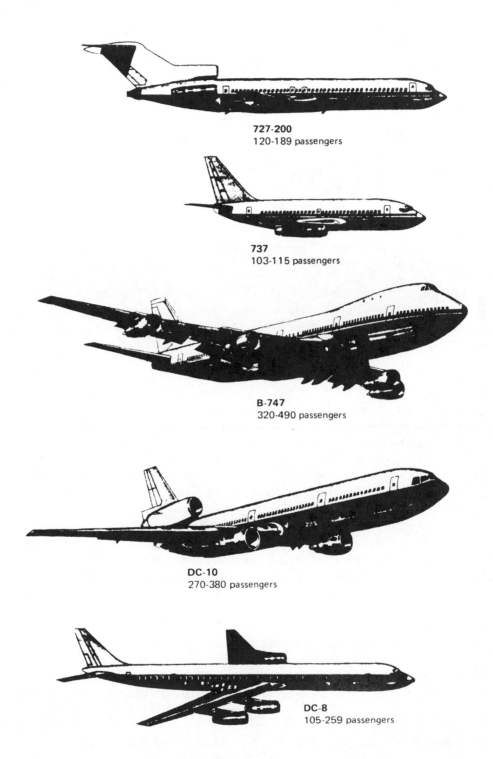

727-200
120-189 passengers

737
103-115 passengers

B-747
320-490 passengers

DC-10
270-380 passengers

DC-8
105-259 passengers

4-11. Silhouettes of some of the jetliners commonly in use today. From Robert M. Kane and Allen D. Vose, *Air Transportation*, courtesy Kendall/Hunt Publishing Company.

DC-9
80-125 passengers

707
121-219 passengers

4-11. Silhouettes of some of the jetliners commonly in use today. From Robert M. Kane and Allen D. Vose, *Air Transportation, continued.*

leasing companies, while the airline escapes an investment in planes. When the lease expires, the lessor gets the plane back and can then lease it again or sell it.

The Supersonics

After the introduction of the jumbo jet and the wide-bodied planes that fly at subsonic speeds, the next logical development seemed to be more speed. It was the supersonic plane, flying faster than the speed of sound. The step took much longer and cost much more than expected. Though a supersonic plane was proposed by President Kennedy as a national priority in 1963, the United States gave up its attempts to produce a supersonic transport (SST) for commercial use after spending $1 billion in development. The supersonic plane was left for a consortium of the British and French governments to develop at a cost of $3 billion. The Russians also have a supersonic, the TU-144, but it has been plagued with economic and safety problems.

Both groups may wish they had never heard of the SST. The British/French version of the SST, the Concorde, has a cruising speed of 1,458 miles per hour at an altitude of 50,000–60,000 feet. (The usual subsonic cruising speed is about 550 miles per hour.) The Concorde needs speeds of 200–215 knots to take off, as compared with 165 knots for subsonics. The noise level on takeoff

and the sonic booms created in flying at such speeds have created airport problems and given rise to opposition from people on the ground under the SST's flight path. Over populated areas, the SST must fly at subsonic speeds. Opposition has also come from some scientists, who contend that flight at high speeds and high altitudes reduces the ozone layer surrounding the globe, allowing excessive ultraviolet light to reach the earth, which is known to increase the incidence of skin cancer.

The SST has a number of other problems as well. It seats only 105 passengers; fuel consumption is two to three times that of a subsonic; the range—less than 4,000 miles—is also a handicap. All this, plus the fact that added speed usually increases operating costs per mile, means the SSTs run at a loss if their use is figured without "creative accounting." Some analysts believe that, if airlines operated SSTs, the added costs would be so high that they would be passed on not only to those passengers flying on the supersonics but to all other airline passengers as well.

For long flights over water and unpopulated areas, the SST is a marvelous machine. Air France has operated in between Paris, Dakar, and Rio de Janeiro; British Air between London and Bahrain, London and Washington, D.C., and London and New York.

For those who can afford to fly the Concorde—or those flying at another's expense (80 percent are business travelers)—there are several advantages. Because journey times are halved, fatigue and jet lag are diminished. The cabin is pressurized to 5,500 feet instead of to about 7,000 feet as in subsonic jets, making adjustment easier for passengers during flight. The air conditioning also balances the humidity, which makes colds, sore throats, and burning eyes less likely.

The Concorde cruises at 50,000 to 60,000 feet, which takes it out of the more heavily traveled subsonic jet levels of 30,000 to 40,000 feet. Usually the higher altitude also keeps the SST out of the jet stream (which extends up to 40,000 to 45,000 feet), and the sky appears as a deep purple. At such heights passengers can see the curvature of the earth.

The bottom line, however, has been huge financial losses for both Britain and France. Only sixteen SSTs have been built. Both Air France and British Airways would like to increase their charter business on SSTs (a flight of sixty-five minutes costs about $40,000) and make up some of their losses that way.

Even though the SST has proved economically unfeasible—mostly because of its small payload—air travel changes will probably call for an improved version, one that can carry at least 250 passengers and have a 7,500-mile range. That kind of plane would be a boon for Pacific basin travel, where current flight times are nine to thirteen hours. Air traffic is expected to double by the year 2000; in the Pacific basin it is predicted to increase four to five times.

The Newest Planes

The newest of the long-range jets are the Boeing 747-400 and McDonnell Douglas's MD-11. Both planes are being built to test the traveler's capacity to sit in one seat for a marathon 16-plus hours, extending over 7,000 to 8,000 miles. A larger derivative of McDonnell Douglas's DC-10, the MD-11, can carry as many as 405 passengers. Boeing's 747-400 can carry 410 passengers and has a range of 8,800 miles. These planes of the

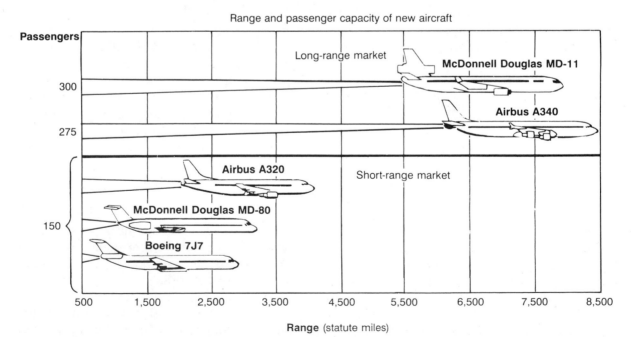

4-12. Comparison of the new commercial aircraft in the number of passengers each plane can carry and the range of each plane.
SOURCE: Adapted from *U.S. News and World Report*, April 20, 1987, pp. 42–43.

1990s will allow endurance flyers to fly nonstop between Los Angeles and Hong Kong, New York and India, or San Francisco and Buenos Aires.

By 1987 Europe and its Airbus Industrie had put about $15 billion on the line to produce a "junior jumbo," the Airbus A-340, a 275-seater with a range of about 8,000 miles, the same as Boeing's jumbo jet, the B-747. Though the A-340 is smaller than Boeing's 747, it will have wider aisles, which means quicker turnaround and greater flight frequencies because of faster loading and deplaning of passengers.

Airbus has also been building the 150-seater A-320, with a 3,500-mile range, to meet the short-range market. Airbus Industrie aircraft, says the maker, have a shorter "footprint" than that of their competitors. An aircraft's footprint is the distance from the takeoff point to the point at which the plane is no longer significantly audible. In other words, the company advertises that their planes are less noisy, a boon to passengers and to people living near airports. "You get home without waking the neighbors."

A smaller aircraft contender is N.V. Fokker, the Dutch aerospace company. In 1989 American Airlines announced it would be buying the 100-passenger, 1,000-mile range Fokkers for use on its short-haul routes. The Fokkers are fuel-efficient and require small cockpit crews.

HIGHWAYS IN THE SKY

Commercial airliners are subject to many more regulations than automobiles, and they fly along airways or air corridors just as cars travel on highways on the ground. Jet Eighty, for example, is a major aerial artery across the central part of the United States. Airways do not necessarily connect cities: they follow radio beams emitted from navigation stations 200 to 300 miles apart. Except for deviations caused by weather conditions, pilots follow the sky tracks from station to station.

More important, perhaps, are international rules designed to keep airplanes well apart. Planes generally must be at least 1,000 feet above or below one another, with ten minutes' flying time between one another, and ten miles on either side.

At takeoff, planes are separated by time intervals of one minute when going in different directions, and two minutes when going in the same direction.

In the sky, commercial aircraft fly at altitudes between 18,000 and 75,000 feet. The air space between 45,000 and 75,000 feet is reserved for the supersonic jets; subsonic planes occupy the next layer down. Most subsonic jets fly at about 30,000 to 40,000 feet, where the thinner air of the higher altitudes offers less resistance to the plane and reduces the amount of fuel needed. The lowest layer is used by turboprop and propeller-driven aircraft. Below 18,000 feet and outside established airways, pilots generally fly on a "see and be seen" basis without radar guidance.

Passengers in a plane coming in for a landing at night will notice lines of white stroboscopic lights. These are sequence flashers that aid the pilot in marking the runway center line. The red approach lights indicate an "undershoot zone," an unobstructed runway section some 1,000 feet long in which pilots should not land.

Effect of the Jet Stream

Do you ever wonder why it takes about half an hour longer to fly from the East Coast to the West Coast than to fly west to east? The answer involves the jet stream. Winds resembling huge streams circle the hemisphere, usually at altitudes of 30,000 to 40,000 feet. These jet streams are established when cold polar air comes into contact with hot air from the tropical regions. They flow generally from west to east, but may flow north to south and meander at times. Airline pilots can ride these streams when flying east but must necessarily buck them when flying west.

Jet streams racing across the upper skies represent tremendous amounts of energy. They determine much of the variation in weather experienced around the world.

Little was known about jet streams until near the end of World War II, when the B-29 Super Fortresses flying toward Japan at higher altitudes were slowed by as much as 200 miles per hour. Later, meteorologists plotted these wind paths and found west-to-east winds traveling as fast as 400 miles an hour, somewhat faster in winter and slower in summer.

These "rivers of air" in the atmosphere are often much longer than the longest river on earth. Some flow completely across the United States or Canada. At times they join with other streams over most of the Northern Hemisphere. A jet stream will curve from the northern to the southern borders of the United States or even from Canada into Mexico. Following the direction of the stream as it advances from the Pacific Ocean helps the meteorologist forecast weather in the United States and Canada. In the winter, jet streams are found over the area extending along the West Coast to the Gulf of Mexico and up through the Carolinas. In the summer they are more likely to be over the Great Lakes.

ROUTING

For long flights computers are used to project the fastest and most fuel-efficient routes (fuel costs make up 25 percent of the total operating costs). The altitudes for most efficient flight are also projected. It was once believed that the highest possible altitude was best, but a jet loaded with fuel burns excessive amounts in the climb to high altitudes. The climb, therefore, is taken in steps; as the plane becomes lighter as fuel is consumed, it is taken higher up. On a long flight, such as the 6,000-mile trip from New York to Tokyo, fuel can initially account for as much as half the weight of the plane (about 50,000 gallons of kerosene). On takeoff a B-747 burns 185 gallons of fuel a minute.

Airlines are doing many things to reduce weight and the drag of the air against the outside skin. TWA reduced the number of pillows and blankets aboard. Paint, bumps, and dents on the outside have also been reduced.

Long-distance flights follow routes different from what would be expected by looking at the usual map of a flat world. Weather and traffic conditions help determine the best route. Flights from Los Angeles to London, for example, may go diagonally across the United States or fly north to Winnipeg, across Canada, over Greenland and

Iceland, then southeast to London. Flying from New York to Tokyo, the flight usually crosses northern Canada, lands at Anchorage, Alaska, and then aims for Tokyo.

The Hub-and-Spoke Concept

The major airlines link their routes together through a hub-and-spoke system, selecting one or more hub cities, into and out of which most of their flights radiate.[3] By linking flights at the hubs and tightly coordinating flight schedules the airline can offer more frequent service and attract more passengers than was true before 1978 when the Civil Aeronautics Board (CAB) tightly controlled all route changes. As of 1986 the airlines had set up some forty-three major hubs in thirty U.S. cities. For example, San Juan, Puerto Rico, is a natural hub for the Caribbean.

The map, Figure 4-13, shows Salt Lake City as a hub and some of the airports being used as hubs. Because Denver is within 90 miles of the geographic center of the United States, it is a popular hub.

An airport chosen as a hub by a particular airline is usually dominated by that airline. In 1986 U.S. Air had an 81 percent share of the market for Pittsburgh; Piedmont (now part of USAir) had 76 percent of the Salt Lake City market. Eastern and Delta carried 95 percent of the Atlanta market.[4]

The airlines that dominate a hub often raise fares for local passengers who are flying short distances. These dominant airlines control most of the gates and terminal facilities, making it difficult for competing airlines to gain entry into the airport. For longer flights fares are competitive because more airlines operate on such flights.

Although the hub-and-spoke concept promotes airline efficiency and provides for rapid change of planes, it has some disadvantages. In bad weather flights tend to back up and passengers miss their connections. Atlanta's Hartsfield Airport, a hub

---

3. *The New York Times,* January 31, 1988, p. 9.
4. "Airline Travel Revolves on Hubs," *Los Angeles Times,* May 4, 1986, pp. 5–6.

4-13. Hub and Spokes.
SOURCE: *Los Angeles Times*, January 31, 1988, p. 9.

A Delta hub at Salt Lake City, top, illustrates the "hub and spokes" of its air routes. Map shows location of some other airlines' hubs around the country.

for Eastern and Delta Airlines, has become notorious for overcrowding, long delays in departures, lost luggage, and angry passengers. As someone put it, "Even to get from heaven to hell you have to transfer in Atlanta."

In less congested hubs, such as Kansas City and Memphis, the hub-and-spoke concept works to the airline's and the passenger's advantage. Less baggage is lost, and the passenger makes a connection at a nearby gate.

Air transit points around the world are a variation of the hub-and-spoke concept. Airports become transit points because of their geographical location and their importance to large populations and concentrations of wealth and power, and sometimes for other reasons. London, Paris, Amsterdam, Frankfurt, Copenhagen, Madrid, and Rome are important European transit points. In Canada, the airports serving Vancouver, Toronto, and Montreal are major transit points. So, too, is Anchorage, Alaska, in the United States. The Dubai International airport in the United Arab Emirates is the second-largest transit airport in the world. Aside from its geographical location, it offers duty-free shopping in a 22,000-square-foot complex, a buyer's oasis that sells caviar, fancy chocolates, and videocassettes for very low prices, and is one of the few places in the Arab world where liquor is openly sold.

The large carriers rely heavily on smaller commuter lines to bring passengers to the large carrier hubs. Regional airlines fly propeller planes that carry ten to sixty passengers between small towns and major airports. About fifty regionals do 85 percent of regional traffic. Franchise-like agreements are set up between the small-plane companies and the major airlines. The commuter line arranges its flight schedule to mesh its connecting flights with the larger partner. The regional pays the major carrier a fee for such services as discounting joint fares, reciprocal ticketing, joint use of gates, frequent-flyer programs, and sometimes for the shared handling of telephone reservations. The commuter line is given priority on the list of connecting flights in reservation computers leased by 85 percent of all travel agents from the major carriers.

MAJOR AIRPORTS

The busiest airports are like giant waiting rooms for people in transit. Seventy percent of the people who fly to Atlanta's Hartsfield Airport, for example, simply land there to change planes. The busiest American airports are in Chicago (O'Hare), Atlanta, Los Angeles, New York (John F. Kennedy and LaGuardia), Dallas–Fort Worth, Denver, San

Francisco, Miami, St. Louis, and Honolulu. The busiest air corridor in the world is that between Chicago and New York City.

As more nonstop service is introduced between more cities, air traffic flows change; some airports gain flights, while others become less important as transit points.

Figure 4-14 shows the most important airports within the United States and their code designations. Some of the codes are easily identified with the city served: LAX for Los Angeles, SFO for San Francisco, CLE for Cleveland, ATL for Atlanta. Other codes are not so identifiable: MSY for New Orleans, IAD for Dulles in Washington, D.C., and so on. Canadian airport codes begin with a Y; YVR is Vancouver, for example.

Figure 4-15 gives the numbers of passengers served by the world's top fifty airports during 1986. The figures change continuously.

Chicago and Atlanta are the world's busiest airports. Despite its crowding, Atlanta's Hartsfield Airport is considered one of the best in the country. Only nine miles from the heart of the city, the airport can accommodate two landings and take-offs per minute. AT&T provides two international calling-assistance centers that give visitors detailed computer-updated information about currency exchanges, car rental availability, lodgings, local transportation, and connecting flights—in eight languages. A twenty-four-hour translation service for forty-five different languages can be connected with the service. The airport employs 30,000 people and, like all other large airports, is a big business that sends economic ripples throughout the area.

Other international airports that receive enthusiastic approval are Paris's Charles de Gaulle and Singapore's Changi.

Airports Around the World

The major airports in Canada are in Vancouver, British Columbia; Calgary, Alberta; Ottawa and Toronto, Ontario; and Montreal, Quebec.

In Latin America the major airports are located in the capital cities. In addition to its capital, Mex-ico's major airports are Cancún on the east coast and Acapulco on the west coast.

Most of the trans-Atlantic flights from America terminate in London, Paris, Copenhagen, or Frankfurt. A number of flights also land or pass through Amsterdam, Lisbon, or Madrid. Rome is another large airport center.

In the Middle East the major air centers are Istanbul, Turkey; Jedda, Saudi Arabia; and Tel Aviv, Israel.

In east Africa the major airport is Nairobi, Kenya. West Africa has large terminals in the Ivory Coast and Senegal. The major airports in South Africa are at Johannesburg and Cape Town.

Hong Kong is a large trading and tourist center with a major airport. Tokyo is the major air center for Japan. Seoul is the same for South Korea. China has its large Beijing airport, Indonesia has Jakarta, and Singapore is a major hub for the Far East.

Flights from the United States to New Zealand and Australia usually pass through Honolulu or Papeete, Tahiti, and sometimes Nandi, Fiji. The major airports in New Zealand are at Auckland and Wellington. Those in Australia are at Sydney and Melbourne.

Most large cities in the western world are not only air travel nodal points but also tourist centers that attract both pleasure and business travelers. In the United States, New York, Miami, and Los Angeles immediately come to mind. Washington, D.C., is a tourist mecca as well as the country's capital. San Francisco's number one industry is tourism.

In Europe, London, Paris, Copenhagen, and Vienna are centers of tourism as well as centers of culture, government, and business.

South of our border, Mexico City, Caracas, and Rio de Janeiro are major travel and transit centers. Tokyo, Bangkok, and Singapore stand out as tourist centers in the Orient. Yet size alone does not create tourist appeal. Places like Bombay, São Paulo, Calcutta, and Jakarta have huge populations, but arouse little tourist interest.

Airport Accessibility

Accessibility of airports to a city's center varies widely. Getting to and from airports can take as long or longer than the actual flight. The ride by cab from Tokyo's Narita Airport to downtown Tokyo or from the São Paulo International Airport to downtown São Paulo costs $50 or more. Late night and early hours may mean expensive cab rides since bus and limousine service is curtailed or shut down. Boston's Logan Airport, on the other hand, is a few minutes from the downtown area. A similar situation applies in Washington, D.C. A number of international airports require one to two hours of travel from the centers

---

4-14. Important United States Airports and Their Abbreviations

Alabama
  BHM Birmingham
Alaska
  JNU Juneau
  ANC Anchorage
Arizona
  TUS Tucson
  PHX Phoenix
Arkansas
  LIT Little Rock
California
  SFO San Francisco/Oakland
  LAX Los Angeles
Colorado
  DEN Denver
Connecticut
  BDL Hartford/Springfield, MA
Florida
  MCO Orlando (International)
  TPA Tampa/St. Petersburg
  MIA Miami
Georgia
  ATL Atlanta
  SAV Savannah
Hawaii
  HNL Honolulu
  ITO Hilo
Idaho
  BOI Boise
Illinois
  ORD Chicago (O'Hare)
  SPI Springfield
Indiana
  IND Indianapolis
Iowa
  CID Cedar Rapids
  DSM Des Moines
Kansas
  TOP Topeka
  ICT Wichita
Kentucky
  SDF Louisville
Louisiana
  MSY New Orleans

Maine
  BGR Bangor
  PWM Portland
Maryland
  BWI Baltimore
Massachusetts
  BOS Boston
Michigan
  DET Detroit (City)
Minnesota
  DLH Duluth
  MSP Minneapolis/St. Paul
Mississippi
  JAN Jackson
Missouri
  MCI Kansas City (International)
  STL St. Louis
Montana
  BTM Butte
Nebraska
  OMA Omaha
  LNK Lincoln
Nevada
  RNO Reno
  LAS Las Vegas
New Hampshire
  MHT Manchester
New Jersey
  EWR Newark
New Mexico
  ABQ Albuquerque
New York
  ALB Albany
  BUF Buffalo
  LGA New York City (LaGuardia)
  JFK New York City (Kennedy)
North Carolina
  RDU Raleigh/Durham
North Dakota
  BIS Bismarck
  FAR Fargo
Ohio
  CLE Cleveland
  BKE Cleveland (Burke)
  DAY Dayton
  CVG Cincinnati

Oklahoma
  TUL Tulsa
  OKC Oklahoma City
Oregon
  PDX Portland
Pennsylvania
  ERI Erie
  PHL Philadelphia
  PIT Pittsburgh
Rhode Island
  PVD Providence
South Carolina
  CHS Charleston
South Dakota
  RAP Rapid City
  FSD Sioux Falls
Tennessee
  MEM Memphis
  BNA Nashville
Texas
  DFW Dallas/Fort Worth
  SAT San Antonio
  HOU Houston
Utah
  SLC Salt Lake City
Vermont
  BTV Burlington
  RUT Rutland
Virginia
  RIC Richmond
Washington
  SEA Seattle
  GEG Spokane
West Virginia
  CRW Charleston
Wisconsin
  MKE Milwaukee
  MSN Madison
Wyoming
  CYS Cheyenne
District of Columbia
  DCA Washington, D.C. (National)
  IAD Washington, D.C. (Dulles)

4-15. Worldwide Airport Traffic Top 50 Airports — 1986	
Airport	**Total Passengers**
1. O'Hare, Chicago	53,338,056
2. Hartsfield, Atlanta	45,191,480
3. Los Angeles	41,417,867
4. Dallas/Ft. Worth	39,945,326
5. Stapleton, Denver	34,685,944
6. Heathrow, London	31,315,300
7. Newark	29,433,046
8. San Francisco	28,607,363
9. Kennedy, N.Y.	27,223,733
10. Tokyo International, Japan	27,217,761
11. LaGuardia, N.Y.	22,188,871
12. Miami	21,947,368
13. Logan, Boston	21,862,718
14. Lambert, St. Louis	20,352,383
15. Frankfurt/Main, West Germany	19,802,229
16. Orly, Paris	18,543,670
17. Honolulu	18,235,154
18. Osaka, Japan	17,694,649
19. Detroit Metropolitan	17,604,583
20. Toronto, Canada	17,136,147
21. Minneapolis–St. Paul	17,073,605
22. Gatwick, London	16,309,300
23. Greater Pittsburgh	15,989,507
24. Charles de Gaulle, Paris	14,427,026
25. Washington National	14,307,980
26. Houston Intercontinental	13,996,015
27. Sea-Tac, Seattle	13,642,666
28. Sky Harbor, Phoenix	13,274,015
29. Philadelphia	12,780,306
30. Orlando	12,495,346
31. McCarran, Las Vegas	12,303,400
32. Fiumicino, Rome	12,241,145
33. Charlotte/Douglas International	11,987,339
34. Mexico City	11,310,871
35. Stockholm, Sweden	10,599,000
36. Kingsford Smith, Sydney	10,114,958
37. Salt Lake City	9,990,986
38. Copenhagen, Denmark	9,971,012
39. Athens, Greece	9,599,651
40. Zurich, Switzerland	9,250,967
41. Tampa	9,198,139
42. San Diego	9,084,438
43. Dulles, Washington, D.C.	8,962,346
44. Changi, Singapore	8,912,233
45. Memphis	8,725,359
46. Baltimore/Washington International	8,670,506
47. Dusseldorf, Federal Republic of Germany	8,493,402
48. Vancouver, Canada	8,385,000
49. Kansas City	8,309,567
50. Amsterdam Schiphol, Netherlands	8,207,969

SOURCE: Airport Operations Council International.

of the cities they serve. London's Gatwick Airport, however, is connected by train to Victoria Station in London. The train runs every fifteen minutes and takes forty-two minutes.

Airport Shortage

Low fares brought on by deregulation, coupled with a strong economy, increased the number of U.S. air passengers from 275 million in 1978 to more than 450 million in 1987. Crowded parking lots, long lines in restrooms, flight delays, and missing baggage were some of the results. More important, jammed skyways and runways increased the possibility of collisions, and the practice of hubbing added to the congestion. Even though the United States has 500 airports that offer commercial air service, more than 80 percent of the passengers use the top forty.

Not one major airport has been built in the United States since 1974, although Denver has a new airport under way, which is scheduled to open in 1993.

The Federal Aviation Administration (FAA) wants more airports but problems abound. Few cities want them; the cost is tremendous. A big new airport can take ten to twenty years to build and can cost up to $3 billion. Moreover, aviation analysts advise that major new airports will require 25,000 to 30,000 acres to provide enough space to avoid noise restrictions. Initially, the money must come from cities, states, and the Federal government. Eventually, the airlines (which means the flying public) pay much of the cost in the form of increased landing fees and airport-lease payments that go to retire bonds issued by a local government — often a city, county, or hybrid-board that operates the airport.

Air travelers within the United States pay an 8 percent tax on every ticket purchased; the tax is supposed to pay for, maintain, and expand airports. The money accumulates in the Airport and Airways Trust Fund. Critics point out that the money is not being used as intended; as of 1987 the fund had accumulated $5 billion. In light of rising congestion and traffic delays, say the critics, safety is being compromised. The FAA has responded that the delays were caused by over-scheduling of flights during the popular departure times, a situation which they say did not compromise flight safety.

DETERRENTS TO FLYING

Despite the obvious time advantages of long-distance travel by plane, a number of disadvantages remain. Among these are the difficulties and vexations in getting to and from many airports, airport congestion, lost or damaged luggage, the decline in security in airport parking lots, and theft in airports. Jet lag (discussed in a later chapter) leaves nearly all long-distance flyers befuddled, some a great deal more than others. At times skyjacking has been a real threat, and in 1985 terrorism played a prominent part in flights to Europe and the Middle East.

Theft in Airports

Theft has increased at major airports. Travelers are warned not to leave their luggage even for a moment. Cars in airport parking lots, which were once considered safe because of security patrols, may have parts stolen, or the entire car may be gone when the owner returns. Thieves usually work with confederates when stealing purses and luggage. International travelers, who are most likely to be carrying large sums of cash, are particular targets.

Pickpockets are constantly devising new gambits to distract travelers and steal from them. One ploy is to drop a large number of quarters near the quarry. As the solicitous traveler helps collect the money, a confederate walks off with the baggage. A Japanese visitor was robbed of $10,000 with this little game at the Los Angeles International Airport. The motto is keep everything in sight and within reach.

Fear of Flying

A major deterrent to flying is fear. One of every six adult Americans — 25 million people — is afraid to fly. The reasons may be explicit or unconscious. Some become anxious at the thought of a plane trip; some become nauseated in flight; others are so miserable over the thought of flying that it colors or overrides all the pleasurable aspects of a vacation trip. A few people absolutely refuse to fly and will go to almost any length in order to avoid flying.

Such fears can be overcome by psychological therapy involving behavior modification. Some psychologists use a form of mild hypnosis. They begin by teaching the person to relax by tensing and then relaxing the various muscle groups of the body. The subject is told to concentrate on breathing or on some pleasant image. After being put into a mild trance, the subject is asked to imagine various experiences about flying, such as purchasing a ticket, boarding a plane, and watching the scenery out of the window. This sequence is repeated several times so that the person finally associates pleasure with each of the actions involved in the trip.

Sometimes subjects are taken to the airport under favorable conditions. By the use of conditioning, the psychologist can teach a person to participate in flight with pleasure. This process may take ten weeks, one session a week, to arrive at that state.

TRANSPORTATION

DISCUSSION QUESTIONS

1. How did the two world wars affect today's long-distance travel?
2. The Boeing Company dominates commercial jet sales. Under what circumstances could the company lose its top position?
3. You own a downtown hotel. A new airport is being recommended on a site 25 miles away. Are you for or against the new airport? What factors influence your decision?
4. As a travel agent, you are dealing with a client who wants to go to Strasbourg, France, which is on the German border. Would you recommend flying via Paris or Frankfurt, Germany?
What information would you need to make the recommendation?
5. As chief executive officer of a large corporation, under what circumstances would you authorize first-class air travel for executives? What about travel on a supersonic jet?
6. Several major airlines operate their route system under a hub-and-spoke plan. What conditions would call for a change in the hub city?
7. As chief executive officer of a major airline, under what conditions would you recommend the development and purchase of a 1,000-seat jetliner?

Part B: Airlines

"In the space age man will be able to go around the world in two hours, one hour for flying and the other to get to the airport."[5] In the past, airlines were classified as commuter, regional, national, and international. They are now classified according to annual revenues. Major carriers have annual gross revenues exceeding $1 billion; national carriers $100 million to $1 billion; large regionals, 10 million to 99.9 million. Medium regionals have incomes of less than $10 million. Some 230 commuter airlines fly relatively short distances. The major or trunk airlines fly nationally and/or internationally.

Flight distances largely determine the size of the plane. Long-distance and heavily traveled routes are flown by the wide-bodied planes—the Boeing 747, the Lockheed 1011, and the Douglas DC-10. The Airbus is used by those European countries that are part of the consortium that builds it; it has been adopted by some American carriers as well.

Regional airlines are likely to use the Boeing 727, 737, 757, and 767 for their shorter distances; these planes lack the range to fly overseas.

Most of the world's airlines of any importance are listed in Figure 4-16, along with the code by which each is known. Aeroflot is by far the world's largest airline, which is understandable since it is the only airline in the Soviet Union.

THE CHARTERS

Operators of charter flights have much more flexibility than operators of scheduled flights. The charter operator may change itineraries or cancel a flight even if it is too late for passengers to make alternative arrangements at a comparable price. In-flight services vary, depending upon how much the tour operator contracts to pay. The worst part

of traveling by charter is that the seating configuration has usually been changed to crowd in more passengers. The *pitch*, the distance between each row of seats, is cut to thirty or fewer inches, compared to forty inches in first class and thirty-four to thirty-six inches in tourist class on regularly scheduled airlines. The width of each seat is such that a 200-pounder or anyone over average size can barely squeeze into it. Crowded planes on long flights also mean long lines of people waiting to use probably dirty toilet facilities.

The charter plane companies did well financially, especially with contracts to fly military personnel during the Vietnam War. With deregulation, the difference between scheduled and supplemental carriers (as the chartered companies were called) tended to blur. Scheduled airlines offered charter flights, and the "nonscheds" began offering scheduled flights.

INTERNATIONAL AIRLINE ORGANIZATIONS

Two international organizations based in Montreal are concerned with airline coordination and safety—the International Civil Aviation Organization (ICAO) and the International Air Transport Association (IATA). ICAO is an association of national governments; IATA, an association of airlines. ICAO, an intergovernmental regulatory agency, concentrates on air navigation and air transport as regards safety and coordination of air services. It is funded by governments, with the lion's share coming from the United States.

In the past a principal purpose of IATA was to get member airlines to agree voluntarily on air fares on international flights. Members generally lived up to the agreements, which kept air fares higher than would have occurred in open competition. There was some cheating, since some air-

5. Neil McElroy, in *Empires of the Sky* by Anthony Sampson. New York, Random House, 1984, p. 18.

4-16. Some Airline Codes

AA	American Airlines	ID	Pan Am/American	PZ	Lineas Aereas Paraguayas (LAP)
AB	Air Cortez	IL	Intercontinental Airways	QF	Qantas
AC	Air Canada	JL	Japan Airlines	QR	Air Florida/Lacsa
AF	Air France	JM	Air Jamaica	QZ	Zambia Airways
AG	Aerolineas/Varig	JN	Rich International	RC	Republic
AI	Air India	JU	Yugoslav Airlines—JAT	RG	Varig Airlines
AK	American/BWIA/Pan Am	JW	Arrow Airways	RJ	ALIA—Royal Jordanian Airlines
AM	Aeromexico	KE	Korean Airlines		
AN	Air National	KL	KLM Royal Dutch Airlines	RK	Air Afrique
AO	BWIA/Pan Am	KM	Air Malta	RO	Tarom
AR	Aerolineas Argentinas	KT	British Air Tours	RY	Arista International Airways
AT	Royal Air Maroc	KU	Kuwait Airways		
AV	Avianca	KX	Cayman Airways	SA	South African Airways
AY	Finnair	LA	Lan-Chile	SF	Air Charter International
AZ	Alitalia	LB	Lloyd Aero Bolivia	SK	SAS Scandinavian Airlines System
BA	British Airways	LH	Lufthansa		
BB	Balair	LM	ALM Airlines	SM	KLM/Sabena/Swissair
BD	British Midland Airways	LO	LOT Polish	SN	Sabena
BW	BWIA	LP	Lacsa/Air Panama	SR	Swissair
BX	Spantax (Spain)	LR	Lacsa	SU	Aeroflot
CB	Air One	LT	LTU German Airlines	TE	Air New Zealand
CF	Faucett-Peruvian Airlines	LY	El Al	TI	Texas International
CI	China Airlines	MP	Martinair	TJ	Oceanair
CL	Capitol Air	MX	Mexicana	TP	TAP Air Portugal
CO	Continental Airways	NI	American International Airways	TV	Transamerica
CP	CP Air			TW	Trans World Airlines
CV	China Airlines/Air India	NW	Northwest Orient	TZ	American Trans Air
DF	Condor	OA	Olympic	UA	United Airlines
DL	Delta Airlines	OC	Air Cal	UN	East Coast Airlines
DM	Maersk Air	OK	Czechloslovak Airlines	UP	Bahamasair
DZ	Davis Airlines Inc.	OP	Air Panama	UR	Empire
EA	Eastern Airlines	OT	Pan Am/Delta/Eastern	UT	UTA French Airlines
EI	Aer Lingus	OV	National Airways	VA	VIASA
EL	Eastern/Pan Am	PA	Pan American	WA	Western Airlines
EO	Aerostar	PC	Air Panama/Faucett	WO	World Airways
EU	Ecuatoriana	PE	Pacific East Air	YH	Aerostar
FD	Delta/USAir	PF	American/ALM Airlines	2A	Ryan Aviation
FF	Tower Air	PI	Piedmont Airlines	3A	Capitol/American Trans Air/BWIA
FI	Icelandair	PK	Pakistan International Airlines		
GL	Global International			1B	Pan Am/Arrow
GU	Aviateca	PL	Aero Peru	2B	Tarom/Austrian Airlines
HA	Hawaiian Air	PR	Philippine International Airlines		
IB	Iberia Airlines				

lines discounted fares or gave extras in amenities and food service or sold tickets through "bucket shops," the forerunners of what are now known as consolidaters, agencies which buy blocks of tickets on certain airlines and sell the tickets at sharply discounted prices.

The stated aims of IATA are as follows:

• *To promote* safe, regular and economical air transport for the benefit of the peoples of the world, to foster air commerce and to study the problems connected therewith;

• *To provide* means for collaboration among the air transport enterprises engaged directly or indirectly in international air transport service;

• *To cooperate* with the International Civil Aviation Organization and other international organizations.

Like ICAO, IATA promotes worldwide air travel and air safety. Figure 4-19 illustrates how the two organizations have worked together since their founding in 1945.

Until 1984 IATA accredited travel agencies. IATA now registers agents on a central record for member airlines to use if they wish.

The IATA Clearinghouse

IATA serves the valuable function of clearing financial balances between airlines and charges between airlines for tickets, catering ground handling, performing maintenance services, even handling aircraft leasing charges. It is estimated that a quarter of all scheduled passengers make connections between different airline companies during a single trip. The company selling the ticket owes some of the money received to other airlines. Enter the IATA Clearinghouse. Head-

quartered in Geneva, Switzerland, each month its computer processes the accounts and either bills or credits a given airline with the amount it owes or is owed. Transactions are either in U.S. dollars or pounds sterling. Each IATA member is notified by teletype of the balance payable to or by the clearinghouse, and settlement is made one week after clearance is completed. Some 250 carriers participate in the clearinghouse arrangements.

International Government Flight Agreements

Flights into and over sovereign nations are regulated by international agreements known as Air Transport Service Agreements, made bilaterally (between two nations) or multilaterally (among several nations). A number of agreements have been reached since the Paris Convention on the Regulation on Aerial Navigation in 1919. One of the most important agreements, that of the Chicago Convention of 1944, formulated the Five Freedoms (also called the Flying Freedoms) that laid down rights of airlines to fly over, land,

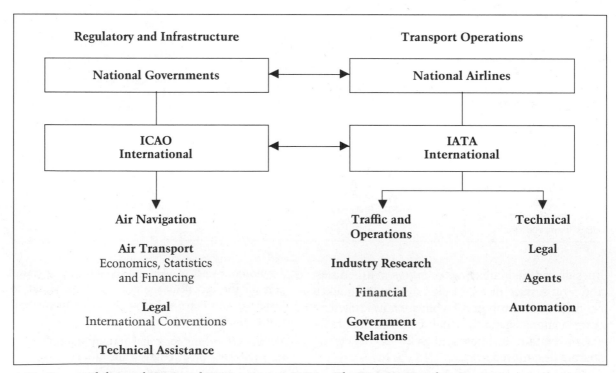

4-17. Responsibilities of ICAO and IATA. Source: IATA—The First Six Decades, Geneva.

depart, take on, or drop off passengers. Over the years three unofficial freedoms have been added to the list. Not all of the freedoms are completely accepted, and the Soviet Union is not signatory to the 1944 agreement. The eight freedoms follow:

- *First Freedom*. The right of an airline to overfly one country to get to another.
- *Second Freedom*. The right of an airline to land in another country for a technical stopover (fuel, maintenance, etc.) but not to pick up or drop off traffic.
- *Third Freedom*. The right of an airline, registered in country X, to drop off traffic from country X to country Y.
- *Fourth Freedom*. The right of an airline, registered in country X, to carry traffic back to country X from country Y.
- *Fifth Freedom*. The right of an airline, registered in country X, to collect traffic in country Y and fly on to country Z, as long as the flight either originates or terminates in country X.
- *Sixth Freedom*. The right of an airline, registered in country X, to carry traffic to a gateway—a point in country X—and then abroad. The traffic has neither its origins nor ultimate destination in country X.
- *Seventh Freedom*. The right of an airline, registered in country X, to operate entirely outside of country X in carrying traffic between two other countries.
- *Eighth Freedom*. The right of an airline, registered in country X, to carry traffic between any two points in the same foreign country.

In 1946 the United States and Britain negotiated a bilateral agreement that put together the Bermuda Principles, so called because the accord was signed in Bermuda. The Bermuda agreement incorporates the spirit of the Flying Freedoms and has become a model for subsequent agreements.

The Helsinki Accord, made in 1975 at a meeting of the European Conference on Security and Cooperation, is a general statement declaring tourism a positive force, one that should be encouraged and facilitated. The Helsinki Accord acknowledged the contribution of international tourism in the development of mutual understanding between people and recognized its value in promoting economic and social well being.

International landing and other flight agreements are used as diplomatic and economic bargaining chips and are not necessarily made in the best interests of the flying public. For example, South African Airways is not permitted to overfly or land in black African nations even though SAA might provide needed flight service. Qantas, the flag carrier for Australia, is not permitted to take on passengers in Honolulu, probably because of the additional competition it would provide for U.S. carriers.

In some regards international tourism pits nation against nation. No nation wants a travel deficit (greater foreign expenditures for travel than income from foreign travelers). One way to increase national tourism income is to gain as many advantages as possible for the national carriers and limit the advantages for foreign carriers.

AIRLINE SAFETY

The Civil Aeronautics Board (CAB) that had tightly regulated commercial aviation was disbanded in phases beginning in 1978. The final phase of deregulation culminated with the complete abolition of the CAB in 1984. Safety and technical oversight of commercial aviation is now under the jurisdiction of the Federal Aviation Administration (FAA). The Department of Transportation (DOT) inherited most of the jurisdictional responsibility of the CAB in 1985. It is to this agency that service complaints are directed.

The FAA is an agency of the DOT and concentrates on passenger safety, aircraft certification to meet safety standards, pilot licensing, and air traffic control. It is the FAA that investigates aircraft accidents along with the National Safety Board and sets standards for design and building of new aircraft and equipment. Its primary concern is to direct air traffic in the federal airway system, which covers 350,000 miles. Aircraft flying above 18,000 feet are constantly monitored by ground-based radar, and air controllers direct air traffic into and out of all sizable U.S. airports.

Flying by commercial jet is perhaps fifteen times safer than driving in a car—but not everywhere. Dakarta, Delhi, and Cairo airports have

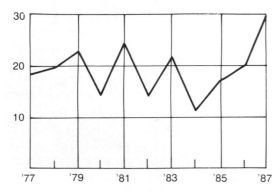

4-18. Accidents at major American airlines, excluding commuter craft.
SOURCE: National Transportation Safety Board.

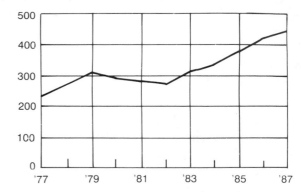

4-19. Number of passenger boardings, in millions, on domestic carriers.
SOURCE: Department of Transportation.

bad reputations for control and safety. The International Federation of Air Line Pilot Associations (IFALPA) marks with a black star those airports that its members consider "critically deficient by international standards." There are many such airports.

Reputation for safety varies from country to country. Veteran travelers avoid the Russian national airline, Aeroflot, like the plague. The odds of crashing on Aeroflot are ten times greater than on U.S. airlines. India Airlines is also much less safe than any U.S. airline.

Air travel in Europe is roughly twice as risky as in the United States; in Latin America, three times more dangerous; in Africa, four times more.[6]

Between 1977 and 1978 the number of airline accidents in the United States did not change dramatically, in spite of the fact that the number of airline passengers during the same period nearly doubled. Figures 4-18 and 4-19 illustrate this relationship.

Airline accidents reached 2,000 in the year 1985, yet the most dangerous part of the flying experience remained the trip to and from the airport by car.

Causes of Airline Accidents

There is good evidence to show that it is safer to fly during the day than at night for the simple reason that the pilot of the plane is not quite as

alert at night as during the day, and of course, the pilot lacks the visibility offered by daylight.

Pilot fatigue accumulates in a vicious circle: being fatigued makes pilots do more work, which in turn makes them feel more tired and anxious about their performance, until eventually the point is reached when the flying skills break down completely. Also, a mild diminution in oxygen content in the air can hasten the onset of fatigue.

In-flight accidents have numerous causes, such as faulty equipment, lack of correct weather information, tornadoes, and wind shear—but the vast majority are caused by cockpit error, or could have been avoided by pilot alertness, good judgment, and skill. Another cause of accidents that could be prevented is the number of small planes—noncommercial planes that are permitted to use already overcrowded airports.

In 1988 a large portion of the cabin ceiling blew off an Aloha plane en route from Hilo to Honolulu. The accident occurred at 24,000 feet, over four miles in the sky. The pilots, a man and a woman, miraculously were able to emergency-land the 19-year-old B-737 at the Maui airport with only one fatality. The cause was metal fatigue, the stress of compression–decompression on the skin of the plane from 90,000 flights over a nineteen-year period. This accident raised the question, should there be a mandatory retirement age for commercial airplanes? Some venerable DC-3s, built in the 1930s, are still in service in South America. In 1988 the average age of the

6. Anthony Sampson, *op. cit.*, pp. 211–212.

U.S. air fleet was about twelve years. Some airlines, Lufthansa for example, have a policy of replacing the fleet continuously. Other airlines fly their planes as long as they meet FAA standards.

Strange things can happen anywhere, but one of the strangest occurred in a flight on a Chinese airline. The pilot put the plane on automatic pilot and proceeded to walk back through the plane. The co-pilot did the same. Somehow the door to the flight cabin closed and locked. The pilots finally hacked down the door with axes while the very astonished passengers looked on.

Windshear has been a major cause of death in air travel. Powerful downdrafts of cold, heavy air acting on aircraft taking off and landing have been largely undetectable. These downdrafts act like a jackhammer, so strong that the pilot is virtually helpless to control the plane. Windshear can suddenly form from beneath a thunderstorm, beneath cumulus clouds, or even from a clearing sky, creating high velocity winds.

To detect windshear the FAA uses the Doppler System, which detects about 97 percent of 30-knot or greater microbursts (the most powerful of the windshear winds). A radar antenna housed inside a dome captures the windshear information and transfers it via computer to meteorologists and air traffic controllers. The controller passes on the information to pilots in the area, who can then delay takeoff, or avoid the windshear area if approaching an airfield.

FLIGHT DELAYS

Why do so many planes arrive and depart behind schedule? The airlines say, "It's because the air traffic control system is obsolete." The FAA blames bad weather and high altitude winds for more than half of all delays. Many of the rest of the delays, according to the FAA, can be laid to the owners of the airports, local governments that allow too many flights to be bunched up at the most popular flight times (early mornings and late afternoons). Given freedom of scheduling, the airlines will schedule their flights to sell the most tickets.

Bunching flight schedules at say 8 A.M. not only results in many flights getting off to a late start; the delays are also passed along through the system to other airports. The hub-and-spoke system requires a cluster of flights to arrive and depart within minutes of one another because of connection requirements.

Sitting on top of the flow control is an FAA computer in Washington that tracks all flights around the country and projects when a particular airport is likely to reach its saturation point. When that happens, the FAA issues "gateholds" to selected flights, requiring them to postpone takeoff. A delay at a major airport such as Hartsfield in Atlanta or O'Hare in Chicago creates a ripple effect of delays at other airports around the country.

DATALINK NAVIGATION

Air safety will be enhanced as satellite-navigation and data communications systems come on line. By 1993 an advanced automated system (AAS) is scheduled to go into operation. AAS is a high-speed computer network that receives positional information from eighteen orbiting satellites. Using this system, a civil aircraft will be able to plot its position automatically within a 300-foot circle any place in the world and calculate its ground speed exactly.

The information will be transmitted in digital code, thereby avoiding the spoken word. The number of aircraft that controllers can handle at one time is currently limited to how fast they can talk. Moreover, voice communication is often misunderstood. The international language for air traffic control is English, but pilots flying to foreign countries receive special lessons in the fractured English that may be used. With a system called *datalink*, now used in military aviation, messages can be flashed between air and ground in the digital code used by computers. Computers will select the best flight plans (as they do now) and will warn controllers and pilots of any deviation from the assigned course. With the new system planes can be scheduled to fly closer together. A constant flow of information will appear on an electronic map displayed on an aircraft cockpit screen. Pilots can see exactly where they are and the location of other planes nearby.

COMPUTERIZED RESERVATIONS SYSTEMS

Almost as valuable as the airplanes themselves are the computerized reservation systems owned by some airlines. Airlines, hotels, and car renters pay fees for bookings. In 1989 American Airlines sold a half interest in its Sabre reservations system to Delta Airlines for $650 million. Delta in turn offered shares to foreign partners for as much as $2 billion. United owns 50 percent of the Apollo system with the other 50 percent split among USAir, British Airways, Swissair, KLM, and Alitalia. In 1988 Apollo took in $450 million.

Besides facilitating reservations, the computer's system enables the airlines to enter data on everything from flight schedules and customer preferences to seat availability and equipment maintenance. A broken arm on seat 20D can be reported en route to the next landing and a repair crew can go directly to that seat and replace the arm. (The capabilities of the computer systems are discussed further in the chapter, The Travel Agent.)

INTERNATIONAL AIRLINES AND HOTELS

An obvious relationship exists between hotels and airlines, especially those flying internationally. Airlines want to assure their passengers of first-class accommodations at the cities they serve. Airlines feed hotels and *vice versa*. Even so, several hotels once owned by airlines have passed into other corporate hands. American, Eastern, TWA, and United all owned large hotel chains that have been sold for financial reasons.

Swissair is an example of the intermarriage of travel business segments. In a joint venture with Nestlé of Switzerland, the airline owns Swisshotel, an international chain of hotels. Swissair also controls Reisburo Kuoni, parent company of Kuoni Travel, which in turn owns Kuoni Hotel Management, a hotel company concentrating on managing hotels in the Caribbean and the Mediterranean regions.

Pan American World Airways was the first to enter into international hotelkeeping on a grand scale. During World War II, President Roosevelt met with Juan L. Trippe, then president of Pan Am. Roosevelt suggested that American interests would be best served if Pan Am would foster the growth of first-class hotels in Latin America. Out of the meeting grew the Inter-Continental Hotels Corporation (IHC). Unfortunately, later financial pressures forced Pan Am to sell the highly profitable IHC.

For a time Allegis, which included United Airlines, Hertz car rentals, Hilton International, and Westin Hotels, was a huge travel conglomerate. Computers linked the hotels, rental cars, and United Airlines. The theory was that customers would take a United Airline flight, rent a Hertz car, and drive to a hotel operated by Allegis. Computers would identify demands for beds, cars, and airplane seats, permitting the company to offer discounts and other incentives. The theory was never really tested because stock raiders forced the breakup of Allegis in 1987.

Figure 4-20 shows some airlines that owned hotels in 1988. The primary market for these hotel giants has been the business person traveling on an expense account, for whom room rates are not a major concern. Pleasure travelers, who pay their own expenses, are more concerned with room rates.

Many U.S. travelers are especially keen on staying at American-operated hotels abroad because they feel that they are safer and can expect familiar standards of comfort. They can also expect to find English-speaking personnel at the front desk and in other key positions. American-style food is usually found on the menu, another preference of many American travelers.

AIR FARES

As the cost of a mode of travel drops, its use usually increases. Air fares are a major part of most long-distance travel decisions, and they vary

4-20. Some International Airlines in the Hotel Business

Airline	Hotel Company	Number of Hotels	Where Located
Aer Lingus	Aer-Lingus Dunfey	47	Omni Hotels are part of the chain.
Alaska Airlines	Golden Nugget Motels (Fairbanks property only, others operated under Alaska Airlines, Inc.)	5	Alaska, USA only
Air India	Partnership with Hotel Corps of India		India
Air France	Meridien Hotels	59	Owns some and manages others
Alitalia, Airways, Lufthansa	European Hotel Corp.	10	Denmark, Portugal, England, USA, W. Germany, Switzerland
All Nippon Airways	ANA Hotels	29	USA, Philippines, Singapore, Australia, Japan
British Airways	Investment in hotels operated by others	40 plus	England
Swissair	Swisshole (jointly owned with Nestlé)		Hotels in Europe, USA, and Far East
Canadian Pacific	Canadian Pacific Hotels	19	Canada, W. Germany
Continental	Continental Hotels	4	Guam, Saipan, Truk, Palau
Japan Air Lines	JAL Hotel System (Nikko)	71	Worldwide. Four JHS-owned, the rest managed or affiliated
Korean Airlines	Hanil Development Co.	3	Korea, Hawaii
Scandinavian Airlines	SAS	15	Scandinavia

widely at any given time. As pointed out by the Air Transport Association of America, while airline fares remained relatively stable between 1960 and 1980, hotel and restaurant prices rose sharply. By 1980, $100 rooms in luxury hotels and $20 meals appeared. In other words, the air fare had become a smaller part of a total vacation expense package—a factor that might encourage longer distances in vacationing.

Deregulation and more efficient operations have reduced air fares drastically. The average ticket price dropped 23 percent after adjustment for inflation, even though full-fare prices rose at double the rate of inflation since 1978. In the period 1978–1988, passengers and airlines saved $10 billion annually, according to the Federal Trade Commission.[7]

Generally, air fares are set to serve two broad markets, the business traveler and the discretionary traveler. Business travelers usually have few

7. *U.S. News & World Report*, October 31, 1988, p. 51.

options in scheduling their trips. They must go now and return at a specific time. Standard air fares are quoted for the business traveler; discount fares attract the discretionary traveler. The disparity between the two can be huge. Fares for two seats, side by side, may vary as much as several hundred dollars, depending upon the discount or special fare being paid by the passengers. Discounted fares are usually highly restrictive: the traveler must go and return as specified. Penalties for not following the schedule can be high. This two-tier system of pricing puts the burden of the fare on the business traveler, who usually accepts the premium charge out of necessity and the fact that the trip is tax deductible. The individual business traveler is courted with frequent flyer bonuses in the form of free trips and other rewards.

Air fare distortion is also caused by *cabotage*, which restricts foreign airlines from engaging in passenger service within a country. For example, Singapore Airlines, which must stop in Hawaii for refueling on its way to and from the United States, is not allowed to drop off or pick up passengers between Hawaii and the continental United States. If foreign airlines were given passenger service within the country, air fares would be more competitive.

On the international scale fares are not determined by distance but by national interest, bilateral and multilateral negotiations, and competition. The People's Republic of China has three sets of air fares, one for residents, one for Chinese visitors from Hong Kong, and another for all foreigners. Rates for foreigners may be double or more than the fares for Chinese residents.

Overbooking and Bumping

Airlines legitimately overbook a number of passengers on a flight for a very good reason. A percentage of passengers who have booked seats do not appear; they are "no-shows." The percentage varies from 2 percent up to 33 percent. Some travelers book more than one flight, then fail to cancel flights not taken. Bad weather, time of day, traffic conditions, and late connections are other reasons for overbooking.

Often more passengers show up than there are seats available, and some passengers are "bumped." If they have a confirmed reservation and arrive at the departure gate at least ten minutes before the scheduled departure time for domestic flights, they are entitled to compensation. Airlines often offer money to confirmed passengers—as much as $400—to take a later flight that is not filled.

Elasticity of Demand

Much, perhaps most, business travel is inelastic. Business people can rarely postpone a trip and therefore take it with little regard for cost. Of course, if air fares rise excessively, they will consider alternate means of travel or not traveling at all. Business people continually balance the cost of their time against the cost of air travel. They may shift to auto, bus, or train if the travel distance is not too long. Numerous travelers between New York and Washington, D.C., for example, have switched from air travel to Amtrak's Metroliner.

Pleasure travel is more elastic; cost looms much larger in the travel decision when the expense comes directly out of the traveler's pocket. A cost-benefit study of the visitor industry in Hawaii showed that a 10 percent reduction in air fares increased the number of visitors to Hawaii by about 15 percent. The same fare reduction also increased the house count in Hawaiian hotels by about 9 percent, and the length of stay rose about 3 percent.[8] (For more information on air fares, see Chapter 6.)

COMPONENTS OF AIRLINE PROFIT AND LOSS

Airlines have both fixed and variable costs. *Fixed costs* are constant and do not change regardless of the amount of business. Examples are the amortization or lease of airplanes, the maintenance of airline-owned or leased terminals, interest on borrowed money, insurance, and pensions. *Variable*

8. "The Visitor Industry in Hawaii's Economy: A Cost-Benefit Analysis," *MATHEMATICA*, 1970, pp. 27–29, 187–203.

costs tend to rise and fall with the volume of sales or number of flights. They include wages and salaries, advertising and promotion, fuel costs, passenger food and drink, and landing fees.

The biggest single cost for airline operation is labor, which typically runs 30 percent to 45 percent of total operating costs for established carriers. Senior pilots for airlines such as United and Delta receive as much as $150,000 and more a year. Flight attendant jobs, once considered fairly low-paying, pay as much as $40,000 a year and provide many fringe benefits.

Inflation has made itself felt in landing fees. Landing and takeoff charges can add up to thousands of dollars per plane, depending on the airport and time of day. A fully loaded 747 may pay $9,000 to land at London's Heathrow Airport.

Once a schedule is set and the break-even point is reached, extra passengers produce large profits. (The break-even point is that amount of income that just covers all costs of creating the income.) Passenger servicing costs such as reservations, ticketing, food, baggage handling, and a small amount for additional fuel rarely exceed 15 percent of the average ticket price. Being able to offer just the right amount of discount tickets that may be needed to fill a plane then becomes highly important. Capacity control, a technique for maximizing sales income by lowering the price of seats according to the expected demand, relies on advances in computers and modeling techniques.[9]

The Load Factor

A key statistic in analyzing an airline's profitability is the *load factor*—the percentage of seats filled on all flights, including planes on low- and high-density routes and those being flown empty to be in position for the next day's schedule.

The load factor, like the occupancy rate of a hotel, is an indicator of efficient or inefficient use. Until 1974 a load factor of about fifty-one was generally considered the break-even point for an airline. In 1983 that figure was 60.3, an increase

caused mainly by rising oil prices. The break-even point is likely to be unique on any given flight because it is determined by the rate structure in effect, the length of flight, the time spent on the ground, and other costs such as wages and salaries.

An airline with the long-haul high-density route, for example, from New York to Los Angeles, has a decided cost advantage over another airline's short-haul, low-density route. The cost of flying a plane is sharply reduced once it reaches cruising altitude. A short flight thus costs more per mile than a long one because a greater proportion of flight time and fuel is consumed in climbing to and descending from the cruising altitude. In busy airports such as O'Hare, Los Angeles, Atlanta, and Kennedy, much time may be spent waiting to take off or land. Every minute's wait adds dollars to personnel, fuel, and other costs.

To keep costs down, the airlines have shifted to the newer two-engine planes such as the B-767, which reduces fuel consumption by as much as 30 percent. Aircraft have also been reconfigured to include more seats, resulting in seats that are smaller and have less leg room for the increased number of passengers.

The Management Factor

The *x* ingredient of profitability almost always boils down to leadership at the top, which is often centered in the personality of an individual. An example was Eddie Rickenbacker, America's greatest World War I flying ace, whose name and personality were associated with the development of Eastern Airlines. United Airlines was assembled under the strong leadership of William Patterson. Best known and most powerful of the airline pioneers was Juan Trippe, who started Pan American and was its head until 1968. It was largely his drive and vision that made Pan Am's famous Clipper Ships—flying boats—the carrier of the American flag across the Pacific and the Atlantic. Visionary, shrewd, and often ruthless, Trippe was the driving force that put together what was for decades the world's best known airline, always pioneering in flight technology and pushing for bigger and better planes. At one point

8. William Farrell, "Low Air Fares Are Here to Stay," *Wall Street Journal*, June 9, 1987, p. 30.

Pan Am had 40,000 employees and owned or controlled the internal airline of China and the viable airlines of Latin America.

Beginning in about 1970, when Trippe was no longer chief executive officer, Pan Am began to decline. By 1983 the company had been forced to sell its headquarters, the Pan Am Building in New York City, and its highly profitable hotel chain, Inter-Continental Hotels. Despite the two sales at $500 million each, the company was still deeply in the red in 1989. Part of the reason for this can be attributed to Pan Am's purchase of National Airlines, a major trunk line. The purchase gave Pan Am major U.S. routes that could feed its international flights, but it also brought big problems when the two airlines were integrated, among them increased labor costs, as salaries for former National employees were raised to Pan Am levels.

Delta Airlines is an example of how an efficient airline operates. For years it has led the industry in profits and, many say, in service. One of the reasons is that during peak periods pilots and gate attendants help load bags to speed up departures, and during the Christmas rush top management pitches in as well. The company places great emphasis on worker participation in the decision-making process and is very concerned with maintaining the "family" feeling. A committee of flight attendants chooses the uniforms for Delta's 6,000 stewards and stewardesses, and mechanics even choose their immediate supervisors. Without a union to prevent job switches, Delta management is free to move employees to different jobs as needed. The company temporarily reassigned 700 pilots and flight attendants to jobs loading bags and taking reservations. With cross-training such as this, all the employees understand how their jobs fit in with the overall company goals.

By 1988, Delta had the most fuel-efficient fleet in the nation by virtue of retiring its older 727s and 737s and replacing them with 757-200s and MD-88s. The 757s hold 187 passengers instead of the 128 carried by the 737s. Delta's revenue per passenger mile was 12.7 cents, nearly 15 percent above the industry average. The airline wants to keep its nonunion standing, and maintains a payscale among the highest in the industry.[10]

Deregulation and Profits

For forty years, from 1939 to the late 1970s, the airline industry was highly controlled and protected. Protected routes, protected profits, protected employees, and protected management made airline operation a kind of cartel. The major airlines even had a mutual-aid pact, an arrangement by which colleagues grounded by strikes were compensated by other pact members.

Deregulation brought major changes in the number of large airlines, which jumped from twenty-two to over eighty. New airlines often employed enthusiastic nonunion personnel; in some cases pilots worked for a third of the union salaries. Some acted as ticket agents and baggage handlers, then climbed aboard to fly the plane. The new airlines could underprice fares because of lower labor costs and more enthusiastic employees. They also used some ingenious methods to gain passengers.

Southwest Airlines sold tickets by automatic vendors that spat out the paperwork in ten seconds. It took credit for starting low-fare flights by staging an up-in-the-air hole-in-the-sock contest. A passenger with a hole in the hosiery won a prize.

Although it eventually failed, Hawaii Express was typical of the fast-start, low-fare airlines. It leased one B-747 and flew only one flight, between Los Angeles and Honolulu, each way, every day. Its kickoff fares were $89.95 one way, which broke down to about 3.6 cents per mile, an unheard-of price in recent airfare history.

To compete with such drastically lowered fares, established airlines under new management resorted to spectacular promotions. In 1981 to 1982, for example, Pan Am offered two seats for the price of one on many international flights, provided a coupon had been picked up on a previous Pan Am domestic flight. Western Airlines offered

---

10. *Wall Street Journal*, July 25, 1988, p. 4.

a round trip to Hawaii for $100 with a similar arrangement.

Most of the new airlines failed to survive. According to Airline Economics, a Washington consulting firm, 198 new airlines were formed between 1978 and 1987. Of these start-ups 160 merged with other airlines or failed. The principal reason for failure was undercapitalization. Existing airlines could underprice the new lines. In some cases the new entrepreneurs misread the market. There were not enough potential customers to sustain a new airline.

Some survivors made it by arranging agreements with a large airline: The small airline fed passengers to the bigger line in return for services such as ticketing and advertising for a fee.

Deregulation not only inspired the birth of many airlines. During 1986 to 1988 a huge consolidation of major airlines took place as airlines bought airlines. United picked up the Pacific routes of Pan Am for $750 million. American acquired Air Cal. TWA took in Ozark. Northwest got Republic. USAir took over Piedmont and PSA, an airline that served California and the Southwest. Southwest bought Muse, and Alaska Airlines absorbed Jet America.

United Airlines lost its role as the largest airline in the world (behind Aeroflot, Russia's monolithic airline). The reason: Frank Lorenzo, a company takeover artist and chief of Texas Air, bought Eastern Airlines, Continental, People Express, Frontier, and New York Air. Using Newark, Atlanta, Miami, Houston, or Denver as hub cities, the new giant controlled about 20 percent of the nation's air traffic. The company flew 588 aircraft to four continents and had about 48,000 employees. It also had a monster debt exceeding $5 billion.

By 1988 the Big Five (Texas Air, United, American, Northwest, and Delta) controlled about 90 percent of the commercial service in the United States. In 1988, according to the Wall Street Journal, eight big airlines controlled 93 percent of the nation's air traffic, and the industry was slipping cozily into the comforts of oligopoly.[11]

11. Wall Street Journal, August 31, 1988; p.1.

AIRLINE PERSONNEL

The U.S. airlines employ 450,000 workers and carry about 40 percent of the world's air travelers who are carried on scheduled airlines.[12]

Economists point out that airlines are labor intensive. It is interesting to note, however, that less than a fourth of the personnel that work for airlines actually ride in the planes. Maintenance workers, aircraft and traffic personnel, passenger personnel, aircraft controllers, and cargo handlers make up the bulk of airline employees; but only the flight deck crew and flight attendants actually ride in the planes.

Airline Pilots

The aristocrats of people transportation are the senior airline pilots of the U.S. scheduled airlines. They are aristocrats in both income and working conditions. Many live in the glamor tradition of the leather-helmeted, begoggled pilot seated in the open cockpit, with white silk scarf flying in the slipstream. Others are business people first and pilots second; they have plenty of time to operate businesses of their own, since the FAA mandates that no commercial pilot may fly more than eighty hours a month. Flying at no cost, these pilots may live in California, fly out of New York, and have a home in Acapulco or Hawaii. Their pay is related to the size of the plane being flown — the smaller the plane, the lower the salary. Pilots of DC-10s, DC-8s, and Boeing 737s receive less than pilots of 747s. Critics of this arrangement point out that personnel flying identical jumbo planes for airlines outside the United States receive less than half the salaries of American pilots. The pilots themselves argue that their vast responsibility entitles them to their salary. That may be true, but it must be said that most of the flying during long-distance flights is done by automatic pilot.

The workload of pilots and flight engineers continues to be reduced as new automatic equipment is introduced. A pilot on the MD-80 can engage

12. Somerset R. Waters, Travel Industry World Yearbook, The Big Picture—1988. New York: Child and Waters, 1988, p. 138.

autothrottles prior to takeoff and the autopilot shortly after takeoff. Once these systems are engaged, the pilot on a routine flight need not touch the manual flight controls and throttles until the plane is rolling on the ground after landing.

Airline Mechanics

Underlying the work of the flight crew are the airline mechanics, about fifteen for each commercial jet, making a total of about 50,000 in the United States. Airplane maintenance takes on increased importance as airplanes are punished by 17-hour days in the air and repeated takeoffs and landings. Maintenance is performed under the pressure of departure schedules and with the knowledge that one mistake can jeopardize the lives of dozens of people (mechanical failure ranks behind pilot error and bad weather as a cause of fatal crashes).

In 1986 mechanics working for scheduled airlines earned between $25,000 and $35,000 a year. Airlines prefer hiring mechanics who have trained in the military because of their extended training and of the discipline required in the service.[13]

Flight Attendants

The dramatic changes that have taken place in air travel can be clearly seen in the way the job of the flight attendant has changed in the short span of about fifty years. In 1930 United Airlines employed eight flight attendants, all women and all registered nurses. During flight they wore white nurses' uniforms, and on the ground they changed to green woolen twill suits with capes and berets. Their salary was $125 a month for 100 hours of work, $1.25 per hour.

One of the first stewardesses described her day's work on a typical flight between Oakland, California, and Cheyenne, Wyoming, during which the plane made five stops. Scheduled flying time at an altitude of 2,000 feet was eighteen hours, but the usual time required was more often twenty-four hours. Stewardesses loaded baggage, dusted the planes, and helped fuel them. They also helped the pilots push the planes into the hangars. The stewardesses, who turned nurses during flight, made sure that the passengers did not open an exit door by mistake while going to the washroom. If all seats were occupied, the stewardesses sat on a suitcase or mailbag in the rear of the plane. They were told to "swat flies in the cabin before takeoff," to keep passengers from throwing "lighted cigarette butts out of the windows," and to carry a railroad timetable in case of plane trouble. In the beginning, transcontinental travel by air included train travel by night because night flying was impossible. When TWA mastered the art of night flying in 1932, it cut the cross-country trip to twenty-four hours. The menu was the same every day, throughout the day: coffee or tea, fruit cocktail, fried chicken, and rolls. Steam chests were used to heat the food and beverages.

Despite the common belief that flight attendants are merely glorified waiters and waitresses, the job still remains one of the most sought after in the business. A spokeswoman for Eastern Airlines says that for every job there are eighty applicants.

In the early years, the job of stewardess (now called flight attendant) was highly prized by young women because the work brought them into close contact with the social and economic elite of the nation. In fact, many a stewardess married into wealth.

Glamor continued to surround the job of flight attendant until the 1960s. Then shuttle flights and larger planes tended to make the attendants on some flights into flying bartenders or hard-pressed waitresses, rushing to complete service before the flight was over. By the early 1970s, about 15,000 of the nation's 35,000 flight attendants belonged to the Air Line Pilots Association (ALPA). This and other unions have prevented the airlines from discharging women because of marriage or pregnancy and on some airlines have given them job security to the age of sixty.

---

13. "Timetables and Risks Put Constant Pressure on Jetliner Mechanics," *Wall Street Journal*, January 3, 1986.

4-21. In those days, the stewardesses, who were registered nurses, also helped fuel the planes and helped the pilots push the planes out of the hangars.

In 1971, as a result of a discrimination suit filed against Pan American by a man, the Supreme Court ruled that a man could not be denied a job as an airline steward because of his sex. Since then, major airlines have sharply increased the number of male flight attendants.

Because all major airlines fly about the same planes, differentiating airlines becomes a matter of marketing and service. Airlines, says one observer, can market only seats, service, and smiles. In this the Asians have excelled. Through-out their six weeks of training, Korean air stewardesses are rigidly conditioned to smile, even during reprimands. Cathay Pacific requires daily eye-contact exercises, with attendants staring into one another's eyes for ten minutes. The "Singapore Girls" of Air Singapore are taught to chant "smile, attitude, humility, and coopera-tion." Service on Air Korea is indeed unforgetta-ble. The cabin crew lines up, bowing and smiling, as passengers enter and leave the plane. Gifts are distributed to business and first-class passengers.

American Airlines, Lufthansa, and Swissair hold courses in transactional analysis.

In the intense competition existing on flights to the Orient, United Airlines hired concierges to give the maximum service to passengers flying first class. Initially, they were instructed to wear white carnations, not knowing that white flowers are a symbol of bad luck in the Far East. Red carnations have now replaced the white.

A new job category, flight service supervisor, has been established. This person, whose job title varies with the airline, is in charge of all luggage handling, flight service personnel, and general service to passengers. The job differs from the job of flight attendant in that it is a management (nonunion) position.

Declines in Service

Deregulation of the airlines led to more airlines, more flights, discount fares, and an explosion in the number of passengers (from 145 million in 1978 to 415 million in 1986). The number of flights during the same period rose from 14.7 million to 19.2 million.

To remain competitive, the airlines cut salaries and cabin crews. The consequences of that action are less service and more passenger complaints.[14] By 1987 many of the nation's 100,000 flight attendants were being asked to take reduced salaries, and newly hired attendants were started at salaries considerably below those of a few years earlier. The strike, which had been effective in gaining increased salaries and benefits, had little effect because management had the option of selling the airline to a competitor with lower labor costs.

FUTURE OF AIR TRAVEL

According to the Gallup organization, 72 percent of American adults have flown at some time in their lives, which suggests that flying, at least in the United States, is a widely experienced phenomenon. Even in developing countries such as Papua New Guinea, the people travel by air to market their coffee and pigs. Given peace and prosperity, the air travel market is likely to continue to grow, even explode, in the next decade or so.

Air traffic growth is of course subject to the vagaries of economics, international tensions, and other relatively unpredictable forces. The average annual growth rate of revenue passenger miles on airlines around the world expanded at a rate of 13 percent from 1960–1973 and then slowed to 6.9 percent from 1973–1982. The Federal Aviation Administration forecasts that U.S. air traffic will grow at an annual average rate of 5 percent through the year 2000. At that time airlines throughout the world are expected to be carrying some two billion passengers a year, about double the number carried in 1987. Other analysts are even more sanguine, predicting annual growths of 7 percent to 14 percent over the next twenty years. A significant relationship between gross national product and American air travel has been reported by Somerset Waters. In both good and bad times, he said, United States air travel growth averages more than twice the average growth of the GNP.[15]

The FAA Looks Ahead

The U.S. Federal Aviation Administration has developed five scenarios that describe the travel picture for the year 2000. By identifying events common to most of the scenarios, the FAA was able to make a number of conclusions about the need for new airports, new types of planes, safety needs, and future noise levels.

Each of the five scenarios was based on a different set of assumptions. Scenario 1 supposed a "limited growth" economy; Scenario 2 was called "Muddling Through"; Scenario 3 supposed a time of rigid resource allocation; Scenario 4 was called "Individual Affluence"; Scenario 5 assumed expansive growth throughout the economy. Even

---

14. Passengers with gripes about lost baggage, refunds, and questionable fares can call the Department of Transportation Consumer Affairs Office—(202) 366-220. Questions about such items as security measures, child safety, and carry-on baggage can be called toll-free: FAA-SURE.

13. Somerset R. Waters, *Travel Industry World Yearbook—1984.* New York: Child and Waters, 1984, p. 9.

with the constraints placed by the limited-growth scenario, the number of plane passengers is predicted to double between 1975 and the year 2000. Using the "expansive growth" model, the number enplaned would increase almost fivefold.

Assuming the worst, the "muddling through" scenario, many general aviation airports would be closed and converted to other uses. All public interstate transportation would be nationalized, and energy and resource rationing would be strictly controlled. The petroleum industry would be nationalized by 1990. Recreational activities would be restricted to those of low-cost and minimal energy use. FAA officials appear confident that air travel will continue to grow, but if there is a general energy crisis, aviation fuel simply may not be available at any cost. Business travel would be cut off, and business people would necessarily resort to telecommunication to get much of their work done. Short takeoff and landing (STOL) aircraft may become popular. A STOL operation between London and Paris is planned. Some passengers may be able to land in Paris before they could have taken off from Heathrow, one of London's airports, by conventional aircraft.

Hypersonics

We now have supersonics; the next step in raising speed levels is the hypersonic, a long-range transport flying at extremely high altitudes and using liquid oxygen as fuel. The possibility of future rocket travel could make any place on earth less than an hour away. Traveling at speeds in excess of 5,000 miles per hour, transcontinental flights would be measured in minutes, not hours. Los Angeles to Honolulu would be an eighteen-minute ride! Such transports could operate at eight times the speed of today's transports; however, they are not expected to be in use before the turn of the century.

The Hypersonic Transport (HST) would attain speeds of six times that of sound, 4,000 m.p.h., when computers would kick in another set of five engines to boost speed. (Military planes were able to fly at five times the speed of sound in 1986.) The plane would have no passenger windows;

they would be eliminated in favor of structural strength. At 4,000 m.p.h. the outside skin of the plane would heat to sizzling temperatures.

Boeing, Lockheed, and NASA are working on advanced airplane design while Pratt and Whitney is researching the supersonic combustion ramjet engine (or scramjet). The Japanese, too, have joined in the race to develop a hypersonic plane. They do not want to be left out of travel between Asia and the United States, for that travel is estimated to increased fivefold by the year 2000, to more than 30 million travelers.

If such planes are built, the military will have a big hand in funding their design and development. The U.S. government announced in 1986 that a "space plane," capable of flying at 25 times the speed of sound, would be developed.

Other future developments in aviation involve economics. By 1995 airframes will be 40 percent composites—plastics reinforced with such new materials as graphite and boron fibers—already used in military planes. Two-engine passenger jetliners, now approved for trans-Atlantic flights, will displace three- and four-engine planes because of concerns for fuel efficiency and easier maintenance.[16]

Some experts see the airline future as the big getting bigger, with a shakedown resulting in ten to fifteen multinational carriers that will compete worldwide, each with farflung networks of hubs for their routes. This assumes that cabotage rights will be traded between nations. The 1988 purchase of 10 percent of Texas Air by Scandinavian Airlines may be a bellwether of mergers to come.

As air travel becomes even more commonplace and crowded, we can expect more criticism of the "same plastic food, the same tiny lavatories, the same narrow rows of seats . . . airports with nowhere style. You can fly a succession of exotic sounding airlines—by Indonesian, Malaysian, Singapore or Colombian—and still find yourself on a Boeing 747 with the same rows of seats, the same non-dairy creamer . . . the airports all appear

16. Marvin Cetron, *The Future of American Business, The U.S. in World Competition*. New York: McGraw-Hill, 1985, pp. 89–95.

THE TOURIST BUSINESS

to be insulated from any known city or land . . . air travel provides a unique and devastating combination—of boredom and terror." Passengers, says writer Anthony Sampson, "are conditioned to eat, to watch films or to buy duty free goods at the same time." Carrying his criticism to the preposterous, Sampson likens a B-747 to the eighteenth-century slave ship—"each carries about 400 people packed equally close."[17]

17. Anthony Sampson, *Empires of the Sky*, New York, Random House, 1984, *passim*.

DISCUSSION QUESTIONS

1. Many airlines own hotels, but until 1984, no hotel chain owned an airline. Then the Hyatt Corporation bought controlling interest in Braniff Airlines. Why had hotel interests not moved into the airline business before that time?

2. Discuss the statement: Pleasure travel is more inelastic than business travel.

3. Some futurists are predicting that public space travel will cost passengers $1 million a ride. If you were in charge of selling such travel, who would constitute your target market?

4. Commercial air travel was once a thrilling experience reserved mostly for the well-to-do. Can you see a time in this country when air travel becomes quite stressful? What would be the causes?

5. Do you think that in the future there are likely to be plenty of well-trained people who want to become commercial pilots at fairly modest salaries? Can the same be said for flight attendants? Explain.

6. The Far East, including the People's Republic of China (Taiwan), Hong Kong, Japan, and Korea, is experiencing rapid growth in air travel. Why?

7. Most airlines in this country are deeply in debt. Even so, are some of them likely to see large increases in their stock prices? What might be some of the reasons for such increases?

Part C: Train, Ship, Rental Car, and Bus

Change in the technology of travel has widespread implications for society. Rail travel influenced the building of towns and cities, caused hotels to be built near rail depots, and opened up the West, among other things. Auto travel produced the motel and a network of highways. The commercial jet created destination resorts in formerly remote and exotic locations, made the rental car business a necessity, and changed the way we look at geography. Since recorded history, ship travel could be fairly comfortable for the wealthy, but not until the development of the railroad in the 1830s was travel comfortable and cheap enough to be within the reach of the masses.

By the 1920s the automobile and the bus began usurping the position of the railroad as the leading common carrier. The auto has since become the predominant mode of transportation for short distance travel. It gives the individual the most flexibility and convenience of any travel mode now available. In California, for example, 95 percent of all travel is by auto.

The auto created and unleashed the urge to travel in North America and Europe. (It has also proved to be a dangerous weapon, killing 40,000 or more Americans each year.) In the advanced industrialized countries the private automobile is a kind of extension of the person; in places such as Southern California it is a necessity, a capsule in which nearly everyone spends a good part of their life, by choice or as a requisite of business. How much of auto travel is properly included in the category of travel/tourism depends upon definition. However defined, the auto in the industrialized world is by all odds the number-one transporter of people, carrying at least four times more people than airplanes, trains, ships, and buses combined. The automobile has become a part of the way of life in the industrialized world, no other artifact in history has so affected people's lives.

Nothing compares with the auto for convenience and ease of getting around. Rental cars are obvious parts of travel/tourism. So too are recreational vehicles (RVs), estimated to number more than seven million. Private auto travel fostered much of the leisure industry. Motels, many hotels, ski lodges, and many resorts live by the automobile; they would not exist without it. In 1985 automobiles accounted for 81.3 percent of all intercity travel in the United States.[18]

Even though the privately owned auto is the predominant travel mode in industrialized countries, travel professionals are not directly concerned with sales or service of cars, hence the subject is not treated further in this book.

Shipboard travel, relatively slow and expensive, has changed its role to passenger cruising. In 1952, the superliner *United States* won the blue ribbon for the fastest trans-Atlantic time. The ship is now in mothballs, and nearly all the trans-Atlantic liners have been modified to cruise liners. Dozens of new ships designed especially for cruising have been built.

The railroad, the automobile, and the airplane have added mobility and glamor to the American way of life. The power, the sound, and the speed represented first by the steam engine, then the auto, and now the airplane, stir the emotions and evoke a sense of awe. The feeling of movement, the pride in ownership of an automobile, the sight of clouds from an airplane provide thrills in what may be an otherwise prosaic life.

RAIL TRAVEL

Rail buffs, young and old, thrill to the midnight whistle of the train, warm to the fellow passenger, enjoy the leisurely meals in the diner, anthropomorphize the engines and trains, memorizing

---

18. *Transportation in America*, 1985 and 1986 Reports. Transportation Policy Associates, Washington, D.C.

THE TOURIST BUSINESS

their statistics and christening them with names—Green Devil, Rocky Mountain Rocket, Royal Blue. The ultimate in American passenger trains was named the Twentieth Century Limited. A visiting French economist, Michel Chevalier, summed it up: "The American has a perfect passion for railroads."[19] Rail travel in this country was a part of the nation's mythology, an icon to progress.

During the depression of the 1930s, however, the railroad began to recede both in use and in the popular imagination. Rail and bus travel reached their peaks during and immediately following World War II. Since then, both modes have declined as a percentage of the total. Auto travel predominates, although as a percentage of travel it is beginning to taper off, being replaced partially by air travel.[20]

Comparative Costs

The disparity between the cost of travel by bus and train as compared to air travel grows each year, as shown in Figure 4-22.

4-22. Comparative Costs: Airplane, Bus, and Train (in Billions)			
	1975	1980	1985
Airplane	$10.30	$23.32	$33.53
Bus	1.17	1.94	2.39
Train	.21	.38	.52

SOURCE: U.S. Travel Data Center, 1986.

In terms of miles traveled (in billions) and percentages of total miles traveled using the "common carriers"—airplane, bus, and train—the figures for the same period appear in Figure 4-23.

The choice of travel mode rests upon the individual's perception of the three C's: Comfort, Convenience, and Cost. The winner for comfort

4-23. Miles Traveled (in Billions)				
Sector	1975		1985	
	Miles	Percent	Miles	Percent
Airplane	136.9	82.4	247.7	89.7
Bus	25.4	15.3	27.1	8.8
Train	3.9	2.3	4.6	1.5
Total Common	166.2	100.0	306.4	100.0

SOURCE: U.S. Travel Data Center.

is probably the cruise ship. The jetliner wins hands down for convenience in terms of long-distance travel. The bus is favored for cost. Air travel by charter plane can be decidedly uncomfortable but this discomfort is offset by reduced cost of fare. First-class air travel can be quite comfortable. Auto travel is the most convenient for short distances and less expensive per person when the car is full.

Given the choice, people who have the money usually choose speed and convenience over cost—provided cost is not exorbitant. When gasoline increased dramatically in price in the United States in 1973 and again in 1979, the increase alone had little long-term effect on automobile travel. The same can be said of air travel. There is, however, a point at which speed and cost vie as considerations; this is seen in the load factors of the supersonic planes. There has been no great rush to get on these flights, even though travel time in the air over the Atlantic is cut by about one-half. (The supersonic planes must fly at subsonic speeds over the United States, and during these flight legs the SST offers no time advantage at all.)

The National Science Foundation found that buses covered about 85 intercity passenger miles per gallon of fuel; the train, 48; the auto, 40; and the plane, 16. Such statistics are subject to a number of qualifications, the principal one being the number of passengers carried by the vehicle. When fuel rises in cost, more attention is paid to the efficiency of various travel modes.

19. *The New York Times*, May 1, 1971, p. 34.
20. Albert G. Gomes, *Hospitality in Transition*, American Hotel & Motel Association, 1985, p. 47.

TRANSPORTATION

AMTRAK

In 1956, the airlines and the railroads carried the same number of passengers. The airline passenger number continued to increase, while the railroad decreased. Between 1929 and 1971, the number of intercity trains operating in the United States dropped from 20,000 to about 185. Amtrak is a pale shadow of what was once the arterial system of the nation.

By the 1960s the United States was faced with the likelihood of a complete collapse of passenger-rail service. This prompted the federal government to give attention to the possibilities of subsidizing passenger trains, as well as supporting and maintaining new rail equipment.

In 1971 the National Railroad Passenger Corporation began operation as a semipublic corporation established to operate intercity passenger trains. The Interstate Commerce Commission defined these trains as ones with runs of seventy-five miles or more. It was a move toward the seminationalization of American railroads. The corporation, known as Amtrak, is directed by a fifteen-member board, eight selected by the President of the United States, three by the railroads, and four by preferred private stockholders.

Between 1970 and 1986 the government invested as much as $10 billion in Amtrak service and facilities. Amtrak seeks to eliminate most of the money-losing runs and to improve others so that they come closer to making a profit. The system was coordinated and fares set without ICC or state regulatory approval, a process which would have been time-consuming and political.

Most major cities are connected by Amtrak. Chicago, a long-time railroad center, is still a major hub. A West Coast north-south route connects San Diego, Los Angeles, Oakland, Portland, Seattle, and Vancouver. The part of the run between San Diego and Los Angeles is a busy commuter route and would probably be more heavily used if the service was faster.

Four east-west routes cross the prairie states, and on the East Coast, Amtrak trains run between Miami and Boston. Connecting service is available from New York to Montreal.

The New York to Washington, D.C., trains are express trains called Metroliners. Amtrak's showcase, they ply the heavily populated northeast corridor six times every business day in each direction. The scheduled travel time is two hours, forty-nine minutes. The other Amtrak trains take only a little longer and cost considerably less, but they offer less leg room and overall comfort.

The northeast corridor accounts for half of all Amtrak's passengers. Amtrak officials point out that their service is much more reliable in bad weather and more convenient to downtown areas than the airline shuttles.

For long-distance travel the cost-and-time difference between trains and planes remains great. In 1986 a train trip between Salt Lake City and Oakland took 27 hours and cost $218 (for a compartment, meals additional). The air fare was as little as $69 for a flight time of less than two hours.

Amtrak offers a number of tour packages for the leisure traveler, tours emphasizing the value of seeing America's sights at eye level. Extensive stopovers and use of good hotels adds to the package appeal. Travel agencies produce about 30 percent of Amtrak's sales, helped by the fact that payment to travel agents is facilitated by the Area Settlement Plan (described in the chapter on the travel agent).

Amtrak maintains a special disk to handle reservations on Canada's VIA Rail, which operates all of Canada's passenger rail service, and Amtrak ticket stock may be used to travel on VIA. The Canadian passenger system has fared no better, possibly worse, than Amtrak. Formed in 1977 VIA Rail has a record of running late; government subsidies amount to two-thirds of VIA's operating costs.

The energy-conservation argument that trains consume less energy per passenger than other means of transportation does not hold because of low passenger loads. On an average Amtrak trip, service was found to be only about one-half as energy efficient as the intercity bus; outside the northeast corridor, Amtrak uses more energy per passenger mile than even the automobile.

Yet Amtrak may be pulling ahead of its unhappy early history. As of 1988 Amtrak revenues covered 69 percent of the operating costs, up from 48 percent in 1981. Amtrak was attracting crowds of passengers, especially on the metroliner runs between Washington, D.C., New York City, and Boston. For the long trips west it was difficult to reserve sleeping space. Amtrak was helped considerably by being included in the Airline Reporting Corporation, the nationwide clearinghouse established by the airlines for collecting and redistributing income from sales made by travel agents. Amtrak is also included on most major airline computer systems used by travel agents, and that permits rapid reservations and ticket generation. Figure 4-24 shows Amtrak's National Rail Passenger System. In 1990 Amtrak will add service between Philadelphia and Atlantic City.

RAIL TRAVEL ABROAD

While the United States tries to rejuvenate rail travel under the aegis of Amtrak, rail service in other parts of the industrialized world is being improved. Rail travel makes good sense in densely populated areas like those in Western Europe and Japan. But even though most of the railroads are nationally owned and subsidized, total mileage and the number of passengers is dropping off. To make up for the decrease, seventeen European nations have banded together to offer American visitors unlimited first-class rail service for a reduced lump sum. This is the justifiably famous Eurailpass. Valid for periods of two weeks to three months, the pass may be used from Scandinavia, down through Italy and the Iberian peninsula, and up through the rest of Western Europe. Greece and Ireland are also part of the Eurail system; and Hungary joined the system in 1988. The other countries are Austria, Belgium, Denmark, Finland, France, West Germany, Italy, Luxembourg, the Netherlands, Norway, Portugal, Spain, Sweden, and Switzerland. By 1989 there were also 75 Eurocity trains—high standard, long-distance trains that provide premium international travel between European city centers.

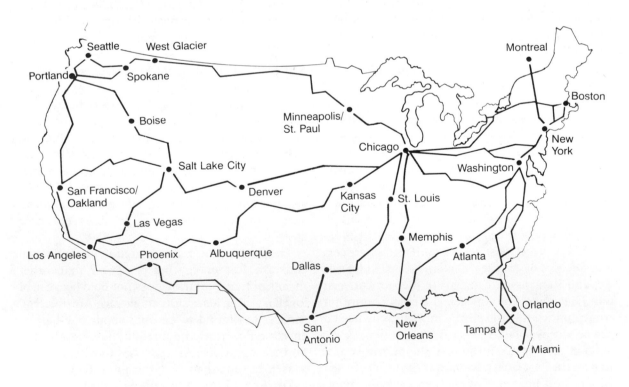

4-24. Major Amtrak Routes.

Purchase of the Eurailpass may be made in the United States from most travel agents. The pass is sold only outside of Europe. Veteran travelers, however, often say that in fact it may be cheaper to travel without the Eurailpass and to buy tickets locally. They add, if one really wants to get to know the people, one should travel second class, which can be all right in some parts of Europe.

A reserved seat is a good idea on any train trip in Europe. A modern express train costs more than the more usual older ones, and additional tickets are needed for a sleeper. The best buy on European trains is a **couchette** — a simple berth for a fixed charge no matter what the class or distance traveled. The fee includes a blanket and a pillow but on some trains there are no sheets, washing facilities, or privacy.

Many European trains provide Wagon-Lits, the equivalent of our Pullman cars. On English trains, compartments similar to Wagon-Lits are known as sleepers. A Pullman in Britain is a seat similar to those in our parlor cars. Second-class rail tickets in Britain are much cheaper than first-class but do not usually entitle the rider to use the dining car.

Veteran train travelers suggest taking food along, especially when traveling second class. A supply of paper tissues and packets of premoistened towels is a good idea too. They also recommend traveling light so that one can get off and on trains easily, and some travelers use collapsible metal carts to transport their belongings quickly. Since drinking water is not available on European trains, a canteen of water is useful, although wine, soda, and fruit juices may be available. If the rest room nearest the traveler's seat is unappealing, perhaps others are better. Nonsmokers can get seats in nonsmoking compartments. It is important for travelers to be sure they are in the right section when boarding a train — different cars may go to different destinations, and they are not always clearly marked.

The International Union of Railroads supplies a schedule of major train service in nineteen European countries. For copies, write French National Railroads, 610 Fifth Avenue, New York, New York 10020. *Cook's Continental Timetable*

can be obtained from Thos. Cook & Sons, 45 Berkeley Street, London, WIA IEB.

Other passes provide other travel bargains. Persons under twenty-six can use an InterRail card for second-class passage in twenty-one European countries. Britain has its own reduced fare ticket, BritRail, which can be booked by one of the major airline reservation systems. A Benelux Tourrail is good for rail travel in Belgium, Holland, and Luxembourg, while a Scandinavian Rail Pass is valid in Denmark, Finland, Norway, and Sweden. Australia offers the Austrailpass; India, the Indrail Pass; Finland, Finnrailpass. For persons sixty-five or older the Senior Rail Card, good in seventeen European countries, offers a sizable reduction in fares. Sweden, Switzerland, and some other European countries offer their own special reduced fares for senior citizens.

Rail travel buffs have a wide choice of trains, from second- and third-class coaches, to the supertrains of Japan and France, to a private car booked on a train in India. The Orient Express, the luxury train that ran from Paris to Istanbul, gradually reduced service, became a third-rate train, and stopped running in 1977.

Two versions of the Orient Express now operate. The nostalgic Istanbul Orient Express has only fans for cooling and uses a steam engine part of the way in its occasional runs between Zurich and Istanbul.

More trips are offered by the Venice–Simplon Orient Express, which runs from London to Venice and Vienna. Its air-conditioned cars are refurbished coaches from the 1920s and 1930s. Actually, two trains are involved in the Venice–Simplon Orient Express, one that travels from Victoria Station in London to the channel port of Folkestone, where passengers take a 90-minute ferry ride over the English Channel. The second train starts at Boulogne, France, and goes on to Venice. The word *Simplon* refers to the Simplon tunnel that links Switzerland and Italy. When not in service between London and Folkestone, the Venice–Simplon Orient Express makes excursion trips out of London.

The Republic of South Africa's Blue Trains are recognized for their luxurious accommodations.

The all-compartment trains run between Pretoria in the north and Cape Town in the south. Although their average speed is less than fifty miles per hour, passengers say they wish the trip took longer.

Traveling by rail can be far from dull. A train that runs south from Lima, Peru, to the mountain mining towns climbs to 16,000 feet. The conductor moves about with an oxygen container, giving wheezy passengers who cannot take the heights a free whiff to sustain\them until the train descends. The trip from Cuzco, the former capital of the Inca empire, up to Machu Picchu is so steep that the train does not spiral up all the way. At points, it goes in reverse to back up a slope in a different direction, then continues moving ahead.

The adventurer's train journey is the six-day, nonstop ride between Moscow and the Pacific on the Trans-Siberian Express, 5,778 miles of it. Travelers can go either "soft" class or "hard" class; the latter have to hire their own bedding.

For the rail-travel buff, some steam locomotives are still in service. In fact, mainland China has a factory that produces them. For the historically minded, there is still a bridge over the River Kwai. Built by Allied POWS for the Japanese at great cost in human life, as in the movie, the railroad continues to carry trains over the river in Thailand.

4-25. This lounge in one of South Africa's Blue Trains exemplifies the luxurious accommodations available to passengers.

Japan's Rail System

The first spectacular rail accomplishment after World War II was Japan's *shinkansen*, the bullet trains, which began operations in time for the 1964 Olympics in Japan. They make the 550-mile run between Tokyo and Osaka in three hours and ten minutes, down from the former rail time of eighteen hours. In addition, they provide a ride so smooth that a passenger can rest a coffee cup on the windowsill and not a drop will spill. Phone calls can be made from the train as it speeds along in excess of 100 miles per hour. In its first decade of operation, there was not one fatal accident on the line. A computerized control center feeds information onto a lighted board that shows the location of every train and the conditions of the track, switches, and wires. The computer automatically stops the train in the event of any trouble, especially an earthquake. Station stops are necessarily brief, as short as two minutes at intermediate stations, so travelers must be ready to move fast or miss their stop.

What was hailed as the world's finest passenger rail system has also been the world's costliest. In 1986 the Japanese government revealed that JNR—the Japanese National Railway—was $234 billion in debt. Only one main line—the Tokyo-Osaka-Fukuola "bullet line—and seven commuter lines were operating in the black. JNR was broken up in 1987, replaced by six regional passenger companies (collectively called Japan Railways) and a company that will lease the three bullet lines."[21] In 1987 a Japanese train reached 249 miles an hour, but it carried no passengers.

French Railroads

The French supertrains have now taken first place in the world rail sweepstakes. The streamlined pride of the French railroad system, Très Grande Vitesse (TGV, very high speed), operates between Paris and Lyons. It can hit speeds of 250 miles per hour with a ride so smooth that a glass of water sitting on an armrest is not disturbed. The most

21. *Los Angeles Times*, December 14, 1986, Part IV, p. 2; and *Wall Street Journal*, May 8, 1987, p. 16.

4-26. A *Très Grande Vitesse* train in the Gare de Lyons in Paris. This is one of the several trains that operate on special tracks between Paris and Lyons and between Paris and Marseilles. Travel on TGV from Paris to Lyons takes only two hours, making these trains faster, as well as less expensive, than air travel.

economically feasible speed is 210 m.p.h. but, to conserve energy, the top speed is held to 186 m.p.h. One problem is that, at 175 miles per hour, it takes three minutes to stop. The problem is minor, because the system runs on its own rail corridor with no rail crossings. The Paris-Lyons line will be extended 55 miles south by 1992.

The extended TGV line will dramatically cut travel time between Paris and the south of France. Paris to Marseilles will be about three hours. A TGV "Atlantique" is planned between Paris and Brittany, and then into southwest France, the Dordogne and Bordeaux regions, putting Bordeaux within three hours of Paris. A Paris to Amsterdam run is also being discussed. The trip, which now takes five and three-quarters hours, would be reduced to about three hours.

Other High-Speed Railroads

Germany is scheduled to have hi-speed trains by 1991; intercity express trains have been tested traveling at 215 m.p.h. The Soviet Union is working on 125 m.p.h. trains between its two principal cities, Moscow and Leningrad.

Efficiency Grows with Payload

As with other forms of transportation, the more seats filled in a train network, the greater the cost-effectiveness. This is particularly true with passenger-rail service in the United States, since union rules fix the minimum number of workers. The same number of brakemen, firemen, engineers, conductors, and, if there is a dining car, galley crew is required whether five or eighteen hundred passengers are aboard the train.

Passenger trains have the distinct advantage over planes and buses of being able to add cars if the passenger load is larger than expected. Up to eighteen cars can be added to the standard travel length, and some of the newer cars can carry as many as eighty passengers.

Depending upon the load factor, fuel costs can be less on trains than on other modes of transportation. Carrying maximum loads, the train is considerably more cost efficient. In 1984, for example, fuel costs were 25 percent of the airlines' gross operating revenues, while on trains they were less than 5 percent. The French TGVs, which use electricity, can travel the equivalent of 107 miles per gallon of gasoline.

FUTURE RAIL SERVICE

For long trips—those of over 300 miles—air travel is so much faster that long-distance passenger-train service is needed only for those afraid to fly or those who can enjoy train travel as an experience.

Rail travel may, however, make a comeback in the United States. Weaning people from their automobiles will be difficult, but the conurbation of America may decrease American reliance on the car. Population around major cities keeps growing and spreading. Solid blocks of population and land development from Boston to Washington, D.C., around the Great Lakes, and in coastal California may make rail travel a sweeter travel option than the car. As airports and roads become more congested and parking a rare luxury, a train ride becomes more appealing and in many instances more time-efficient.

4-27. Food service aboard a *Très Grande Vitesse* train is similar to that aboard a jetliner.

Magnetic Levitation

The Maglevs are coming—not aliens from outer-space, but superfast trains suspended in air and propelled by magnetic force. Trains will soon be traveling at speeds up to 300 miles per hour, lifted off the ground on a cushion formed by magnetic forces and pulled forward by magnets. Maglevs, as they are called, will run more quietly and smoothly and can climb steeper grades than the conventional train. Maglevs were developed first at Massachusetts Institute of Technology (MIT), and research and development have been going on in Germany and Japan.

Japan Railways has a prototype that travels at more than 310 miles per hour on a five-mile track. A consortium of three German multinationals have a Maglev they call Transrapid; it is projected to link a 185-mile line from Frankfurt to Dusseldorf. The company also hopes to build a Philadelphia-to-Pittsburgh line that would take less than two hours.

In 1987 a Japan Air Line affiliate HSST, a Nevada Corporation, began building the first commercial Maglev, a four-mile connection between downtown Las Vegas and the Strip, the city's biggest hotel and gambling area. The trip will take 3½ minutes and the train's speed could exceed 120 miles per hour.

Other corridors with heavy passenger traffic—between Boston and Washington, Los Angeles and San Diego, Los Angeles and Las Vegas, and the Texas Triangle of Dallas, Houston, and Austin—are being considered for Maglev routes.

Maglev trains will roll out of the station on wheels. Once a speed of about 30 m.p.h. is reached, the magnetic forces generated will lift the train from the tracks. The train can then zip along floating on its magnetic cushion, without the usual friction of wheels on tracks. Near the end of the trip the train will slow down, lower its wheels onto the track, and roll into the station. Riders on the Japanese three-car prototype say there is a floating sensation and the visual sensation is spectacular because of being so close to the ground.

The train is propelled by electromagnets near the tracks that constantly change polarity to pull on the train's magnets and move the train forward. Advances using superconductivity will make Maglev's even more efficient and less costly to operate.

High hopes for a Maglev-type rail service running between Ontario, California and Las Vegas, Nevada collapsed for lack of funds. Florida has similar hopes for a high-speed train connecting Miami, Orlando, Tampa, and probably the Cape Canaveral area and Jacksonville by 1995. Using magnetic levitation the 230-mile trip between Miami and Disney World would take one hour.[22] Funding would be similar to that which made the transcontinental trains of the 1860s possible: real estate development rights. The state of Florida would give builders development rights to thousands of acres of real estate in communities served by the train and would accelerate the process of obtaining permits for developing the land. Presumably property values would soar and the railroad would be able to develop the land or sell it for hotels, shopping centers, offices, and new residential communities.

TRAVEL BY SHIP

Immigration, trade, and war were the principal reasons for undertaking water travel until about

22. "Florida Hopes For a High-Speed Train by 1995," *Wall Street Journal*, October 2, 1986, p. 6.

the 1830s, although some ocean travel in the ancient world could be considered as pleasure. Though the first cruise is believed to have taken place in 1844, and there were several around-the-world cruises in the 1920s, the real cruise-ship boon occurred in the 1960s and 1970s. Between 1964 and 1974, twenty-six new, moderate-sized ships entered the cruising business. The airplane, which caused the demise of most transoceanic passenger service, actually helped stimulate the cruise business. As early as the 1950s, most of the passengers for some Mediterranean-based cruise ships arrived at the embarkation point by plane. Today, thousands of air passengers join Florida- and San Juan-based cruise ships each week. Air/cruise plans have made cruising an option for millions of potential new passengers.

The only oceangoing U.S. flagships in service—three of them—cruise among the Hawaiian islands. Major American ports for cruise ships are Miami, New York, San Juan, Port Everglades, Los Angeles, San Francisco, and New Orleans. From West Coast ports, cruises sail to the Mexican Riviera—Puerto Vallarta, Manzanillo, Zihuatanejo, and Acapulco. Sailing north, cruise ships move along the American coast to Prince Rupert in Canada, and to Ketchikan, Juneau, Skagway, Valdez, and Anchorage in Alaska.

The Mediterranean, especially the Aegean, is Europe's "Caribbean." Piraeus, the port serving Athens, is the embarkation point for such Greek isles as Crete, Mykonos, Rhodes, and Santorini. Europeans also cruise the fjords and North Atlantic coast of Norway and the Baltic Sea.

The North Cape, the northernmost land in Europe, is a popular cruise destination. Along the Baltic stops are made at such cities as Stockholm, Helsinki, and Leningrad.

Cruises are announced several months in advance of departure. The fly/cruise package is the most popular. Costs for cruising are about the same as the total cost for a land/air package that includes hotels, meals, and air transportation—about $200 and up a day per person. The cruise passenger may also have less fear of visiting a foreign destination than if he or she traveled by plane, because evenings and nights are spent on the boat.

Pay-up time for trips is usually about two days before disembarkation, and personal checks are rarely accepted. The purser is the credit manager and treasurer for the crew. Tipping is expected in the dining room, cabin, and public rooms. If wine or cocktails are served by request at a table, the wine steward is also tipped.

About 70 percent of the cruise passengers originate in Canada and the United States. The Cruise Line International Association (CLIA), a marketing and educational organization of thirty-three major cruise lines serving North America, estimated that 3.5 million passengers took cruises from American ports in 1987–1988. Throughout the world, the deep-water cruise ships produced sales of about $5 billion in 1987.

Travel agents book 98 percent of all passengers taking cruises offered by the members of the CLIA. A big-ticket item, cruises bring them sizable commissions.

In view of these figures, cruise lines are optimistically building ships. Mass marketing, especially by the Carnival Cruise Line, has tapped into new markets by using TV. The "Love Boat" television series, which ran for many months, also helped cruising appear exciting and romantic.

In addition to cruises, there are many point-to-point shipping services around the world—passenger ferries linking Ireland and England; other ferries serving England and Continental Europe; trips on the Inland Waterway of Alaska; cruises between the islands of Japan; cruises on the Nile River; and barge travel on canals in England, France, Sweden, and elsewhere.

Pleasure cruising has become a major "destination" for tens of thousands of North Americans who, once aboard a cruise vessel, can experience a cocoonlike existence devoid of problems and filled with bodily pleasures. Food and drink are bountiful—up to six meals a day. Diversions aplenty are laid out on twenty-four-hour programs. The passenger can sally forth at exotic ports and return to mother ship at night, safe and secure.

Over 80 percent of the cruise market is for trips of seven days or less, and cruise passengers spend more per day on a short cruise than on longer ones. The short-cruise passenger gets younger each year. Older folks may take cruises of two to three weeks, while the round-the-world cruise is usually for the elderly, who have the leisure and the money (up to $200,000 for a luxury suite) for such a long trip.

Cruise passengers tend to be repeat customers. The solicitous service can be most gratifying. The typical cruise ship sailing from an American port is owned and officered by northern Europeans, manned by southern Europeans, and filled with middle- and upper-class Americans. The round-the-clock appeal to bodily pleasures amidst generally agreeable fellow passengers can be addictive.

The Cruise Ships

Between 150 and 200 cruise ships (depending upon definition) ply the oceans. Sea voyages can be taken on a variety of sizes and kinds of ships, from freighters to huge ocean liners. Yacht charters also cruise the Caribbean, the Aegean, and seasonally, the coast of New England. Experienced sailors can negotiate a bare-boat charter and sail a yacht without benefit of a professional crew. Freighters carry only a few passengers, itineraries are subject to change, and reservations are usually made up to a year in advance.

The day of ocean liners sailing back and forth across the Atlantic is over. Only the Queen Elizabeth II makes regular Atlantic crossings, from May to November. The trip between New York and Southampton, England takes five days each way. The great liners had large cabins for first-class passengers, smaller for other classes. When the airplane put the liner out of business, the liners were converted to cruise ships, smaller cabins were installed, and different classes eliminated or minimized. The *France*, once the pride of the French, is an example. The 70,202-ton ship was built in 1961 by the French. It was bought by the Norwegian-Caribbean Lines for the bargain basement price of $18 million, renamed the *Norway*, and refitted from a two-class ship into a one-class floating entertainment emporium at a cost of $40 million. Passengers have a choice of lively lounges, a disco, and a 665-seat theater. The *Norway* cruises from Port Everglades or Miami on

an itinerary that includes St. Thomas in the Virgin Islands and a stop at a Bahamian island, San Salvador, which is owned by the cruise line. The 2,133 passengers the ship can carry are transported to the island for a day of beach life by two 400-passenger boarding craft, themselves carried aboard the ship. *Norway* cruises do not include a transit of the Panama Canal, however; the ship is a few inches too wide to make it through.

The even larger *Sovereign of the Seas*, like the *Norway*, is owned by a Norwegian company. At 74,000 tons it carries as many as 2,282 passengers, making it the world's largest cruise ship. This $200 million monster has style to match its size: 14 stories, 18 elevators, splashing fountains, grand staircases, and a five-story centrum (atrium) that adds to the illusion of a floating hotel.

A cruise ship is like a floating resort in other ways. The rooms are air-conditioned and have private baths. The guests are housed, fed, and entertained. Because they do not have the option of leaving, however, guests are likely to become critical as the cruise goes on. One ship sales manager commented, "The first week out, the passengers are busy overeating; the rest of the cruise they are busy complaining about the food."

Some cruise ships even employ a "hotel manager" who is responsible for the food and beverage operations, housekeeping service, and launderers. The ship's purser offers banking services, safety deposit boxes, postal services, and customs and immigration help. Food and beverage managers arrange private parties and food and beverage service à la room service. The larger cruise ships have about four crew members (including the "hotel" staff) for every ten passengers.

The *Queen Elizabeth II*, commissioned in 1969 and refurbished in 1987, will probably never again be duplicated because of the enormous cost. To build a similar ship today would cost between $300 and $400 million. A 67,140-ton superliner, the *QE II* was moved from the class market to reach the larger mass market. In addition to a gymnasium, miniature golf course, and five nightclubs, it offers an array of celebrities and lecturers. There are also a shopping arcade, six bars, a

4-28. The Royal Caribbean Cruise Line's *Sovereign of the Seas*, the world's largest cruise ship, sails weekly from Miami on seven-day cruises to the Eastern Caribbean. The 2,282-passenger vessel calls at Labadee (Royal Caribbean's private resort on Haiti's north coast), San Juan, and St. Thomas. The *Sovereign* has two swimming pools, twin dining rooms, a casino, cabarets, and lounges, a shopping mall, and twin cinemas.

casino, and a theater, an IBM computer training center, special deck areas for teenagers and children, and air-conditioned kennels for pets. The crew needed to run this hotel numbers 900. Luxury suites on the vessel sell for up to $200,000 for the Pacific cruises.

To keep a ship from capsizing in rough weather, its center of gravity must be kept low. The *QE II*, which is thirteen stories high, has a low gravity because all of its superstructure above the second deck is made of aluminum. Stabilizers on the sides of the ship automatically work off a gyroscope, moving in and out as necessary to keep the ship on an even keel.

Considering that the ship is 973 feet long and has a beam of 106 feet, its top speed of 32 knots is remarkable. The ship is so wide that it has but five inches to spare on each side when it moves through the Panama Canal. It is owned by Trafalgar House PLC, a London-based conglomerate that includes upscale hotels.

The born-again cruise ships have undergone a series of name changes, some ships having had their names changed as many as four times as the vessel passed from one owner to another. Several have been literally cut in half and had a section added so that they can carry more passengers.

New ships especially designed for the cruise market are also being built. Unlike the old ocean liners, the new ships provide ocean views for nearly every cabin, enough dining seats for everyone to eat at one time, more luxury, and public rooms with wide picture windows instead of portholes.

Point-to-point transoceanic liners often had three classes—first, cabin, and tourist. The newer cruise ships charge according to the location of a cabin—inside or out, what deck the cabin is on, and how close it is to midship where passengers experience less rolling. Generally, the higher the deck, the higher the fare. The word *posh*, according to one story, was coined by the British to describe the choice cabins on the England to India run, that is, the coolest ones. These cabins were port when outward bound from England and starboard on returning home: Port Outward, Starboard Home—posh.

The optimal size of a cruise ship depends upon the market. The ship that is too large for one person may be too small for another. The ideal ship is one that is booked to capacity and is profitable.

Unfortunately for the United States, all but three U.S. cruise ships were built abroad and sail under flags other than American. Three main reasons explain this condition:

1. U.S. labor costs for ships, officers, and crews, forced up by the maritime unions, are too high to compete in the world market.
2. U.S. ships are not permitted to operate casino-type gambling.
3. To fly the American flag, a ship must be built in the United States, and the cost is much higher than in competing nations. Many foreign shipyards are government subsidized to keep workers employed.

As a result, the cruise ships that sail from U.S. ports are registered under foreign flags. Many are flags of convenience, representing registration in countries such as Liberia, Panama, and the Bahamas, which have relaxed policies and lower taxes. Cabotage laws protect American ships engaged in coastal shipping by prohibiting foreign vessels from transporting passengers or cargo from one U.S. port to another unless the routing includes a "distant foreign port."

The liner *United States* illustrates the dismal record of U.S. passenger ship travel. Built in 1952, the 990-foot ship originally carried almost 2,000 passengers and a crew of 1,000. It cost $79.5 million, of which $44.5 million was paid by the government. Between 1959 and 1969, the federal government paid $118.5 million in operating subsidies. In 1973 the Maritime Administration (part of the U.S. Department of Commerce) purchased the ship for about $4.6 million.

The number of small United States cruise ships, mostly sailing coastal and inland waterways, has increased, but total employment of Americans (about 10,000) in the cruise business will remain relatively small and be confined to jobs in reservations and sales for foreign cruise lines with U.S. offices. Some Americans are also employed as pursers, social directors, entertainers, and lecturers. The main reason why more Americans are not employed is the high wages and salaries expected by Americans as compared to other nationals.

Amenities on Board Ship

Passengers usually have little basis for complaint about the food on passenger ships. The ship lines, recognizing the importance of meals in a closed environment, usually spend a great deal of time, thought, and money on providing the best in food and service. A menu will never be repeated on a 100-day around-the-world cruise. As might be expected, food service aboard ship reflects the ownership. Dutch ships feature Dutch food; Greek ships, Greek food. On a ship with a mixed crew, the food sometimes is also mixed.

Passengers on cruise ships elect to take a first or second sitting in the dining room. First sittings usually begin at 7:00 A.M. for breakfast, at noon for lunch, and at 7:00 P.M. for dinner. Second sittings, which tend to attract younger crowds, are at 8:30 A.M., 1:30 P.M., and 8:30 P.M. Passengers choose a table for two, four, or six people and may request table assignments prior to sailing. If one's table mates are not congenial, the maitre d' can arrange a change.

Although the tendency is to believe that a ship's food and sanitation precautions are exemplary, about 30 percent of the ships inspected by the Public Health Service fail to pass, *prima-facie* evidence that shipboard travel can present health hazards.

The fun of the cruise begins the moment one steps aboard. Bon voyage parties, often arranged prior to sailing, are held in the passenger's cabin or in a public room. The first day out, the first meal is usually a buffet. The captain's cocktail party is a mixer that allows passengers to meet each other and be introduced to the captain and other key officers. There is usually a captain's dinner and, near the end of the cruise, a sort of "New Year's Eve" party at sea with noisemakers, funny hats, and complimentary champagne. VIPs may be invited to sit at the captain's table.

Virtually all passengers are given the same service, which means that all enjoy the same privileges, food, and social activities, no matter what they pay.

Several ships now have their own Cruise Phone using credit card phones installed by Comsat Maritime Services. The caller inserts a credit card, dials a number for a phone on land, and the equipment sends a signal up from an antenna on the ship to one of the satellites of Inmorsat, a consortium involving more than fifty countries. The satellite then beams the signal down to a giant dish antenna, where it is routed through the regular telephone system. The Atlantic, the Caribbean, and the Mediterranean each have their own telephone area codes.

Social hosts and hostesses engineer all sorts of fun and games. Games of chance, such as horse racing with miniature play horses or films of actual races, bingo, and a daily pool on the ship's mileage are offered. The U.S government proscribed shipboard gambling, including slot machines in 1952. This interdict on gambling on American ships has been one more boon for ships sailing under foreign flags and is undoubtedly a huge source of income. The *Queen Elizabeth II* reluctantly added a casino in the late 1960s, then had to double its size in 1972.

Cruise ships also provide almost continuous entertainment, which can include charm classes, language lessons, computer classes, dance classes, port-of-call briefings, bridge, table tennis, and shuffleboard. Many ships have gymnasiums and organize exercise classes as well as other sports. All cruise ships feature live entertainment, sometimes with name performers. Usually there are two nightly shows, plus late-night bars and discotheques.

Cruises are promoted and sold on the basis of health, relaxation, and self-indulgence. Theme cruises are popular, with almost any theme imaginable offered—culinary cruises, historic-dimension voyages, exploration cruises to little-known places, stock market seminars, movie festivals and music festivals, as well as cruises devoted to art, golf, astrology, tennis, photography, beauty counseling, and even witchcraft.

Cruising Can Be Profitable

At least one cruise ship magnate has acquired a billion dollars in assets. Ted Arison, principal owner of the Carnival Cruise Lines, did it by recognizing the vast market represented by low rollers and young vacationers and being first to use TV advertising widely to promote his "fun ships." The line woos travel agents with free seminars and easy-to-sell air/cruise packages.

Enterprising and innovative, Arison is the Conrad Hilton of cruising. At the age of 42 he was operating a small leased Israeli cruise ship between Florida and the Caribbean when the Israeli government impounded the ship because the owners were in debt. Arison had passengers booked for the cruise but no ship. Reading that the Norwegian Caribbean Lines *Sunward* was not in use, he called its owners in Oslo and arranged to use the ship in place of the impounded Israeli ship.

In 1974, he had one ship, the *Mardi Gras*, an aging fuel-inefficient ship that by necessity sailed slowly to save fuel. He filled the ship with discos, a casino, and other distractions. The crew dubbed it "Fun Ship," a label that became the trademark and marketing theme for all Carnival cruises.

Carnival Lines keeps prices about 20 percent lower than the competition. It offers just one class of service and a schedule of fly/cruise packages of four days and seven days. Marketing is done via national TV. Carnival cruises sail 51 weeks a year at full capacity. The break-even point is reached when 68 percent of the rooms are filled. The company pays no corporate income taxes because its ships are registered in Panama. In 1988 Carnival purchased part ownership of the Admiral Royal Caribbean Cruise Line. It has also opened an 876 room hotel/casino, The Crystal Palace, on Cable Beach in Nassau, the Bahamas.[23]

The company is planning "Project Tiffany," which will add three luxury liners carrying about 700 passengers each, and will be marketed under a different name. Ultimately, Arison hopes to have four brand names, segmenting the markets as has been done by Marriott, Holiday, and others among hotel chains.

An Optimistic Industry

Cruising has surfaced as one of the hottest vacation items. As of 1988 the average load factor was 90 percent, which is high indeed. (Some ships run a load factor exceeding 100 percent, possible because ship occupancy is based on two in a cabin; however, many cabins have pull-down berths for additional passengers.) Southern California represents the single largest cruise market in the world. The rest of the North American market continues to grow; as discretionary income increases elsewhere, the world market is almost certain to grow as well.

More than 30 million Americans could take a cruise (according to such criteria as age and income) but only about 4 percent have ever done so.

23. "Carnival Cruise's Spending Spree," *The New York Times*, August 8, 1988.

Surveys show that 50 to 60 percent of the public would like to go on a cruise. To meet the expected demand, more and bigger ships are being planned. Forty new ships had their champagne christening between 1980 and 1989, and by the end of 1988 some 80,000 berths were for sale.

RENTAL CARS

Waiting at nearly every sizable airport in the world are one or several car rental agencies, a significant segment of the travel/tourism business. Revenue for such cars in the United States exceeds $8 billion a year.

The hurried business traveler is likely to rent a car, speed out of the airport, do his or her business in a day or two, return to the airport, and hop on a plane to return to home base. The pleasure traveler, frequently with a choice of a dozen or so rental car agencies, is likely to rent a small car for a week or more and constitutes about 30 percent of the rental car market.

The traveler at any large airport may have a choice of renting a car from a dozen or more highly competitive companies. The larger companies do 50 percent or more of their business with large corporate accounts, accounts that receive sizable discounts under contract.

The big four rent-a-car company agencies in the United States are Hertz, Avis, National, and Budget. Most of the larger rental car companies have undergone several changes in ownership, being bought and sold like a commodity, with huge profits made and large debts acquired. High turnover among employees is common. Avis is unusual in being employee-owned (but also heavily in debt). Hertz, the largest agency, is owned by U.A.L., parent of United Airlines. The agencies maintain some 525,000 rental cars that are usually new and are sold after six months to reduce maintenance costs and help avoid breakdowns.

Adventures in Rental Cars

"Getting there is half the fun" is a slogan once used by an airline. If that is true, getting around once one has arrived, can be the other half of the fun. In a rented car it can be adventuresome, if not downright dangerous. Many a nice, friendly person becomes a kamikaze pilot once in the driver's seat. Tourists driving cars in Rio de Janeiro are likely to last one day before recalling that caution is the better part of valor and returning the car to the rental agency. About the only way to slow down the Mexican driver is to build sharp risers across the road, which can cause a broken spring or worse when driven over at any speed.

Driver instructions are often minimal or non-existent in foreign countries. The owner's manual quite naturally is written in the area's language, and the driver may start backing up instead of going forward.

Getting off a plane in Madrid, suffering with jet lag, a visitor driving a rented car should be prepared to get lost. Street signs, usually part of a building, are barely visible, and at a busy intersection there is little time to search for them. In Cairo traffic jams are normal, and even the natives get lost.

Where driving is on the left, as in the United Kingdom and a number of British Commonwealth countries, drivers must glue themselves to the left until they become accustomed to the change. The person who daydreams may be driving head on into a car in the right lane. Engaging in a traffic circle is particularly tricky for Americans, who are never quite sure who has the right of way.

Another problem in some foreign countries is that the rental cars may be long past their prime — gasoline fumes may stream into the driver's seat, gears may shift only under duress, and little things such as car jacks may have long since disappeared.

Problems of Renting Cars

Car rental companies have a number of practices not calculated to build repeat customers — for example, excess charges for dropping off a car at a place other than the one where it was picked up or for failing to refill the gas tank before returning the car. Misleading advertising that fails to specify extra costs is another charge leveled at the rental companies. Travelers who take advantage of express drop-off service often find that their charge card has add-on charges they did not anticipate. Pressuring customers to buy collision insurance is another criticized practice since many customers are covered by their own car insurance. More than $1 billion of the industry's gross annual revenue comes from collision damage insurance, which some critics aver is mostly profit for the car companies.

Often the car rental company may not accept cash payment; a charge card gives the company recourse if there is an accident or theft.

Value-added taxes, which are nonrefundable, can be considerable in many European countries. France adds 28 percent to the rental charges made by the rental car company. Belgium adds 25 percent, Sweden has a V.A.T. of 23.4 percent, Germany and Denmark add 22 percent, Norway and the Netherlands 20 percent. One can avoid paying the V.A.T. by leasing a car, but lease conditions vary from country to country.

Some 5,000 rental car companies operate in the United States. About 75 percent of their sales take place at airport counters that are leased from the airport, the cost of which is passed on to the customer. Travel agents account for half or more of car rental reservations for some of the large car rental companies.

MOTORCOACHES AND INTERCITY BUSES

Although the intercity bus was a major player in both business and pleasure travel for many years, its place has been largely usurped by the airplane for long distance travel and by the private automobile for short distances. Yet intercity buses serve more communities than rail or air, and for relatively short distances are usually cheaper than air travel. In many communities the bus is the only option for public transportation.

In the travel lexicon buses and limousines that transfer passengers between airports and hotels are said to be providing ground transportation. A distinction is sometimes made between buses and motorcoaches, the latter being vehicles that are custom-designed for tour operators and contain a toilet and possibly an upper deck. Motorcoach tours are growing in popularity, especially among those of moderate means and older people. Hosted tours include the services of a tour host who meets an individual or group at each destination and makes local arrangements, but does not accompany the tour. Tour escorts accompany escorted tours. The escorted motorcoach tour is convenient and hassle-free. The pre-planned itinerary allows the traveler to sit back and enjoy the scenery in a comfortable motorcoach. There are no luggage problems, and travel is with a group likely to be of similar age and circumstance.

Motorcoaches are also used for city sightseeing and for city package tours that may include hotel accommodations, meals, and entertainment.

Any group such as a school or club can charter (hire) a bus from a charter operator. Combination bus and air package tours or cruise-motorcoach tours (intermodal tours) have become popular. Group tours using chartered motorcoaches can be arranged by travel agents. Financial risk is comparatively low and returns can be high.

Until 1982, when motorcoach operators were deregulated, two companies—Greyhound and Trailways—had virtual monopolies on most intercity markets. Deregulation brought in hundreds of competitors (many of whom soon failed). The National Tour Association, to which most motorcoach brokers belong, set up escrow accounts, to protect consumers in the event of bankruptcy of one of its members.

In 1986 Greyhound Corporation sold its domestic bus operation, ending the company's seventy-three years in the U.S. bus business. The new owners, a Dallas-based investor group (GLI), retained the Greyhound name. Greyhound had become a conglomerate in consumer products, food and financial services, cruise ship operations, and Canadian bus services. The transaction included about 3,000 buses and a nationwide route system that totaled about 70,000 miles. Principal reasons for the sale were the rejection of wage offers Greyhound made to its employees and the fact that the number of passengers had declined by almost half. The purchasing company was free to negotiate new contracts or hire non-union employees.

In 1987 Greyhound bought most of Trailways, which had serious financial troubles. The new owners immediately began upgrading service, replacing old buses with new, relocating stations and upgrading others, and arranging to add service to smaller communities that had been cut out over the previous dozen years. They arranged with smaller, independently owned bus companies to act as feeders to Greyhound. With Greyhound's help these independent entrepreneurs may obtain favorable interest rates to start up a business and lower insurance rates to run it. The new companies operate with vans, some with up to 20 seats (as compared to Greyhound's 43 to 47 passenger buses). The small companies receive a proportionate share of the total ticket cost and act as agents for Greyhound, receiving a commission of 10 percent to 15 percent of each long-haul ticket sold. The installation of a badly needed modern computer system for handling reservations and ticketing provides information to agents about seats available for each trip and helps with the correct routing of small packages that Greyhound carries in the underbellies of buses. About 22 percent of the company's revenues comes from this package service.

The major reasons for selecting bus travel over other modes of travel are convenience and economy. Bus riders tend to be older and to have lower incomes. Bus service is available in virtually every town of 1,000 people or more, and a passenger station or ticket agent for bus service is at hand in each of these communities.

Most people do not choose bus travel for long trips, although there are a few aficionados who are thrilled by sitting in a bus hour after hour, even day after day.

Travel by bus for pleasure purposes varies widely within the United States and around the world. The convenience and economy of bus transportation between some destinations highly favors the bus over other modes, including the private automobile. For example, there is regular bus service between most sizable communities in New England and New York. In the heavily populated northeast corridor, it is often easier for travelers to ride the bus than to drive their automobiles into the city. Intercity bus travel, according to the American Bus Association, is far safer than travel by auto.

Types of Bus Service

In addition to routes between towns and cities, bus travel includes:

- Local route service
- Charter, tour, and special services
- Commuter service
- Airport service
- Urban and rapid transit service

Of major interest to travel planners are charter and sight-seeing bus services, here and abroad.

The granddaddy and giant of the specialized travel service is Gray Line. Founded in 1910, Gray Line is a franchise operation based in New York. The company assembles packaged tours, arranges rail and air transfers, and contracts for rental cars and limousines. Its major service, however, is sightseeing trips by bus. When a traveler arrives at a destination and wishes to see the town and major tourist attractions, a Gray Line is usually ready to serve. The 200-member organization carries about 40 million passengers a year in such widely diversified trips as around-the-town in Paris to around-the-country in Thailand. In the United States Gray Line's biggest market is Los Angeles, followed by San Francisco, then Manhattan. American Sightseeing International, the number two sight-seeing company, offers services similar to Gray Line.

DISCUSSION QUESTIONS

1. Intercity bus travel, usually the least expensive public travel mode, has experienced a flat sales curve over the past several years. As president of a bus company serving a single state, what would you do to create new business?
2. As a member of Congress, would you vote for continued large subsidies for the operation of Amtrak? What are your reasons?
3. Why is it that European trains seem to be so much more popular than the Amtrak system trains?
4. As marketing director for a cruise line operating out of Miami and cruising the Caribbean, what are your target markets? How would you reach them?
5. Suppose that for some reason the price of gasoline doubles within a short period of time. How would such an increase affect bus travel? Train travel?
6. It is said that another ship of the size and luxury of the *QEII* will never be built. Why not?
7. What has happened to cause the number of American shipping and cruise lines to decline drastically?
8. The U.S. interstate highway system is a marvel of design that provides a number of advantages for auto travelers. What value does the system have for American society other than helping people move rapidly between two points?
9. What circumstances could cause a sharp decline in the importance of the privately owned automobile?
10. When, if ever, and under what conditions will there be widespread use of Maglev trains in the United States?
11. The cruise business is highly optimistic about the future. Is that optimism justified? What circumstances could seriously depress the cruise business?
12. What is the future for the intercity bus business?

FIVE

TRAVEL ACCOMMODATIONS

HOTELS, MOTELS, AND RELATED ACCOMMODATIONS

Travel implies hotels and related public accommodations. Travel and tourism as it is known today could not exist without them. In almost any civilized part of the world there are overnight accommodations for public rental. Much of travel hinges on the quality and availability of an area's hotels. A third-world country, no matter how poor or remote—be it Nepal, Bolivia, or Haiti—usually has at least one first-class hotel. According to one estimate, there are close to 10 million rooms (including motels) worldwide, approximately 2.73 million of which are in the United States.[1] The worldwide capacity of hotels and similar establishment is shown in Figure 5-1.

Hotels support, participate in, and extend trade centers, government centers, entertainment centers, and theme parks. New York, Chicago, and Los Angeles are examples of trade centers; Washington, D.C., and the state capitals are examples of government centers.

In cities and resort destinations, hotels and the activities taking place in them constitute a large part of the cultural landscape. Hotels say a lot

5-1. Worldwide Capacity of Hotels and Similar Establishments in 1986		
Region	Rooms (000)	Percent of Total
World[1]	9,935.7	100.0
Africa	246.5	2.5
Eastern Africa	38.4	
Middle Africa	15.2	
Northern Africa	98.9	
Southern Africa	51.1	
Western Africa	42.8	
Americas	3,654.7	36.9
North America[2]	2,857.3	
Central America	299.8	
South America	398.7	
The Caribbean	98.8	
East Asia and the Pacific	842.4	8.5
Europe	5,007.9	50.2
Eastern Europe	295.8	
Northern Europe	824.5	
Southern Europe	1,922.4	
Western Europe	1,931.2	
Other[3]	31.0	
Middle East	86.8	0.9
South Asia	97.5	1.0

[1]World: 158 countries and territories.
[2]North America: Canada and U.S.
[3]Other: Israel.
SOURCE: World Tourism Organization

---

1. Somerset R. Waters, *Travel Industry World Yearbook. The Big Picture—1988.* New York: Child and Waters, 1988, p. 125.

about a city, help define it, provide character, add to or detract from its reputation, and constitute a considerable part of its architectural profile. What would New York City be without its skyscraper hotels and its 100,000 guest rooms? What would Orlando, Florida, be without its 60,000 guest rooms? Paris would not be Paris if it lacked luxury hotels. Honolulu would not be Honolulu if it lacked its fleet of hotels facing on Waikiki Beach. In fact, Hawaii tourism growth can be measured in hotel rooms, from only a handful of first-class guest rooms in 1960 to 60,000 in 1988. Singapore's rise to financial eminence can also be tracked by the construction of first-class hotels. Casino hotels "are" Atlantic City and Las Vegas.

The kind of accommodation offered to pleasure travelers becomes an integral part of the travel experience. Some travelers want only deluxe hotels; the reputation of the place reflects on the traveler's self-image. Other travelers, who want to meet the local people and learn their culture, seek out the bed-and-breakfast place in Wales or spend a week with a sheep farmer in New Zealand. The auto tourist wants convenience to the highway and a quick getaway in the morning.

The nature of hotels changes to reflect social and financial change. The tremendous growth in conventions and meetings in the 1950s prompted the construction of many convention hotels, several with over 1,000 rooms, built to serve convention groups. Conference-center hotels are specialized properties built in response to the training and meeting needs of corporations. Resort condominiums, made possible because of rising middle-class incomes, spawned the new business of rental condos, by which condo owners rent their property to the public through a management company.

Types of Accommodations

Depending upon pocketbook and taste, travelers have a variety of accommodations to choose from, ranging from sleeping in a six-foot capsule (with television) in Tokyo to dining with a duke in Britain. Young hikers are delighted to have a place to spread their sleeping bags and find cold running water in a youth hostel, for which they will pay only a few dollars. (The nonprofit American Youth Hostel Association has a membership of nearly two million.)

The traveling salesperson may be pleased with a minimum motel accommodation at $30 or less a day. The traveler with a family will find a Holiday Inn, with its swimming pool and moderately priced restaurant, highly satisfactory at $50 a day. The affluent may be pleased to spend $300 a day at the George V in Paris, while the traveler who wants complete luxury and a taste of status will be happy to spend $400 per day living like a laird, with a laird, in Scotland.

According to *Lodging Hospitality* magazine, lodging customers fall into these categories:

- 20 percent are business travelers
- 19 percent are attending a conference
- 29 percent are on vacation
- 4 percent are on government or military business
- 8 percent are on a weekend trip
- 17 percent have other personal or family reasons to stay
- 3 percent are relocating

Hotels can be classified in several ways: according to room rate charged (budget, mid-scale, upscale, or luxury); purpose of guest stay (resort or pleasure, business, convention, conference); or length of stay (transient, residential). All-suites apartment motels, sometimes high rises, may include a living room/sleeping area and kitchenette and serve complimentary breakfast and offer a gratis cocktail hour. Figure 5-2 lists and briefly describes the kinds of overnight accommodations and rates that are found worldwide.

The large hotels are mostly run by management companies such as Hilton, Hyatt, Western, and Marriott. Some management companies also take equity positions in some of the hotels they manage. Airline-owned hotels usually set up their own management subsidiaries. Motels tend to be independently owned but covered by either a franchise agreement such as Holiday or a part of a marketing/referral group such as Best Western.

TRAVEL ACCOMMODATIONS

5-2. Types of Overnight Accommodations		
Transient hotels	Price is for room only.	Inexpensive to very expensive
European plan	All meals included in one price (usually resort hotels).	
American plan (AP)		
Resort hotels	Dinner and breakfast included in one price.	
Modified American Plan (MAP)	Same as AP; European terminology.	
Full pension	Same as MAP; European terminology.	
Demi-pension	Breakfast included in one price.	
Hotel garni	Hotel has no restaurant except breakfast room; mostly in Europe.	
Casino/hotels	Cater to gaming customer, usually offer entertainment. Suites often complimentary to high rollers.	Inexpensive to expensive
Conference centers	Similar to hotels but catering to groups for educational meetings. Some are resorts or are attached to a university.	Moderately expensive
Health spas	Hotels or resorts with emphasis on weight reduction or medical treatment.	Expensive to very expensive
Rental condominiums	Found mostly in resort areas; completely equipped apartments.	About same as moderate to high-price resort rooms
Motels/motor inns	Provide bedroom, bath, and parking; rooms are usually accessible from parking lot. Convenient for auto travelers. Usually adjacent to highways.	Inexpensive to moderately expensive
All-suites	Apartment motels; breakfast often included in the room rate.	Moderately expensive
Guest houses	Resemble small, inexpensive hotels.	Inexpensive
Bed and breakfast	Guest lodged in private homes; breakfast included.	Inexpensive to expensive
Pensions	Found in Europe; similar to boarding houses or guest houses.	Inexpensive
Hostels	Appeal mostly to young travelers. Minimal amenities. Guest often required to help with work.	Inexpensive
Campgrounds	Appeal mostly to families who travel in RV's.	Inexpensive
Castles, chateaux, and mansions	Lavish accommodations and meals.	Very expensive

SOURCE: *The Hotel and Restaurant Business*, Fifth Edition. Van Nostrand Reinhold, New York: 1989.

The residential hotel is essentially an apartment building, offering maid service, a dining room, food service for rooms, and possibly a cocktail lounge. Some of the better-known hotels, such as the Hotel Pierre and the Plaza in New York City, rent a large number of suites on a permanent basis, which makes them at least partially residential in character. The Waldorf Towers, a part of the Waldorf-Astoria Hotel, is also residential in character.

Airport hotels are located in or near airports for the traveler who is between flights or is holding a business meeting or for some other reason wants the convenience of being near the airport.

The acme in facilities and services is found at the handful of luxury health spas, which charge as much as $3,000 a week for a suite. Food cost for the operator is low. The guest gets to eat less while being manicured, pedicured, and tutored in such esoteric subjects as body control and yoga.

A "budget motel" has been defined as one with rates 20 to 50 percent below the area's Holiday Inn. The largest of these chains, Days Inn, is headquartered in Atlanta. Motel 6 has about 500 motels, but the numbers change daily. Most budget motels do not offer food service; Days Inn is an exception. Its attached restaurants offer free meals to children twelve and under when accompanied by an adult guest.

Until about 1950, most resort hotels were seasonal, open either in the winter or summer. Many still are, but most resorts in Florida, California, Hawaii, and the Caribbean remain open the year round, with low seasons in the spring and fall.

Megaresorts

The size and complexity of large resort properties took on new dimension in the middle and late 1980s, when several megaresorts were built in Hawaii. These destination resorts, made possible by billions of Japanese yen, are of a size and scope not previously seen. The swimming pools are immense, embellished with islands, water slides, fountains, and waterfalls. The Waikoloa Beach Resort on the big island of Hawaii (managed by Hyatt) has a concrete swimming pool that covers almost three-quarters of an acre; sand for the beach was imported from another island. A Hyatt property due to open in 1990 will have a pool patterned after the magnificent Grecian pool at Hearst Castle in San Simeon, California.

Destination resort hotels are invariably located on or near a scenic beach or mountains. Some of the new luxury resorts are part art collection, part Disneyland. The Westin Kauai purchased all of the production of a Chinese marble quarry. The $360 million Hyatt Waikoloa gives the guest a choice of three means of transport from lobby to guest room: walk down a sweeping, columned staircase, travel by boat over a mile-long system of canals, or ride via monorail to one of three guest-room towers.

What makes these new properties distinctive are their immensity in acreage and the variety of attractions they offer. The Westin Kauai has a large collection of oriental art and 500 landscaped acres on which there are a mile of canals that guests can explore by outrigger canoes or motor launches, passing a shoreline populated with monkeys, zebras, wallabies, llamas, and other animals.

At least one golf course is standard in the big resorts. The smaller resorts cater to the independent traveler (I.T.); the larger ones necessarily depend heavily on group business. The Ritz-Carlton and Four Seasons chains are both building luxury hotels in Hawaii, with luxury room rates on the Big Island and on Maui.

The Japanese own more than a third of the 60,000 hotel rooms in Hawaii, hotels in Guam, Micronesia, and several large properties in California. In 1988 the Seibiu Saison Group paid $2.15 billion for the Inter-Continental Hotel chain, originally put together by Pan American Airways in the late 1940s.

Casino Resorts

Casino hotels—while relatively few in number—play a colorful and important part in the financial well-being of a few hotel companies. Places such as the Principality of Monaco, the tiny independent state on the French Mediterranean coast, Biarritz on the French west coast, and Baden Baden in Germany were known for casino gambling prior to the twentieth century. Las Vegas, Reno, and Atlantic City are products of a relaxed view toward gambling in this country, starting with Las Vegas when casino gambling was legalized in 1931. The idea of extravaganza entertainment and huge luxury hotels built around casinos is an American idea. Today Las Vegas has a population of half a million and about 60,000 guest rooms. Forty-to-fifty percent of the Hilton Hotels' profit came from "gaming" in Las Vegas.

Atlantic City—located where one-quarter of the U.S. population is within a 300-mile range—was fading fast as a destination until casino gambling was legalized by the state of New Jersey in 1976. The result has been startling. The number of visitors to the city climbed from 2 million to 30 million a year, making it the largest tourist destination in the nation (if cities like New York and Los Angeles are not considered tourist destinations). The phenomenal number of visitors to Atlantic City are mostly day trippers. Over half arrive by car; another 45 percent by bus. Many are lower income people coming to break the monotony of life and take part "in the action." By 1990 the place will have about 20,000 hotel rooms; one hotel that is being built will reportedly cost nearly a billion dollars. Where gambling exists, the question of morality is outweighed by the billions of dollars in gaming profits and the creation of tens of thousands of well-paying jobs and billions in tax revenues that accrue to the local and state governments.

Rental Condominiums

Rental condominiums are increasingly important in the hospitality field. Derived from the Latin, *condominium* means "joint domain" or "joint ownership." The condominium owner actually has full ownership of a unit in a complex, usually sharing in the cost of taxes and the maintenance of jointly used facilities and services, including the cost of security and upkeep and maintenance of grounds, roads, and recreational facilities such as tennis courts, parks, and marinas. These services and facilities are often managed by an independent company. The condominium agency may contract to rent the unit when it is not being used by the owner. Each owner can sell his or her unit independently of the other owners.

The concept is believed to have originated in Milan, Italy, and reached the continental United States via Puerto Rico. In 1958 the Puerto Rican government approved condominium ownership and obtained Federal Housing Authority approval for mortgage loans in 1959. The concept has spread to all corners of the United States. On the island of Maui, in Hawaii, for example, there are many more condominium apartments than hotel rooms. Condominiums have special appeal because of tax advantages, property appreciation, and the fact that the condominium is cared for in the owner's absence.

For some travelers, accommodations may be secondary to the services offered. The more than 110 fishing and shooting inns of Scotland exemplify services that are more important than the accommodation itself.

Accommodations in Private Homes

Bed-and-breakfast accommodations are widespread in Britain, Ireland, and the United States. Hundreds of home owners put out their "B & B" signs in Britain. Farmers' wives sometimes set themselves up as modest innkeepers and provide a room, bath, and a hearty breakfast. The quality of the offering varies greatly. B & Bs recommended by the local tourist authority are invariably clean, the homes pleasant, the breakfast complete with eggs, bacon, orange juice, coffee or tea, and toast. The proprietors are often retired, and the guests offer a welcome source of income, as well as the possibility of minimizing loneliness. At the lower end of the B & B scale, the beds sag, the rooms are not too clean, and one bathroom may be shared with ten other guests.

At the extreme upper end of the private-home innkeeper are the estate owners who take in guests. The estate owner may be titled; the home, a castle; the park surrounding the home may cover a thousand acres or more. The entire affair is luxurious and is the essence of good breeding. The visitors are treated as guests in a lovely home. They are treated to drinks or tea on arrival, and dinner is a lavish affair of several courses with wine. Vegetables and fruits are likely to come from the estate gardens. The cost is likely to run more than $300 a night for two, breakfast included. This kind of experience is available in stately homes in England and Scotland, chateaux in France, and mansions in Austria.

Much of the Austrian countryside in the summer becomes a vacationland for Germans from the north. *Zimmer Frei* ("room free") signs seem to be on every other farmhouse. Austria becomes a nation of small innkeepers until fall sets in.

Bed-and-breakfasts in the United States are much more elaborate than the basic British variety; the residences may be virtually small hotels (without a hotel license, bar, or restaurant as such). Room rates in many are as high or higher than in neighboring hotels. But in rural areas, as in parts of New England, they may be the only accommodations for miles, and they offer a way to get to know people and places different from the traveler's home area.

In varying degrees, hotels depend upon travel retailers (travel agents and tour operators). Some resort hotels receive as much as 90 percent of their business through tours and travel agents. Larger hotels may get 25 to 30 percent of their reservations from a travel agent and another 20 percent from tour operators. Some hotels could not survive without tour business.

RESTAURANTS

The amount of the restaurant business classified as travel/tourism-related depends heavily upon definition. Using a definition of food eaten in restaurants by persons twenty-five miles or more from home yields enormous figures. The figure for food served in restaurants to persons away from home for at least one night is much lower but totals billions of dollars a year.

Depending upon location, restaurants may receive half or even all of their business from the traveler. The international traveler to the United States spends close to $6 billion in hotels and restaurants each year. Denny's, the largest of the coffee shop chains, has restaurants located on major highways and operates 24 hours a day. It is safe to say that three-fourths of its business comes from travelers. Half or more of the customers in luxury restaurants in New York City may come from out of town. Hotel/motel restaurants probably have 80 percent or higher patronage from their own guests, all travelers.

Restaurants are classified in different ways: according to service offered—self service to full service, fast food to elaborate French service; according to markets served (low-end, mid-scale, and up-scale). Traditional classifications are fast food, cafeteria, coffee shop, family style, dinner house, and luxury.

Food service accompanies and serves travel modes: dining cars on railroads are an important part of rail travel. The Howard Johnson chain, built beside turnpikes in the eastern United States, were a landmark in road travel. Inflight food service can be minimal, as on SAS flights in Stockholm, where the air traveler picks up a boxed snack on entering the plane, or it can be a five-course dinner offered in first class on some trans-Pacific flights by some of the oriental airlines.

In broad perspective, the commercial restaurant business can be divided into fast food (fast service) and "other." Fast-food restaurants featuring the hamburger do more than half of all commercial restaurant sales. Most also offer chicken in one form or another, and many have added salads, some prepacked or on buffets. Most are part of chains and/or franchiser companies. Highway travelers favor fast-food restaurants because they can be found on, or just off, major highways. They are usually clean, have quick service, and offer moderately priced food. Mass advertising has emblazoned their names and images into the general public's minds. Children traveling with the family often demand a stop at McDonald's or Kentucky Fried.

CONVENTIONS AND GROUP MEETINGS

"The Americans of all ages, all conditions, and all dispositions constantly form associations." The writer, Alexis de Tocqueville, a widely quoted commentator about the American scene, made this remark in 1831. His judgment is as valid today as it was then. In 1987 convention and meeting delegates were expected to spend $30.3 billion.[2]

While more and more manufactured goods can be produced by fewer and fewer people, the number of persons engaged in management, finance, sales, higher education, and a variety of technical positions has grown steadily. We have a special eagerness to exchange information and pass on,

2. Somerset R. Waters, *Travel Industry World Yearbook. The Big Picture—1988.* New York, Child and Waters, 1988.

even to our competitors, ideas that in other countries are retained entirely for the benefit of the person who has them. Many industries formerly located in downtown sections are now on the outskirts of the metropolitan areas, making it necessary for their management and technical people to travel to a meeting to do business and exchange information. Large corporations with plants scattered all over the country must bring their technical and managerial personnel together frequently.

The real impact of group business did not hit American hotels until the 1950s. By the late 1960s, most of the large downtown hotels were getting at least 40 percent of their business from conventions and group meetings. The International Association of Convention and Visitor Bureaus reported in 1988 that the number of conventions held in 1980 through 1987 more than doubled, while attendance increased 67 percent. Some hotels and destination resorts receive as much as 80 percent of their business from conventions and other groups. The gregarious American character, jet travel, and the desire to keep abreast of one's field in a pleasurable setting are responsible for the "multibillion-dollar American ritual."

Jet travel and tax deductions for business purposes make it easy for Americans to express their desire to get together with others or exchange information, look for a new job, buy new merchandise for their businesses, and have fun doing it.

As many as 100,000 delegates attend some national gatherings—enough to fill hotel rooms for miles around. What makes conventioning even more interesting to hotel managers is that conventions often can be scheduled to fill low-occupancy periods, weekends, and off-seasons. Also, once a convention has checked in, most of the guests take most of their meals in the hotel.

Much of the convention business has quietly merged into the vacation business. The independent businessperson may have his or her spouse as an officer in the company; both travel to a business meeting at business expense, which is tax deductible. The executive going to a business meeting has expenses paid; the small extra cost for double occupancy of a room makes the trip relatively inexpensive for the spouse.

With group air fares, today's convention is likely to be a family affair. Spouses accompany over half of the conventioneers to New York City, while about 75 percent of the convention-goers to Florida bring their spouses. Group meetings for a company's salespeople are likely to be a combination of entertainment and sales pitch. Philco-Ford, for example, chartered thirty jets to carry 5,000 appliance and electronic dealers and their spouses to such places as Puerto Rico, Hawaii, Las Vegas, and Paradise Island in the Bahamas. The entertainment may cost $300,000 for the group.

Role of the Trade Show

Trade shows and exhibitions are closely related to the convention business. Many of the trade associations get the bulk of their income from conducting a convention-trade show each year. The National Restaurant Association receives much of its budget from this source.

Space for shows may be rented for less than $1 per square foot and sold for up to $9 per square foot. The difference is largely profit for the associations. Convention bureaus join with hotel associations to build up convention business. Municipalities also join in to promote convention sales.

Visitor and Convention Bureaus and Centers

Visitor and convention bureaus seek to attract affluent visitors and are therefore natural allies of the hotel/restaurant operator. Across the country, these centers and their cousins, convention centers, engage in marketing and public relations to bring business to the areas they represent.

Those representing larger cities with several thousand guest rooms compete for the larger conventions and group meetings: groups representing professions such as teaching, medicine, and law; governmental groups such as city councilors or tax collectors; trade groups such as plumbers or junk dealers; and union groups. Political conventions, especially on the national level, bring thousands of visitors to an area.

Once booked, groups and conventions hold to the convention date regardless of the weather. The convention segment itself, however, is somewhat seasonal, depending upon location. For the United States as a whole, the high months for major conventions are generally March through November.

Convention bureaus may act as housing bureaus, assuming the complete responsibility for accommodating a large group, allocating rooms among various properties in an area. A bureau may also manage a convention center, selling exhibit space, arranging for registration and side trips, providing for buses between hotels and the convention center, helping with news releases, and working with the media of the area.

A number of salespersons are employed within a convention bureau such as the Anaheim Convention and Visitors' Bureau. Each is responsible for up to 1,000 groups, keeping files on meeting dates, names of association executives, and other information of value in soliciting the groups to come to an area. Convention and visitor bureau management has become a highly specialized area of management expertise. Those engaged in it share several traits and problems with hotel managers. To move up in their careers, they must usually move on to larger centers. The top jobs are highly political since there are many bosses to please.

Convention bureau work is closely related to hotel sales work and calls for alertness, a pleasant personality, and the ability to relate easily to association executives. It is also an asset to be able to type so that one can avoid the necessity of employing a secretary to work with an account executive. Convention bureau work can be rewarding financially and otherwise, and can offer a more stable career than hotel management.

Convention Centers

Convention centers are facilities designed to provide space for exhibits and meetings. Their goal is to attract more visitors — convention groups, conferences, and trade shows — to a city or area. The multipurpose conference center can accommodate entertainment presentations, recreational events, and consumer-related events. Community residents can also be served through local meetings, exhibitions, and educational, social, cultural, artistic, athletic, and religious functions. Large open spaces that can easily be blocked off for individual exhibits are the principal architectural feature. Food services and an amphitheater are usually included, plus massive space for parking. One center, the San Diego Convention Center, for example, can provide food service for 6,000 people at a single setting.

McCormick Place in Chicago is one of the largest of the convention centers. Other cities with convention centers having 300,000 square feet or more of space include Las Vegas, Houston, New York, Louisville, Anaheim, Dallas, Atlanta, Tulsa, Atlantic City, Detroit, Philadelphia, Cleveland, New Orleans, Washington, D.C., San Diego, Rosemont/O'Hara, Los Angeles, Indianapolis, Kansas City, and Salt Lake City.

Convention centers vie with one another to attract large convention groups. Close relations and support are needed from the hotel/motel association, the Chamber of Commerce, and the funding organization, usually a government agency with the power to tax.

Cities that formerly were not considered convention towns have gotten into the act. Houston is one of the new convention centers. Its Astrodomain includes the 52,000-seat Astrodome, the 57-acre Astroworld amusement park, the 16-acre Astrohall, and a 1,500-room hotel-motel complex. San Diego has two convention centers: the newer and larger, costing about $150 million, is funded by the San Diego Port Authority. The older center receives support from a city and county room tax of 7 percent levied on guest room sales. The two convention centers are managed independently of each other and are not formally joined with the San Diego Convention and Visitor Bureau. The bureau, however, considers itself the marketing arm for the centers.

The San Diego Convention and Visitor Bureau employs sixty full-time employees and calls on an additional forty-five part-time people to help with registration of visitors. A number of the full-time employees are salespeople who call on trade shows and groups who might be interested in visiting San Diego. The most important group is the American Society of Association Executives, the members of which influence thousands of travel decisions. The San Diego Bureau is headed by a 70-member board of directors and has 1,500 members—people from government, the hotel and restaurant business, and others interested in San Diego tourism.

Hotel managers and marketing directors work closely with their convention office staff, jointly planning budgets, promotion trips, and future efforts. Hotel/restaurant owners and operators are prominent on the centers' boards of directors, since they can extend and magnify their marketing efforts by working with and through the convention office. Convention offices mobilize and focus the components of tourism, helping to fill guest rooms and restaurant seats and attracting literally thousands of people who would not otherwise come to a city or area.

Most of the larger offices belong to the International Association of Convention and Visitor Bureaus, an organization with some 180 U.S. members and fifteen or so members from other countries. Dozens of small communities have one or a few people, many of them part of the local Chamber of Commerce, assigned to promote visitor spending.

Convention and visitor center funding often comes from a tax on hotel rooms, typically 6 to 10 percent. Bureau budgets can exceed $1 million a year. The Las Vegas Convention and Visitor's Authority has a budget of $13 million a year generated by a 6 percent tax on guest rooms in the city. Of the sixty principal convention centers, reports show that most operate at a financial loss made up by public funds—local, state, or federal.

In-Hotel Convention Management

Within the hotel, the sales department personnel are responsible not only for attracting a convention but for making sure the convention runs smoothly once it has started. This is a full-time job for at least one person; in the large hotels it requires several people. Within a large hotel there may be a Director of Sales (DOS), three more

national sales managers, and a Director of Tours and Conventions. This last person is the first-line liaison between a group and the hotel, seeing to it that all functions move as planned and all facilities and services within the hotel work to satisfy the group guests.

Rooms assigned to the officers of a large convention are often complemented by the hotel; sometimes meeting rooms also are made available without charge. The convention group can then rent to purveyors and others if they wish.

Chain Control of Conventions

A sizable part of the convention business is controlled by the larger chains, those with large hotels in the principal cities. Hilton, Hyatt, Ramada, Loews, Sheraton, and a few of the other larger chains can afford a big staff of convention sales specialists whose principal business it is to cultivate and sell key people in the large national associations. Conventions for some of the large national groups, such as the National Education Association and the American Medical Association, are planned at least five years in advance, some even earlier. The American Chemical Society selects its convention sites ten years in advance. Most of these associations move the annual meeting from place to place to equalize travel distance for members from all parts of the country. Some go abroad to Canada, Mexico, or the Caribbean. Another reason for moving conventions is to add interest and fun to the national meeting by holding it in a new place each year.

Only the larger hotel chains have the budgets necessary to make and continue the contacts needed to influence the location decisions of these associations. In this sense, the chains have a real competitive advantage over the independents. Moreover, the very large hotels that can accommodate large national groups are mostly managed by the chains; the chains therefore compete more with each other than with the smaller or independent hotels.[3]

3. For a comprehensive discussion of hotels and restaurants, see *The Hotel and Restaurant Business*, Fifth Edition, Van Nostrand Reinhold, New York, 1989.

DISCUSSION QUESTIONS

1. In what ways do the hotels of a city or community represent that city or community?
2. The all-suite motel offers the traveler what advantages that are not offered by a hotel or motel?
3. About what percentage of the world's hotel rooms are found in Europe? In Africa?
4. Why are most large hotels managed by hotel chains?
5. What is the future of the casino hotel? Will there be many more by the year 2000? Why or why not?
6. What are the advantages of owning and operating a bed-and-breakfast accommodation? What are the disadvantages?
7. The most successful hospitality business of all time is McDonald's. Why?
8. Would you be successful as a manager of a convention and visitor bureau? Why or why not?
9. Why is it that the Japanese are willing to invest as much as $400 million in a resort in Hawaii, much more than has ever been spent before on a single destination resort?
10. Will the restaurant business become more tourist-oriented in the future? Explain.

SIX

THE TRAVEL AGENT

The travel agent is an important nexus in the travel chain, the link in the series of events that stimulates travel and makes it convenient and satisfying. Ideally, the agent is a well-traveled professional who stays current on schedules, accommodations, entertainment, and costs. The travel agent acts as the sales intermediary, an agent for airlines, railroads, car rental companies, and cruise ships. The agent also brokers tours and may package some for the agency's own account, especially the less complicated ones that use motorcoaches for tours in the general area. Figure 6-1 shows the travel agent's relationship to the traveler client and the various travel suppliers and services for which the agent acts. The agent is both responsible to the client and also in a fiduciary relationship with the carriers and other suppliers from which a commission is received on sales. Commissions average about 10 percent on domestic flights and 11 percent on international flights, and are also received on rail, bus, and car rental sales and on making hotel reservations.

The average agents are owners or employees of a relatively small business. If employees, their income will be modest and the work demanding, but it will also be exciting and probably enjoyable. Even as owners agents will probably never get rich, but they will enjoy inexpensive travel and will travel widely.

The American Society of Travel Agents (ASTA) found that the typical U.S. travel agency has annual sales of under $2 million; a full-time staff of three to six people; and a mixture of travel sales: cruise, package tours, hotel reservations, airline tickets, car rentals, and often rail tickets.

In the United States and Canada the number of travel agencies more than tripled between 1970 and 1987, climbing from 6,700 to 30,000. Agency sales in 1987 were $38 billion. Suppliers (public carriers, hotels, car rental companies, and tour packagers) increasingly depend upon travel agents to book business.

Thousands of people take travel courses, many with the expectation of going into the business. Many, including a surprising number of retirees, do it because they want to travel; others study the field because they want an income-producing sideline. The attractions are several—free airline passage or a 75 percent discount on travel, hotel rooms free or discounted 50 percent, passage on trans-Atlantic ships for a quarter of the lowest-priced accommodation and on cruise ships for half the lowest rates. Agents are also invited on free or heavily discounted familiarization trips by countries, resorts, airlines, and hotel chains.

THE TOURIST BUSINESS

AGENTS AS PROFESSIONALS

Travel agents are business people selling travel services. A more descriptive term would be *travel advisers* or *consultants*; perhaps *brokers* is even more apt. Agents are entrepreneurs in the sense that they are usually in business for themselves, and professionals because they have the skill and training to draw on a particular body of knowledge in a meaningful way, in order to help travelers get the pleasures, conveniences, and experiences they want.

A good agent is something of a personal counselor, a psychologist, and an expert in the art and science of travel. Agents not only know the advantages and disadvantages of various modes of travel, their costs, and their schedules, but in many cases they also act as counselors in adjusting travel services to fit the personality of the client. As a professional the agent follows a code of ethics which may not always favor her or him economically.

Travel agents must base their recommendations on the answers to such questions as: How old and energetic is the client? Should the client's travel schedule be arranged for arrival at a destination in the early evening or in the morning? What about the effect of crossing time zones, the effects of altitude in some cities, the dangers of food poisoning in certain areas? The list of considerations stretches on and on.

Agents must learn to keep their cool under pressure—when flights are delayed, tickets lost, clients sent to wrong destinations or ticketed on an expensive flight when a cheaper one was available, and on and on.

Learning the Ropes

To get a foothold in the travel agency business usually means first performing such routine tasks as filing, bookkeeping, making sales reports, answering the telephone, taking messages, and so on. It would be poor judgment to permit a newcomer to ticket a complex trip; that would allow too many chances for error. Gradually the novice learns to handle reservations and domestic ticketing.

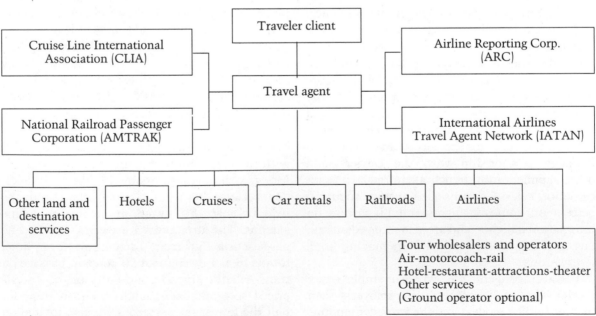

6-1. The Travel Agent: Nexus in the Travel Transaction.

Many travel agency managers and owners refuse to employ inexperienced personnel, relying on other agencies to do their training for them. One technique for in-house training is to request new employees to appear half an hour before opening time, a period that is used for training. Personality, motivation, and basic intelligence are the prime ingredients on which training is based.

Many agency operators are pleased to take on newcomers as outside salespersons who make sales calls on their own to interest groups in patronizing the agency for which they work.

Larger agencies encourage their in-house staff to specialize—to concentrate on commercial sales, vacation sales, or group sales. Others assign certain staff to service overseas sales.

After working for three months, the novice travel agent becomes eligible for the training offered by several airlines, particularly the large domestic trunk lines. American Airlines, which is typical, offers a curriculum that covers schedules, the *Official Airlines Guide*, itineraries, reservations, routings, preparation of tickets, special fares for excursions, construction of fares, and credit card sales. Free transportation is provided to and from the airlines' schools.

British Air has a ten-day regional program—four days of classes and six days of travel in Great Britain. Travel agent training is also offered by the Airline Reporting Corporation, which represents domestic airlines, in cooperation with the American Automobile Association, the American Society of Travel Agents, the Association of Bank Travel Bureaus, and the Association of Retail Travel Bureaus. The International Passenger Ship Association provides two separate one-day seminars covering the sale of ship travel. All are excellent training for the novice or moderately experienced agent. Community colleges also provide travel agent training.

Familiarization Tours (Fam Trips)

Quite naturally, many, perhaps most, agents are themselves wide travelers, taking every opportunity to visit new and different places. Special familiarization tours ("fam" trips) are often arranged for agents at little or no cost. Airlines and tourist agencies are pleased to arrange trips to the areas they represent, most of them at reduced or minimal cost to the agent. One year's work as a *bona fide* agent is required for reduced-fare air travel. The longer agents travel, the better informed they are and, presumably, the better travel agents they become.

A sense of geography is also part of their equipment. Every year, names that have been unfamiliar to the general public suddenly become *the* places to go. In recent years the Seychelles (islands in the Indian Ocean), the Algarve (southern Portugal), Costa del Sol (Spain), and Saint Martin (in the Caribbean) have become names to conjure with and part of the agent's bag of knowledge.

Description of the Agent's Job

The successful travel agent's range of knowledge needs to be large and constantly growing. A job description would include all of the following elements:

1. Prepares individual preplanned itineraries, personally escorted tours, and group tours; sells prepared package tours. Nine of ten agencies plan group travel.
2. Arranges for hotels, motels, resort accommodations, meals, car rentals, sight-seeing, transfers of passengers and luggage between terminals and hotels, and entrance to special attractions such as music festivals and the theater.
3. Handles and advises on the many details involved in modern-day travel, such as travel and baggage insurance, language study material, traveler's checks, auto garages, foreign currency exchange, document requirements (visas and passports), and health requirements (immunization and other inoculations).
4. Uses professional know-how and experience, such as schedules of train connections, rates and quality of hotels, whether rooms have baths, whether their rates include local taxes and gratuities. The traveler could spend days or weeks making phone calls and writing letters to secure this information and, even then, it still might not be right.

5. Arranges reservations for special-interest activities such as religious pilgrimages, conventions and business travel, gourmet tours, and sporting trips. Corporate and business travel account for half the travel agency business; nine of ten agencies report handling corporate accounts.

Entering the Business as an Owner

As with any business, specialized skills and temperament are requisites for success in the travel agency business. Like the restaurant business, the travel business is relatively easy to enter as an owner; similarly, it is also a business in which it is easy to fail. Inadequate financing, lack of business skills, and poor location are factors for failure. Moreover, travel agency owners are responsible for the actions of their employees on the job. In some cases they have been held liable for the actions or defaults of travel wholesalers from whom they have bought tickets. Before striking out as an owner, the individual should work in an agency to see if he or she will enjoy the detail and associated stress.

A prospective agency owner can start an agency in a new location, buy an existing agency, or become a partner in an existing agency and pay for the partnership in installments out of income. An owner who may wish to retire gradually or spend less time in operations may welcome an experienced partner who is willing to take on management responsibility.

The travel agency franchise is another way to get into the business. Uniglobe, a franchiser, had 650 locations in 1988; the franchise fee was $42,500 plus a percentage of sales. Its total sales for 1988 exceeded $1.7 billion. The Uniglobe franchisee usually rents the office space and must have a year of agency experience or employ someone who does. All agency offices use the Apollo computer system and are connected to the central computer via phone line. When a franchised office is not manned, incoming calls are switched to the central office, which is manned around the clock. Thus, unlike the clients of most travel agencies, which do business from 9:00 to 5:00 five days a week, Uniglobe customers can make travel reservations at any time.

The chances of failing as a fledgling agency owner are greatly reduced as a franchisee of an established company. Advertising as a group is less expensive per member, and the franchise group may provide other marketing advantages.

Ask Mr. Foster owns most of the travel agencies under that name but also licenses established agencies under an arrangement similar to a franchise. The licensed agency takes on the Ask Mr. Foster name and pays a percentage of commission income to the Carlson Company, the owner of Ask Mr. Foster. An advertising assessment is also made. Advantages to the licensee are the national advertising and overrides paid by carriers and tour wholesalers for getting preferred status from Ask Mr. Foster agencies.

The large franchisers negotiate overrides (commissions above those normally given) with carriers and other suppliers, and these overrides can be passed on to franchisees; according to the franchisers, they more than make up for the cost of franchise fees. Franchisers claim other advantages. Uniglobe, for example, offers a master contract for accounting services at a fixed price, lower than what the independent agent can negotiate.

Outside Sales Personnel

Outside agents, people who work at their own schedule to solicit business, can bring in large travel sales by soliciting corporations, churches, schools, and other groups for their travel business. The agency services such accounts and pays the outside agents 20 to 50 percent of the commission. Commissions paid outside personnel are on a sliding downward scale for repeat sales of the same account.

Many outside salespersons work part-time, out of their homes. The agency may write their tickets and do the bookkeeping for them. If qualified, the outside salesperson can use the agency office part-time for such work. Outside salespersons may cultivate specialized groups and develop sizable sales from them, especially for tours or meetings.

From the agency owner's viewpoint, outside sales can be a significant addition to income with low overhead costs.

The Airlines Reporting Corporation (ARC)

Travel agents who are agents for airlines and cruise lines must be appointed by them to be able to issue their tickets. The airlines and cruise lines established *conferences*, regulatory bodies that set standards that travel agencies had to meet in order to be appointed and act as sales agents for the carriers.

The Airlines Reporting Corporation (ARC) is made up of domestic airlines and controls most ticketing for domestic flights. For international flights the regulatory body is the International Air Transport Association (IATA), whose members are U.S. and foreign airlines with international routes. Its subsidiary, International Airlines Travel Agency Network (IATAN) is responsible for appointing travel agents in the United States to represent some 135 airlines from 109 countries and sell international tickets. The cruise conference is the Cruise Lines International Association (CLIA), composed of the major cruise lines worldwide. The National Railroad Passenger Corporation, known as AMTRAK, controls rail ticketing in the continental United States.

To get and keep an ARC or IATAN conference appointment, the travel agent must provide information concerning promotional methods, the physical setup of the agency and its location, and financial and personal data. The agency must also be bonded. Strict control of storage and use of ticket stock (blank tickets) is maintained, for ticket stock is equivalent to money.

The Area Bank Settlement Plan

Simplifying travel agency operation is the Area Bank Settlement Plan established by ARC. Under the plan, the agencies appointed by ARC can use a common ticket stock in selling all airline tickets. Ticket sales are computed weekly and one total payment (along with sales documents) is mailed each week to an area bank set up under the Area Bank Settlement Plan. The bank forwards payment to the airlines on whose stock the tickets were validated. The airlines, in turn, pay other carriers whose services appear on each ticket. By this process the travel agency writes only one check weekly to cover total sales of airline tickets for the previous week. Figure 6-2 diagrams the process.

AIR FARES

Thousands of air fares are changed by the airlines each day, and it is essential for a travel agent to keep track of them. One airline trumpets a lower rate between cities X and Y. Within hours, other airlines competing on the same route announce they will match the lower fare. Most of the discount fares announced are limited to a certain number of seats on a flight. That limit depends upon demand. If more passengers than usual book space at a given moment, the number of discount seats is cut back. If fewer seats are being sold, discount seats are added.

When a tour group requests a discount, the airline decides whether to accept or reject the discount. If rejected, the group may fly with a competitor, Airline Y, filling its discounted seats and possibly driving potential full-fare passengers to Airline X.

To find out how many discounted seats are being offered by Airline Y, Airline X may resort to the invidious strategy of phoning in reservations to Airline Y until told only full-price seats remain. Once Airline X has learned the number of discounted seats available on Airline Y, it cancels the reservations.

Air fares directly reflect competition. A coast-to-coast flight served by several competing airlines can be cheaper than one crossing a single state line. Depending upon location, fares may be higher on Tuesday, lower on Wednesday, and downright cheap on Saturday, reflecting the patterns of business travel. A requirement that a passenger remain at a destination over Saturday is designed to get full-fare from the business traveler who does not want to cut into his or her weekend

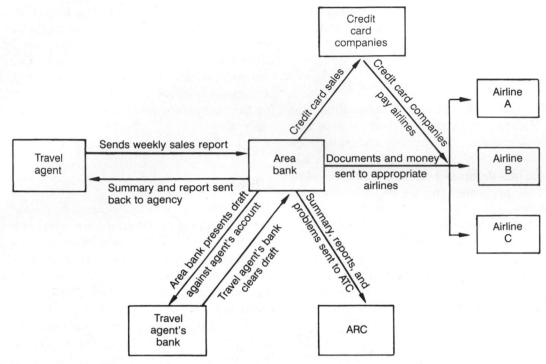

6-2. Area Settlement Plan.
SOURCE: From *Travel Career Development*, Institute for Certified Travel Agents, 1987.

at home. Price per mile varies from less than five cents to upwards of fifty cents even though a particular airline may need fifteen cents per mile to break even.

Classes of Fares

Basically there are three classes of fares: economy, business, and first-class, all of which may be discounted. Price differences hinge on section of the plane, passenger seating space, level of attendant service, and cost of meals served. First-class passengers receive the best service, seating, and amenities—at a price. On some airlines first-class fares can be double those of economy. Pan Am and British Caledonian began offering a service just below first-class in 1978, calling it business class. By 1987 more than forty-five airlines had business class, offering services, space, and amenities that were the equivalent of first-class a few years earlier. First-class seating has been reduced in number so that some B-747s now offer sixteen

or fewer seats of that class. Pan Am has built a reputation for its first- and business-class seats. Airlines such as Air Korea, Japan Air Lines, and Singapore Airlines provide expensive gifts to first-class passengers; others provide limousines for airport transfers and special reservation and check-in lines. Crystal and china and multi-course meals are served to business- and first-class passengers. Experienced and attractive flight attendants are picked to care for those who want, need, and can afford the extra attention and room.

The following list reflects some of the complexity of airline fares:

- *Economy*. This rate is lower in the winter than in the peak summer season. An extra charge is made for cocktails, wines, and movies, if any.
- *Excursion Rates*. These rates are available for trips that last fourteen to twenty-one days and twenty-two to forty-five days.
- *Advance Purchase Excursion Fares (APE)*. These fares are offered between selected cities within the

United States, Canada, and Mexico. Tickets must be purchased sixty days in advance. The traveler must stay at least twenty-two days and no longer than forty-five days.

- *Inclusive Tour (IT)*. A land package must be purchased along with the air travel.
- *Youth Fares*. These fares are offered by major airlines for passengers between twelve and twenty-one years of age and must be for a round trip. Seats are not confirmed until five days before departure.
- *Open-jaw Routing*. This routing is arranged by some airlines so that the traveler can fly from one city and return from another without having to buy two expensive one-way tickets.
- *Short-stay Tour Packages*. In these packages, the traveler receives a number of bonus gifts and services, for instance, "Belgium with a Bonus."

A number of special fares are also offered. Late night fares, for example, are at least 25 percent less than day fares. Flights during the middle of the week may be less than those taken on the weekends.

Triangle flights are offered by some airlines, so that the traveler can take a large loop flight at about the same cost as flying directly from one city to another. For example, the traveler can fly to New York from Los Angeles via Mexico City for a little more than flying from Los Angeles straight to New York.

Bucket Shops and Consolidators

So-called bucket shops that sold heavily discounted tickets operated before deregulation, selling bargain-priced tickets largely to ethnics who were visiting their homelands. These ticket sales were outside of IATA agreements, but were tacitly ignored. Since deregulation, discount houses operate openly, buying up blocks of seats that might not otherwise be sold. The discount brokers, now called consolidators, sell to travel agencies and/or the public directly.

Fare Wars and Capacity Control

With deregulation and airline mergers, fare wars heated up and discount fares became prominent.

Some fares were so low as to be hard to believe—and virtually impossible to get. The airlines raise or lower the number of discount seats available on each flight on a daily, even hourly, basis depending upon customer demand reflected in an airline's computer. They call this practice capacity control or inventory management. The floating inventory makes purchase of a discount seat something of a crap shoot for the airline and the customer. To arrive at fares, analysts study 14–30 and 330-day projections of reservations by time of day, day of week, and time of year. (Hotel marketers use a similar process, but not in such detail.)

COMPUTER RESERVATION SYSTEMS

All but the smallest travel agencies are computerized, on-line with one of the major airline reservation systems, and for a good reason. The computation of some airline fares is no job for amateurs. Some of the joint fares, the variations between twenty-one-day excursions and other types of group fares, are so complicated that most travel agents refer particular fare computations to an airline. Many irate travelers have found that their friendly travel agent or even the airline clerk has figured the fare so that it costs more than necessary. Unless the agent is really on top of the frequent fare changes, the best fare may not be the one offered.

The information and capabilities of the computerized reservations system are awesome. American's Sabre system, the largest of them, is connected to 50,000 terminals in 12,000 travel agencies worldwide. It contains 25 million airline fares, 40,000 of which are updated each day. Using Sabre, a travel agent can call up schedules of 650 airlines around the world and directly make reservations on more than 300 of them. Airline computer systems also contain information about trains, cruise lines, and climate information for major cities around the world.

As a computer Sabre can do math calculations and create client profiles. By pressing a button the agent can learn if a repeat client prefers vegetarian meals, a nonsmoking seat, or pays by American

Express card. The agency books can be kept using Sabre, and the computer can also be used as a word processor to print itineraries.

Travel agencies lease computer terminals and automatic ticket-writing machines from one of the airlines: TWA's system is called PARS; American Airlines uses Sabre; United Airlines has Apollo; and Delta has DATAS II. A number of foreign airlines such as Swiss Air, Scandinavian Air, and Japan Air Lines also lease their computer reservation systems.

Automated "back office" systems are marketed for computerized travel agency in-house operations; these systems interface with the leased reservation systems from the airlines. The back room system records travel sales, notes the commission, credits the agent who made the sale, completes reports, and is available for market analysis.

Computer reservation systems (CRSs) owned by airlines play a role in airline competition. Those airlines that own the CRS have a competitive advantage because their flights are displayed on the computer first, which introduces bias in their favor.

Hotel Reservations

The major hotel chains are included in some of the computer inventories. The hotels assign a number of rooms to a CRS for sale; as a room is sold, it is subtracted from the inventory. Toll-free 800 phone numbers, paid for by the hotel company, are also used for making hotel reservations. They account for about a third of the hotel reservations made in the United States. Hoteliers report that 25 to 40 percent of all reservations placed through their central reservations offices are from travel agents. Some hotel companies report as high as 80 to 90 percent agency-generated telephone reservations for offshore and resort properties.

The hotel chains are likely to spell out what is commissionable and what is not. Commissions are usually paid on extended-stay accommodations, that is, when clients booked by a travel agency extend their stay at a hotel. A commission of 10 percent on meals is applicable only if clients are booked on a full or modified American plan, that is, for two or more meals. No commissions are applicable on drop-in meals if clients are booked on a European plan.

The major airlines that own hotels are quite naturally interested in selling hotel space as well as airplane seats. The major airlines also book large amounts of space at the better-known hotels, even though a particular airline may have no financial interest in the hotel. In this way travelers can be sold an airline ticket and a reservation to a particular hotel at the same time — an advantage to the traveler. Only after the booked block of rooms has been sold out does the airline need to make individual requests for additional rooms. The traveler, in effect, bypasses the travel agent and purchases both ticket and room at the same time through the airline.

Huge travel agencies such as Ask Mr. Foster and franchisers can bargain with airlines and hotel chains for preferred rates, discounts, or other advantages. This places the independent agent at a disadvantage. To counteract this disadvantage, groups of travel agencies within a region have established cooperatives to gain overrides on commission. The coops also may engage in advertising and promotion and conduct education and training programs.

Some travel agencies expand their product line and sell traveler's checks, travel books and maps, and even luggage. The one-stop agency can take quickie passport photos, a valuable service for travelers going abroad. Tours sold can be those prepackaged by a wholesaler or those assembled in-house if the agency has the capital and know how. Some agencies expand their income by providing in-bound services for arriving travelers to the area, a specialized business in itself. Each product or service can translate into a profit, or a loss.

At least half of the larger travel agency's business is the business traveler. An agency may make deals with corporations to handle all of their travel, perhaps giving a rebate on sales to the corporation. An agency can even set up offices in the corporation and the corporation's facilities.

Ticketing may be done on site or through the primary agency location.

Some 1,000 travel agents sell only cruises and deal directly with cruise lines. Rather than handle a multitude of small sales, they concentrate on the "big ticket" cruise sales that mean fewer clients but bigger commissions per client. Many agencies concentrate on sales to a particular ethnic group—sending Jewish travelers to Israel, Irish to Ireland, Korean to Korea.

Corporate Travel Management

More than 80 percent of domestic air travel is discounted for the person who can schedule the trip several days in advance. The business traveler, however, lacks this discretionary planning time and has to fly almost immediately and pay the full fare, which may be more than double the discount price.

To expedite planning and reduce the cost of travel, numerous companies have established their own corporate travel management departments and/or appointed a person as corporate travel manager. Corporate travel managers create and operate travel offices that help establish written travel policies for their companies, help budget travel and entertainment expenses, negotiate travel discounts with travel vendors, and are at the center of the travel communications network of the corporation. Travel managers book and troubleshoot trips, which are often arranged by external travel agencies, limousine companies, car rental firms, and hotels.

KINDS OF TOURS

The typical travel agent is concerned with booking different kinds of tours. These include the following:

1. *Special-interest tours*. A package tour is designed to fit the requirements of a particular group of travelers, for example, special-interest groups such as gourmets, accountants, students, or art lovers. Package tours may be either escorted or unescorted. They are advertised in brochures that contain the cost, terms, and conditions of the offered package.

2. *Escorted tours*. An experienced tour director travels with the group and handles all basic details—hotel reservations, transportation, sight-seeing, baggage, customs, language translation when necessary, and so on. The tour director is responsible for maintaining the overall schedule of the tour. By and large, escorted tours are "all inclusive."

3. *Foreign Independent Tours and Domestic Independent Tours (FIT or DIT)*. These more flexible tours enable the traveler to purchase an arranged package with transportation, transfers, sight-seeing, hotel accommodations, and usually some meals, but the tourist does not travel with a group led by a tour director. Sight-seeing excursions may or may not be arranged. The predetermined cost allows the traveler to budget most expenses in advance. The basic advantage of a package tour is convenience. Also, because the package is arranged by a specialist who buys in large volume, the suppliers—the hotels, sight-seeing companies, and others—are anxious to please the tour director by providing high-quality service for those who have bought the package.

4. *Group inclusive tours (GIT)*. A group tour is usually composed of fifteen or more people traveling together who are members of a club, business organization, or other affiliated group, and who have pooled their purchasing power to realize savings, particularly on transportation. Group tours are offered to almost any destination.

Charter Flights

Late 1966 saw the beginnings of the Inclusive Tour Charter (ITC) in the United States. ITC is a large part of some agents' business. By chartering an entire aircraft from one of the supplemental carriers, the cost per traveler is drastically reduced for longer trips. (It often represents little saving for shorter trips.) The categorization of charters is more important for descriptive purposes than for any substantial difference in operation.[1]

---

1. These descriptions used courtesy of the Institute of Certified Travel Agents, taken from *Travel Career Development*, by Christopher Hooson and Nona Starr, Wellesley, MA: Institute of Certified Travel Agents, 1983.

Single Entity Charter

An individual, company, or organization (or agent acting on their behalf) can charter transportation directly from the equipment owner. The charterer bears the full cost and does not pass it on to the individual passengers. For example, a company that needs to fly ten executives from Kansas City to a secret meeting in Bloomington, Indiana, might find it less expensive and quicker to charter a small plane than to send all ten by scheduled airline. If an airline has a small airplane available, the company will pay a flat fee covering all costs of the flight: pilot, gas, landing fees, and food or beverages served.

Another variation might involve incentive travel. A company might reward employees who attain certain levels of productivity and performance by flying them to Disney World and back on an air charter at the company's expense. A travel agent who negotiates a single entity charter on behalf of a client bears little risk of financial loss and is not a principal in the charter agreement.

Affinity Charter

If an organization or club decides to offer a trip to its members, it may decide to use group rates on scheduled transportation or to charter. The organization usually works with a travel agent or directly with the tour operator who has signed the charter agreement with the equipment owner. The cost of the charter is prorated among the participants, who are either members of the organization or the family of members. Here, the organization enters into a contractual agreement with the charterer, and a travel agent acting as intermediary is not usually financially liable. Organizations that cannot fill an entire plane, ship, train, or bus may take advantage of split-affinity charters, through which blocks of seats or accommodations fewer than the total number available can be purchased, usually from affinity-tour operators.

Charter Tours

A travel agent or tour operator offering a single tour or a program of tours can choose between securing group rates on scheduled service or

chartering. Both arrangements directly affect cash flow, since payments to suppliers are often due well before deposits and other payments are received from clients. The group space blocked on scheduled service can usually be increased or decreased to some extent with payment of a penalty. Once an agent or tour operator decides to charter, however, he or she is responsible for the full amount of the charter price regardless of how many bookings are received. Tour charters are sold directly to individual members of the public through travel agents. They represent, of course, the greatest opportunity for profit or loss for the charterer.

Transportation Only

Single entity and affinity charters can be combined with hotel accommodations, sight-seeing tours, and other land arrangements to produce a tour. Both charters, however, can also be offered by themselves as transportation only. For example, a group of forty season ticketholders in Waco, Texas, may decide to charter a bus to transport them to every home game of the Dallas Cowboys. Frequently, too, single entity, affinity, and even tour charters will offer remaining seats on air, bus, or rail charters to those who want transportation only as a fill-up measure, even though the rest of the group has purchased other tour arrangements.

Seasoned travelers (and those not seeking rock-bottom fares) usually forego bargain charter flights because they are known for flight delays, inconvenient locations in airports, small seating spaces, and full loads of passengers.

Tour Wholesalers

The tour business is growing rapidly and constitutes a major part of many agents' work and income. The agents can put tours together themselves, but they are more likely to use those assembled by specialists who wholesale them to the travel agencies.

Around 80 percent of all overseas tour expenditures are for tours that have been put together by fewer than 100 tour wholesalers in North America. Package tours of various prices, lengths, and purposes are assembled by direct negotiation with airlines, shipping lines, hotels, restaurants, and other travel-affiliated services. These tours are then sold to the travel agents who, in turn, sell them to the traveler.

Most tour wholesalers also operate tours themselves. In recent years some of the tour wholesalers have also purchased ownership or interest in resort hotels. Similarly, some of the hotel chains have purchased tour wholesalers or set up their own tour sales companies. The advantages to the hotel owners are plain—all the tour groups can be routed through the owners' hotels.

For the traveler, a tour offers advantages and disadvantages. Among the advantages are known cost and savings, a known itinerary and no responsibility for making reservations, and guaranteed entrance to attractions when they are part of the tour package. Tour participants are also given preference for theater and other entertainment. Many travelers love the camaraderie developed during a tour; others would rather avoid it.

Traveling via a tour removes much of the challenge of travel, welcomed by many, missed by others. Tours are inflexible; the free independent traveler (FIT) makes his or her own schedule. Tour travelers often complain about obnoxious people in tour groups, too much togetherness, too little time for shopping or being on one's own, and the too-fast or too-slow pace of travel. In some countries—Russia, for example—to travel as an FIT is quite difficult.

Tour Operators

Most of the largest tour operators belong to the United States Tour Operator Association (USTOA), an association with strict eligibility requirements. The National Tour Association (NTA) has some 450 tour operators, primarily those who offer escorted tours within North America. Over 2,000 suppliers (hotels, airlines, bus) and attractions belong as do 400 public-sector organizations such as government travel offices and convention and visitor bureaus.

Services offered by tour operators vary widely and are limited only by the imagination. The tour operator buys a variety of ground services at various destinations from specialized ground-service operations. Services may include meeting clients with fanfare and ceremony upon their arrival at a destination. In Hawaii, for example, the tour operator is on hand to place the traditional leis around the necks of visitors as they arrive in the airport building. The lei with its traditional kiss unnerves some visitors, but the custom is pleasant to most. The ground operator may be on hand for travelers who have been on the plane many hours and need the reassurance, and sometimes the physical support, of an escort to the waiting tour vehicle. The operator makes all the arrangements for transporting the luggage from the airport to the hotel.

Tour operators may accept complete responsibility for the tour, from beginning to end. The tour would then cover all expenses that the traveler would ordinarily have to pay—porterage, baggage gratuities, accommodations, air fares, meals, sight-seeing, and entertainment. Prices for a tour package range from $100 to $20,000, and tours may last from a few days to three months.

Tour operation involves a multitude of details and demands a variety of skills, including sales ability. Tour operators must be administratively capable and able to speak and write well. They must have the talent for visualizing the step-by-step details of a complicated tour arrangement. They are constantly planning for the future and anticipating changes in markets and tour details. At times they work under tremendous pressure. Some tour operators own their own transport; most lease or contract for transport services.

Some tour operators concentrate largely or completely on certain travel destinations. Tours only to Hawaii, for example, are offered by Mackenzie, All Travel, Robinsons', Hawaiian Holidays, Island Holidays, and Tradewind. Three of the major wholesalers own hotels in Hawaii.

Tours can be short but hectic. Gambling junkets fly from New York or Pennsylvania to Las Vegas or the Bahamas, some in two-day packages. The bulk of Atlantic City gamblers travel by bus from nearby cities. Possibly the most hectic, or at least the most demanding, is the tour for Japanese billed as a honeymoon package. JAL flies the couple from Tokyo to Honolulu at night. They spend the day on Waikiki, the night in a hotel, then the next day on the plane back to Tokyo.

Tour wholesalers can be local, national, or international. The local wholesaler packages tours for the area, then sells them to retail travel agents wherever possible. The wholesaler may have regional offices in other countries. If a market area does not justify a complete office, the wholesaler may arrange to be represented in an area. The best known of the tour wholesalers are the Thos. Cook and American Express companies.

Tour wholesalers have the same problems as many other businesses—many go broke. In 1986 at least eighteen tour wholesalers became defunct, some leaving several million dollars behind as debt. The United States Tour Operators Association (USTOA) has set up a protection fund that reimburses or otherwise protects clients of tour operators that have failed.

Foreign Independent Tours

Travelers who buy a tour do not necessarily travel in a particular tour group. Large numbers of tours are classified as foreign independent tours (FIT), the other meaning for the term FIT. Travelers purchase a completely planned itinerary and may have a string of coupons that serves to buy all of the services needed on the trip, but they are not part of a scheduled tour group. Parts of the tour will be taken with other tour groups; travelers may move from one group to another for portions of the trip. The FIT travelers benefit by being able to purchase a completely planned trip and, in many instances, get the package of travel accommodations, services, ground transportation, and entertainment at a total price that is less than if they had assembled the package for themselves. Domestic inclusive tours (DITs) are another type of tour.

The Tour Leader

Tours are usually led by a mature person, very often a schoolteacher or college professor or some-
one who is semiretired and enjoys travel. The job is seldom taken on as a career because the compensation is nominal. The leader engages in the work because he or she enjoys travel and the challenge of shepherding a group of people from the time they leave a point of departure until they return. Tour leaders are often called tour escorts or tour managers. Within a city the tour leader may be called a tour guide. In Europe the escort is often called a courier.

The tour leader who takes a group from the United States to Russia may expect a courier employed by Intourist to take charge once the group arrives in Russia and remain with it until the group leaves.

The job of tour leader is not for just anyone. It calls for both managerial and problem-solving skills. Who knows when one member of the tour will go on a drinking binge or become ill? What happens when a flight is missed or canceled? What is to be done when baggage is lost or stolen? Where are the best and most reliable shops? What can be done to quiet the noisy tour member who upsets the other tour members? Who gets the choice seat in the bus? What happens if the only food available is unacceptable to some tour members for religious reasons?

Should a tour leader expect tips? How far may the tour leader go in hustling the group? Should the tour leader expect a percentage from shopkeepers, as is the custom with many tour leaders?

The tour leader's job can be minimal or highly exasperating, simple or very complicated. The tour leader aboard a cruise ship may find the job very relaxing. On the other hand, the tour leader taking a group on safari across Africa may very well run into numerous problems, including illness and frayed tempers, to name just two.

Time Conversion

Many travelers have missed airplane connections and confused their entire schedules by incorrectly determining the day and the hour. Travelers and travel agents must be aware of time zones and how to convert from one to another. Flying east, one hour is added to the time with each zone crossed, as seen in Figures 6-3 and 6-4. Moving from Los Angeles to Denver, travelers set their watches ahead one hour, another hour in Chicago, and another in New York. In other words, when it is 12:00 noon in Los Angeles, it is 2:00 P.M. in Chicago and 3:00 P.M. in New York. In London and Paris, it is 8:00 P.M., a time difference of eight hours.

Flying from east to west, the conversion is reversed. Travelers subtract hour after hour as each time zone is crossed. A person in New York calling someone in Los Angeles should realize that it is three hours earlier on the West Coast. The same person in London calling at 8:00 P.M. should know that it is 3:00 P.M. in New York but only 12:00 noon in Los Angeles. Daylight savings time, which is not observed everywhere, creates further problems.

A day is gained or lost as the international date line, located in the Pacific, is passed. Going east, travelers lose a day. Moving west, they gain one.

TRAVEL AGENCY PROFIT AND LOSS

A rule of thumb for computing the gross profit of a travel agency is to multiply gross sales by 10

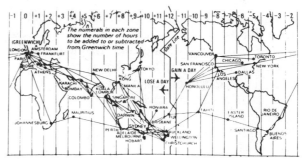

6-4. The world is divided into twenty-four time zones with a one-hour time difference between each. Each time zone represents fifteen degrees of longitude. An invisible line in the Pacific Ocean, called the international date line, separates one day from another. At the precise moment Monday begins in Time Zone 1, on one side of the line, Monday is just ending in Time Zone 24 on the other side and Monday is at various stages of completion in all other time zones around the world.

percent. If an agency grosses $2,000,000 in sales a year, its gross profit for that year would be $200,000. The net profit would vary after all expenses were paid. In part the profit depends on how much salary the owner pays himself or herself. If a corporation, the owner should take a large salary, leaving less profit to be taxed at corporate rates. The owner is well advised to think of various ways of reducing overall profit in perfectly legal ways that present certain tax advantages. Some of the ways of doing this include the following write-offs:

- Drive a company-owned car and charge all or most of the expenses to the company.
- Have the company cover the cost of a life insurance policy on the manager.
- Arrange for the company to provide loans at no interest to the manager.
- Arrange a medical insurance plan paid for by the company.
- Institute a profit-sharing plan that permits a percentage of the profits to be tax-sheltered until the beneficiary retires and is in a lower income bracket.

Subchapters of the Internal Revenue Service Code allow a business entity to operate as a corporation but permits it to avoid paying corporation taxes. This is a form of business entity which

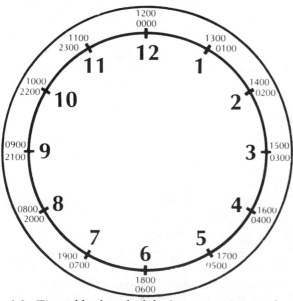

6-3. Timetables for schedules between countries show times using the twenty-four-hour clock shown here.

in most cases fits a travel agency operation well, at least during its early stages of growth. Tax laws and their interpretation change frequently and a tax expert is needed to keep abreast of them.

Bookkeeping/accounting is an on-going process, usually summarized monthly in the form of a profit-and-loss statement and a balance sheet. The monthly statements also compare financial results with previous months' figures. Accounting can be done in-house manually, by computer, or by an outside accounting firm. The American Society of Travel Agents has an excellent book, the *ASTA Travel Agency Accounting and Information System*, designed especially for small and medium-sized travel agencies.

A typical statement of accounts for a travel agency is seen in Figure 6-5. A particular agency might have other special accounts and some of those listed may not apply, but in general all agency statements will include more or less the same items.

A comparison of this year's sales with last year's is a good means of determining progress or lack of it. A third column could put all income and expenses in the form of ratios to sales, another technique for getting a handle on expenses and profits.

Danger: Cash Flow Problems

The nemesis of travel agencies, the sneak-up-and-strike-you-dead problem, comes from extending credit to clients and finding one day that credit accounts have accumulated to the point that it is necessary to borrow heavily from a bank. Obviously, extending credit to clients is an attraction and a service, but it must be handled very carefully. Numerous high-volume agencies have found themselves in serious financial difficulty, and many have failed because of granting excessive credit to clients.

Payments to airlines must be made every week—whether the agency has been paid or not. Many travelers buy their trips on credit and sometimes wait several months before paying the bill. Too many sales like that and the travel agency has no alternative but to borrow from a bank. Paying high rates of interest on loans soon offsets the commission that may be forthcoming eventually.

Corporations can be more serious credit offenders than individuals. Many companies delay payment of all bills for ninety days, a deliberate policy that permits them to operate on interest-free money. The company may be highly profitable and still operate on such a policy. The travel agent knows that the company is solvent and that eventually he or she will be paid, but the agent cannot afford to subsidize the corporation by extending credit for travel purchases.

How Much Is a Travel Agency Worth?

The value of a travel agency hinges on its ability to produce profits, now or later. It may also have value as a tax shelter for a person in a high-income tax bracket who wants a tax write-off for several years but expects that the agency will gradually increase in value and eventually be sold at a profit; such profits of course are taxed as capital gains and not as earnings. Usually the buyer is interested in an agency that will produce a livelihood immediately or within a short time. He or she will want a record of past sales and commissions for at least three years. From such records, the buyer can see if the trend of sales and profits is up, down, or flat. He or she will also analyze the sales mix to learn what percentage of sales is of minimal profit (point-to-point commercial air sales) and what percentage produces higher profits (tours, hotel reservations, car rentals, and large-ticket vacations).

The location is always important. If the agency depends upon volume commercial sales, a street-level location is an asset. Is the neighborhood changing for the better or for the worse? Are the agency's clients moving into the neighborhood or out of it? Is the character of the neighborhood attractive, or at least suitable, for the clientele?

A rule of thumb regarding the value of an agency was proposed by Laurence Stevens, a travel agency expert, in *The Travel Agent* magazine. His contention is that a retail travel agency is worth

6-5. Travel Agency Financial Statement

Acct. No.	Title	January	January Last Year
_____	Commissions earned	_____	_____
	Other income	_____	_____
	Total revenue	_____	_____
_____	Sales commissions	_____	_____
	Total sales expense	_____	_____
_____	Salaries	_____	_____
_____	Overtime	_____	_____
_____	Other wages	_____	_____
	Total salaries	_____	_____
_____	Payroll taxes	_____	_____
_____	Retirement plan	_____	_____
_____	Group life insurance	_____	_____
_____	Employee activities	_____	_____
_____	Travel meetings and entertainment	_____	_____
_____	Automobile expense	_____	_____
_____	Dues & subscriptions	_____	_____
_____	Other insurance	_____	_____
_____	Promotion & entertainment expense	_____	_____
_____	Tour material & bulletins	_____	_____
_____	Advertising	_____	_____
_____	Postage	_____	_____
_____	Stationery	_____	_____
_____	Minor equipment purchase	_____	_____
_____	Telephone & telegraph	_____	_____
_____	Computer lease	_____	_____
_____	Legal services	_____	_____
_____	Data processing services	_____	_____
_____	Other professional services	_____	_____
_____	Equipment rent	_____	_____
_____	Office rent	_____	_____
_____	Office repairs & maintenance	_____	_____
_____	Heat, electric & water	_____	_____
_____	Depreciation furniture & equipment	_____	_____
_____	Furniture & equipment repair & maintenance	_____	_____
_____	Freight & express	_____	_____
_____	Messenger service	_____	_____
_____	Exchange & service charges	_____	_____
_____	Cash overages & shortages	_____	_____
_____	Bad debts	_____	_____
_____	Miscellaneous expense	_____	_____
	Total general expense	_____	_____
	Net before overhead	_____	_____
	Overhead	_____	_____
	Net income before taxes	_____	_____

somewhere between 4 and 10 percent of its average annual gross sales. In other words, an agency grossing $1,000,000 with a favorable sales mix that produces maximum profits would be worth up to $100,000 to the buyer. Some agencies would be liabilities from the date of purchase. Stevens recommends a provision in the contract that permits the buyer to participate in the business during a transition period. The buyer would naturally be interested in retaining customers and building new business while becoming familiar with the agency. Stevens also suggests that the seller may wish to receive payment over a number of years to avoid having to pay very high taxes for the year of the sale.

Cost Analysis

As with any business, travel agency management must perform cost-accounting and cost-analysis. Profitability of a particular travel agency is much related to the type of business it does, the so-called business mix. As seen earlier, commissions vary from 3 percent for services performed for an industrial organization to 20 percent or more when the agency puts together and sells a chartered flight.

The cost of doing business varies widely also. The cost of booking a short domestic air trip, for example, is much higher proportionately than booking overseas travel. Booking an overseas tour can mean $500 or more in profit. The operation of a travel agency has the same problem any business selling a service has—it must determine which items are most profitable and which are least profitable. When all costs are considered, some may result in a dead loss. Travel agency managers or owners sometimes concentrate on tour sales where the percentage of profit can be as high as 20 percent, double the 10 percent paid by the airlines for domestic flights.

The travel agency manager is urged to break down income from sales so that what is selling, what it costs to sell each item, and the profit from each sale can be studied. The breakdown as seen in Figure 6-6 illustrates a method of analysis that

will produce useful information from which management can make decisions.

A word of caution—it is often impossible to sell only those travel packages that are most profitable. The usual travel agency must provide domestic airline sales even though such sales are less profitable than tour or charter sales. Domestic air sales will produce revenue that helps the agency meet fixed costs: rent, some salaries, telephone, computer, and other costs. Such sales might be considered necessary to help reach the break-even point in the agency operation.

The travel agency is one of the most labor intensive of businesses, a fact that makes labor cost control a continuing concern. Laurence Stevens asserts that labor costs in a travel agency must be kept below 50 percent of revenues. An agency with a gross income of $1,000,000 could expect a $100,000 in gross profit, which means that salaries should be no more than $50,000, one reason why travel agencies are considered to be low-profit businesses.

The Future of Travel Agents

The travel agent of the future undoubtedly will have ready access to more information in the computer. He or she will be able to call up not only fares and alternate routes, but also weather forecasts around the world, current events at major destinations, and snow conditions at ski areas. Instant information on available rooms at major hotels around the world will be possible by pressing the appropriate computer button. The day may come when photographs of facilities can be called up by computer.

The sales tools of travel agents will increase in sophistication. American Express's vision of the travel office of the future can be seen at the EPCOT Center at Disney World. Two people may seat themselves before a console activated by touch and by responding to inquiries from the computer, they may zero in on the type of trip and destination they would like. Videotaped scenes of twenty-seven vacation destinations around the world can be called up for the viewers to observe.

THE TRAVEL AGENT

6-6. Sales and Commission Income				
	Sales $	Commission income		Time Cost
		% of Sales	Amount $	at $ Per Hour
Transportation (FIT)				
Sea				
Air—domestic				
Air—foreign				
Rail				
Bus				
Hotels/meals (FIT)				
Sight-seeing and sidetrips				
Transfers (FIT)				
Cruises				
Conducted tours				
College tours				
Reservation costs/income				
Other sales (traveler's checks, etc.)				
Total				
Destination				
Domestic				
Hawaii				
Canada				
Mexico				
Caribbean				
Europe				
Africa				
Asia				
Australia/New Zealand				
Pacific				
Round the world				
Near East				
Combination trips				
Total				

A number of changes, however, do not favor the small, independent travel agency. Several businesses tie in nicely with the travel-selling business and have moved into the field, creating additional competition for the travel agency. A number of banks offer travel services as a part of their services. Already in the business of loaning money, banks are ready to make travel loans as well. Having a travel agency within the bank itself is a convenience for the customer. The American Society of Travel Agents opposes banks entering the travel business, viewing them as unfair competition. The Society has gone to court to prevent banks from operating as travel agents.

In California, where so many new ideas are fostered, large department store chains, such as May Company and Bullocks, have installed travel agencies within their stores.

The stay-at-homes who do not want the travail of travel see a different future. Isaac Asimov, the science fiction writer, proposes travel without terrorists, jet lag—or real challenge. He sees a teletravel agency of the future that

lets your mind do the walking . . . you get hooked up to a machine that emits signals which stimulate the brain's sensory areas. The (teletravel) agent dials an office in Paris, say, and you request a stroll along the Left Bank. The Paris office dispatches an android that relays all sensory data into your brain. You see, hear and smell through it. You feel the uneven pavement under your (its) feet, the gentle wash of air over your (its) swinging arm. Turn your head to the left, and the robot obligingly looks to the left. The result (says Asimov) is so realistic that you can easily fool yourself into believing you are actually there.[2]

Less futuristic changes in travel are already here, and many pose problems for the travel agent. One trend not favoring the travel agent is the airline practice of negotiating bulk fares directly with corporate customers, thereby circumventing the travel agent and reducing the airlines' marketing costs, said to amount to 25 percent of the cost of the airline ticket.

With the use of a $100 program the individual traveler can turn a personal computer into a full reservation and ticketing system that works in the office or at home. In Scandinavia persons wishing to fly SAS can use personal computers to make reservations for flights, hotels, and limos. In the United States a personal computer can allow one to plug into the electronic *Official Airline Guide*, which displays all airline schedules. The computer can make reservations and pay for tickets directly through a link to Thos. Cook travel agencies.

American Airlines has EASY Sabre, a personal reservations system that is on-line with fourteen computer networks. For an hourly fee the individual, using a personal computer and communications modem, can call up flights for more than 650 airlines worldwide and find out the quickest routes between cities and more than 25 million air fares. Hotel rooms can be reserved at more than 12,000 hotels and cars from some twenty rental car companies.

Automatic ticketing machines at airports, railway stations, and hotel lobbies are another threat to the agency. Run a credit card through a slot, punch in the destination, carrier, and departure time — and out pops a ticket.

Frequent-flyer and frequent-hotel guest plans also by-pass the travel agent. In 1981 American Airlines introduced the first frequent-flyer plan, since copied by many other airlines. The plans reward the frequent flyer (mostly persons flying for business purposes) for flying with the airline offering the plan. Several airlines provide free hotel rooms. Holiday Inns, in 1983, began to offer a frequent-guest plan by which participants are awarded points each time they are a guest.

The small agency, like the small independent hotel or motel, will probably be viable in certain markets for many years. The "superagencies," the large franchised groups, the agencies that are part of conglomerates such as American Express, will probably gain greater clout with the carriers and receive higher commissions and other favored treatment.

The huge travel companies can offer greater service to the traveler — for a price. American Express offers a Platinum Card to their most affluent and big-spending customers. Costing $250 a year, the card provides a toll-free, 24-hour number to call when in need of help or a ticket. The Personalized Travel Service (PTS) is officed in Phoenix but writes tickets and sends them via Federal Express and courier service to the buyer, wherever that person may be. PTS is a kind of on-call concierge, ready to help out with any travel-related service (such as the request from a new bridegroom who wanted a six-foot teddy bear in the bridal suite. The bear was there in two hours).

A perhaps minor threat to the independent travel agency is the travel club. The travel club arranges trips at a discount and brings people of similar interests together through travel. Travel club managers bargain with suppliers for discount prices. Some clubs concentrate on last-minute

2. Marvin Cetron, *The Future of American Business*. New York: McGraw-Hill, 1985, pp. 27 and 28.

bookings, especially cruises. Like a hotel room, a cruise cabin is a highly volatile product. If not sold, the income from that cabin is lost forever. The cruise line operator thus discounts last-remaining rooms at 50 percent or more. Suppliers advertise their "clearance sales" only through the travel club, whose members must be ready to take the trip on very short notice. Clubs such as Ports of Call, headquartered in Denver with some 60,000 members, offer their own charter packages using their own aircraft.

In the future, travel agencies will specialize and more will become part of chains or franchises. The American Automobile Association has more than 1,000 travel offices; the Ask Mr. Foster chain has more than 500. The trend toward travel conglomerates and huge travel companies that operate multiple offices in a number of cities seems inevitable. Vertical integration also seems likely; even now, hotel companies own travel agencies that feed business to hotels within the system. Government permitting, airlines are also likely to buy or create multi-office travel agencies.

The small independent travel agent, like the small restaurant owner, will probably always have a place, especially in small communities. The travel agency business will probably continue to include numerous small agencies that make only modest profits. The small independent will be competing against the larger, multi-officed agency that can develop its own tours and has the capital to invest in the best accounting and office equipment. The smaller agency is disadvantaged by being unable to negotiate prices and overrides with the suppliers.

The travel agent of the future will certainly be more sophisticated, will use up-to-the-minute marketing techniques, analyze products, and emphasize those that are most profitable. Travel and education will help agents become better informed about specific destinations and the requirements of special market segments. Whatever happens, we can be sure that the job of the travel agent will continue to demand intelligence, reliability, and a desire to serve the public. The whole world is the agent's field of study—its geography, peoples, politics, foods, and histories.

PROFESSIONAL ASSOCIATIONS

The largest association of travel agents is the American Society of Travel Agents (ASTA), headquartered in New York. ASTA has twenty-four chapters, each with its own elected officers and appointed committees.

The more than 20,000 ASTA members in the United States and 128 other countries make about 80 percent of all travel agency sales. Allied members include airline and steamship companies, railroads, bus lines, car rental firms, hotels, and government tourist offices.

Founded in 1936 as the American Steamship Travel Association, ASTA has sponsored such activities as conferences on travel matters, research into travel preferences, and work with various governmental agencies concerned with travel. The society also conducts a number of training courses and seminars. Those persons who wish to acquire full membership in the society must have three years of experience in the travel field.

A splinter organization is the Association of Retail Travel Agents (ARTA). A number of agents, who felt that ASTA and other associations representing retail travel agents were not aggressive enough, formed ARTA.

Travel agents can upgrade their jobs and increase their professionalism by taking a basic course in the mechanics of being a travel agent, available by correspondence from ASTA. In 1964 the Institute of Certified Travel Agents (ICTA) was established in Wellesley, Massachusetts, to provide an advanced educational program for travel agents. The Institute offers a certification program leading to the degree of CTC, Certified Travel Counselor. To receive this designation, the candidate must pass examinations covering travel agency business management, passenger traffic management, marketing and sales management, and international travel and tourism. A research paper is required. The candidate must be twenty-five years old and have five years of experience in a travel agency.

TRAVEL AGENCY REFERENCE BOOKS AND GUIDES

Travel agencies must have a number of references handy for quick access to information about destinations, accommodations, tours, and flights. Computerized reservation systems provide information on flights, flight times, and fares, which change so frequently that printed information may already be outdated when published. Travel guides provide the hotel, restaurant, and destination information that is part of every travel agent's armamentarium. Most are published annually or semi-annually—a few come out quarterly. Most of their cost is covered by paid advertising. The few that do not accept advertising are expensive to buy.

Several guidebooks rate hotels and motels. The one with the widest circulation is published by the American Automobile Association and is sent to their approximately 22 million members. The *AAA Tour Book* editors select a limited number of motels, motor inns, and resorts to receive their top accolade, the Five Diamonds award. The AAA tour books are published annually in twenty-five regional editions. For all editions, approximately 18,000 properties are approved and listed. AAA accepts advertising but does not make it a condition for rating.

The *Mobil Travel Guide*, also published annually by Rand McNally, has seven regional editions and gives some 5,000 restaurants and 16,000 hotels, motels, and resorts one- to five-star ratings. There is no advertising. The guide uses some 100 inspectors to check lodgings and sample restaurants.

Both the AAA and Mobil guides compile an enormous amount of information: not only where to stay and where to eat, but also data on geography, history, and places of interest.

In Europe the Michelin guides have the highest prestige and have been known to make or break restaurants and hotels with their ratings. Their top ranking is three stars. Michelin has also begun publishing guides to selected areas in the United States.

Armed with these information resources, the travel agent attempts to provide the client with recommendations for travel based on the latest, most accurate information possible—recommendations that fit the client's needs.

TRAVEL AGENCY FRANCHISE SYSTEMS

Cardillo Travel Systems, Inc.
5710 Hannum Ave.
Culver City, CA 90230

Express Travel
5 Penn Plaza
New York, NY 10001

International Tours, Inc.
5001 E. 68th St.
Oklahoma City, OK 74136

Jewelcor Travel
15 S. Franklin St.
Wilkes-Barre, PA 18701

Tenholder Travel
2801 Itaska
St. Louis, MO 63111

Uniglobe Travel (International), Inc.
90-10551, Shellridge Way
Richmond, B.C.
Canada V6X 2W9

TRAVEL INDUSTRY ASSOCIATIONS AND ORGANIZATIONS

Airlines Reporting Corporation
1709 New York Avenue NW
Washington, DC 20006

Air Transport Association of America
1709 New York Avenue NW
Washington, DC 20006

American Automobile Association
8111 Gatehouse Road
Falls Church, VA 22407

American Bed and Breakfast Association
P.O. Box 23292
Washington, DC 20026

American Bus Association
1025 Connecticut Avenue NW
Washington, DC 20036

American Car Rental Association
1750 Pennsylvania Avenue NW
Washington, DC 20006

American Hotel and Motel Association
888 Seventh Avenue
New York, NY 10106

THE TRAVEL AGENT

American Society of Travel Agents
1101 King Street
Alexandria, VA 22314

American Tour Managers Association
8909 Dorrington Avenue
West Hollywood, CA 90048

Association of Retail Travel Agents
25 South Riverside
Croton-on-Hudson, NY 10520

Cruise Lines International Association
17 Battery Place
New York, NY 10004

Federal Aviation Administration
800 Independence Avenue SW
Washington, DC 20591

Gray Line Sightseeing Association
7 West 51st Street
New York, NY 10019

Institute of Certified Travel Agents
P.O. Box 56
148 Linden Street
Wellesley, MA 02181

International Airline Travel Agency Network
2000 Peel Street
Montreal, Quebec
Canada H3A 2R4

International Air Transport Association
26 Chemin de Joinville
P.O. Box 160
1216 Cointrin-Geneve, Switzerland

International Association of Amusement Parks
and Attractions
4230 King Street
Alexandria, VA 22302

International Association of Convention and
Visitors Bureaus
P.O. Box 758
Champaign, IL 61802

International Association of Tour Managers
(North American Region)
1646 Chapel Street
New Haven, CT 06511

International Civil Aviation Organization
International Aviation Square
1000 Sherbrooke Street W
Montreal, Quebec
Canada H3A 2R2

National Air Transport Association
4226 King Street
Alexandria, VA 22302

National Association of Business Travel Agents
3255 Wilshire Boulevard, Suite 1514
Los Angeles, CA 90010

National Passenger Traffic Association
516 Fifth Avenue, Suite 406
New York, NY 10036

National Railroad Passenger Corporation (Amtrak)
400 North Capital Street NW
Washington, DC 20001

National Tour Association
P.O. Box 3071
546 East Main Street
Lexington, KY 40596

Pacific Asia Travel Association
228 Grant Street
San Francisco, CA 94108

Society of Incentive Travel Executives
271 Madison Avenue, Suite 904
New York, NY 10016

Travel Agents Computer Society
238 Main Street, Suite 302
Cambridge, MA 02142

Travel and Tourism Government Affairs Council
1899 L Street NW, Suite 607
Washington, DC 20036

United States Travel and Tourism Administration
U.S. Department of Commerce
Washington, DC 20230

United States Travel Data Center
1899 L Street NW, Suite 610
Washington, DC 20036

World Tourism Organization
Calle Capitán Haya 42
Madrid, 20, Spain

THE TOURIST BUSINESS

DISCUSSION QUESTIONS

1. Why do so many people want to become travel agents?

2. Travel tickets may soon be sold through home computers and vending machines. Will such sales be a serious threat to the travel agency business? Explain.

3. Do travel agencies have to lease a computer to remain competitive? Give reasons for your answer.

4. Suppose you have almost no assets (capital). How could you become a travel agency owner?

5. Suppose you want to sell an inexpensive two-week tour to Great Britain. Who would be a good market for such a tour? How would you let them know about its availability?

6. How important is the travel agent in the customer's travel destination choice?

7. Travel agents, like many business people, want to become more professional. What are some of the things they can do to achieve this?

8. How do travel agencies most commonly get into serious financial trouble?

9. When a travel agency is bought, what are the advantages to the buyer of having the previous owner work in the office for a period of time?

10. Suppose you hear that a certain airline is in trouble financially. Would you as a travel agency manager stop booking passengers on the airline? Why or why not?

11. As an agency owner, you make a mistake in writing an itinerary and your client misses the plane. What would you do to compensate the client for the inconvenience and probable additional cost?

12. As a travel agent selling trips abroad, how important is it for you to have actually been to the destinations you are selling? Support your answer with reasons.

13. What kinds of temperaments and aptitudes are important to becoming a skilled travel agent? Are there some people who would never do well as travel agents no matter how much training they had?

14. What aptitudes and training are needed to become a travel agency manager as compared with being one of the agents in a travel agency?

15. What are some advantages in purchasing a franchise in order to enter the travel agency business? Are there any disadvantages?

16. Selling tours is much more profitable than selling airline tickets. Why shouldn't an agent specialize exclusively in tour sales?

SEVEN

TOURIST DESTINATION MARKETING

Destination marketing is the overall effort to identify what it is a destination has to offer (the product), what groups of people would have the time, money, and desire both to travel to and to enjoy the destination (the target markets), and how best to reach and convince those people to come to the destination (marketing). Destination marketing involves market research and sales and includes trying to find out how to convince travelers to stay longer and spend more.

A destination can be any geographical unit that can be viewed as having a common image, a city such as Miami or San Diego, a state such as Missouri, a region such as New England, a country such as Brazil, or group of countries such as Western Europe.

A maximum number of visitors often is not the desired goal. Mass tourism can be self-defeating. Instead, the goal is often quality tourism, that is, selective promotion to reach the big spenders. Statistics needed to reach the target markets include information such as average length of stay, per capita expenditures, and number of visitors according to season.

Destination marketers may rely on a number of enterprises outside the immediate control of the individuals directly involved to increase the number of visitors to an area or facility. Airlines are a principal factor in destination advertising and in providing transportation. Government promotion and advertising can be a critical factor. Government policy regarding tourism is likewise important. This chapter only touches on the several ramifications of destination marketing, inlcuding its important component, market research.

LEVELS OF TOURISM MARKETING

Who are tourists? Why do they travel? Which destinations do they select and for what reasons? Answers to these questions are constantly being sought by governments, land developers, public carriers, and resort owners. Some of the answers are easily observable; others must be secured through research. Armed with such information, people who sell travel and tourism then set about trying to communicate with their target markets using advertising, promotion, and other means. With target markets identified, investors can make a decision whether to buy or build tourist-related businesses. People already in business can expand.

Tourism marketing is conducted on several levels: city, state, region, and country. Figure 7-1 shows some of the levels. Cities such as Los Angeles, New York, and Las Vegas market tourism through visitor and convention bureaus and other organizations. Each of our fifty states has its own tourism marketing offices. Regional promotional offices such as the European Travel Commission and the Pacific Area Travel Association are active. The World Travel Organization (WTO) takes in most of the Free World nations and has a primary purpose of fostering and facilitating travel among its member nations.

Because national tourist offices (NTOs) want more people to visit their countries, they set up major branches of their national tourist offices in cities around the world. Los Angeles alone has more than thirty such offices. Where separate tourist offices are not maintained, consulates act as their country's travel representatives. Over 100 sovereign nations belong to the World Tourism Organization, an indication of the widespread interest in tourism, promotion, and development.

State tourist offices promote their states either as destinations or as pass-through places worth a stopover. The first purpose of any visitor and convention bureau is to convince more people to visit its locale. More than thirty such bureaus exist in California alone, a few staffed with thirty or more people.

In addition to government-affiliated destination promoters, travel suppliers, carriers, and attractions promoters are all eager to convince more people to visit "their" destination. Eastern Airlines, for example, played a significant part in developing Miami Beach as a tourist destination by advertising heavily in the New York metropolitan area. Airlines commonly provide free travel for travel writers, travel agents, and others who will interest the public in particular vacation destinations.

Regional Marketing

Tourist destinations may be specific, small areas (Nantucket, for example), towns or cities (Miami Beach), or states, regions, or nations. Los Angeles is a tourist destination that is also part of southern California, California, and the West. Cape Cod is a destination that is also part of Massachusetts and New England. Disney World is a destination, a part of central Florida, Florida, and the Southeast. Planning and promotion of a destination can be done at a local area level or at some larger regional or national level.

New England—comprising Maine, Vermont, New Hampshire, Massachusetts, Rhode Island, and Connecticut—is by history and image a regional destination area. It can be planned, packaged, and sold as a region, just as any of its parts, such as the White Mountains, Boston, or the Mystic River, can be planned and sold as entities. Similarly, Myrtle Beach, South Carolina, can be planned and sold as a destination and also gain advantages from being planned and sold as a part of the Golden Strand and as part of South Carolina. California is sold by both regional and state

Global level: World Tourism Organization

National/regional level Example: European Travel Commission

National level Example: Britain

Regional level Example: New England

State Level Example: Florida

Community/City Level Example: New Orleans

7-1. Levels of Tourism Promotion and Development.

promotion. States such as Nebraska and North Dakota that are primarily pass-through or bridge states usually have at least a few destinations that can be packaged into a state image.

Creating an overall image for a region can add to the appeal of its component parts. Advertising New England helps Boston as well as tiny Rangeley, Maine. Perhaps more important, thinking regionally leads to regional research, planning, and control. Although particular areas within a region may be saturated with tourists, regional planning may divert tourists to those areas that need and welcome them. Regional promotion can be directed to build tourism off-season and during the shoulder periods, the relatively low volume seasons on either side of the high season. Analysis of a region may suggest that parts of it be seeded with a tourist attraction to promote regional growth. Other areas of a region may wish to discourage more visitors. Route 28 on Cape Cod exemplifies an area with excessive tourism during the summer months, while other parts of Massachusetts welcome more tourists. Furthermore, a region may have the finances to develop new markets, whereas a smaller part of it may not. For example, it may be economically expedient to promote New England as a whole in Japan, but excessively expensive to promote single destinations within that region for the Japanese.

State Tourism Marketing

State tourist offices are charged with bringing more visitors into their state and convincing them to stay longer and spend more. In 1987–1988 the states appropriated $284 million to carry out this charge. Alaska, for example, where tourism is a major industry, spends close to ten million dollars a year to attract some 780,000 visitors to cruise the Inland Waterway, travel the few Alaskan highways, fish and hunt, and view the magnificent scenery.

Each state has a travel office funded by that state. For example, Hawaii Visitor's Bureau (HVB) has five divisions: marketing, visitor satisfaction, research, finance, and membership. State tourist offices conduct research to identify visitors demographically and psychologically. Some of the findings are surprising. In Alaska during the month of July, for example, Germans and Swiss were second in numbers using the Alaska Highway, the 1,490-mile road from Dawson Creek, British Columbia, to Fairbanks, Alaska. (The trip takes seven days.) The largest number using the highway were Californians. This kind of information enables tourist offices to target markets and aim their advertising to reach the people most likely to entice to the state.

State budgets for tourism vary according to the pressure put on state legislatures and the political philosophy of the party in power. Figure 7-2 shows the state tourism budgets for 1987 to 1988. In 1988 Illinois set aside $20.5 million for tourism development and promotion; New York State, $21.54 million; Hawaii, $13.66 million. State tourism expenditures bear little relationship to size of population. Alaska, with about 500,000 people, spent $9.3 million on its tourism budget in 1987, while California, with the largest U.S. population, spent only $7.6 million.

Tourism promotion spending by states also does not correlate very highly with reported tourism income. Figure 7-3 shows tourism spending for trips over 25 miles from home in 1985.

According to the Travel Industry World yearbook, California ranked first in tourism spending with $59.54 billion. Florida ranked second, New York third, Texas fourth, and Illinois—with the second highest budget—seventh.

Another function of a state tourism office is to call attention to the economic value of tourism to the state. Economic impact studies are commissioned, and the results brought to the attention of voters and public officials. It may come as a surprise to many Californians, for example, to learn that tourism (according to the state tourism office) is the number-one source of income for the state; in fact, California's tourism earnings are more than eleven times those of Hawaii.

Although government tourist offices tend to concentrate on promotion and advertising and to ask for ever-increasing budgets, tourist offices can function with minimal budgets if the directors look upon themselves as catalysts rather than as advertisers. An office can concentrate on developing

7-2. Budgets of U.S. State Tourism Offices		
State	1987–88 (millions of $)	Rank
Alabama	$ 5,111,638	22
Alaska	9,346,800	10
Arizona	3,375,900	31
Arkansas	2,753,324	32
California	7,622,000	14
Colorado	8,697,700	12
Connecticut	2,150,000	37
Delaware	1,216,400	48
Florida	10,723,551	7
Georgia	9,200,000	11
Hawaii	13,665,000	3
Idaho	2,017,000	40
Illinois	20,500,000	2
Indiana	2,107,287	38
Iowa	1,495,533	46
Kansas	1,222,331	47
Kentucky	4,003,800	25
Louisiana	4,314,453	24
Maine	2,640,000	33
Maryland	3,580,609	28
Massachusetts	10,173,972	8
Michigan	10,889,400	6
Minnesota	5,851,700	20
Mississippi	1,680,000	45
Missouri	5,243,038	21
Montana	3,854,865	27
Nebraska	1,168,142	50
Nevada	3,937,263	26
New Hampshire	1,895,056	41
New Jersey	8,101,000	13
New Mexico	2,099,700	39
New York	21,543,300	1
North Carolina	6,772,641	16
North Dakota	1,187,000	49
Ohio	6,362,553	18
Oklahoma	4,460,353	23
Oregon	2,417,147	34
Pennsylvania	12,130,400	4
Rhode Island	1,864,000	42
South Carolina	6,980,298	15
South Dakota	2,300,500	36
Tennessee	9,390,400	9
Texas	11,969,274	5
Utah	3,535,800	29
Vermont	1,745,800	44
Virginia	6,539,000	17
Washington	2,400,000	35
West Virginia	1,789,841	43
Wisconsin	6,317,000	19
Wyoming	3,423,463	30
Total	**$283,766,232**	
Average	**$ 5,675,325**	

SOURCE: U.S. Travel Data Center, Survey of State Travel Offices, 1987–88.

7-3. Domestic Tourism Spending in U.S. States for Trips Over 25 Miles from Home—1985		
State	Tourism Spending in State (billions of $)	Rank
Alabama	$ 3.24	36
Alaska	1.68	45
Arizona	8.08	18
Arkansas	3.46	32
California	59.54	1
Colorado	9.19	16
Connecticut	4.84	28
Delaware	1.24	48
Florida	34.14	2
Georgia	9.59	14
Hawaii	5.11	27
Idaho	1.82	44
Illinois	15.89	7
Indiana	5.46	25
Iowa	3.55	31
Kansas	3.41	33
Kentucky	4.39	30
Louisiana	6.97	22
Maine	3.20	37
Maryland	7.99	19
Massachusetts	10.38	12
Michigan	13.14	8
Minnesota	9.55	15
Mississippi	2.53	39
Missouri	9.14	17
Montana	1.37	47
Nebraska	2.35	41
Nevada	12.70	9
New Hampshire	2.88	38
New Jersey	23.70	5
New Mexico	3.33	35
New York	30.32	3
North Carolina	10.39	11
North Dakota	1.20	49
Ohio	12.56	10
Oklahoma	5.32	26
Oregon	4.53	29
Pennsylvania	17.09	6
Rhode Island	0.93	51
South Carolina	6.21	24
South Dakota	1.06	50
Tennessee	6.88	23
Texas	28.72	4
Utah	3.41	34
Vermont	2.26	43
Virginia	9.72	13
Washington, D.C.	2.26	42
Washington	7.05	21
West Virginia	2.39	40
Wisconsin	7.46	20
Wyoming	1.51	46
Total	**$444.00**	

Note: Foreign visitors spent $12 billion in the U.S. in 1985, bringing total tourism spending in the U.S. to $456 billion.
SOURCE: Travel Industry World Yearbook.

special-interest literature and working with the private sector to bring more visitors to the state. In one instance an expenditure of only $3,000 ultimately brought many millions of tourism dollars into the state of California. The sum was used to establish and organize an annual trade fair at which European and other travel wholesalers met with travel suppliers. Dozens of wholesalers and suppliers now arrive annually at a particular hotel to meet each other and conduct business in a single convenient, comfortable, and pleasant place. This arrangement is good for them and good for the state.

State tourism offices take the lead in establishing a state advertising theme such as New York's, "I love New York." Sometimes an entire marketing campaign is built around the theme. The "I love New York" theme was the centerpiece for TV ads featuring Broadway stars. The casts of some Broadway shows traveled to Rio de Janeiro and to Dallas promoting New York State, especially New York City, as a fun place to visit. In part, the campaign was an attempt to counteract the negative image which New York City had acquired. The campaign was reported to be highly effective.

Florida has the slogan "When you need it Bad, We've got it Good." Hawaii's theme is "The Hawaiian Islands: Where the World wants to be." Texas builds on its history with "Texas—Come Live the Legend." The Virgin Islands uses "Beyond the Blue Horizon." Georgia says, "This Way to Fun." Massachusetts builds its advertising around "Make It in Massachusetts." New Mexico states, "Where the Southwest Began, Land of Enchantment."

National Tourism Offices (NTOs)

Like a state tourist office, a national government's interest in tourism depends much on politics and political pressure. With a few exceptions, national governments have recognized tourism as an economic force. Accordingly, they have increasing national tourism budgets, and several nations—among them Canada, Australia, Morocco, Egypt, and Indonesia—have raised the status of the office of tourism development and promotion to cabinet rank. National tourism office (NTO) budgets vary widely. Canada in 1984 had a budget of $26.2 million; the United Kingdom, $42.3 million; and Spain, $51.3 million. The amounts spent on research, investment, promotion, and planning also vary widely. About two-thirds of the NTO budgets in Europe are spent on planning and investment, and 23 percent on promotional activities. Canada spends heavily on market research. Some other countries spend almost nothing.

NTO budgets for many areas are small, and tourist officials must spend their limited funds judiciously. Bringing in travel writers and arranging familiarization trips for travel agents have been found to be very cost-effective. A well-written article on an island group, for example, placed in the Sunday travel section of a leading newspaper, arouses the interest of hundreds of people, and does so less expensively and more effectively than paid advertisements.

Books by writers such as Robert Louis Stevenson and James Michener have spread the gospel of the South Pacific. Paul Gauguin painted Tahiti onto the world's vision. Travel writers spread the word in articles for newspapers and magazines. A destination may also benefit greatly when it serves as the setting for a movie; *South Pacific* and *Mutiny on the Bounty* left indelible feelings about islands like Hawaii and Tahiti.

Tourism offices must also alert travel agents to the beauty, the romance, the mystery of a country. Brochures help, but slide or movie presentations made in person by a representative of a national tourist office are considerably more effective. Nothing, however, is quite as effective, say the travel experts, as the familiarization trip, by which a number of travel agents are transported, courted, wined, dined, and indoctrinated into the wonders of a destination. Transportation is provided free by an airline that serves the area.

MARKET POSITIONING

Destinations—be they nations, states, cities, or smaller entities—"position" themselves in the minds of their target markets by defining themselves so that the potential traveler has a fairly clear-cut picture of what the marketer wants to sell—the benefits of the destination—and understands where the destination compares with competing destinations. The marketer defines the product to be sold and then transmits this definition in the form of an image to potential travelers.

A hotel marketer, for example, positions the hotel somewhere along the continuum that starts with budget property and ranges to luxury property. Each category offers a range of benefits including prestige, convenience of location, services, amenities, and status of clientele. Examples of market positioning of lodging properties are as follows:

Budget:	Motel Six
Economy Limited Service:	Roadway Inns
Lower Mid-Range:	Holiday Inns
Upper Mid-Range:	Sheraton Hotels
Luxury:	Ritz Carlton

Each market position projects a certain image to the potential guest, an image that is reinforced in every practicable way including the quality of employee service, the room rate, and the location as part of a glamorous setting.

A national tourist office must determine, preferably by research, which groups of people are the target markets, how to reach those target markets, and what kind of image to project into the minds of the target markets to convince them that they should travel to the destination. Exotica appeals to some markets; price appeals to other markets; convenience may be number one; climate is all important for most destination resorts. Friendliness of the residents can be a primary attraction. Architecture, history, interesting terrain, native foods, local crafts—the list goes on and on. Each can be fed into the image equation that determines market position and sets the particular destination apart from other destinations in the minds of the potential traveler. (The technical term is *product differentiation*.)

How does the particular destination differ significantly and beneficially from similar destinations? Target marketing and market positioning by means of product differentiation are combined to form the image that the marketer strives to create and project. That image hopefully triggers the desired response, a decision to travel to the destination.

STATE TOURISM MARKET RESEARCH

Most state tourism offices (STOs) conduct annual research projects to identify visitors, determine how much each spends, figure the total visitor expenditures, and determine where the visitors come from, so that advertising and promotion can target appropriate markets. The State of Hawaii provides a good example of the kinds of research data collected annually by state tourism offices.

Total expenditures by visitors to Hawaii indicate the industry's importance to the state. In 1987, the 6.6 billion dollars from tourist spending accounted for a third (33.7 percent) of the gross state product (which had a preliminary estimate of $19.6 billion by the Department of Business and Economic Development). If we consider total exports of Hawaiian products, visitor expenditures accounted for almost two-thirds (63.6 percent) of the gross state product.

Figure 7-4 shows that lodging was the major category of expenditure among westbound visitors, accounting for 38 percent of all categories combined.

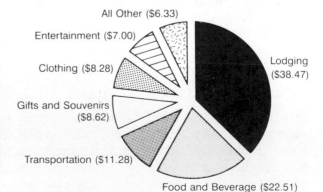

7-4. 1987 Per Day Visitor Expenditures by Categories for All Visitors.
SOURCE: Hawaii Visitors' Bureau.

Expenditures by visitors from the different mainland regions of the United States show different spending patterns. As indicated in Figure 7-5, visitors from the New England states spent $124.82 per visitor per day, the highest among all regions. The lowest averages were among visitors from the west north central regions ($90.78) followed closely by visitors from the Pacific Coast states ($92.85).

Advertising and promotion can be targeted by city as well as by state. Figure 7-6 shows the top ten U.S. metropolitan areas from which visitors to Hawaii came in 1987. Six of the top ten metropolitan areas are in the State of California.

It is also helpful for a state to know where foreign visitors are coming from. Figure 7-7 shows that Japan accounts for more than 20 percent of all visitors to Hawaii. All other Asian countries combined accounted for almost a fourth (22.6 percent) of all visitors in 1987. The Asian count, the Japanese, soared to 1,313,000.

Canadian visitors maintained a slight lead over Australians. Australia's 218,000 visitors, coupled with New Zealand's 117,000 (up to 19.4 percent), propelled Oceania's proportionate share to 6.4 percent of all Hawaii's visitors.

At 66,000 the United Kingdom is the largest European originator. However the number of visitors from West Germany more than doubled in 1987; the 63,000 West Germans almost equaled the number from Great Britain.

Since the Japanese are such an important tourism segment, the tourism office wanted to know whether they were part of an organized tour. Figure 7-8 shows that most Japanese visitors traveled with an organized tour group. The groups tended to be less structured than in former years and allowed members to purchase optional tours after arriving in the islands. Repeat visitors accounted for a third of the market. As Figure 7-9 shows, almost two-thirds (60.7 percent) of the Japanese were traveling for pleasure, while nearly a third (31 percent) visited Hawaii on wedding/honeymoon.

The tourism office also did a demographic breakdown by age. More than half the Japanese visitors were in the 20 to 29 year age bracket. Most (79 percent) were married. Clerical office workers were the largest (29 percent) occupation category.

Most vacation destinations experience a typical volume-of-visitor curve that results in high, low, and shoulder periods. Hawaii is idiosyncratic in that each month of the year shows visitor volume to be almost the same. The exceptions are the summer months of June, July, and August, which show a somewhat higher volume of visitors, as seen in Figure 7-10.

How do states collect this information? Most do so by questionnaire. Each year, the Hawaii Visitors' Bureau (HVB) conducts a Visitor Expenditure Survey. In 1987 the Visitor Expenditure Survey was based on a sample of 1,386 completed visitor expenditure diaries. The diaries were distributed daily among westbound air passengers to Hawaii through the course of the year, collected on their departure, and edited extensively.

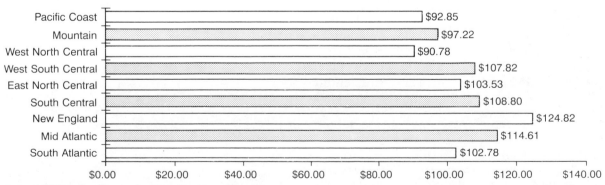

7-5. 1987 Expenditures by U.S. Region of Residence.
SOURCE: Hawaii Visitors' Bureau.

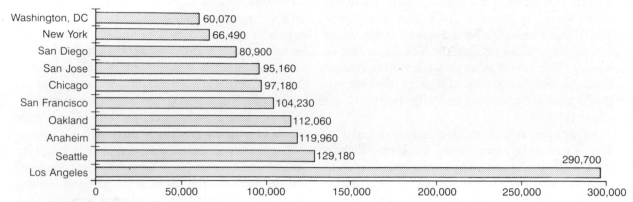

7-6. 1987 Visitors by Top Ten U.S. Metropolitan Areas.
SOURCE: Hawaii Visitors' Bureau.

Visitor counts and demographic data are collected from a combination of monthly reports supplied by the carriers and surveys conducted by the HVB on carriers arriving from the U.S. mainland. In 1987 about 62 percent of the North American passengers disembarking in Hawaii completed the HVB's Passenger Information Form from which a 10 percent systematic sample was taken and analyzed by the bureau.

TOURISM CANADA MARKETING

An illustration of how national tourist offices market a country is reflected in the marketing efforts of Tourism Canada, the Canadian government's tourism office, one of the most effective NTO programs.[1]

Tourism Canada conducts on-going tourism research, the purpose of which is to attract more visitors to Canada, primarily from the neighboring United States. (Canada is the most popular foreign destination for Americans, representing 47 percent of the 30 million international trips

taken by Americans.) International tourism contributed $6.3 billion to the Canadian economy in 1987.

Tourism Canada concentrates its marketing efforts in the four U.S. census regions which it has found to produce three-quarters of all American travelers to Canada:

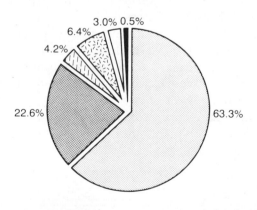

7-7. 1987 Breakdown of Visitors to Hawaii by Country.
SOURCE: Hawaii Visitors' Bureau.

1. The remarks in this section are based on "U.S. Pleasure Travel Market," 1986; "Tourism Canada, Spring 1988 Overseas Advertising Plans"; "Pleasure Travel Markets; Japan, United Kingdom, West Germany, France, 1987"; "Tourism Canada, Ottawa."

TOURIST DESTINATION MARKETING

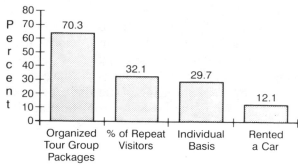

7-8. 1987 Japanese Visitors to Hawaii.
SOURCE: Hawaii Visitors' Bureau.

- East North-Central (20.3 percent): Illinois, Indiana, Michigan, Ohio, Wisconsin
- Mid-Atlantic (22.4 percent): New Jersey, New York, Pennsylvania
- Pacific (20.6 percent): California, Oregon, Washington
- New England (11.8 percent): Connecticut, Maine, Massachusetts, New Hampshire, Rhode Island, Vermont

The data base for target market identification was developed from the most comprehensive travel market study ever conducted in Canada or the United States: a total of 9,000 personal, in-home interviews, averaging 50 minutes in length, con-

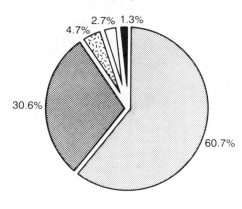

- ▦ Pleasure/ Sightseeing
- ▨ Honeymoon
- ▧ Business and Pleasure
- ☐ Other Reasons
- ■ Business

7-9. 1987 Purpose of Trip by Japanese Visitors.
SOURCE: Hawaii Visitors' Bureau.

ducted in each of the nine U.S. census divisions, amounting to 1,000 interviews per division.

Based on this data base, the researchers classified the U.S. visitors who traveled into Canada into three primary markets: those touring Canada for pleasure; those who came primarily to enjoy the outdoors; and those who came to enjoy Canadian cities. Three smaller markets were also identified: those who came to cruise, visit a theme park, or visit a resort. (A large number of visitors came for the purpose of visiting friends and relatives, but this group was not considered a target market for purposes of advertising because advertising is not needed to induce them to travel to Canada.) Figure 7-11 shows the breakdown of trip nights to Canada. Among the pleasure tour visitors, one trip in five involved a package deal. The trip lasted eight days on average and was planned one to two months in advance. The most attractive Canadian regions for a tour trip in order of appeal were the Pacific Coast, Quebec, Ontario, the Canadian Rockies, and the Maritime Provinces.

The outdoors trip was generally the family vacation, typically lasting three to four days and taken fairly close to home. The city market was made up of those who took an extended weekend getaway lasting an average of three days. Cities with the greatest appeal for this group were Toronto, Montreal, and Vancouver.

Using the data base derived from the 9,000 interviews allowed the tourism office to describe three groups making up the target audience:

1. **Touring group:**
   Age: 40 to 64
   Job: Professional/Managerial
   Education: College or further
   Income: $30,000 or more
2. **Outdoor group:**
   Age: 21 to 39
   Job: Professional/Managerial/Technical
   Education: College attendance or further
   Income: $20,000 or more
3. **City group:**
   Age: 21 to 49
   Job: Professional/Managerial/Technical
   Education: College attendance or further
   Income: $30,000 or more

THE TOURIST BUSINESS

To reach these target groups, selected magazines were used, magazines whose readers fit the description of the target markets as close as possible. Magazines selected to reach the touring market were

Sports Illustrated (select issues)
New York Times Magazine
Life
Money
Travel & Leisure
National Geographic Traveler
Time
New Yorker

The outdoor market was reached by advertising in

Better Homes and Gardens
Architectural Digest
The Atlantic
House and Garden
Gourmet
Vanity Fair
Business Week

And the city market was reached by

Newsweek Executive
Smithsonian
Sunset
Town & Country
Travel/Holiday
Vanity Fair
Business Week

Altogether, the magazine advertising budget for 1988 was $11,970,803 (in U.S. dollars). Tourism Canada also chose to run its ads in specific issues, at those times when the target markets were planning for travel. Figure 7-12 shows the magazines selected by Tourism Canada and the time slots that were used in the 1988 U.S. consumer advertising program.

GLOBAL OR SPECIFIC PROMOTION

National tourist office (NTO) directors are confronted with the question, "Must I target all markets separately, or are there global appeals that attract all potential visitors?" Although some features and qualities of tourist destinations appeal to nearly everyone, other features and qualities appeal to highly specific markets and must be carefully targeted to be effective. These specific features are then accented in promotional literature and other media. In the language of marketing the NTOs must "differentiate their product" to make it stand out from similar products. Their product (their country) must offer special qualities and features; for example, Indonesia features its Balinese dancers; Japan, its kabuki theater; Norway, its fjords; China, its Great Wall; England, its stately homes.

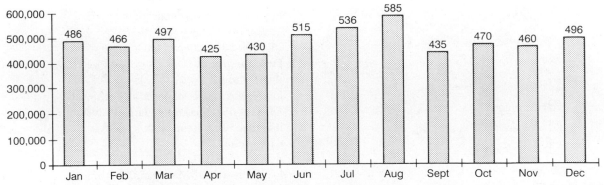

7-10. 1987 Total Overnight and Longer Visitors by Months.
SOURCE: Hawaii Visitors' Bureau.

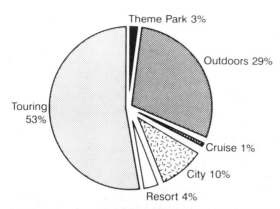

7-11. Canada's Trip Type Mix: Percent of Total Trip/Nights to Canada Excluding Visiting Friends and Relatives and Close-to-Home Leisure.
Source: U.S. Pleasure Travel Market, 1986.

These qualities and features might be considered global in their appeal. Other qualities and features must be tailored to particular markets. A study of Thai tourism showed this to be particularly true. Five visitor groups to Thailand—French, Japanese, English, Chinese, and Spanish—were questioned about the features and qualities of Thailand that appealed most to them in advertising about the country.[2] The French favored learning about cultural differences, the beauties of nature, and advertising for pictures of local people at work or leisure.

The advertising features which the English believed more effective were shopping, night life, special events, architecture, transportation within the country, foods of Thailand, and plants and animals.

The Chinese and Spaniards added tourist services to the list of important advertising appeals. In other words, to reach each national group of potential visitors effectively, advertising should be somewhat tailored to each group.

Interestingly, the same study showed that those who were devising the Thai promotional materials (advertising directors and NTO directors) had different ideas from the tourists as to what advertising appeals were most effective. This difference

2. Prin Laksitanand, "Aspects of Thai Tourism Marketing as Seen by Tourism Directors, Advertising Directors and Five National Groups of Tourists." Dissertation study for U.S. International University, San Diego, 1989.

suggests that promotional literature should be based not on what NTO directors and advertising specialists believe to be important but what the visitors themselves believe is important in attracting them to a particular destination.

Starting in June, 1986, the United States and Canada reached a five-year agreement that allowed Tourism Canada and the U.S. Travel and Tourism Administration to undertake jointly funded travel market research in overseas countries. During October and November of 1986 about 1,500 personal, in-home interviews, averaging 50 minutes in length, were conducted in Japan and in the United Kingdom, West Germany, and France. It was learned that almost 14 million people of 18 years or older had taken a vacation of four nights or more in the preceding three years to an overseas destination, or intended to take one in the upcoming two years.

Figure 7-13 shows the population 18 years or older, the incidence of the target market, and its size.

The overseas travelers tend to be better educated and more affluent than the general population. Japanese overseas travelers typically took an all-inclusive package vacation during the summer months and went to the Far East/Asian destinations or to Hawaii, Guam and/or Samoa. The four preferred activities were sight-seeing in cities, shopping, dining out, and taking guided excursions as part of a tour.

The French placed sampling local foods as the number-one activity while abroad; dining out was number two. It seems the French preoccupation with cuisine is well founded. The Germans, like the French, also chose dining out and sampling local foods as the top two activities. The British placed shopping first followed by taking pictures/filming and dining out.

Tourism Canada found two highly specific target markets in Japan: young single women, age 20 to 29, and young honeymooners. The young women, typically employed as "office ladies," saved money for marriage and an overseas trip before marriage. These women make the decision for the honeymoon destination, and 76 percent decided on an overseas destination.

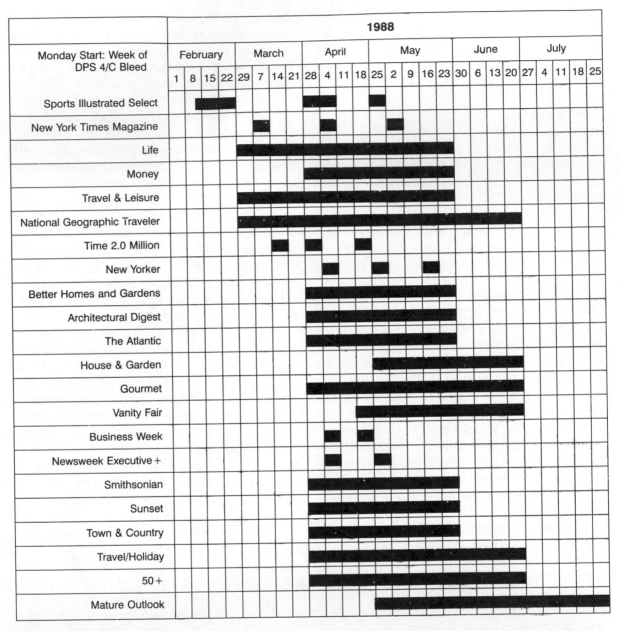

7-12. Magazine Summary.

A "silver age" market, comprised of men and women over the age of 50, was also targeted. Tokyo subway posters were used as a means for reaching the general population. In addition, ads in appropriate magazines were used to reach both the young women and the silver agers.

Government Marketing: The Bahamas

In the Bahamas the government has effectively encouraged tourism by providing tax incentives and tax holidays on imports, and by allowing the expatriation of profits. It appears to be convinced

TOURIST DESTINATION MARKETING

of the effectiveness of private enterprise and has gone so far as to give the ministry of tourism quasi-private status, allowing it freedom of action not enjoyed by other ministries. Those hotels taken over by the government because they were not doing well have been placed under management contracts with such well-known chains as Resorts International, Canadian Pacific, and Trust Houses Forte.

The Bahamas' location, within an hour's flight of Florida, the natural beauty of the islands and their warm weather are largely responsible for the country's touristic appeal, attracting more visitors than any other Caribbean destination. Casino gambling and laws that make Nassau, the capital, a tax haven are also attractions. Proximity to Florida and corrupt officials, however, have also made parts of the Bahamas a smugglers' base, first for smuggling rum into the United States during Prohibition and now as a way station for Colombian drugs.

Tourism is one of the few business choices available in the Bahamas. The soil is unsuitable for agriculture, and attempts to set up small industry have not worked out. Tourism will probably continue to provide 80 percent of the national income. For this reason, two hotel/restaurant schools operate in Nassau. One is a two-year program operated by the government, the other is a branch of the University of the West Indies, offering a bachelor of science degree.

An independent nation since 1973, the Bahamas has a government that seems genuinely concerned about spreading the benefits of tourism across the islands. Recognizing the need for attracting productive personnel, the tourism ministry is set up as a corporation so that the usual civil service rules do not apply; personnel can be hired and fired without the usual civil service red tape.

As in Puerto Rico and Hawaii, the ministry is trying to disperse tourism throughout the populated islands rather than allowing it to concentrate in Nassau and Freeport. To this end twelve research companies undertook a comprehensive study of the islands in 1980. The purpose was to identify propitious locations for tourism development. The World Bank committed $18 million for developing an infrastructure in the places the companies selected.

In 1975 the establishment of a People to People program helped increase the return rate of visitors. Designed to help visitors get to know Bahamians and want to return to the islands, the program has apparently been successful when it has been used. Operated by the Bahamian Ministry of Tourism, the program is patterned after the "Meet the Danes" program and a similar program offered by the French. Hundreds of volunteer hosts have been enlisted, Bahamians who agree to meet and entertain visitors with similar interests. These volunteers show their guests the sights, take them to service club meetings or to church, and often offer them a Bahamian meal.

Representing a cross-section of occupations, the volunteers are blue-collar as well as white-

7-13. Market Size				
	Number of Interviews	Population 18 Years or Over	Incidence of Target Market	Size of Target Market
Japan	1,519	88,900,000	5.3%	4,710,000
United Kingdom	1,618	41,300,000	4.9%	2,020,000
West Germany	1,481	48,100,000	8.9%	4,280,000
France	1,484	40,500,000	7.1%	2,880,000
			Total travelers:	13,890,000

Source: Tourism Canada.

collar workers, carpenters and electricians as well as teachers and lawyers. Selected because they are friendly people, the volunteers are asked to entertain visitors about once every two months. The only requirement is automobile ownership.

Visitors learn about the program from hostesses at the various hotels, through brochures distributed at the tourist information centers, at the airport, from travel stories, and by word of mouth. Some volunteers meet visitors aboard the cruise ships that make Nassau a regular stop.

Problems with tourism still exist in the Bahamas. Operating costs remain extremely high; labor and energy costs and the cost of repairs and maintenance are well above the average for world hotels. Prices of everything are inordinately high by American standards, locally produced foods being no exception. Middle-level restaurants are scarce. Since almost all the restaurants add a 15 percent service charge, there is little inducement for service personnel to extend themselves for the customer, and few do. It has been said that Bahamian supervisors are more eager to be popular than effective and may find themselves without a job should their popularity wane.

As in most developing countries, interruptions of power and the water supply can be expected periodically except in those resorts (as on Paradise Island) that have independent water and power supplies.

A new problem in Bahamian hotel operations appeared when unions moved into government-owned hotels. Some union leaders were also members of parliament, which could result in government and union interference, accompanied by featherbedding and high operating losses.

The government seems committed to the notion that given enough advertising there will always be a tourism market. A study funded by the Ministry of Tourism in 1979 found that in the United States alone approximately 19 million persons would like to travel to the Bahamas. If, using effective advertising and promotion, only 10 to 15 percent of this market could be triggered, the present Bahamian inventory of rooms would be filled. New markets are also being pursued, especially in the United Kingdom and Germany.

Perhaps enough advertising will indeed make it "Better in the Bahamas."

Travel/tourism has indeed been good for the Bahamas, producing over a billion dollars a year income for the country and employing 80 percent of the labor force. Bahamian per capita income is $7,200, highest of any country in the Western Hemisphere south of Florida. Well aware of its dependence on tourism, the government allocates $20 million annually for tourism advertising and promotion.

Complaints that individual tourists make to friends about ill treatment at a destination seem to have comparatively little effect on visitor numbers, provided that mass advertising and promotion is continuous. If the media pick up on widespread discourteous treatment and other problems, especially those involving personal safety, however, tourist numbers plummet. This has happened in the past in Puerto Rico, the Virgin Islands, and Jamaica. It could well happen in the Bahamas.

HOTEL MANAGEMENT AND DESTINATION MARKETING

The management of a resort property may have to take the lead in marketing the area where the resort is located. Although management may believe that marketing should be undertaken by the chamber of commerce or the city, county, or state government, this does not always happen. In such cases the resort management spearheads destination marketing. The Sheraton Hotel at Steamboat Springs, Colorado, was such a case. Sheraton took over an existing hotel, added to it, and was dismayed to find that occupancy was low throughout the summer and as low as 8 percent during July.

Steamboat Springs was a well established ski resort. Sheraton's management asked: What did Steamboat Springs have that would attract summer visitors? Groups of six to eight people from the local community were asked the same question.

"What do you do in the summer? What's it like up here in the summer?"

Responses included: "Aw, it's great, we go horseback riding, white-water rafting. We have trail rides at twilight. We go swimming."

Some forty to fifty activities emerged from the questions. Steamboat Springs was a real cowboy town, very friendly and warm. How could the place be marketed? "The Way-It-Was Days" was the result—a package of trail rides, white-water rafting, western shopping, and water slides. From June to the middle of September each weekend offered a different experience. One weekend it was the mountain men who camped out as was done by mountain men who came to town in the 1860s. Indian dances, a drama festival, playlets, and staged gunfights in the street were featured on other weekends.

A market positioning statement was developed, proclaiming Steamboat Springs the friendliest, most western resort area in the country with the Sheraton at the center of it. Costuming, menus, and entertainment all reinforced this position.

Sheraton enlisted support from the airlines, the hotel employees, and the local people. The hotel did not wait for others to produce guests, but took control of its own destiny, created its own program, and with the help of the community, did its own destination marketing.

The Sheraton Hotel underwrote the entire promotion, and it proved an excellent investment. Summer occupancy climbed from 8 percent to 58 percent.[3]

Seasonality Problems

Most resort destinations experience high and low seasons. The problem is dealt with by doing everything possible to raise occupancy during the off-seasons (often called shoulder periods because of the shape of the occupancy curve). Large hotels have built convention centers that can attract visitors during the off-season. (The Greenbrier, one of the best-known resort hotels in the world, has 65 percent of its guests as convention attendees.) Another method of beating seasonality is follow the example of Malta's Seasonality Pilot Project, carried out between 1982 and 1984. Thirty per-

cent of the promotional budget of the Maltese national tourism office was allocated to attract winter traffic. In Rhodes, the capital city, special individual and group trips for students and senior citizens were organized. Special tourist events were arranged and charter flights by Cypress Airways offered. Malta experienced an increase of 17.2 percent in tourist arrivals for the five-month low season.

MARKET SEGMENTATION

Markets can be divided in a number of ways. Dividing travelers and potential travelers into demographic and socioeconomic segments enables those who sell travel services to pinpoint markets for specific destinations more effectively. Demographic classifications include the following:

- age
- sex
- educational level
- marital status
- family income
- spending habits
- family size and composition
- occupation
- place of residence
- second-home ownership
- automobile ownership

Senior Market Segment

The senior travel market is a good example of a market segment. Persons over 65 number about 32 million in the United States, more people than all teenagers. Since people are living longer, healthier lives, the senior market is expected to comprise 20 percent of the U.S. population by the year 2000. Seniors are not "big buck" spenders traveling on expense accounts, but they travel the year around and stay longer at a destination than other travel market segments.

The senior travel market is divided: 5 percent are big spenders, 10 percent live only on social security. The other 85 percent, according to the

---

3. Taken from: "Marketing a Destination Area," David A. Troy, in *The Practice of Hospitality Management*, Avi Publishing, Westport, 1986, pp. 433–438.

publisher of the *New England Senior Citizen/Senior American News*, fall somewhere in between, with more disposable income than almost any other category except for upper income families. These people learned frugality while growing up and insist on value for their money. Developing their trust and confidence takes time: consistency and repeated ads are more significant for them than is true for other markets. One-shot ads do not work.

Hotel and restaurant operators should understand the preferences of seniors. They rate cleanliness high and tend to prefer menus that include fish, poultry, high-fiber foods and complex carbohydrates, low sodium foods, and decaffeinated coffee. Buffets are popular.

Special-interest Segments

For some destinations, only the affluent with disposable time or special-interest groups are viable markets. The South African Tourism Board, for example, has decided that its principal growth market for tourism is the United States. An income pyramid points up the limited market segment available as a tourist market to South Africa. At the top of the hierarchy of family income in the United States are the 10 percent (8.3 million) who have incomes of $50,000 and more. These high-income families are prime travel markets.

South Africa appeals to the nature lover, especially those interested in the national wildlife parks, of which South Africa has close to 100. The market for South Africa further defines itself as veteran travelers who have already been to Western Europe, the Caribbean, and other places closer to home. South Africa is thus for the widely traveled who are looking for another country, another extraordinary travel challenge.

To reach this market requires strategic promotion. Advertising in *Audubon* magazine reaches millions of bird lovers. The *National Geographic* magazine is for the connoisseur of exotic destinations. *Modern Maturity*, the magazine of the American Association of Retired Persons, reaches 22 million older members. FM radio would be a much better medium than AM radio, since lis-

tener studies have shown that FM radio attracts more affluent and educated listeners than AM radio does. Rail-travel buffs would very likely be interested in South Africa's Blue Trains.

Can a South African hotel chain afford to spend $100 in advertising and promotions for each new guest it attracts? The answer is yes, if that guest spends enough with the chain to recover the $100 plus, in the form of profit. This is exactly what was done by the Southern Sun hotel chain of South Africa. The chain spent $200,000 in radio, television, and newspaper advertising in the southern California market. The result was 2,000 package tour guests and a net profit for Southern Sun hotels.

Like any other investment, advertising and promotion by whatever means can be in any amount and can be justified if there is a reasonable return on that investment.

Proving that a certain expenditure per visitor produces so many visitors can be very difficult. In the case of the Southern Sun hotels, proof was self-evident: 2,000 package tours were sold to Californians. On the other hand, the Bahamas tourist organization has spent as much as $18 for every visitor to the Bahamas and believes it to be cost-effective. That spending by the Bahamian government is responsible for producing so many visitors to the Bahamas is not as clearly proven. Motivation for travel to the Bahamas could be a result of a variety of factors, including recommendations by friends, bad weather in the United States, or cheap air fares.

Psychographic Segmentation

Travel consumers can also be grouped psychographically—that is, according to their psychological make-up. Emphasis here is placed on values, attitudes, feelings, and desires. Psychographic description includes such factors as

- self-image
- attitude toward travel
- attitude toward marriage
- value placed on security
- value placed on status

- need for change and adventure
- concern for creature comforts
- value placed on material versus experiential things

The behavioristic approach, which is similar and which often merges with the psychographic, emphasizes finding out when people travel, what they enjoy doing when they travel, and what can be done to induce them to travel to a particular place.

Two groups may be demographically similar but psychographically quite different. Why, for example, do Californians and New Yorkers travel so much more than others in the same income and educational level? Demographically, they may not be much different from similar people from Omaha. Psychologically, the travelers may be quite different. Name almost any remote spot in the world, and there you will find at least some New York tourists. One of the great surprises in the travel world was the emergence of Californians as the principal market for the fly-cruises out of far-away Miami. Apparently, New Yorkers and Californians place high value on mobility and new experiences. As a group they also find the time and have the money to engage in extensive travel.

Demographic research is largely a matter of describing the external characteristics of a group based on data that are usually easy to find, classify, and understand. Group A is middle-aged, lives in the midwest, and went to high school. Group B comes from the northeast, is over sixty, and has an income in excess of $25,000. This type of data can be collected in libraries, by questionnaire, by phone, and by personal interview.

Psychographic research can take a variety of forms. It can be collected using in-depth interviews, focus groups, word-association tests, projective techniques, and other psychological testing techniques, most of which are subject to investigator bias or the inherent unreliability of the technique or instrument used. Feelings and attitudes are qualitative and labile. Nevertheless, pleasure travel is associated with emotions and attitudes, and to predict or influence pleasure travel, the researcher must try to understand the mindsets of travelers.

Demographic Segmentation

Demographic research involves counting and classifying. Most research done by governments emphasizes demographics—counting visitors and classifying them in various ways.

Those using the demographic approach usually try to select a representative sample from a certain "universe" of people, then count and analyze the sample. If the sample is indeed representative, the larger universe is also delineated. For example, the question may be, how many people go to Cape Cod during a summer season? It is not practical to count each and every visitor to Cape Cod because of the cost and time involved. It may be practical, however, to collect data on every tenth person on a given day. If every tenth person is representative of the other nine, we have a good sample. Describing the sample also describes the universe.

It is possible, in some destinations, to count and describe every visitor because every visitor is required to complete a questionnaire before entering. The Bahamas does this. Hawaii achieves almost the same result by asking visitors to complete the questionnaire while en route on the plane.

One way of collecting data on visitors traveling to a state by automobile is to photograph license plates as the cars pass under an automatically operated camera. Another method is to invite visitors to stop at a welcome station for free refreshments. Vermont provides information centers; those who stop are requested to complete a questionnaire.

Origin and destination studies are often conducted by state governments at entry points into a state. With the help of a roadblock set up by the state police, a sample of visitors is asked to complete a questionnaire. As implied by the term, origin and destination studies are used to determine where the visitors started their trip (usually their home town) and their destination. Such studies often record an estimate of what the travelers think they will spend or have spent each day and how they will spend it. The studies may include reactions of visitors to a particular place, what they liked or disliked, and how they spent their time.

Probably the most common method of conducting demographic research is to send questionnaires by mail to selected persons. The sample selected, however, is likely to be biased. Moreover, less than 10 percent of those who receive the questionnaire respond. To overcome this defect, some research firms enclose $5 or $10, asking the recipient to "sell a small bit of his or her time." In this way, more people respond, making the sample broader and more representative of the universe being studied.

Special-interest Markets

An especially effective form of demographic market research pinpoints special-interest groups. Literally hundreds of special-interest groups constitute potential travel markets. Among the more obvious of such groups are golfers, scuba divers, horse-riding enthusiasts, and music lovers. Less obvious are such groups as botanists, butterfly fanciers, gourmet cooks, bicyclers, amateur archaeologists, and calligraphers. Literally hundreds of thousands of people are entranced by traditional dancing, wine festivals, and music festivals. Advertising in special-interest magazines and newsletters and on television programs of interest to particular groups is one way of informing these receptive groups of the related attractions at a specific destination.

Honeymooners have long constituted a special market, filling some resorts, especially during June, the marrying month. Japanese honeymooners travel in large numbers to Guam, Hawaii, and Palau. The *Wall Street Journal* reports that the airlines that fly from Tokyo to Honolulu are filled with newlyweds bound for their honeymoon—but only on certain days, since many Japanese still follow an ancient custom of marrying only on designated lucky days. At other times the Hawaii-bound planes are nearly empty. To fill in the gaps Northwest and United offered special tour packages for nonhoneymooning passengers traveling on nonlucky days.

The single woman, recently out of high school or college and perhaps living with her family, may look upon travel as an escape, an adventure, or a trip to romance. She is a growing travel segment.

Retired and semiretired persons constitute a vast special travel market, especially in this country. Elderhostel, a Boston-based organization, has experienced phenomenal growth since the late 1970s, with more than 230,000 participants each year. Its travel-study programs for persons sixty and older generate a tremendous amount of travel. One-week courses are offered at a wide choice of university campuses in the United States, Canada, and Mexico. Two- and three-week programs are also available in Israel, Scandinavia, and other European countries. Participants are accommodated in campus housing during periods when regular students are on vacation. The programs combine morning classroom instruction with travel in the vicinity in the afternoons and weekends. Travel/study trips include canal, river, and sea trips, and even two round-the-world cruises.

A practical example of identifying a special-interest market was given by Leo Le Bon, owner of Mountain Travel, a tour company based in Albany, California. Mountain Travel arranges for travelers in groups of fifteen to visit some of the most remote spots in the world, places such as the Himalayas in Nepal. No place, says Mr. Le Bon, is off limits except the North Pole and Antarctica. His clients are "up-market—lawyers, doctors, intellectuals," a market that Le Bon judges to be only about 20,000 Americans. He believes that although about 200,000 Americans travel to Africa and Asia, only about 10 percent, or 20,000, are really keen on adventure travel. Even with such a small total market, Mountain Travel grows at roughly 20 percent a year.[4] The company depends heavily on word-of-mouth advertising and editorial exposure. Advertising costing about $100,000 a year is placed in *Smithsonian* and *Natural History*, whose readers might include those interested in adventure.

4. Joe Nunzio, "The Faint of Heart Need Not Apply," *Advertising Age*, April 25, 1983; p. M–10.

The "Bargain" Market

Travel sections of many Sunday newspapers carry dozens of ads, nearly all appealing to the bargain market, offering flights, tours, and cruises at low prices. Some destinations are built on the inexpensive package vacation. The Dominican Republic, the Spanish-speaking republic that shares the island Hispaniola in the Caribbean with Haiti, is one instance; a cheap, all-inclusive week of low air fares, sun, sand, and casino night-life brings nearly 800,000 visitors a year. Tourism has rocketed to outpace the country's traditional dependence on sugar, coffee, and cacao. The cheap package made possible by 60-cent-an-hour wages is responsible for the republic's 16,000 hotel beds.

Finding Markets

Sociological changes produce new travel market segments, people who are potentially interested in and have the wherewithal to travel. Young marrieds are such a group. In the past they were too involved in raising families and had such limited incomes that they could not travel. But by the middle 1970s the wives of more than half of the newly married couples worked and considered their incomes to be supplementary to those of their husbands. Their income was at least half as much as that earned by the husband—money that could be used for travel, automobiles, expensive houses, recreational vehicles. Newly marrieds became a major market segment for air travel.

DESTINATION MATURATION AND MARKET CHANGES

As destinations mature, their markets tend to change; in other words, as a destination becomes more popular, the kind and number of visitors change. Typically, as time passes, places that were originally frequented by one or a few social groups tend to attract different groups. In the late 1800s, Nice on the French Riviera was the winter spot for the English upper classes. Today, it attracts the middle class; the upper classes have gone elsewhere. Whereas only people with leisure time and considerable wealth could afford ship travel to Hawaii before World War II, today the jet brings the middle class from all over North America and more recently huge numbers from Japan.

Distant destinations may first be discovered by the elite or the explorer/affluent types. Travel then becomes easier to that destination, and the economically elite are replaced by the educated, adventuresome middle classes, who in turn are followed by the mass/charter traveler. Honolulu and Puerto Rico are good examples of this market shift. When only the leisured and wealthy could arrange a vacation at Waikiki, the psychological climate at that resort was quite different from now, when jets can and do drop off a package-tour group of 400 persons.

Like most restaurants and hotels, many destinations have life cycles: they are born, mature, and decline. There are no mystical reasons for such cycles. Social, political, and economic change have widespread effects. New forms of transportation, political realignments, and the redistribution of wealth influence choice of vacation destinations.

Détente with the Russians facilitated a sharp rise in the number of American visitors to Russia and to the Russian satellite countries of Rumania and Hungary. U.S. friendship with the Japanese, along with that country's spectacular economic growth following World War II, has played a large part in the tremendous increase of Japanese visitors to Hawaii and to the West Coast. These factors also account in part for Guam being a major honeymoon resort for the Japanese. West Germany's economic growth has facilitated widespread travel by the Germans.

Some social classes have a history of travel that is adopted by the other classes as they procure increased leisure time and vacations with pay. The English have long been among the world's greatest travelers—for empire building, for seeking culture, and for searching for adventure. The upper classes of England led the way in touring Europe; its middle classes have now adopted parts of Spain for vacations and second homes.

Typically, the guest stay has shortened. The person who came to spend the season has been replaced by the transient and the day tripper. Residents feel different about a long-term middle-aged or older visitor who owns a great house, has servants, and belongs to an exclusive country club. The younger crowd, which has replaced the former long-stay guest, fills the streets, jams the roads, favors the discotheque, and perhaps frequents fast-food restaurants and campsites. Attitudes on the part of residents toward transients are quite different from those formed toward long-term guests.

The Grand Canyon is an example of such change. At one time, guests necessarily came by train and stayed several days. By 1975 the canyon might have seen as many as 15,000 new people each day, few if any staying long enough to become known to the employees or to the residents of the village.

Allocentrics and Psychocentrics

Stanley C. Plog, a behavioral researcher, has divided travelers into "psychocentrics" and "allocentrics," classifications that may help to explain why so many destinations change their character in the space of one summer.[5]

"Allocentric"—having one's interest and attention on other persons—is used by Plog to describe people who are highly curious, who thrive on stimulation and change. When he did research for the airlines and others interested in learning why certain people do not fly, Plog found that some people are ridden with vague and generalized anxieties that make the unfamiliar threatening. To them, little problems are big. They are inhibited and unadventuresome. Plog labeled them *psychocentric* or centered on self. Figure 7-14 compares the psychocentrics and allocentrics.

Allocentrics are likely to fly rather than drive. At their destination they want to explore, to discover;

they will probably rent a car and go on their own. Tours, on the other hand, are for the psychocentrically inclined.

"Allos" tend to accept challenges, meet the residents, try out the food and drink, look for the new experience. The allocentric would go to China or Nepal; the psychocentric would prefer a nearby state park.

Further research revealed another dimension: energy level. The high-energy allocentric is the hiker, the biker, the diver. The low-level allocentric is still curious and adventuresome but forgoes the more demanding schedule. A week at the Edinburgh festival or a group tour to Russia would be more suitable for that person. The low-energy psychocentric is quite content to stay home. The high-energy psychocentric will take a European tour, but one that is completely arranged. At a resort the allocentric plays tennis; the psychocentric plays golf, using a golf cart. The allocentric gets bored at a resort with the beach as its only attraction.

As a destination becomes more commercialized, its unique qualities, those qualities that attracted the allocentrics, become diluted. It becomes more mundane, appealing to the less adventuresome. According to Plog, the distances involved and the differences in culture between the Caribbean and North America make it safe to say that parts of the Caribbean have a long way to go before they approach the psychocentric status of Miami Beach. Parts of Puerto Rico, however, are probably already old hat to the much-traveled sophisticated New Yorker. As travel becomes easier and relatively less expensive, the Caribbean may not appeal to the allocentric, but it will have added appeal for the great mass of travelers classified as "midcentrics." The midcentrics are those people who are in between the extremes, really neither adventuresome nor fearful of travel—the kind of person who constitutes the bulk of the population.

Plog believes the Caribbean is now attracting midcentric people. The allocentrics are seeking out such exotic places as the South Pacific, Africa, and the Orient. The homebodies go to Cape Cod or a nearby state or national park. If they become

5. Stanley C. Plog, "Why Destination Areas Rise and Fall in Popularity" (Paper presented to southern California chapter of the Travel Research Association, Los Angeles, October 10, 1972).

7-14. Travel Characteristics of Psychographic Types	
Psychocentrics	**Allocentrics**
Prefer the familiar in travel destinations.	Prefer nontouristy areas.
Like commonplace activities at travel destinations.	Enjoy sense of discovery and delight in new experiences, before others have visited the area.
Prefer sun 'n' fun spots, including considerable relaxation.	Prefer novel and different destinations.
Low activity level.	High activity level.
Prefer destinations they can drive to.	Prefer flying to destinations.
Prefer tourist accommodations, like heavy hotel development, family-type restaurants, and tourist shops.	Tour accommodations should include adequate to good hotels and food, not necessarily modern or chain-type hotels, and few "tourist" type attractions.
Prefer familiar atmosphere (e.g., hamburger stands), familiar type entertainment, absence of foreign atmosphere.	Enjoy meeting and dealing with people from a strange or foreign culture.
Complete tour packaging appropriate, with heavy scheduling of activities.	Tour arrangements should include basics (transportation and hotels) and allow considerable freedom and flexibility.

Source: Stanley C. Plog.

more adventurous, they may go to Honolulu, the Caribbean, Europe, or Mexico. Figure 7-15 shows the distribution of the various types.

Plog's correlation of travel destinations and personality types is a valuable hypothesis that is nevertheless open to qualification and testing. For example, travelers on a package tour of the Orient could represent several psychographic groups, some of whom would not be allocentrics as suggested by the model. The tour could be highly structured, traveling by first-class air and by ship. Even though the tour touched such exotic spots as Bangkok, Bali, and Fiji, the security and scheduling provided might appeal to midcentrics as well as allocentrics.

What is allocentric changes with time and circumstance. An example is Tibet, a place that until recently was not open to visitors. A plane trip to the North Pole is now commercially available. The perceived challenge and cost is a major determinant in psychographic positioning and no doubt varies widely among individuals.

MARKET PROFILES

The airlines and airplane manufacturers conduct market research to determine how many new planes will be needed and what groups of people will become airline passengers. Using open-ended, relatively unstructured interviews and group sessions, some researchers start with the usual demographic and socioeconomic information but also include parental background and childhood influences.[6] It was found that children of college-educated parents are likely to take more vacations than those whose parents are not college trained. It was also found that former Boy and Girl Scouts are more likely to travel a good deal and are more likely to take a chance on a resort they have never been to before.

6. Emanuel N. Denley, "Travel's Not So Far Away," *Proceedings of the Eastern Council for Travel Research 1969–1970 Conference*, 1971, pp. 46–54.

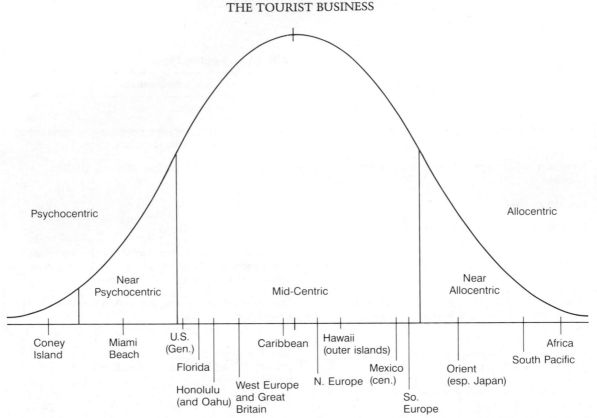

7-15. Psychographic positions of destinations. From "Why Destination Areas Rise and Fall in Popularity," a paper presented by Stanley C. Plog to the southern California chapter of the Travel Research Association, Los Angeles, 1972.

People who like do-it-yourself projects are likely to spend less money on a vacation and to travel by car rather than by plane. Persons who go to the movies, the theater, and to concerts travel greater distances than those who stay home most of the time. Being active in civic and fraternal organizations is also associated with frequent travel. Persons with greater salary expectations travel more than those who expect less.

Subjects have also been classified as "passives" and "creatives." Creatives tended to play golf while the passives tended to go hunting and fishing. Creatives flew to their vacation spot; passives tended to travel in their own car. The creatives were more likely to use a travel agent and stay at a city or resort hotel. Once back from a vacation, creatives were likely to start planning their next one. The creatives were more likely to own a sailboat, take sports instruction, and to favor American, United, or Pan American as airlines.

THE MARKET POTENTIAL INDEX

The basic figure in any tourist feasibility study is the number of people who can be expected to use the facility at a given price.

Tourism research may require highly sophisticated concepts and techniques. An example is the Market Potential Index developed by the United States Travel Service (USTS). The index ranks countries in terms of their potential for providing travelers to the United States. This model can digest information from eleven variables and produce suggestions as to where promotional dollars can best be spent to reach the candidates and influence them to visit the United States.

The pilot study for the Market Potential Index centered on the Mexican market. It used a sample of 4,000 adults residing in Mexican cities with populations of 10,000 or more to learn which segments of the population travel here and which do not. In this study income and place of residence were found to be the important variables in the Mexican market for travel to the United States.

Variables that affect travel to the United States were found to include

1. The financial ability of individuals in a country to travel
2. The authority of individuals to choose to travel to the United States
3. The political and economic relationship between the United States and a given country
4. The cost and ease of travel between the country and the United States
5. The social/cultural relationships existing between a country and the United States

The Market Potential Index showed that there is no simple one-to-one relationship between advertising and promotional expenditures and the number of visitors and their expenditures at a destination. As pointed out by William Dircks, Director of Research and Analysis for the USTS, numerous factors in addition to advertising and promotion affect tourist expenditures. The travel promoter needs to view the entire group of prospective travelers in terms of their alternatives in choosing a travel destination.

Misleading Statistics

Travel statistics must be carefully interpreted to have meaning for decision makers. For example, the statistic that the Bahamas rank fourth as a tourist-generating country to the United States may mean nothing more than the fact that relatively few Bahamians take a number of shopping trips to Miami each year. Numerous people crossing the Canadian or other borders for one-day visits or for shopping purposes also artificially inflate travel statistics.

It is quite possible that even though tourism may show a 5, 10, or 15 percent growth each year over a period of years, the attitudes of the tourists toward the destination are such that they would not return. The area may, without knowing it, be relying completely on one-time trippers. Perhaps the tour oper-

ators do not care, but they should know the nature of their market. Most tourist areas that show a solid growth over a number of years build upon repeat visitors and favorable recommendations.

A finer analysis of the typical questionnaire can yield some enlightening results. Visitors who stay for one week at some destinations tend to be highly enthusiastic about the area; if they remain for two or three weeks, the glamor begins to pale. Some resort operators who realize this do not want guests to stay more than one week; they realize that when long-stay guests become bored, they do not hesitate to denigrate the resort to their friends. Long-term guests may also be a source of irritation to newly arrived guests.

The researcher can help discover what really pleases and displeases the traveler. Too little of that type of research has been done. Too much reliance has been placed on hunches by advertising agencies responsible for selling an area.

Travel Media Writing

Travel writers for newspapers and magazines have a tendency to omit anything unfavorable about a destination or travel mode partly because they are in the business of romancing travel and partly because most professional travel writers are hosted by the airline, travel office, and lodging facility about which they write. Who is going to bite the hand that feeds him or her? There are exceptions. Travel writers for the *Wall Street Journal*, *Washington Post*, and *New York Times* are forbidden to take travel freebies. Some, like the *Los Angeles Times* and the *Dallas Morning News*, do not allow their staff members to travel "on the house," but buy reports from freelance writers and syndicated writers who have no such qualms. Most travel writing thus tends toward the "ain't it just wonderful" style and can be highly misleading for the travel agent who wants the unvarnished truth.

DESTINATION IMAGE RESEARCH

Research done for the Canadian Government Travel Bureau revealed that people go through three phases before they take a vacation. The first, a dream phase, is when they speculate about the ideal vacation. The second phase is concerned with gathering information and exploring the possibilities of realizing their dream vacation. The last phase is when dreams face realities and practical travel decisions are made. In order to be effective, the advertising for each phase must be different. The dream phase calls for "image" advertising; the second phase, for "inquiry" ads, those that offer information; the third phase consists of "hard sell" advertising, such as "Fly to Montreal" or "Capture Canada."

Motivational research can be used to discover the image projected by a destination. Canada, for example, learned that the image of the country was a limited one and prospective tourists were somewhat misinformed. Canada was not perceived as the friendly, rapidly growing country seen by Tourism Canada. Rather, the image of Canadians was of a somewhat staid and conservative people; Canada as a whole was viewed as remote and lacking in excitement. The total image was weak and not well defined; it tended to attract older people. Once Tourism Canada knew the country's image, it could change its marketing efforts to alter the image to a more positive one.

Another example of image research was conducted by Marketscope Research Company and sponsored by American, Eastern, TWA, and United airlines, together with the Port Authority of New York and New Jersey. The airlines and the Port Authority were concerned that New York had experienced a lower rate of economic growth than the rest of the nation and that domestic air traffic at New York had declined as a percentage of the nation's total since 1950.

Thirty-five hundred telephone interviews in seventeen cities throughout the United States were conducted to determine attitudes toward New York as opposed to other destinations. It was learned that New York ranked worst in social unrest, air traffic congestion, and cost of hotels and restaurants.

Although New York was considered the leading city for art, culture, entertainment, and sightseeing, it had developed a poor reputation for delays at the airports and inconvenience in ground transportation. It was also considered one of the most dangerous places to visit because of crime,

tension, and (at that time) student unrest, and there was some reaction against the size, density, and congestion of the city. Overall appeal to both pleasure and business travelers had declined.

Such image studies provide information about how particular groups or markets actually feel about a destination—information that can be compared with what the promoters think is true. If the area is viewed as a place for fun and frolic, promoters can aim their advertising at groups who want that kind of entertainment. Areas that project images of rest and relaxation can be promoted among those markets. Ill-defined images can be sharpened by advertising, and unfavorable attitudes toward an area can be changed by advertising something different.

THE VEBLEN EFFECT

Thorstein Veblen, a prominent American social theorist and economist who died in 1929, called attention to *conspicuous consumption*, the practice of purchasing things or experiences because of the status they might bring. Being able to say, "I spent a week at Caneel Bay Plantation" or "We go to Switzerland every year for the skiing" may be examples of conspicuous consumption. A number of resort hotels, deluxe cruises, and first-class flights are attractive at least partly because of the Veblen effect.

Instead of supply and demand determining the cost of a product, the Veblen effect sets up new demand curves based on exclusivity and prestige. Certainly the purchase of very expensive automobiles and huge homes are examples of conspicuous consumption. The higher the cost of an experience or product, the more desirable it may become—up to a point.

Professor Floyd Harmston devised the Veblen demand curve in Figure 7-16. If price P_1 is charged, quantity Q_1 is purchased. If the price increases to P_2 according to the demand curve D_1, the quantity purchased should decrease to Q_2. This does not happen in the Veblen curve because the buyers attach new importance to the product and actually buy a large quantity, Q_3. In effect, the new price has enhanced the quality of the service or the experience offered. The demand curve, instead

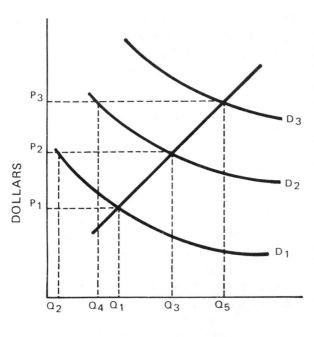

7-16. The Veblen demand curve. Courtesy Professor Floyd Harmston, University of Missouri.

of shifting downward, has shifted to D_2 because of the Veblen effect. Decreasing the price causes only a small increase in the amount purchased since the movement will be along the new demand curve D_2. Increase the price further to P_3, and the curve again shifts. Instead of a decrease in demand to Q_4, the demand actually increases to Q_5.

Diamonds are perhaps the best example of the Veblen effect. They may be "a girl's best friend" simply because they are so highly priced. Demand for SST travel probably partakes of the Veblen effect. It would be interesting to see whether increasing the ticket price would reduce the demand or actually increase SST ticket sales.

THE ENGEL CURVES

Economists like to classify goods into those that are preferred and those that are nonpreferred. Travel is seen as a "preferred superior good" in that more is undertaken as incomes increase. The Engel curves reflect the difference between "nonpreferred superior goods" and "preferred superior

goods." As incomes rise, these goods are purchased more—but at different rates. The rate of purchase of the nonpreferred superior goods accelerates at a decreasing rate while that of preferred goods accelerates, as seen in Figure 7-17. The Engel curve illustrates what has actually happened in travel growth, especially over the last twenty-five years. As more families reach higher income brackets, both in this country and around the world, the demand for travel experience increases at a faster rate than does income.

MARKET IDENTIFICATION AND ADVERTISING

Decision makers in the travel business are constantly confronted with the question of where and how to advertise and promote their businesses. Millions of dollars in advertising are spent each year in travel-related businesses without the spender ever knowing much about the sales generated from such investment. The problem is to identify the market or potential market clearly and aim the advertising at well-identified groups

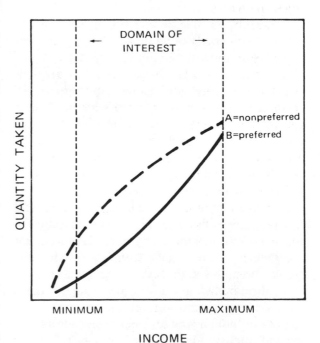

7-17. Engel curve shapes. Courtesy Professor Floyd Harmston, University of Missouri.

of people. This is easier said than done. The advertiser may have a good fix on present consumers but be unaware of trends that are changing the market. And markets do change.

Some advertisers concentrate on developing new markets; others concentrate on established markets. An airline may have been granted a new route; consequently a disproportionate percentage of the advertising budget is allocated to penetration of the market for that new route.

The big spenders in tourist promotion are the airlines. The effect of airline advertising is fairly immediate; airplane seats are filled or not filled. Knowing that the break-even load factor for a particular airline may be 58 percent, the decision makers have a clear target as to what they are trying to do—raise the load factor. Each airline has presumably studied its market and knows its customer by age group, income bracket, educational level, and place of residence. Presumably, the medium that best reaches the market is also known, be it television, magazine, newspaper, or some other. Airline policy regarding percentage of income devoted to advertising varies among airlines and with time.

Although people in the advertising field feel that anyone who does not value advertising and promotion for tourism is completely naive, some skeptics want hard data in the form of cost-benefit studies to justify advertising expenditures for travel and tourism. In reply to statements that tourism expenditures within a state have increased by a certain percentage as the result of advertising, critics suggest that such growth in expenditures would have occurred anyway, advertising or no advertising.

State travel promotion budgets vary widely and are not necessarily correlated to the importance of tourism to the economy of a state. California, for example, is said to enjoy a $59.54 billion income from tourism—yet, for several years, the state allocated no budget at all for promoting it. Puerto Rico's travel promotion budget for 1981 was $9.482 million, a very high per capita advertising expenditure.

Allocation of the advertising budget to various media is an inexact science, as witnessed by the wide variations in how the advertising dollar is spent. It is difficult to determine the relative effectiveness of various media in attracting tourists.

According to a study conducted by the Newspaper Advertising Bureau, "friends" led the list of most influential sources for vacation travel planning. Magazine articles were next in importance, followed by travel agents, newspaper articles, and newspaper ads. Television advertising was still less influential.

National promotional budgets vary widely, as might be expected. The airlines spent more money on newspapers than on any other medium. Television was next in importance and gaining rapidly in favor. Some states allocate a sizable portion of their budget to television advertising. Some states use radio, others do not. Some decision makers arrange destination familiarization tours; others believe strongly in printed material, and distribute literally millions of maps and pieces of descriptive literature.

The individual resort is hard-pressed to promote and advertise on its own. The operators can build guest lists based on guest histories developed from registration and other information. Periodic mailings are made to those guest lists. The operators can hold cocktail parties in a community where they have a concentrated market. They lack the budget, however, to do much newspaper or magazine advertising. Television advertising is usually precluded completely because of cost.

Independents may join one of the promotional groups that advertise a certain class of hotel. They may join their local chamber of commerce and be included in the chamber's advertising efforts. They may prevail upon the local government to advertise their area and benefit in that way. If they are relatively small and isolated, they must appeal to a relatively small group of people who like to "get away from it all." Independents that are part of a resort complex such as Las Vegas or Miami Beach benefit from the advertising done by the airlines, the convention bureaus, and government advertising for such areas. They may need to do no advertising, getting a "free ride" on the area or airline advertising.

Costs/Benefits of Tourist Office Expenditures

National and state tourist offices justify their existence and budgets in terms of income derived from their efforts and expenditures. Funded studies purport to show that every dollar spent by the office results in X number of dollars of income to the area and to the government. Such studies can be costly; almost necessarily they produce only rough estimates of benefits. The Ministry of Tourism in the Bahamas offers a good example of the kind of estimates being made. Islands as such offer a demarcated area and economy that reduces the amount of error. According to a study done in 1981 by the ministry, for every dollar it spent, between 30 and 35 dollars of income were generated for the Bahamian economy. The ministry also estimated that 57 percent of the total government income was generated by tourism. Each visitor is known to spend an average of between $325 to $350; each cruise ship visitor spends about $50 while ashore. The government also collects about $20 million in gambling licenses and taxes, as well as a $4 departure tax from each visitor. Although much of what hotels import is tax free under the Hotels Encouragement Act, which provides for a number of tax concessions to hotels for up to twenty years, import duties are collected on almost everything else that is imported.

The statement that, for every dollar spent $30 to $35 return to the economy, is very misleading. The assumption made is that tourist expenditures come largely as a result of the ministry's efforts. Of course, this is not true. Word-of-mouth advertising, the efforts of travel agents and tour operators, airline promotion and advertising, and a number of other forces bear on the visitor's decision to visit the Bahamas. If all of the activities of the ministry ceased, undoubtedly tourism to the island would decline sharply, but it certainly would not disappear.

Cost per Visitor

Skepticism about advertising is hard to overcome because of the difficulty in obtaining accurate data concerning traveler motivation. It is relatively easy to place an ad in the *New York Times* travel section and include a coupon that a respondent may send in to request a state brochure. A follow-up study will show that a certain percentage of those who requested the brochure actually visit the destination advertised. A cost-per-inquiry study or a cost-per-visitor study shows that it may cost anywhere from a few cents to many dollars to attract a visitor, if indeed the advertising was the direct agent of the decision to visit a state.

Cost-per-inquiry studies are commonly done to justify advertising and promotion expenditures, but of course they do not uncover the matrix of motivation existing in the mind of the traveler. A person may have become interested in visiting Mexico as a result of seeing a particular movie, reading any number of books on the subject, taking a Spanish class, or hearing a neighbor talk about a similar visit. The fact that he or she wrote for a brochure and later took a trip may be incidental to the forces that formed such a decision to travel to Mexico.

According to Victor B. Fryer, Travel Information Director for Oregon, the only answer to those skeptical of advertising is a very comprehensive and expensive in-depth survey of vacationers to find out why they went to a particular place. It might take a psychoanalyst's couch to arrive at the real reason.

Regardless of the vagueness associated with effective advertising, advertising and promotion are generally accepted as important, and advertising and similar expenditures for tourism increase year after year. Particular states or destinations may shift their advertising from one agency to another and shift their medium from magazine to television or back again without any real facts to justify such shifting. This kind of juggling is likely to continue because of the cost in time and money of learning how to use advertising most effectively.

Identifying Market Trends

Travel researchers are interested in identifying a market and measuring its size, but they also want to know the changes that are taking place within it. Is the market growing in size? Who is leaving the market? Who is entering it?

For basic economic data, researchers usually turn to available government or local bank statistics on a destination. In some cases it would be impossible to collect such information without the assistance of a government unit.

Researchers are interested not only in actual numbers but in noting how the mix changes with time. Suppose a travel-oriented company is interested in how the travel mix is changing. It could commission a study that explores how many people in selected occupations procure passports; it could compare these figures over several years to determine the travel trends for different occupational groups. The information is valuable for such companies as airlines, travel agencies, and international hotel chains.

The researcher and market decision maker also want to know the geographic origin of the market for a particular destination area and how that market is changing. With such information advertising budgets may be allocated to reach a present market or to develop new ones.

THE MULTIDISCIPLINARY NATURE OF TRAVEL RESEARCH AND MARKETING

Identifying and developing markets for travel is a multidisciplinary effort. In the past, marketing research was done by marketing experts from business schools, economic analysts, statis-ticians, and accountants. More recently, the behavioral sciences have become involved in travel research. In many destination areas, political considerations are overriding factors in determining if the area will be attractive to a particular market, and political scientists are needed to identify political trends that will affect the viability of an economy.

Changing lifestyles and other social changes may alter the travel mix drastically in the next few years. That in turn will change the type of tourist facilities needed. Travel research in the broad sense is a prerequisite to construction of a facility and to marketing it once it is built. It is needed as a barometer and sensing device to take regular readings of what is happening in the travel world.

TRAVEL DATA RESOURCES

The Travel Research Association, Business Research Division, University of Colorado, lists Indexing Services, Bibliographies, and Finding Guides to Travel Periodicals and Travel Trade Associations. Various yearbooks that contain travel information include *Yearbook of Railroad Facts*, *Air Transport Facts and Figures*, *Automobile Facts and Figures*, and *Handbook of Airline Statistics and World Air Transport Statistics*. The *Travel Industry World Yearbook*, published annually by Child and Waters, New York, is an excellent compilation of tourism statistics.

DISCUSSION QUESTIONS

1. What are the differences between demographic and psychographic information?
2. As a director of a state tourist office with a million-dollar budget, how would you allocate it for a maximum increase in the number of visitors to the state?
3. The Veblen effect relates to the urge to buy status goods, whether in the form of travel or a pair of shoes. As operator of an expensive European tour, how would you capitalize on the Veblen effect?
4. As director of tourism for a city that has an ambiguous image, how would you go about sharpening the image and making it more pleasing?
5. Define *marketing*, in broad terms.
6. Suppose you enjoy doing marketing and public relations. What would be the advantages of working with a visitor and convention bureau as compared with working in a hotel sales office?
7. Alaska, with only a fraction of the population of California, has a tourism budget about twelve times as large as California's budget. As Alaska's tourism director, how would you justify your budget?
8. In what ways can a hotel sales department work with a local visitor and convention bureau?
9. As director of tourism for the Republic of South Africa, a country which has a poor reputation because of discrimination toward its black population, would you sponsor familiarization trips to the country for travel writers?
10. You have been asked by a state office of tourism to develop several special-interest tours to the state. Choose a particular state and outline what tours you would develop.
11. You are director of tourism for the Tonga Islands, a poor island nation of 100,000 people in the Pacific. Your budget is only $100,000 a year. What would you do to promote tourism?
12. Give two examples of emerging travel markets.
13. Where does product analysis fit into the total sequence of the marketing effort?
14. In travel research, much emphasis is placed on "sampling a universe." Explain what is meant by this term.
15. Where are some likely locations for a state to conduct an origin and destination study?

EIGHT

TRAVEL AND CULTURAL GEOGRAPHY

According to the National Geographic Society, most Americans fail geography literacy tests. This finding was based on an international study that compares U.S. citizens with people in other countries in locating various countries on a map. Fewer than half of the Americans surveyed could identify the United Kingdom, France, South Africa, or Japan. Only 25 percent were able to locate Sweden.[1]

Many people do not realize that Rome is about the same distance north of the equator as New York City; that London, England, is farther north than Vancouver, Canada; that Oslo, Norway, and Anchorage, Alaska, both border longitude 60°.

Travel geography is based on physical geography, which encompasses the seven continents, twenty-one oceans and seas, and depending upon definition, 159 countries. Travel geography concentrates on those aspects of geography that facilitate travel and make it more interesting. Knowledge of the continents, countries, and oceans of the world adds dimension to life and is requisite for the travel professional. Travel professionals need to carry elementary political maps in their heads—maps showing the states of the United States, the provinces of Canada, the countries of Europe, the locations of

the major cities and transit points of the world. It's called locational geography.

Depending on how a sovereign nation is defined, there are more than 200 countries. The Bureau of Census identifies 45 countries as developed, 163 as developing.

As discussed here, travel geography concentrates on areas most visited by Americans. These areas include the United States, where about 90 percent of American travel takes place, followed by Canada, Mexico, Western Europe, and the Caribbean. Since about 1970 the Pacific Rim countries of Japan, South Korea, Hong Kong, and Taiwan have become major industrial nations with a consequent sharp rise in business travel by residents and visitors. Travel for pleasure has also increased to these countries.

Even though the developing nations (also referred to as third world nations), contain three-fourths of the world's population, relatively little travel takes place to these countries or within them. This situation is changing, however, with the increase in transnational investment and business operations; moreover, as some third world countries industrialize, a larger percentage of their population acquire discretionary income that can be used for travel. This is especially true of the newly industrializing economies in the

---

1. Peter S. Greenberg, "America's Travel IQ," *Los Angeles Times*, September 18, 1988.

Western Pacific Rim countries. Sub-Saharan Africa, most of Latin America, and much of Asia are experiencing little or no economic development. Despite their huge populations, there is little promise in the way of travel growth. Most travel in the Soviet bloc nations takes place within and between those countries.

Some third world countries, however, attract sizable numbers of American and European visitors. Egypt, Morocco, and Kenya in Africa, and the Bahamas and several Caribbean islands are examples.

Travel geography also encompasses cultural geography—what all those more than five billion people are like out there, something of their ethnic and social codes, and what they expect from and dislike about foreign visitors. The subject is briefly introduced in this chapter.

THE UNITED STATES

Travel geography is concerned with the places where people go for business and pleasure and the ways they get there. Since Americans travel most in the United States, we will look at its travel geography first.

Although it is useful to know the names of the principal mountain ranges, rivers, and lakes and details about population, it is more useful to know the principal airports, something about air travel times between major transit points, and the geography and natural attractions of popular destinations.

Figure 8-1 shows the major airports of the United States, airports that are important because they serve large population centers and have become travel nodes because of their location. Chicago is a good example. Long a travel exchange point, first as a railroad center, now also as an air travel center, it serves a large section of the Middle West. New York City has three major airports that serve as an air travel hub for domestic and international travel. Atlanta, Miami, Los Angeles, San Francisco, and Seattle are important hubs for similar reasons. Denver and Salt Lake City are hubs serving the mountain states and connecting the West with the rest of the country. Dallas and Houston serve the Southwest; St. Louis and

Kansas City, the heartland; Detroit, the Great Lakes region. Of the two airports serving Washington, D.C., one has domestic flights; the other, international.

At times the airlines themselves decide to make new hub-and-spoke flight arrangements, and these change traffic flows. St. Louis and Charlotte, N.C., are examples of such new hubs. (See Chapter 4 for a discussion of the hub-and-spoke concept.) The forty-eight states of the continental United States are shown in outline in Figure 8-2. Alaska and Hawaii appear separately, in the lower left-hand corner. As a student of travel, the reader should be able to fill in the names of the fifty states, something few people can do without a little preparation. As an aid, look at the U.S. map in Figure 8-3, which contains the abbreviations for the states.

Notice that the map in Figure 8-2 is regionalized. Some regions—New England, the Southwest, the Far West—have commonly accepted boundaries. The Heartland—the Central States—is less well defined. This region is included in what is referred to as the Middle West or Midwest, a region in north-central United States that includes states in the upper Mississippi Valley and those bordering on the Great Lakes. To test your understanding, complete the outline map in Figure 8-2 by drawing heavy lines around the eight regions.

In addition to the fifty states, the United States is associated with various islands. Nearest is Puerto Rico, which is a separate commonwealth whose people are U.S. citizens. The U.S. Virgin Islands in the Caribbean are governed as U.S. territories. The Pacific territories are the islands of American Samoa (population 35,000, capital, Pago Pago); and Guam (population 116,000, capital, Agana). The U.S. also has several client states in Micronesia. The Marshall Islands and Palau have declared themselves sovereign republics. The Northern Mariana Islands are a commonwealth and remain a U.S. territory. There is also the Federated States of Micronesia. All are heavily dependent upon U.S. aid.

From "sea to shining sea" the U.S. offers a sweep of unparalleled natural beauty—lakes,

8-1. Major airports of the United States.

8-2. Outline map of the United States.

8-3. Map of the United States with state abbreviations.

mountains, streams, rivers and gorges. There are deserts for desert lovers, wilderness areas, and caves.

Hawaii has unpolluted and healthful tropics, and Florida is subtropical. For those who prefer a Mediterranean climate there is Southern California. The forty-nine national parks encompass spectacular scenery that attracts crowds each year. In addition, there are hundreds of state and local parks.

Although the United States lacks the stately homes of aristocrats, such as the palaces of Versailles, Buckingham, and Windsor, it has the magnificence of the capitol in Washington, D.C., the southern plantations, and the state capitols and the old mansions of the wealthy in the northeast. Hearst Castle in California, a conglomerate of buildings, has a collection of great art purchased from Europe by William Randolph Hearst over a lifetime. Its location on a mountain overlooking the Pacific Ocean is unrivalled. For awesome national beauty the United States has the Grand Canyon, Yosemite, Yellowstone, and Mount Denali in Alaska (formerly called Mt.

McKinley, Denali has the greatest vertical free-rise in the world: 18,000 feet straight up, compared to Mt. Everest's 10,000-foot sheer rise).

The world's most successful commercial travel attraction is Walt Disney World in Florida, visited by some 22 million people each year. Disneyland in California, which changed the nature of theme parks forever, attracts 12 million, followed by Sea World in Florida with 4 million, and the Universal Studios Tour near Los Angeles with 3.8 million.

In this country there is an enormous range and diversity of tourist attractions. We tend to think of tourist attractions like Disney World in Florida and Arizona's Grand Canyon. However, there is also plenty to see and do, for example, in Kentucky—there are the Mammoth Cave National Park at Cave City, the Kentucky Saddle Horse Museum in Lexington, and the race tracks of northern Kentucky. To attract tourists in Mississippi there are antebellum mansions and the birthplace of Elvis Presley; in Massachusetts there is Plimoth Plantation, first home of the Pilgrims; in Nebraska there is the Strategic Air Command, one of the state's leading attractions; and in Missouri there is the huge Gateway Arch in St. Louis, the number one state tourist attraction.

To provide an idea of the range of attractions, a list follows, which shows three of the top ten attractions in each state as reported by state tourism officials.[2]

Alabama. Alabama International Motor Speedway, Talladega. Bellingrath Gardens and Home, Theodore. Birmingham Zoo.

Alaska. Portage Glacier, Anchorage. Inside Passage, Southeast Alaska. Mendenhall Glacier, Juneau.

Arizona. Grand Canyon National Park. Lake Powell/Glen Canyon National Recreation Area, Page. Petrified Forest/Painted Desert National Park, Holbrook.

Arkansas. Ozark Fold Center, Mountain View. Great Passion Play, Eureka Springs. Buffalo National River.

California. Disneyland, Anaheim. Knotts Berry Farm, Buena Park. Universal Studios, Universal City.

Colorado. Rocky Mountain National Park. U.S. Air Force Academy, Colorado Springs. Mesa Verde National Park Mesa, Cortez.

Connecticut. Mystic Seaport Museum, Mystic. Mystic Marinelife Aquarium, Mystic. Mark Twain Mansion, Hartford. Barnum Museum, Bridgeport.

Delaware. Hagley Museum and Eleutherian Mills, Wilmington. Rockwood Museum, Wilmington. Winterthur Museum and Gardens, Winterthur.

Florida. Walt Disney World/The Magic Kingdom, Lake Buena Vista. Walt Disney World/Epcot Center, Lake Buena Vista. Sea World, Orlando.

Georgia. Georgia's Stone Mountain Park, Atlanta. Callaway Gardens, Pine Mountain. Savannah Historic District and Waterfront.

Hawaii. National Memorial Cemetery of the Pacific, Punchbowl, Oahu. U.S.S. Arizona Memorial, Pearl Harbor, Oahu. Polynesian Cultural Center, Oahu.

Idaho. Sun Valley Ski Resort. Peregrine World Center for Birds of Prey and Snake River Birds of Prey Area, Boise area. Hell's Canyon National Recreation Area, western Idaho.

Illinois. Sears Tower, Chicago. Museum of Science and Industry, Chicago. The Art Institute, Chicago.

Indiana. Auburn-Cord-Duesenburg Museum, Auburn. Amish Acres, Nappanee. The New Indianapolis Zoo, Indianapolis.

Iowa. Amana Colonies. Excursion Boats on the Mississippi River. Iowa Great Lakes Area.

Kansas. Sedgwick County Zoo, Wichita. Kansas Cosmosphere and Space Center, Hutchinson. Topeka Zoo, Topeka.

Kentucky. Mammoth Cave National Park, Cave City. Kentucky Horse Park, Lexington. Race Tracks, northern Kentucky.

Louisiana. French Quarter, New Orleans. Louisiana Downs Race Track, Bossier City. Mardi Gras, New Orleans.

Maine. Old York Village, York Village. Kennebunkport-Portland Area.

Maryland. Inner Harbor, Baltimore. Ocean City. Historic Annapolis.

Massachusetts. Plimoth Plantation, Plymouth. Old Sturbridge Village, Sturbridge. Hancock Shaker Village, Hancock.

Michigan. Straits of Mackinac area. Winery Tours and Wine Tastings, Paw Paw, Leelanau/Old Mission Peninsulas. Sleeping Bear Dunes National Lakeshore and the Pierce Stocking Scenic Drive, Empire.

Minnesota. Itasca State Park, Mississippi River Headwaters, Lake Itasca. Ironworld U.S.A., Chisholm.

Mississippi. Historic Antebellum Homes, Statewide. Vicksburg National Military Park, Vicksburg. Elvis Presley's Birthplace, Tupelo.

Missouri. Gateway Arch, St. Louis. Mark Twain Home and Museum, Hannibal. Pony Express Museum, St. Joseph.

Montana. Glacier National Park. Virginia City and Nevada City. Custer Battlefield National Monument, Crow Agency. Grant Kohrs Ranch National Historic Site, Deer Lodge.

Nebraska. Strategic Air Command (SAC), Bellevue. Museum of the Fur Trade, Chadron. Fort Robinson State Park, Crawford.

2. SOURCE: "Focus 500 United States Canada, The Top Tourism Attractions in the U.S. and Canada," *Travel Agent Magazine*, April 17, 1989 (New York).

Nevada. Hoover Dam/Lake Mead, Boulder City. Reno. Lake Tahoe. Highway 50, "The Loneliest Road in America," Fernley to Ely.

New Hampshire. Mt. Washington (reachable by the first cog railway in the world). Franconia Notch State Park (site of the Great Stone Face and the first aerial tramway in North America). Lake Winnipesaukee.

New Jersey. Atlantic City. Statue of Liberty/Liberty State Park, Jersey City. Meadowlands Sports Complex, East Rutherford.

New Mexico. Santa Fe Plaza, Santa Fe. Taos Indian Pueblo, Taos. Carlsbad Caverns National Park, Carlsbad.

New York. Niagara Falls. Corning Glass Center and Museum, Corning. Olympic Attractions, Lake Placid.

North Carolina. Blue Ridge Parkway, Western North Carolina. Biltmore House and Gardens, Asheville. Cherokee Indian Reservations, Cherokee. Seashore, Cape Hatteras.

North Dakota. Fort Union Trading Post National Historic Site, Williston. Fort Abraham Lincoln State Park, Mandan. International Peace Garden.

Ohio. Amish Region, Tuscarawas/Holmes Counties. German Village, Columbus. Portside Festival Marketplace, Toledo.

Oklahoma. Remington Park, Oklahoma City. National Cowboy Hall of Fame and Western Heritage Center, Oklahoma City. Wichita Mountains Wildlife Reserve, Lawton.

Oregon. Multonomah Falls and Columbia River Gorge Scenic Area. Sea Lion Caves/Hatfield Marine Science Center, Oregon coast. Mt. Hood.

Pennsylvania. Independence National Historical Park, Philadelphia. Carnegie Institute's Museum of Art and Museum of Natural History, Pittsburgh. Valley Forge National Historical Park.

Rhode Island. Newport Mansions. Benefit Street's Mile of History, Providence.

South Carolina. Charleston's Historic District. Historic Plantations, Homes, and Gardens. Cherokee Foothills Scenic Highway #11.

South Dakota. Mount Rushmore National Memorial, Black Hills. Badlands National Park, Interior.

Tennessee. Great Smoky Mountains National Park, eastern Tennessee. Opryland USA, Nashville. Grand Old Opry, Nashville.

Texas. Alamo and Spanish Missions, San Antonio. Big Bend National Park. LBJ Ranch and National Historic Site, Stonewall.

Utah. Arches National Park, Moab. Bryce Canyon National Park, Bryce Canyon. Capitol Reef National Park, Torrey.

Vermont. Fall Foliage, statewide. Ben and Jerry's Ice Cream Factory Tours, Waterbury. Granite Quarries, Barre.

Virginia. Colonial Williamsburg. Mount Vernon. Jamestown Festival Park, Jamestown Island. Monticello, Charlottesville.

Washington. Space Needle, Seattle. Mt. Ranier National Park, southeast of Tacoma. Hell's Canyon, Clarkston.

West Virginia. Jamboree USA, Wheeling. Greyhound and Horse Racing, statewide. Historic Park.

Wisconsin. The Northwoods. Wisconsin Dells Area. The House on the Rock, Spring Green. The Great River Road.

Wyoming. Yellowstone National Park. Jackson Hole in Grand Teton National Park.

Mountains are formed by volcanoes and by the collision of the great tectonic plates undergirding the oceans and continents. When two plates come together or slide under one another, the land above is crumpled upward to form mountains. The continental United States has two great mountain systems, the Appalachian range that extends from southern Quebec in Canada to northern Alabama, and the Western Cordillera, a complex of mountain ranges and high plateaus that includes the Rocky Mountains. The cordillera is a part of the massive chain of mountain that stretches north into Alaska and south the length of Latin America.

The Blue Ridge Parkway, a beautiful 355-mile-drive, runs along part of the southern Appalachian Mountains in the states of Virginia, North Carolina, and Tennessee, feeds into the Great

Smoky Mountain National Park, which attracts more than 10 million visitors each year.

The immense variety of natural and other tourist attractions in the United States makes a detailed discussion of travel geography impossible. To get a general picture, this book will focus on each region and its attractions separately, with the reminder that regional definitions vary.

U.S. Regions

New England is well recognized as comprising Maine, New Hampshire, Vermont, Massachusetts, Rhode Island, and Connecticut. It is a region known for its early American history, gorgeous fall foliage, old inns, and lakes and ocean views. In historic Boston and its vicinity are Bunker Hill, the Boston Common, Harvard University, and the USS Constitution. Lexington and Concord, famed in the American Revolution, are nearby. Cape Cod, Nantucket, and Martha's Vineyard are favorite vacation areas. Salem, Newburyport, and Old Mystic recall sailing days. New England also has beautiful rural scenery, from the Green Mountains and White Mountains to Maine's rocky coastline. Acadia National Park near Bar Harbor, Maine, and the fishing villages on the coast are memorable. Deerfield Village, Old Sturbridge Village, and Plimoth Plantation recreate colonial life.

The heavily populated Northeast—New York, Pennsylvania, New Jersey and Delaware—is known for its urban centers of New York City, Philadelphia, and Atlantic City. Fast-paced New York City is one of a kind, our largest city, with thousands of restaurants and the largest aggregate of hotel rooms anywhere. Atlantic City, in neighboring New Jersey, has gambling casinos that attract thousands. Upstate New York has the Finger Lakes region and the Adirondacks for summer vacations. Awesome Niagara Falls is shared with Canada. Philadelphia is home to the Liberty Bell and Constitution Hall. Valley Forge is not far away, and Gettysburg National Military Park is the largest battlefield shrine in the United States.

The Mid-Atlantic states include Maryland and adjacent Washington, D.C., Virginia, and West Virginia. The District of Columbia, home of the Capitol, has other famous government buildings, the Lincoln and Jefferson Memorials, the Library of Congress (largest library in the world), the Smithsonian Institution, the National Gallery, and the Washington Monument. Mount Vernon, home of George Washington, can be reached by a pleasant boat trip from Washington. Williamsburg, Virginia, is a museum town not to be missed by anyone interested in colonial America.

The Southeast—North Carolina, South Carolina, Georgia, and Florida—has Charleston with its beautiful antebellum homes and its coastal islands. Great Smoky National Park and the Blue Ridge Parkway pass through three states. The popular entrance/exit points are Gatlinburg, Tennessee, and Front Royal, Virginia.

The South (also called the Deep South) includes Alabama, Mississippi, Tennessee, Kentucky, Arkansas, and Louisiana. New Orleans has creole charm but is miserably hot and muggy in the summer. Some of the antebellum mansions are open to the public; a few have been converted to B & Bs. Mammoth Cave in south-central Kentucky is well named: its cave system, which is entered by elevators, stretches more than 300 miles. Its Snowball Dining Room is 267 feet below ground.

The Midwest and Plains states include Ohio, Indiana, Illinois, Michigan, Wisconsin, Missouri, Iowa, Minnesota, Kansas, Nebraska, South Dakota, and North Dakota. Chicago is the great trade and transit point for the area. The tallest building in the world, the Sears Tower, is in Chicago. St. Louis and Kansas City are also rail and air hubs. Detroit is the auto-making center. The Great Lakes are the outstanding natural feature of the region, so huge that storms can capsize ships in their waters. Lakeshore communities attract tourists for water sports and fishing. Every state has at least one tourist attraction. South Dakota, for example, has Mt. Rushmore National Park, 9,620-foot-high rock carved with giant heads of Presidents Washington, Jefferson, Lincoln, and

Theodore Roosevelt. The region is also noted for its rich farmland and sweeping prairie.

The Southwest, usually thought of as including Oklahoma, Texas, New Mexico, and Arizona, has a diverse geography that includes vast plains, mountains, and desert. Arizona has the Grand Canyon National Park, a 217-mile canyon that averages 7 miles in width, created over millennia by tons of water rushing down the Colorado River and the uplifting of land.

The Carlsbad Caverns National Park, in southwestern New Mexico, is a series of limestone caves that offer a three-mile walking tour and return by elevator. Southwestern culture is heavily influenced by that of Mexico. The central downtown section of Santa Fe, New Mexico, has been preserved much as it was under Mexican rule. Texas has the famous Alamo, huge ranches, and modern cities on a scale with the state's vast size.

The Mountain States of Nevada, Utah, Colorado, Wyoming, and Montana are shaped by mountains and desert. Las Vegas is virtually one large tourist attraction. Bryce/Zion National Parks, in southwestern Utah, are multi-colored canyons with unusual geological forms. Other national parks abound in this thinly populated region.

The Far West—California, Oregon, and Washington—has the Cascades and part of the Sierra Nevada as part of the Western Cordillera. The mountains provide several ski slopes, and exciting viewing. Lake Tahoe, which borders California and Nevada, is a year-round resort area with gambling on the Nevada side. Yosemite National Park in California covers 1,189 square miles and contains Yosemite Falls. California has several stands of majestic Sequoia (redwood) trees, a tourist attraction in themselves. San Francisco and its Golden Gate Bridge are one of a kind. To the south is Carmel/Monterey with gorgeous ocean views. For the historically minded, there are twenty-one Spanish/Mexican missions in various states of repair, vestiges of the days when Spain, and then Mexico, ruled the area.

San Diego, home port for many naval vessels, is also noted for its fine zoo. Eighteen miles south is the Mexican border town of Tijuana, visited each year by millions of tourists.

California is unusual in its range of scenery and climate. It is possible to swim in the Pacific Ocean and then drive two hours inland to ski in the mountains. Coastal temperatures are mild, while in Death Valley temperatures soar to 120°F and even the crows gasp for breath.

Oregon's majestic coastline has miles of crashing surf. Inland are mountains for skiing and wilderness areas for camping. Along the Columbia River on the Oregon/Washington border runs the Columbia River Scenic Highway, one of the great scenic drives in the United States. Puget Sound and the San Juan Islands near Seattle, Washington, are great places for boating, while Seattle's opera has become world famous.

Hawaii

Hawaii, our fiftieth state, seems like an international destination because of its remoteness, ethnic make-up, and tropical environment. The map of Hawaii in Figure 8-4 outlines the major islands and the principal airports for the state. Honolulu is a transit point for the Pacific Basin. A number of airlines fly nonstop between the Orient and Oceania and the United States, but it is more comfortable to break the trip and stop overnight in Honolulu. Most flights land in Honolulu on Oahu, and it is necessary to backtrack to get to other islands.

The state of Hawaii consists of a chain of five major and 127 minor islands. Oahu is the business, educational, tourism, and military center of the state, and about three-fourths of the state's people live there. There are so many cars on the island that if all were on the road at one time, there would be complete gridlock. Tourists can shop in Honolulu, relax on Waikiki Beach, and visit the Polynesian Cultural Center for an introduction to Polynesian culture.

Two-thirds of the approximately million residents of Hawaii are of Asian, Polynesian, or Pacific descent. Those of Japanese background control much of the business and politics.

The big island of Hawaii provides a bubbly, burning volcano that erupts every year or so, spewing lava that runs down to the sea and slowly

8-4. Travel destinations in Hawaii.

adds to the island's territory. The island has two huge mountains, Mauna Kea and Mauna Loa. The southernmost tip of the island is also the southernmost part of the entire United States. On Maui, tourists can visit the huge crater of the volcano Haleakala or stay at one of the many resorts on the island.

Alaska

Because of its location, immense size, and extensive natural beauty, Alaska is a special case in American travel geography. Alaska's natural beauty will remain even though its salmon and haddock come and go and the price of timber rises and falls.

Visitors tend to fall into one of three groups: those who arrive by ship—generally retired, older, and fairly affluent travelers; adventurous families who come via the Alaska Highway from the "lower forty-eight" and Canada; and those who come by air, a middle-aged and middle-income group.

For most people the immensity of the forty-ninth state is difficult to comprehend: one-fifth the size of the "lower forty-eight," it turns Texans

tongue-tied when it comes to the word "biggest." Two-and-a-half times larger than Texas, it covers four time zones. The coastline is greater than that in all of the continental United States. Climate varies widely largely because of the warming influence of the Japan Current that sweeps north and east from the mid-Pacific.

Anchorage, strategically located on the polar route between Europe, the United States, and Japan, is a major international airport city. About halfway between Europe and Asia (7½ hours flight time), the Anchorage International Airport is a logical break point in intercontinental travel (see Figure 8-5). Containing half of Alaska's population, Anchorage is the state's only real city, a relatively sophisticated metropolis. Because it sits on Cook Inlet, the Japan Current spares it the severe winter weather of the interior, where temperatures drop into the minus 40°F range.

The engineering marvel of World War II, the Alaska Highway is one of the adventure roads of the world. Driving the 1,500 miles from Dawson Creek, British Columbia, to Fairbanks, Alaska, takes about seven days. The Canadian segment of the highway is mostly gravel, with paved sections near larger towns. The Alaskan section is all

THE TOURIST BUSINESS

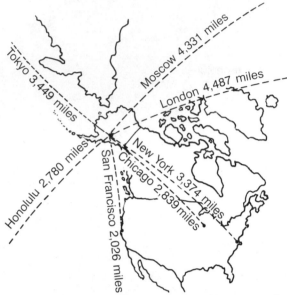

8-5. Distances to major world cities given in air miles measured from Anchorage, Alaska.

paved. Seasoned north country residents prefer to drive the highway in winter, when it is less crowded and the road surface is smooth and frozen, free from dust and flying gravel.

Unique to Alaska is the long ferry route provided by the state, the Alaska Marine Highway, which runs the Inside Passage or Inland Waterway between the coastal islands and the mainland. Residents of the little towns served by the "highway" see nothing strange about its name. To them it is the only surface transportation into or out of their communities.

Of the several villages and towns served by the highway Sitka stands out. Picture-postcard beautiful, it is protected from the open sea by a series of islands. Its simple little Russian Orthodox Church, an architectural beauty, is a reminder of the days when Sitka was the capital of Russia's territory. On a hill in Sitka one of the greatest real estate coups in history took place when the United States purchased what is now Alaska for 2 cents an acre.

The graphics of Alaskan tourism center on the totem pole, that expression of the wood carver unique to the natives of the northwestern United States, British Columbia, and Alaska. Paris has its Eiffel Tower, London its Big Ben clock. Alaska has its totem poles. The totem pole appears in tourist literature, enlivens hotel lobbies and brochures, and is prominently displayed in almost every museum. The original totem poles were commissioned by Native American families or chiefs to commemorate an event, to make a statement, and sometimes to deride another family who failed an obligation, such as repaying a debt. Old photographs show numbers of totem poles standing before waterside villages facing toward the sea, the first thing seen by a visitor. Clan symbols like the raven, the eagle, and the frog stared out from the brightly colored poles.

A fascinating rail trip can be taken between Anchorage and Fairbanks via the Alaska Railroad. The train runs daily from mid-May through mid-September, and once a week during winter. It passes through Denali National Park and Reserve, Alaska's best-known wilderness recreation area. Traveling the park road almost assures the visitor of seeing one or more grizzly bears, moose, fox, caribou, or Dall sheep. Mount Denali (formerly Mt. McKinley) dominates the area and well it should. From base to summit it is the tallest mountain in the world (the Himalayas start at higher elevations).

CANADA

After the USSR, Canada covers the largest area in the world, yet most of the 26 million Canadians live within a hundred miles of the 3,986-mile border that adjoins the United States. Not surprisingly, the greatest international travel by U.S. residents and by Canadians is between the two countries. Figure 8-6 is a tourism map of Canada.

Known for its natural beauty, Canada has thousands of lakes, rivers, and streams, as well as the Canadian Rockies, which are even grander than the U.S. Rockies. Canada has the St. Lawrence Seaway, a system of rivers, canals, and lakes from the Atlantic through to the Great Lakes. Niagara

8-6. Map of Canada.

Falls in the Niagara River is shared between Ontario, Canada, and New York state. Vancouver and Victoria Island are much like Seattle, Washington, in both climate and scenic beauty. The Canadian Ministry of Tourism, however, is concerned that the average U.S. resident perceives Canada as only rustic and rural. In fact, the majority of Canadians live in metropolitan centers with cultural amenities that equal or excel those in the United States. Actually, only a little more than 4 percent of the whole country is under cultivation, and it is estimated that only 7 percent ever can be.

Canadians, like Americans, are a multicultural society, with people of British and French background predominating, though many others come from Western Europe and more recently, Eastern and Southern Europe and Asia. Canada's largest cities are as ethnically mixed as U.S. cities.

Geographically, Canada can be divided into five regions: the Atlantic or Maritime provinces; Quebec and Ontario, the nation's population core; the Prairies; the Mountain West; and the North. Politically, the country is divided into ten provinces and two territories.

Quebec is predominantly French and Catholic. It is proud of its French heritage, and has even, at times, called for separation from the rest of Canada. Montreal, the capital of Quebec, is the world's largest French-speaking city after Paris and Kinshasa (capital of Zaire in Africa).

Excellent air, rail, and road systems serve the country. Major gateway air terminals are at Vancouver, Calgary, Montreal, and Toronto. Toronto experiences the most air travel, domestic and international, and is Canada's leading city in population and income. The people of Toronto and Montreal have learned to live with cold winters. Each city has a huge underground concourse of shops and restaurants. The metro, Montreal's excellent subway system, links shops, art galleries, and theaters.

The Maritime provinces of Prince Edward Island, Nova Scotia, and New Brunswick are popular summertime vacation spots for Canadians and for Americans from the east coast. Nova Scotia has the most developed tourist industry; no part of the province is more than thirty-five miles from the sea.

The U.S. and Canada are each other's best trading partners. Vancouver and the rest of British Columbia are magnets for Canadians as well as Americans. The climate is similar to that of Seattle and the state of Washington.

Coast to coast, Canada can be enjoyed by traveling the Trans-Canada Highway. Just under 5,000 miles long, it is the world's longest paved road. The other notable highway is the 1,500-mile Alaska Highway, two-thirds of it in Canada. VIA Rail is similar in concept to Amtrak, and similarly operates at a huge deficit.

To escape the long winters, many Canadians travel to the Bahamas and the Caribbean, southern California, and Hawaii. Britain, the ethnic home for 45 percent of Canadians, is a summer destination.

MEXICO

Mexico and the United States share a border that extends from California east through Arizona, New Mexico, and part of Texas, a border crossed by millions of Americans and Mexicans each year to shop, do business, eat, drink, and experience a decidedly different culture by merely crossing a border. Tijuana, eighteen miles south of San Diego, gets the most border crossings, estimated

at close to 23 million a year. Other border crossings such as El Paso, Brownsville, and Laredo, Texas, see other millions of visitors going to and coming from Mexico. The five million visitors who are other than day-trippers mostly fly to resort destinations. Cancún, on the Yucatan Peninsula is the most popular, attracting more than a million people a year. Its palm lined beach— twelve miles long—is three and a half hours by jet from New York City, two hours from Houston. It is also a gateway to the well-known Mayan ruins of Chichén Itzá, 75 miles east of Mérida. Chichén Itzá is 45 minutes by plane from Cancún. Uxmal, 48 miles south of Mérida, is a second choice, the location of a most impressive Mayan structure known as the Palace of the Governor. Tulum, one of several Mayan ruins on the Mexican coast, is a day trip from Cancún.

Mexico City, called locally México, is the premier city of the country, politically, economically, and culturally. Growing from only 1.8 million people in 1940, Mexico City now has over 18 million people and the population grows by 700,000 each year through births and migration of the poor from rural areas of Mexico. At the time of the Spanish conquest in 1521, Mexico City was larger than any European city. The city today is larger than even the Tokyo-Yokohama urban complex. Located on a plateau ringed by mountains, the city is ill-equipped for such demographic eminence. Unhealthy smog is said to be worse than that of any other city. A 1988 Reuters News report stated that 2 million people are estimated to relieve themselves in the open for lack of facilities, producing 110 tons of human waste a day. Once dried, it rises into the air along with exhaust fumes and a host of noxious gases.

Two of Mexico City's many attractions stand out, one a site of ruins, the other perhaps the most impressive of all cultural museums. Thirty-five miles north of the city is Teotihuacán, founded in 150 B.C., a city that dominated Mexico until A.D. 700. Among its vast ruins are two massive pyramids, about which one guide book comments, "to miss them would be like visiting Egypt and not seeing the pyramids there." The other marvel is modern—the National Museum of Anthropology, which is fascinating even to the non-museum-goer. Constructed of a series of chambers encircling a patio, the museum portrays the various civilizations of Mexico's past, including the Olmecs, the Mayans, the Toltecs, and the Aztecs. The last were the dominant group at the time Cortez the Spanish conquistador arrived by ship from Cuba. The museum also includes rooms showing the lifestyles of Mexico's several ethnic groups.

Mexican weather is determined largely by altitude, for mountains dominate Mexico's landscape. The Sierra Madre divides in the southern state of Oaxaca and runs north, forming two plateaus. On one of these is Mexico City; at about 7,000 feet the city can be quite cool in the winter. The coastal areas are warm to hot most of the year. South of Mazatlán on the west coast it is hot most of the year, while Acapulco is warm from December through April, and quite hot and humid the rest of the year. Summer is the rainy season.

Except for Cancún off the Yucatán Peninsula, most of the resorts are on the west coast of mainland Mexico, the "Mexican Riviera." As Figure 8-7 shows, these resorts stretch south from Mazatlán through Puerto Vallarta, Manzanillo, Ixtapa/Zihuatanejo, and Acapulco, to the newest government-built resort, Huatulco.

8-7. Map of Mexico with major tourist destinations.

Like Cancún on the Yucatán Peninsula, the Bahias de Huatulco (Bays of Huatulco), a twenty-mile stretch of beach, is a government-planned resort, slated to be the biggest resort development in Mexico by the end of this century. Puerto Vallarta is being expanded by Nuevo Vallarta, which will double the hotel capacity of the area within a few years. For many years Acapulco was the resort capital of Mexico. That title has shifted to Cancún because of its easy access to U.S. cities and because the quality of Acapulco has declined.

North Americans and others fly to Cancún, on the Yucatán Peninsula and to the "Mexican Riviera," which extends south along Mexico's west coast to Huatulco, below Oaxaca.

Baja California (Lower California) extends southward 1,500 miles from the U.S. border. The only major city is Tijuana, which has a population exceeding one million. At the southern tip of Baja, at Cabo San Lucas, are several expensive resorts. For the adventurous, there is a 1,800-mile road to drive from Tijuana to Cabo San Lucas.

Mexico has a population exceeding 70 million and considerable wealth in oil, but it also has enormous debts brought about by incautious borrowing. The country is plagued by corruption in the government. Bribery, the *mordida* (bite), is an unfortunate but accepted practice in government and business. Drug trafficking is a major problem in some areas. Visitors are advised to avoid driving at night and to stay away from some parts of the country.

A caveat about private auto travel in Mexico: Drivers must buy Mexican insurance because Mexican authorities do not recognize United States auto insurance policies.

Despite these problems, Mexico attracts tourists because of the beauty of its countryside, its rich pre-Columbian and colonial heritage, its ethnic variety, its abundance of decorative arts, and its masterpieces of mural art.

EUROPE

Technically, Europe is a continent, part of the Eurasian landmass. It is separated from Asia by the Ural Mountains on the east and the Caucasus Mountains and the Black and Caspian seas on the southeast.

Is England a part of Europe? In British usage, Continental Europe is sometimes contrasted with Britain. An arm of the Atlantic Ocean, the English Channel, separates northern France from southern England. (At one time swimming the English Channel, about 20 miles wide at its narrowest point, was a great achievement. Later an American did it both ways, nonstop.)

As of 1993 Continental Europe and Britain will be closer together, linked by Eurotunnel *le plus gigantesque peage du monde*, the biggest tunnel in the world. The twin-bore rail tunnel is being dug under the channel between southeast England and northwest France. It will be 30 miles long and is forecast to carry 30 million passengers —and their cars—on special trains.

The Eurotunnel, which will further bind Europe together, is good news for rail travelers in that there will be through services from Edinburgh to Milan. The completion of the tunnel will come just in time. The road systems of Europe, especially northern Europe and Britain, are overcrowded, as are the airways. Europe will rely more heavily on a growing network of higher-speed trains for larger-distance travel; and with the problems of getting to and from airports and jammed airways, preference for rail travel between Europe's major cities will increase.

Western Europe follows Canada and Mexico as the most popular travel destination for Americans. Over half of U.S. travelers abroad head for Western Europe. Americans especially favor Britain (officially the United Kingdom of Great Britain and Northern Ireland) for pleasure travel. The U.K. is made up of England, Wales, Scotland, and the Province of Northern Ireland. Ireland, or Eire, is an independent country. Wales is referred to as a principality, Scotland as a country with a capital city, Edinburgh. Once the center of an empire, today Britain is part of the British Commonwealth of Nations, a large group of nations and dependent territories around the world, united by a common allegiance to the British crown.

France usually follows Britain as a popular American destination in Europe. France has the largest territory of the West European countries, whereas West Germany has the most people. Germany ranks third for American visitors, largely because so many U.S. service people are stationed there.

Figure 8-8 shows the number of U.S. citizens traveling to the twenty countries that attracted the most U.S. visitors in 1986. (Canada, which always has the most U.S. visitors, is not included.) The United Kingdom heads the list of European countries, followed by West Germany, France, the Netherlands, Italy, Switzerland, and Spain. The rankings change over time because of costs, the effects of marketing, terrorism politics, and other factors.

In 1986 France reported the most international tourist arrivals (36 million), followed by Spain, Italy, Austria, the United Kingdom, Germany, and Switzerland.

Russia, the Union of Soviet Socialist Republics, occupies part of Europe and much of Asia. Made up of 15 constituent republics, it occupies nearly one-sixth of the world's land surface. Relatively few Americans, 200,000, traveled to Russia in 1988, although the figure is expected to increase.

To keep the European countries in perspective, think of all of Sweden as having about the same population as New York City and all of Scandinavia about the same number of people as California.

Europe has its micro-states, the smallest being Vatican City, where about 1,000 people live within .2 of a square mile. Andorra, in the Pyrenees Mountains between France and Spain, has about 34,000 people; Liechtenstein, between Austria and Switzerland, 26,000. San Marino, the village atop a small Italian mountain, has 21,000.

Counting the mini-countries, Europe includes thirty-one countries. The island Republic of Malta, in the Mediterranean, and Iceland, in the Atlantic, are also sometimes considered part of the European region. Figure 8-9 is an outline map showing the larger countries of Europe. The reader might try filling in the map with the first two letters of each country. Figure 8-10 is the same map with the names of countries included.

8-8. U.S. Citizen Air Departures to Foreign Countries in 1986 Top Twenty by Ranking (excluding Canada)			
Rank	First Port of Entry	U.S. Citizens 1986	Percent of Grand Total
1.	Mexico	2,237,549	15.7
2.	UK England	1,788,610	12.5
3.	Bahamas	970,956	6.8
4.	West Germany	950,295	6.7
5.	Japan	777,749	5.4
6.	Jamaica	612,267	4.3
7.	Dominican Republic	489,392	3.4
8.	France	459,820	3.2
9.	Bermuda	369,203	2.6
10.	Netherlands Antilles	348,608	2.4
11.	Netherlands	305,496	2.1
12.	Italy	289,035	2.0
13.	Korea	258,426	1.8
14.	Switzerland	255,722	1.8
15.	Spain	194,767	1.4
16.	Hong Kong	193,017	1.4
17.	Ireland	189,387	1.3
18.	Belgium	186,122	1.3
19.	Brazil	175,985	1.2
20.	Barbados	175,852	1.2
Total (Top twenty):		11,227,718	78.7
Grand Total:		14,275,234	100.0

SOURCE: Nettleton Travel Research Center, Inc.

8-9. Outline map of Europe.

Much of the continent is mountainous, especially eastern and southern France, Switzerland, southern Germany, Austria, northern Spain, and northern Italy. The Alps are the best known of the mountain ranges in Western Europe. Other ranges are the Pyrenees, the Sudeten, the Erz, the Urals, and the Caucasus. The Balkan Mountains extend from Western Bulgaria to the Black Sea.

European weather varies widely depending upon latitude, altitude, and the presence of large bodies of water. Of particular importance to

8-10. Map of Europe with names of countries.

Western Europe is the Atlantic Drift (the diffusion of the Gulf Stream) that moderates European climate and is responsible for much of Europe's rain. The Mediterranean is Europe's Caribbean, ringed by vacation spots and dotted with islands.

A popular way to see Europe is by rental car, often included as part of a travel package. Much of continental Europe is served by multilane, divided highways, many segments of which are toll roads. Britain's motorways have London as their focal point, and Paris is the center point of France's superhighways. Among the toll roads that radiate from Paris, one leads south to Dijon, Lyon, and Marseilles. One branch runs to the Cote d'Azur (the French Riviera) and resorts of Nice and Monte Carlo. Another branch goes all the way into Spain, then down the coast of Spain to Valencia.

The German autobahns have no real speed limit and more high-speed driving occurs there than in any other country. From Frankfurt, Germany's major international airport, a traveler can rent a car and drive the autobahn down through Stuttgart into Munich in Bavaria, then on to Salzburg, Austria, and east to Vienna. Another route heads directly south from Frankfurt, past Heidelburg and Freiburg and into Switzerland. Italy's principal toll road, the autostrada, runs from Milan to Rome and Salerno. A separate branch skirts the Adriatic coast and reaches the heel of Italy at Taranto. Once the motorist leaves the superhighways, however, driving times can be long because of narrow winding roads and the necessity of passing through innumerable towns and villages.

Air travel to Europe is made easy by numerous airlines and frequent flights. Every country of any importance has at least one airline that connects with the continent. Nearly all fly to one or more of the national capitals of Europe.

Heaviest air traffic to and from Europe takes place on the trans-Atlantic routes. Direct daily or weekly flights reach Europe from a number of U.S. cities. New York City to London routes carry the most passengers, but numerous direct flights are scheduled from as far away as Los Angeles. Flights go not only to London but to Paris, Frankfurt, Amsterdam, Glasgow, and Copenhagen.

A problem with intra-European air travel is its cost. Fares on European airlines have been much higher than for comparable flights outside of Europe. Travel packages that include intra-European flights usually offer less expensive air travel.

On the other hand, rail travel within Europe can be fast, efficient, and a travel bargain. Frequent schedules and spotless trains are the norm in several European countries. The best trains are part of the Eurocity network that operates in nine countries and ranges from Barcelona in the south to Hamburg in the north. London is connected by rail and ferry to Rotterdam as part of the network. A great many Americans see continental Europe via the Eurail system, which covers more than 100,000 miles of rail lines. (For more about European rail travel, see Chapter 4.)

Britain

The traveler landing in London has the largest museum city in the world to explore. Two airports serve the international traveler, Heathrow and Gatwick. Both have links into the heart of London. Gatwick to Victoria Station is a thirty-eight minute train ride. Heathrow to Piccadilly Station is forty minutes by underground (subway). Heathrow is one of the five busiest airports in the world.

Most Americans who fly to the United Kingdom arrive and depart from the airport at London, Glasgow, or Belfast. They seldom travel by air within Britain. Seeing Britain by rental car and by rail are the preferred means of transport. Although Britain has twenty-nine international airports, few of them are served by direct flights from the United States.

Tourists can travel to most parts of Britain by rail. BritRail passes can be booked by travel agents who subscribe to the computer service PARS (the TWA computer service) or APOLLO (United Airlines service). Travel agents can also book BritRail pass at any one of fifty railway stations in London. Most stations for the larger trains have tourist information centers where accommodations can be reserved for a nominal fee. Some offices, however, are several blocks away from the station.

Literally hundreds of trains have been cut from the schedule, however, and it is impossible to reach some of the more picturesque areas of Britain by train. The Scottish Highlands around Inverary has no train service, and most of the Cotswolds is reachable only by car or by infrequent buses.

A large number of ports serve the sea traveler in Britain and Ireland. Southhampton was once the predominant port for the great Atlantic steamers. Portsmouth is a well-known naval base. The Dover-to-Calais route is well known to travelers between London and France. Jet-foil service is offered between Dover and Ostende, Belgium, and hovercraft service is available between Calais and Dover between Dover and Boulogne.

The United Kingdom is surprisingly small, about the size of Oregon. It is about 600 miles from northernmost Scotland to southernmost England. At its widest part, the country spreads 250 miles from the west coast of Wales to the east coast of England. The Irish Republic and Northern Ireland share an island about 300 miles north to south and 200 miles east to west.

England

London is the epicenter of England and once was capital of the British Empire. London is the money market, the political center, the city where legitimate plays rise or fall, the shipping and trade center of the British Isles. Few capitals dominate their respective nations as London does England.

London has been described as a collection of villages run together. Within London are two cities, the City of London and the City of Westminster. The visitor recognizes the City of London, the financial center, because nearly every male is wearing a bowler hat, carrying an umbrella, and maybe a briefcase. It is home to the Bank of England and the Stock Exchange.

The West End is like New York City's Fifth Avenue along Central Park. It's where the well-to-do people live and includes Mayfair and St. James.

London is large, larger than New York City, Paris, Rome, or Berlin, about thirty miles in diameter. To get around London most people take the underground. It is the easiest and the least expensive way. Compared to the New York subway, it is more attractive, more pleasant to use, and much safer, though it too is noisy and boring.

London taxis are mostly diesel fueled and roomy. The cab drivers, a race apart from New York's cabbies, are mostly restrained, quiet, and polite.

London's legitimate theater is generally considered the best in the world and costs about half of New York City's. There are more than forty live theaters.

Several great museums are in London. The British Museum, the grandparent of museums, is best known and very crowded. The best examples of Greek art are there, purloined by Lord Elgin. The Rosetta Stone, key to the ancient Egyptian hieroglyphics, is also there. In the National Gallery are portraits of the nation's famous people.

Besides being a bustling city, London is known for its parks, most of them a legacy from the royalty and nobility. What are now Hyde Park, Regent Park, and Kensington Gardens were once owned by the Dukes of Devonshire, Bedford, and Westminster. Westminster is still a large London landlord. History abounds. At the Marble Arch, on one side of Hyde Park, a gallows once stood.

Undoubtedly London's biggest tourist attraction is the royal family: their palaces, their guards, and their antics. Tourists line up at Buckingham Palace to see the changing of the guard—and hope to see the Queen as well. When not in residence there, she may be at Windsor Castle. The Government supports the royal family to the tune of $40 million a year, an investment in tourism as well as tradition.

Britain's number-one place to visit is the Tower of London, beside the Thames River, a grisly reminder of bygone royal power. The crown jewels of England, on display in the Tower, are a major attraction. At Westminster Abbey, where the great and powerful of the British Empire have been buried, the steady procession of visitors are wearing the stone floors down. Nearly every tourist thrills to the chiming of Big Ben. Parliament buildings and Big Ben have become London's trademark, much as the Eiffel Tower is to Paris.

THE TOURIST BUSINESS

The British Empire is now a shadow of its former self, but its panoply and pageantry remain. No one, not even Hollywood, rivals the British in pageantry. A sense of history pervades the place. The Guard regiments on duty in downtown London provide an unmatched tourist attraction. The Changing of the Guard, the Trooping of the Colors, and the Opening of Parliament, are events that warm the cockles of the hearts of the British Tourist Authority.

London is for shoppers as well as museum-goers. Harrods stocks everything from prams (baby buggies) to potted partridge, and Fortnum & Mason specializes in fine groceries. Saville Row gets the nod of gentlemen's tailors (who do the make-to-order kind). The best buys in Britain, according to the British, are to be found in Marks and Spencer, the clothing and food store chain found in most British cities.

Hampton Court Palace, on the outskirts of London, is a major tourist attraction. (It also attracted Henry VIII, who appropriated it from Cardinal Wolsey, who had built it for himself.) It can be reached by road or by boat on the Thames River. That river leads northward to the university town of Oxford and beyond, a wonderful river for boating, with plenty of riverside towns to stop at for a rest.

Windsor Castle, an excursion out of London, is awesome in dimension. The public school of Eton is nearby, best known of all private schools. The place is suitably medieval and the boys appear in period dress.

Among England's other large cities are Manchester, Liverpool, and Sheffield, all in the industrial north.

England is divided into counties. Those nearest London are called the home counties. The Midlands are the central counties. The hilly Cotswolds, part of the Midlands, are a tourist attraction with their villages of honey-colored stone.

A road map of England shows London to be the hub of the country. Eight of the major motorways, the M system, converge on the city from around the country. The M1 starts with London and heads north into Scotland. The M5 starts south at Plymouth and joins the M6, then heads north to Scotland. The M4 stretches east and west, from Cardiff, Wales, on the west to London on the east.

The motorways that form spokes to London's hub allow high speed travel in and out of London once the driver reaches the ring road that circles the city. (Paris and Rome have similar ring roads.) Once away from the superhighways, however, picturesque winding roads—slow by American standards—pass through innumerable villages.

The number two attraction in Britain, not surprisingly, is Stratford-upon-Avon, Shakespeare's home. The village sits beside the little Avon River, northwest of Oxford. Popular tourist spots are Ann Hathaway's cottage and the beautiful church on the edge of town.

The southwest is England's favorite playground. Appropriately, the tip of England, in Cornwall, is called Land's End. East of Cornwall is Devon, with coasts on both the English Channel and Bristol Channel. Torquay is one of the better known beach towns on the English Channel. Devon is home to the famous Devon Teas, a baking powder biscuit covered with jam and heavy clotted cream.

East of London is Bath, popular since its founding by the Romans for its curative hot springs and since the eighteenth century, for its Georgian style of architecture.

Oxford and Cambridge, north of London, date back to the Middle Ages and are England's renowned university towns. Architecturally, Cambridge is the more interesting of the two because of its variety of building styles ranging from Norman to modern. Not far from Oxford is Blenheim Palace, home of the first Duke of Marlborough and his heirs. Impressive in its own right, the palace gained further fame as the birthplace of Winston Churchill.

Going east from London on the M2 the tourist reaches Canterbury, famous for its cathedral that has been a shrine for centuries. Nearly every high school English class includes some reading of Geoffrey Chaucer's *Canterbury Tales*, the fictionalized story of a group of pilgrims on their trip to Canterbury from London about 1390.

The poet Wordsworth and others celebrated the Lake District, in northwest England, in verse and prose. A mountainous area occupied by lakes, it attracts visitors who water ski, fish, hike, or pony trek through the region.

The British pay homage to history by preserving its remains. Castles and mansions, even whole villages have been taken over by the government or by the conservation societies, the National Trust or the Scottish Trust. The London-based National Trust owns or protects nearly two hundred historic buildings, 416 miles of unspoiled coastline, and more than a half million acres of land. It oversees thirty complete villages and hamlets, castles and abbeys, and lakes and hills. It owns parts of inland waterways, bird sanctuaries, nature reserves, wind and water mills, and working farms. It has coastal waterways, conservation camps, gardens, gift shops, and restaurants. It even owns a section of Hadrian's Wall, the wall built by the Romans to protect England. Many of its properties can be rented by visitors for a few days or weeks.

The National Trust includes many stately homes, whose owners cannot afford to maintain them. By giving them to the government or the National Trust, the owners can continue to live in a section of the mansion, while the rest is open to the public.

Garden and flower lovers adore England. The damp, mild climate makes the country ideal for roses, rhododendrons, azaleas, and a host of other flowers and shrubs. No matter how small the house, it usually has a little flower garden in front of it. Many stately homes include an orangerie and greenhouses for growing plants, fruits, and vegetables year-round. Mansion owners often feel obligated to keep large gardens: formal clipped gardens, gardens with ponds, gardens with "follies" (buildings with no special purpose other than to embellish the grounds), gardens with gazebos, puzzle gardens with mazes designed to lose the stroller, French gardens, Italian gardens, miniature and massive gardens. Garden shows are not only for horticulturists, they are social occasions for everyone.

Kew Gardens in London is the biggest and best known. The Rothschild forest garden, about 100 miles southeast of London in St. Exbury, is said to be the finest forest garden in the world. Its thousands of rhododendrons and azaleas are well worth a visit between March and June.

Every history buff will thrill to walking Hadrian's Wall. The wall crosses seventy-three and a half miles of hills and plains, from the North Sea to the Irish Sea. Built by the Roman Emperor Hadrian's legionnaires starting in A.D. 122, the wall marked the boundary between Roman domination of what is now England and the north, which was left to the wild Picts and Scots. The methodical Romans built a fort every five Roman miles and at every Roman mile put up a milecastle, a small fort with barracks for a garrison of eight to thirty-two men. Turret watchtowers were built between the milecastles. Legionnaires built the wall, and provincials manned it. Their enlistment period was twenty-five years.

What is left of the wall—and many stretches of it are intact—runs from Bowness-on-Solway on Solway Firth to Wallsend in the east. The Cheviot Hills and Scottish border are to the north, and the Lake Country is just south. Newcastle-upon-Tyne, near the eastern end of the wall, is the nearest large town.

Wales

Wales, on the west of Britain, extends out into the Irish Sea. Like Scotland, it is a nation within a nation. Tourism is big business. A geography pedant's paradise, some of the place names are almost unpronounceable to an outsider.

There is a Betws-y-Coed, no relation to the popular song of a few decades ago ("Betty Coed Has Eyes of Blue"...) The capital city, Cardiff, is easy enough to pronounce.

Wales is small, about 8,000 square miles, with a total population of about 2.8 million. Most of the people and industry are in the south. Anglesey Island in the north is connected to the mainland by a bridge. The north is also known for the Snowdonia, a mountainous region where hiking, pony-trekking, and mountain climbing are popular. The mountains are small but grand and were used by the conquerors of Mt. Everest as a training ground. The Welsh seacoast has numerous sandy bays and quiet towns. Freshwater fishing is the most popular of outdoor sports. Some of the riverside hotels even own fishing rights along the banks on which they sit.

All road signs in Wales appear in both English and Welsh. Train service is good, except on Sundays when nearly everything closes down.

About 20 percent of the population can speak Welsh, a language that bears little resemblance to English although both come from the same roots. The Welsh have a long memory. The last Welsh prince, Llywelyn, was killed in 1282, and in 1536 Wales was merged into the English state. Even so, a sizable number of Welsh think of themselves as Welsh first and members of the United Kingdom second. A separate TV channel in the Welsh language operates twenty-two hours a day.

Wales is castle country, most of them built by the English to keep the Welsh under control. Of the more than two hundred castles, most in ruins, about 100 are open to visitors.

Caernarvon Castle in the north is the most restored and best known. It houses the Regimental Museum of the Royal Welsh Fusilliers and is also the scene of the investiture of the Prince of Wales. Conway, farther north, has town walls flanked by twenty-one towers and pierced by three gateways. Its castle was built in the late thirteenth century.

Cardiff Castle is really a pseudo-castle since it was built in the Victorian period. In August, Cardiff Castle sports a resounding military tattoo, Britain's first and largest military marching performance. From London, Cardiff is a two-hour trip by high speed train.

Scotland

The ballad that includes the line, "You take the high road and I'll take the low road and I'll be in Scotland afore you," tells much about the Scottish love of country. The singer, who was about to be hanged on an English gallows, was referring to going back to his home around Loch Lomond by way of the "low road," the spirit world.

Scots around the world, wherever they are, harbor a mystical warmth for their homeland. Climatically, the country is less than idyllic. The temperature seldom climbs above seventy de-

grees; skies are overcast much of the year, and more than enough rain falls. Yet Scotland exudes romance.

Part of the reason is its geography—hills and dales, lakes and valleys, surrounding oceans. Scotland is small enough that at one time the Duke of Sutherland could travel all the way across its northern section on his own land.

Scotland has many brooding castles with romantic names—Inveraray, Cawdor, Elair, Glamis, Edinburgh, and Sterling. Several castle and mansion owners take in guests on a discreet, prearranged basis, with payment made to a London tourist office. Some farmers also take in guests, and it is well worthwhile to reserve a stay with them in the local tourist office. Most fishing and hunting must be prearranged with the person owning the land or fishing rights along the streams, and a permit can be very expensive.

Only as little as one-fourth of the land is suitable for the usual agriculture. But oats do grow and constitute a staple food, oatmeal, for which the Scots are well known. The land is also good for sheep, which produce the fine wool for which Scotland is famous.

The North Sea bounds Scotland on the east, the Atlantic on the west. Traditionally, Scotland is divided into the Lowlands, in the center of the country, and the Highlands, the northern half. The Uplands are in the south. The Highlands have been sparsely populated since "The Clearances," in the eighteenth century, when the huge landowners decided it was more profitable to raise sheep and cattle than to allow the small farmers, the crofters, to eke out a marginal living on relatively small plots of land. (The Clearances was one of the reasons there are more Scots living abroad than in Scotland itself.) The landowners hastened the crofters' departure by burning their homes, sometimes neglecting to check whether anyone was still inside. Even today 80 percent of the land is owned by 7 percent of the people. Aristocrats and the wealthy own an ample supply of lovely lochs for fishing and boating, mountains, and moors.

Considered some of the most romantic of mountains, the Highlands are not really high at

TRAVEL AND CULTURAL GEOGRAPHY

all as mountains go. Inverness is the northernmost town of any size in the Highlands. The Highlands call Scots from around the world. They provide natural beauty; bountiful Scottish breakfasts, fishing and hiking, shopping and touring of stately homes, and accommodations ranging from private homes (bed and breakfast) to Gleneagles Hotel, one of the best. Gleneagles and St. Andrews are the most famous of Scotland's numerous golf courses.

In the Lowlands, consisting of grassy hills and dales, are Scotland's two major cities, Glasgow and Edinburgh. The Lowlands holds two-thirds of the population, and nearly all of the industry. Just about everyone has heard of Loch Lomond, longest of the Scottish Lakes, about an hour's drive from Glasgow. (In Scotland the bays are called *firths* and the lakes, *lochs*.)

Loch Ness is home to Nessie, the Loch Ness Monster, which has appeared from time to time, apparitionally or otherwise, since the seventh century. The lake is deep and dark, just right for a monster that may or may not exist.

On the west coast, the Solway Firth is shared by Scotland and England. Merging with the Firth of Clyde, it leads inland to Glasgow, the major manufacturing city, with about 900,000 people. The region of Scots poet Robert Burns is not far to the south.

On the east coast, the Firth of Forth is overlooked by Edinburgh Castle, official residence of the reigning British monarch when in Scotland. Edinburgh (pronounced Edinboro) is Scotland's capital, a major tourist attraction because of its marked architectural style and beautifully landscaped gardens and squares.

South of Glasgow are the southern Uplands, where fishermen gather along the banks of the rivers Tweed, Fay, Dee, and Spey to angle for salmon. The tourist cannot simply march up to a stream and fish. Acres along the rivers are owned or leased.

Perth (pronounced Pearth by the Scots) is the base for exploring the Highlands. Aberdeen, on the northeast coast, is a base for the North Seas oil drilling. It is a city of granite; most of the public buildings, schools, and many homes are made of that stone. Balmoral Castle, summer retreat for the British royal family, is nearby.

Off the jagged coast of western Scotland are some six hundred islands called the Inner Hebrides and the Outer Hebrides. Some are still completely owned by a noble family to whom all residents pay rent. Skye is the largest and most popular and is a short ferry ride from Kyle of Lochalsh. The Inner Hebrides include the islands of Islay, Jura, and Mull. Part of Jura has its own microclimate that permits the development of subtropical gardens.

Farther south, in the Firth of Clyde, lies the island of Arran and Brodrick Castle, ancestral home of the Dukes of Hamilton. As with many castles, this one is now owned and maintained by the National Trust of Scotland. Reachable by ferry, Arran comes alive with summer visitors.

North and west, out in the Atlantic, are the Outer Hebrides. To the northeast are the Shetlands, home of the Shetland pony. Now popular as a pet, it was bred to be no higher than 42 inches at the shoulder so that it could work in the mines. Of the more than 100 Shetland islands only twenty-four are inhabited. It is easy to see why fewer than 12,000 people live there. Short summers and constant wind prevent most farming, although sheep thrive and provide the wool for Shetland woollen goods.

Off the northeast coast of Scotland are the Orkney Islands. Of the sixty-seven outcroppings that can be accurately called islands, twenty-six are occupied. The islands can be reached by air from London, Edinburgh, or Aberdeen, or by P & O steamer from Scrabster, Scotland, 6 miles away.

Warmed by the Gulf Stream, the islands seldom experience snow, but gale-force winds are frequent, usually from mid-September until May. Winds and ocean salt spray are blamed for an almost treeless environment, similar to that of Iceland. Londoners are more likely to know Miami than the Orkney Islands. It is cheaper for them to fly on a package tour for two to Miami than to travel to the Orkneys.

The islands still show traces of Viking invasion and habitation. A few Norse words may even creep into an islander's conversation, and on the Shetlands tourists enjoy the Viking celebration of Up-Helly-Aa.

THE TOURIST BUSINESS

A favorite auto tour of Scotland heads north from Prestwick Airport, Scotland's major international gateway, to Fort William, loops around the Highlands to Inverness and south, ending up at Edinburgh.

Among Scotland's unique tourist attractions is the Scotch Whiskey Trail in northeast Scotland, centered around the rivers Spey, Avon, and Livet. The distilleries along the seventy-mile trail themselves are not too different from one another. But it is the spirit of the thing, especially since at many distilleries the guest is treated to something completely un-Scotsmanlike, a free dram of whiskey. Visitors should allow at least an hour for each of the five malt distilleries on the trail. Incidentally, because of high taxes, Scotch whiskey costs more in Scotland than in the United States.

The BritRail pass, or a special Scottish rail pass, gets the traveler around much of Scotland. A few crack trains, the Intercity 125s, run between Edinburgh, Glasgow, and London. The 500-mile run to Edinburgh can be done in less than five hours, with the trains reaching speeds of 125 mph.

BritRail advertising can be misleading. Although it suggests that the rail traveler can enjoy a first-class meal, served in style and lavishly prepared, most trains include only a stand-up snack bar with little or no hot food. Passengers with first-class BritRail passes may find that many trains have no first-class coaches and no food service. Particularly exasperating is the experience of boarding a train only to find all seats occupied so that one is forced to stand.

Like food service, baggage service also has largely vanished. Left Luggage rooms mean a sizable charge and often a wait in line both to check in and to check out bags. A few stations have coin-operated luggage lockers.

Yet the train guards (conductors) in Scotland are extremely polite, even solicitous. They stand ready to advise you on the better buys in accommodations and which hotels to avoid as "too pricey." A guard on the Edinburgh-London run closes each announcement with "And God Bless You."

Ireland

The Republic of Ireland, which occupies the southern part of the island of Ireland, includes five-sixths of the land and two-thirds of the people. Known as the Irish Republic, it is a land of small towns and villages connected mainly by narrow roads. The tourists who drive will have to remember to drive on the left side of the road and to refrain from honking the horn after 11:30 p.m. until 7 a.m.

Visitors head for Dublin, the country's capital, which sits on the Liffey River. Ireland's designation as the Emerald Isle is a result of the frequent rain, which comes in off the North Atlantic and bathes the grass and trees. The North Atlantic Drift, the warm currents sweeping north from the Caribbean and across the Atlantic, keeps the weather mild. Seventy percent of American visitors to Ireland are of Irish extraction.

Ireland's rail travel was greatly improved in the 1980s. The 150 miles between Dublin and Cork takes only 150 minutes, and there are ten trains daily between the cities. Within Dublin there is DART (Dublin Area Rapid Transit). Bus services feed the twenty-five modern stations. The Eurail pass is currency on the overnight passenger ship service between Cork and Rosslare, as well as the French ports of Le Havre and Cherbourg. The crossing takes 18 to 22 hours, depending upon the port used.

The Irish pub, often named after its owner, is a national institution featuring Guinness stout, a dark, creamy brew much too bitter for many beer drinkers, and Irish whiskey. For a jumpstart to inebriation, try a Guinness followed by a shot of whiskey; this combination may account for some of the famous Irish blarney. The visitor need not look far for a pub; there are about 11,000 of them.

Ireland's northeast corner is part of the United Kingdom of Great Britain. Because Northern Ireland is a land torn by strife between its Catholic minority and Protestant majority, it has not had the kind of tourism enjoyed in the Irish Republic.

France

France follows Britain as the most popular European destination for North Americans. As the political and cultural center of the country, Paris is also France's travel epicenter. Most international flights use the Charles de Gaulle Airport, north of Paris, while most domestic flights use Orly, south of the city. Although Paris is farther north than Quebec City, the Gulf Stream and the Mediterranean Sea produce a temperate climate.

For many Paris cab drivers and hotel receptionists it is open season on naive tourists. The cab driver may go the long way round to drive up a fare, and a hotel receptionist may refuse to acknowledge a room deposit made at the airport. On the buses, some drivers refuse to return change due. Yet the charm of Paris overcomes these shortcomings.

The French topography is varied, long stretches of coast, several beautiful rivers, and mountain ranges. Europe's highest mountain, Mont Blanc, is in France. Marseilles, France's largest port and second largest city, is not nearly as popular a vacation destination as the coast farther east, which the French call the Côte d'Azur. A series of coastal resort towns, starting with Saint Tropez and running east through Cannes, Nice, and the principality of Monaco, are part of this French Riviera. Cannes boasts that it is second in the country (after Paris) in its wealth of luxury, first-class hotel rooms. This city of 72,000 people has 4 four-star luxury hotels and more than 125 restaurants. Cannes is also known for its international film festival.

Paris and the area that surrounds it is on an island, the Isle de France, in the Seine River. Paris has four railway stations: Gare du nord, Gare de l'est, Gare de Lyon, and Gare de l'Austerlitz. French supertrains, the TGVs, all depart from the Gare de Lyon. France also has a well-developed road system, including several toll superhighways.

About two hours away from Paris by car or train is the Loire Valley, the "Garden of France" where visitors can see a number of magnificent chateaux. The Loire Valley has the fine towns of Orleans, Tours, Samur, Angers, and Nantes. Orleans is famous for Joan of Arc, and at Tours the French stopped the Moslem drive into Western Europe in 732.

Wine devotees make pilgrimages to the Bordeaux region in the west of France; Burgundy lovers go to the Burgundy region, which has Dijon as its historic capital. The northwest coast of France has Brittany, Normandy, Piccardy, and French Flanders.

Smart travelers do not rent cars in France, since the French government adds a 28 percent tax to the bill. And the surcharges don't stop. Paris hotels have a 15 percent service charge and an 18.6 percent value added tax per room per night. Just as the visitor is about to leave by air, there is another tax as a security surcharge for every departing passenger. (The French are not alone in slapping on extra charges. Hotel rooms in New York City get an 8.25 percent city sales tax, a 5 percent city hotel room tax, and a $2.00 per room per night "city service fee.")

Americans generally overlook Strasbourg, a city that has both French and German roots. For 900 years prior to Louis XIV's rule, the city had a German-speaking population. The city and its province changed hands between France and Germany several times thereafter. The sauerkraut with sausages featured in the restaurants bespeaks a German heritage, while the waiters hold forth in French. Walking along the river, in the old sections of the city is like walking straight back into history several hundred years. (The Rhine is a couple of miles away.)

Luxembourg

France's neighbor to the north is a little bit of history, the tiny Duchy of Luxembourg. Its capital, also called Luxembourg, has 100,000 inhabitants. It is easy for the driver to get lost there because of the one-way streets.

The size of the duchy, 999 square miles, is fairly easy to remember. It is dense with walking paths. Its people number 355,000. Luxembourg's castles and battlements reflect the wars of the past. In 1867 the great nations of Europe agreed to its neutrality but this did not stop a German takeover during World War II. Many young men who were conscripted into the German army deserted and joined fellow citizens in the resistance. The older generation remember those days well and do not especially welcome German tourists. Luxembourg is the co-capital of the European Common Market, headquarters of the Court of Justice of the European Communities, and the General Secretariat of the European Parliament.

West Germany (Federal Republic of Germany)

Divided after World War II, Germany became two nations—West Germany and East Germany. North Americans flying to West Germany are most likely to land in Frankfurt. Figure 8-11 shows Frankfurt as a hub with spokes radiating to other European cities and major airports throughout the world. Flight times to other German cities are less than an hour, to Paris a little over an hour, to London one hour and thirty-five minutes, and to New York eight and a half hours. Berlin, the former German capital, is surrounded by East Germany, but easily reached by the autobahn or plane.

Germany's rivers are important waterways. Bonn, the capital city, is near the Rhine River, principal river artery of the country. The Rhine begins as a brook in the Swiss Alps, flows through Lake Constance, and then north, forming the frontier between Germany and France before it crosses Germany and flows through Holland. River trips on the Rhine are popular with Europeans. The Elbe River reaches the North Sea at Hamburg, Germany's principal port. Across the base of the Jutland Peninsula the Kiel Canal connects the North Sea to the Baltic Sea. The Danube, longest river in Central Europe, links Germany and southeastern Europe. Picturesque villages and vineyards line the Moselle River as it flows north to join the Rhine.

Germany has excellent rail and road systems. The autobahns, the first superhighways, have no speed limits. Wise tourists stay out of the fast lanes unless they are going 90 miles an hour or faster. Europabus, run by the German Federal Railways, is a good way to see the countryside and to take tours of the castles in the Rhine-Main area and other scenic parks of Germany.

Nearly 20 million of Germany's 61.4 million people are concentrated in the large cities, of which the biggest are West Berlin, Hamburg, Munich, and Cologne. The country is about the size of Oregon.

Southern Germany presents a much more pleasant climate than that in northern Germany. Munich, the capital of Bavaria, which lies along the Austrian border, is the place in which 60 percent of all Germans would prefer to live. So too do a

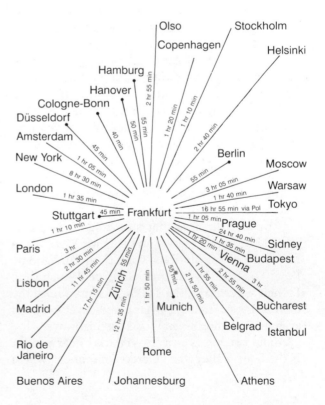

8-11. Frankfurt, Germany, as a travel hub.

number of foreign nationals. Two hundred thousand of the city's 1.2 million people are Turks, Yugoslavs, Italians, Greeks, American Spaniards, French, Britons, Japanese, and other non-German people.

Here Ludwig II built the fairytale castle of Neuschwanstein that is said to be the inspiration for Disneyland. Munich, is nicknamed *millionendorf*, "the village with a population of a million," because it is surrounded by fields and woods. Famous for its beer festival, Munich is also called the city of love of life.

The Netherlands

Despite the fact that the Netherlands has one of the highest population densities in the world, the people enjoy a high standard of living. Popularly known as Holland, the country is crossed by drainage canals, and its rivers are interconnected with artificial waterways. Dikes and dunes hold back the sea from the 40 percent of the land that is below sea level.

The capital and largest city, Amsterdam, is a major commercial and artistic center of Europe. The museums of the city house major collections of art. The city, which is built on piles, is crossed by 40 canals. Many of the city streets are lined with quaint, attractive houses. The city has many fine restaurants. An added attraction is that there are a number of Indonesian restaurants, Indonesia once having been under the control of Netherlands.

The country is a mecca for garden-minded tourists, who come to view the fields of fabled Dutch bulbs and other gardening attractions.

Switzerland

Switzerland is situated in south-central Europe, and two-thirds of the country is covered by mountains, lakes, or forests. The Alps, a mountain chain that runs approximately east and west through the southern part of the country, constitute about 60 percent of Switzerland's total area.

The Jura Mountains, a spur of the Alps, stretch from the southwest to the northwest and cover 10 percent more of the land area. In the remaining 30 percent, a plateau between the two ranges, Switzerland's large cities and industrial activity are concentrated.

Cog railroads and cable cars go to the middle heights of mountains, and there are well-defined paths to hike on. Comfortable huts are spotted throughout the mountains. The Matterhorn shares with Mt. Fuji in Japan the accolade, "the most photographed mountain in the world." The Jungfrau, 13,640 feet, is one of the most beautiful mountains anywhere. Just below its summit a restaurant and cafeteria entertain tourists above the clouds.

Think of an "in" place to ski and Switzerland leaps to mind: mountain village, lively inns, and unexcelled ski facilities. The cognoscenti choose the Swiss Alps not only for the skiing but for the civilized pleasures that go with a Swiss vacation. Where else can downhill skiers experience runs up to fourteen miles long? From Zermatt, for example, one can ski to Italy for lunch, then ski back to Zermatt in time for supper. St. Moritz and Gstad are internationally known ski centers.

Little Switzerland has three international gateway airports: Zurich, Geneva, and Basel. Switzerland is a little more than half the size of Maine, and nothing is very far from the main roads and railroads. Throughout the country travel is quick and highly scenic by car or train. The superb electrified rail system covers 3,000 miles. The Glacier Express is one of the most spectacular train rides to be found. (It is not very "express," since the train takes seven and a half hours to go 170 miles.) Running between Saint Moritz in southeastern Switzerland and Zermatt in the southwest, the train goes up and down and around and through; it moves through 90 tunnels, one going for nine miles through solid rock. On several steep slopes the engine is engaged to the track by rack and pinion.

All large Swiss towns have efficient bus systems with frequent schedules. In Geneva special bus lanes mean a bus from the airport is faster and cheaper than a cab, which can be expensive.

Americans traveling to Switzerland need have no language worries: most Swiss speak some English and are likely to understand German, Italian, and French as well. That is because Switzerland has German, French, and Italian areas. Lugano is in the Italian part; Geneva is in the French part; and Zurich is in the German part. A fourth language, Romansh, is spoken by a small group of people in eastern Switzerland and neighboring parts of Italy.

Switzerland is an armed camp. Unseen by the tourists are numerous guns and closed-off military depots. No fewer than 650,000 fighting troops, about 10 percent of the total population, can be mobilized within 48 hours. (A similar percentage applied to the United States would mean a military of 23.5 million.) Every bridge of any importance in Switzerland is marked for demolition, and someone is trained to blow it up on command. Three giant fortresses, continuously manned, are likened to underground ant colonies, forming networks of tunnels, caverns, bunkers, and surface installations. Each is spread through tens of square miles. As the Swiss put it, "Switzerland does not have an army. Switzerland is an army."

With a population of 400,000, Zurich is the nation's largest city and its leading banking and financial center. Geneva enjoys an international reputation for culture and sophistication and is home to the World Trade Center and the United Nations.

Geneva is also headquarters for more than 140 international organizations; the bureaucrats knew what they were doing when they selected the city. The Rhine River rises in the heart of Geneva as it leaves the Lake of Geneva. The city also is astride the winding river called the L'Arve and, as a backdrop, has the Alps, with Mt. Blanc the highest peak in Europe at 15,771 feet.

Basel, second largest of Swiss cities, is beside the Rhine River and like Zurich is a business and corporate headquarters city. Switzerland's capital is Bern.

Switzerland is one of the few industrialized nations that does not run a travel deficit (more money spent by nationals than is taken in from visitors). Tourism brings Switzerland about $3 billion a year. The Swiss National Tourist office headquartered in Zurich maintains twenty-four offices abroad.

The six million Swiss are hardworking, tidy, and thrifty, so much so that their per capita income is substantially greater than that in the United States. The same qualities apply to Switzerland's tiny neighbor Liechtenstein, and with the same results.

Liechtenstein

Wedged between the Swiss and Austrian Alps is the tiny Principality of Liechtenstein, fifteen miles long and a little over eight miles wide. Atop one of its mountains, Naafkopf Peak, the visitor can see Lake Constance in Germany and Switzerland as well as parts of Austria and Liechtenstein itself. It is the only spot in the world from which the tourist can view four countries at once.

Liechtenstein has the highest per capita income in Europe. Moreover, it has no jail, no army, no airport, no divorce, and practically no taxes. Its industry makes, among other things, pillows and quilts and false teeth. Eight thousand foreign corporations have nominal headquarters in the city, mainly to avoid home taxes and to have a place to launder money.

The ruling family bought the country to acquire the title of prince that went with it. Liechtenstein has eleven communities, each at one time ruled by an earl. Now it is a constitutional monarchy with a democratic parliament. The ruling prince has a collection of 1,400 art masterpieces, many displayed in his 124-room castle perched above the capital, Valduz. Each year the Prince hosts a huge party for the people; they in turn invite him and his family to an annual party.

Austria

Think of Austria and you think of Mozart and music, skiing, *zimmer frei* (bed and breakfast), the architecture of the Austro-Hungarian Empire, and hearty food. The three principal tourist cities are Vienna, Salzburg, and Innsbruck, which are linked by excellent bus and rail service.

The 7.6 million Austrians are noted for their cleanliness, punctuality and hard work. Tourists applaud those Austrian housewives who take in summer guests (mostly Germans) for their neat homes and their flower boxes overflowing with blooming geraniums.

Three-fourths of Austria is mountainous; much of it, like Switzerland, is as well maintained as alpine meadows. Scenic finger lakes lie to the north and east of Salzburg. Bavarian Germany is just north, and Lake Constance is shared with Switzerland.

Much of the charm of Salzburg ("salt town") is due to its former rulers, princes of the Catholic church, who believed as much in the pleasures of life as they did religion. The old town of Salzburg wisely prohibits auto traffic and with its cathedral and palace is an unforgettable place. Travel in Salzburg is by trolley.

Vienna is nearly everyone's romantic city, with coffee shops and the 2,600-room Hofburg Castle where Austrian officialdom presides. Like the city of Washington, D.C., Vienna is built in concentric rings, the center of which is St. Stephens Cathedral. Music lovers go to great trouble to secure a seat at a performance at the Opera House. Seats at the numerous coffee houses are easy to come by, however, and the justly famous Viennese pastry goes down just as easily. Three imperial palaces grace the city. Schonnbrunn Palace in the city's outskirts has been described as "the purest realization of the melody of Austrian baroque." Half the size of the Hofburg Palace in the heart of Vienna, it has 1,441 rooms.

Tourists line up to see the famous white Lippianzer horses practice or perform at the Spanish Riding School in Vienna. Formal performances are sold out months in advance. Tourists also line up to see the crown jewels that date to the time of Austria's empire, which was disbanded following Austria's defeat in World War I.

Trolley-car travel in Vienna is fast, efficient, and inexpensive. One line reaches an old part of the city, Grindzig, where violins and accordions play to entertain guests drinking wine served in mugs. Nearby are vineyards that are part of Austria's wine-growing industry.

Italy

A familiar comment about Italy is that it is shaped like a boot, the toe pointed to kick the island of Sicily, also belonging to Italy (see Figure 8-12). The country is long and thin, the north on a level with Quebec, the southern tip with North Carolina. Northern Italy shares the Alps with Switzerland and may experience three months of snow while Sicily basks in a subtropical climate.

The Germans are the most numerous of Italy's visitors. The French come second, and U.S. visitors are third. Venice on the Adriatic attracts the most tourists. Rome, to which "all roads lead," in central Italy, is second. Florence, directly north of Rome, is third. During the summer Venice entertains 100,000 visitors a day, the majority boarding a *vaporetto*, a 150-seat boat that carries passengers up and down the Grand Canal, to view the

8-12. Major tourist destinations in Italy.

architectural wonders of the city. Venice's two-and-half miles of brick and marble homes and palaces rest on millions of wooden pilings driven into the mud of the sea. For years the museum city was slowly sinking into the sea but then was rescued by massive donations from abroad. History permeates the city and recalls the days when Venice, not England, ruled the sea, where 16,000 men labored in the dockyards and could build an armed galley each day.

About an hour away from Venice, at the base of the Italian Alps, is Verona, famed in Shakespeare's *Romeo and Juliet*. With the largest extant Roman amphitheater, which seats 25,000, it offers an open-air setting for opera, a Shakespeare festival, ballets, and concerts.

Rome, which is second to Venice in attracting visitors, is Italy's best-known city, once capital of the mighty Roman Empire. Rome completely surrounds Vatican City, which is only 108.7 acres in size, but which attracts more visitors than most large nations. St. Peter's Basilica overpowers the viewer, aesthetically and in sheer size, the largest and most awesome church in the world. Reminders of Rome's past are everywhere—the Colosseum, the Forum, and the Pantheon.

Rome is the principal air gateway to Italy, via the Leonardo da Vinci Airport. It is reached by a circular road, the Grand Raddardo Anulare, twelve kilometers from the city center, which allows motorists to bypass the central city or enter it at convenient points. Roman auto drivers seem to think they are charioteers careening around the dozens of monuments remaining from ancient Rome. Four of Europe's superhighways extend into Italy, and the Italian autostradas (superhighways) are toll roads connecting the different parts of the country. The Stazione Termini, the main railway station serving Rome, is Europe's largest.

Ranking third as a tourist attraction is Florence, the premier city of Renaissance Italy. Florence is famed for its magnificent art and its Renaissance architecture and is as crowded as Venice during the summer months. To the north of Florence are industrial Milan and Turin. Another large city, Naples in the south, attracts visitors to the ruins of Pompeii, a Roman city buried in A.D. 79 by the eruption of Mt. Vesuvius. The Italian Riviera bordering the Mediterranean coast is a geographical continuation of the French Riviera.

Another attraction for tourists is the wonderful Italian food. Italian wines are also a favorite of many visitors.

Scandinavia

Denmark, Norway, and Sweden, and sometimes Finland, Iceland, and the Faroe Islands, are collectively called Scandinavia. All have high standards of living, including health care and education, among the highest in the world. Together their population is not as big as that of Mexico City. All the countries experience a travel deficit, because the amount of money spent by residents traveling abroad is more than the amount of money spent by visitors visiting their countries. Visitors to Scandinavia are likely to fly Scandinavian Airlines, a joint venture owned by Norway, Sweden, and Denmark. U.S. passports are required, but visas are not needed. Copenhagen, Denmark, is the hub city and transfer point for much of the air travel to Scandinavia from America and Britain.

Don't be surprised to see cars driving around Sweden and Norway with their headlights on during the daytime. In 1967 a law was passed in Sweden that switched driving on the left side of the road to driving on the right side. Since there was concern that the change would cause accidents, a temporary rule required drivers to turn on their lights even during the day. Because casualties were reduced, the practice of leaving headlights on became law.

Scandinavian schools require English as a second language. The bilingual skills of the people add to the ease of visiting the region.

Denmark

This small and charming kingdom consists of a peninsula and more than 450 islands of which only a hundred are populated. The low-lying countryside is a biker's paradise during the summer. Copenhagen is the capital, with 1.7 million people, a third of the country's total; it is located on the island of Sjælland. Jutland is a peninsula, extending north and sharing a southern boundary with Germany. Only a few miles of the Öresund, a strait off the Baltic Sea, separate Helsingör in northern Denmark from Halsingbörg in southern Sweden. Danish food is excellent, and the hospitality of the people is notable.

Sweden

Stockholm, Sweden's capital and largest city, is the location of its legislature and the royal palace. Sometimes called the Venice of the North, Stockholm's 700,000 people reside on twenty islands with water surrounding them. The water is so clean that salmon can be caught in the heart of the city. A leading tourist attraction is a preserved warship, the *Wasa*, which had the distinction of sinking on the occasion of its launching in 1628. It sailed a total of 300 meters and then foundered in Stockholm's harbor. Raised from the mud between 1959 and 1961, it is now a museum.

One of Stockholm's islands is graced by Millesgarden, a garden of sculptures in which the figures seem to fly off into space, in sharp contrast to Oslo's famous sculpture garden, Vigeland, in which the figures are blocky and earthbound, depicting humanity's struggle in rising from an evolutionary past.

Göteborg, Sweden's second largest city, is the home of the Volvo manufacturing plant. The city is connected by a narrow canal, the Gota canal. The 347-mile trip by canal to Sweden's west coast takes three days.

Norway

Norway is graced by magnificent geographical features. The fjords, which are long, narrow, deep inlets, wind in from the sea between steep cliffs and slopes. There are also inland fjords nestling between high mountains. Some of these fjords seem especially made for cruise ships, which appear during the long, sunlit days of summer. Norway also has one of the most spectacular train rides in Europe, running in an east-west direction over a mountain range between Bergen and Oslo.

Finland

About the size of England and Scotland, Finland has 4.5 million people and lies alongside Russia. The countryside resembles that of northern Minnesota. Generally it is flat, with dozens of lakes surrounded by forests and farmland. Helsinki, the capital, is noted for its many forested parks within the city. It is located on the Gulf of Finland. Relatively few Americans visit the country except as part of tours or on the way to Russia flying Finnair.

Iceland

Iceland is better known to Americans, partly because of the American airbase near Reykjavik, the capital and only sizable city in the country. Another reason for Iceland's familiarity to many Americans is that Icelandic Air has underpriced New York to Europe flights for a number of years. Iceland is an interesting country geologically, because of its volcanic activity.

Greenland

A country for the travel connoisseur who enjoys the natural beauty of fjords and icebergs, Greenland has a cool to frigid climate.

The native Greenlander, the Inuits, create beautiful and imaginative figurines from stone, whalebone, and walrus tusks. They also make sealskin clothing, handbags, and miniature kayaks.

From the air, Greenland, the world's largest island, appears to be one big chunk of ice. An ice sheet that is about 14,000 feet deep in places covers more than four-fifths of the land area. The small fringe of land on the west coast is where most of the population resides. The average summer temperature is about 50°F, but it is changeable.

Spain

Spain, the most popular tourist country in Europe in terms of visitor numbers, welcomed 51 million tourists in 1987. Most of the visitors are other Europeans seeking sun and a relatively inexpensive vacation. Many come in chartered planes to live in the coastal towns of Costa del Sol and Costa Brava, inexpensive relative to the French and Italian coasts. Spain, which shares the Iberian Peninsula with Portugal, also includes the Balearic Islands in the Mediterranean (Mallorca, Ibiza, Formentera, Minorca) about an hour's flight from Barcelona, and the Canary Islands off the northwest coast of Africa. The map, Figure 8-13, shows the air gateways and major roads leading into Spain from Portugal and France.

The Pyrenees help define Spain by barricading it from the rest of Europe to the north. Some peaks rise to over 10,800 feet. The Principality of Andorra, only 15 miles across, lies on the border between France and Spain, toward the eastern end of the Pyrenees. The Strait of Gibraltar, the passage connecting the Atlantic and Mediterranean, is about 8 miles wide at its narrowest point, a convenient ferry trip between Spain and Morocco.

Madrid, the capital of Spain, has a population of over 3 million. It is a modern city, but it also has historic sections with narrow, winding streets. Barcelona follows Madrid in population. Museum towns such as Toledo and Avila are more interesting for the historical-minded. Seville is a tourist center and is the site of Spain's largest cathedral. The Alhambra, on the outskirts of Granada, bespeaks southern Spain's Moorish heritage. Cordova has a unique architectural feature, a cathedral built within a mosque. Possibly the most awe-inspiring attraction in Spain is not promoted by the national tourist office. "El Valle de los Caidos," or the Valley of the Fallen, was chiseled out of solid rock by thousands of Republican prisoners, who were the losers in Spain's terrible civil war which took place in the 1930s. Hundreds of soldiers who died in that war are buried there high in the mountains, a spectacular but eerie site.

Many of Spain's castles have been converted into inns called *paradores* ("stopping places") by the Spanish government. The experience takes the tourist back to the Middle Ages.

Portugal

West of Spain is Portugal, which comprises about 15 percent of the Iberian Peninsula. Portugal is one of the poorest of the Western European nations and one of the most interesting touristically. The roads are good; the castles and palaces, some of which take guests, are built-in tourist attractions. Lisbon, the capital, is a beautifully laid out city on the Tagus River, which feeds into the Atlantic Ocean.

South of Lisbon is the Algarve region, which has a Mediterranean-type climate that can be hot in the summer. Oporto, home of port wine, is on the Atlantic, to the north of Lisbon. The island of Madeira is a favorite resort destination of the British.

For those who want "aristocratic" accommodations Portugal offers 200 country homes through the organization Turismo de Habitação, a national program designed to boost tourism in less visited places. These private homes, many of them fazendas owned by Portuguese nobility, are reserved through regional tourist offices or the Portuguese National Tourist Office in Lisbon. The "super-deluxe" category are estates that produce rave reviews from guests.

Politically part of Portugal are the Azores, an archipelago of nine main islands scattered in the North Atlantic, between 700 and 1,200 miles west of Lisbon. The islands have a mild climate year round and are a place to enjoy dramatic landscapes and an abundance of bird life.

8-13. Air gateways and major roads leading into Spain.

Greece

The ne plus ultra for travelers interested in classical Greece, Athens is home to about four million of Greece's total population of over nine million people. After visitors to Athens have settled in, they are likely to look for the highest point in the city, the Acropolis, the site of the Parthenon, a temple dedicated to the goddess Athena. Ancient Athens was built around the Acropolis. Sadly, modern Athens is so smog-ridden that the air is accelerating the deterioration of the ancient buildings.

Modern Athens is a bustling place, which spreads out to reach the port of Piraeus, embarkation point for most Aegean Island cruises. Cruise ships sail from island to island, the most popular stops being Delos, Mykonos, Santorini (also called Thera), Rhodes, Crete, and Corfu.

Altogether there are some 1,400 islands, 200 of which are inhabited by small farmers, fisher folk, and those catering to tourists. The island of Rhodes has fortifications surrounding its old city, which were built in the fifteenth and sixteenth centuries as a defense against the Turks. The island of Delos is a famous archaeological site. Several other Aegean islands have museums.

From Athens the visitor can travel by car or bus to Marathon, namesake of long-distance running, where the news of a victory over the Persians in 490 B.C. was carried to Athens by a runner. The Temple of Poseidon, god of the sea, is 44 miles southeast of Athens. Or the visitor can travel 100 miles west to Delphi and perhaps learn the future from the oracle. Olympia, the Peloponnesus Peninsula, which forms the southern part of Greece, was the site of the first Olympic games, which were held in 776 B.C. Today Olympia is the home of a museum of Olympic Games and of an international Olympic Academy.

Geographically Greece belongs to Europe, forming the southern extremity of the Balkan peninsula. Summers can be extremely hot, especially in some of the narrow streets of Athens.

EASTERN EUROPE

The few tourists who visit the Soviet Union visit the European part, so that country is included with Eastern Europe. The bulk of travel in Eastern Europe (Bulgaria, Czechoslovakia, East Germany, Hungary, Poland, Rumania, Albania, and Yugoslavia) has been within and between these Eastern Bloc countries and the Soviet Union. Visitors from the rest of Europe and North America have increased whenever political tensions have eased. New hotels are desperately needed in the area. In 1988 Moscow had a total of only 10,000 beds; other leading Eastern Bloc capitals were also short of beds to meet the summer season demand. A promising note: several international chains are being allowed to manage or co-manage joint venture hotels. Inter-Continental, a subsidiary of Japan's Saison Group, the French chains Accor and Pullman, and the American chains Marriott, Radisson, Sheraton, Ramada, and Holiday Inns International have management contracts or joint venture deals in Eastern Europe.

The World Tourism organization map (Figure 8-14) shows the Eastern Bloc countries. Hungary leads in the number of international tourist arrivals, and their numbers are expected to increase when Hungary becomes a part of Eurail. Yugoslavia has long been popular with the Germans and British, who have favored Dubrovnik, the medieval city on the Adriatic Sea. Rumania, Bulgaria, and the Soviet Union have sizable summer resort destinations on the Black Sea, but these are used mainly by their own peoples.

East Germany (German Democratic Republic)

Following World War II, East Germany became part of the communist bloc. The notorious wall dividing West Berlin from East Germany is not a real barrier for tourists, most of whom visit East Berlin as day-trippers. East Germany has a population of 17 million, and its capital is East Berlin. Travel prices, including hotel rooms, are much less than in West Germany. Principal cities of historical and architectural interest are Potsdam, Leipzig, Dresden, and Weimar.

East Germany has built a luxury hotel, and Western travelers are welcomed. The Baltic sea-coast attracts domestic travelers to its resort

8-14. Major tourist resorts of Europe and the Mediterranean.

towns. The government does not publish tourism statistics though it is obvious that travel between East and West Germany has increased sharply since 1985.

Hungary

Hungary is probably the most sophisticated country in the Eastern Bloc, the sophistication left over from pre-World War II days. Opera-goers in Budapest, the capital, arrive in dark suits and gowns, more formally dressed than opera-goers in New York City. Straddling the Danube River—Buda on one side, Pest on the other—Budapest stretches along about 18 miles of the river. Most non-communist visitors to the city come by train or plane by way of Vienna. Hungarian food is delicious, and the city has thousands of restaurants. However, those run by the government offer indifferent service.

Lake Balaton, which is the largest lake in Europe, is a leading resort area.

THE SOVIET UNION

As the major rival of the United States, the Soviet Union holds special interest for North Americans. Almost all travel arrangements within that country are made by Intourist, the government tourist organization. In operation since 1929, Intourist books all major hotels for visitors. Every visitor coming to the USSR must have hotel space booked before applying for a Soviet entry visa.

Americans are traveling to Russia in increasing numbers, almost all via tours originating in New York City or in London. The tour groups usually first land in Moscow and then travel to Kiev or Leningrad, or else go south to Georgia and the Black Sea, Russia's resort playground.

Moscow has a huge tourist hotel called the Cosmos. The Leningrad is a 730 room property that overlooks the Neva River, which runs through Leningrad. Intourist directly controls and manages a number of hotels, those which are set aside for foreign visitors. Municipally controlled hotels are mostly for Soviet citizens. Soviet citizens pay a nominal rate, six to nine rubles, to stay in Soviet

hotels. Trade Unions have their own resort hotels, more than 300 of them in the Republic of Georgia, which borders the Black Sea. Intourist negotiates with Aeroflot, the national airline, for tour seats, and with the national railroad for train berths for use in package tours.

Service personnel display a range of friendliness to visitors, from a glum and stony-faced demeanor to one that is open and eager to please. The latter are a small minority. Questions may be answered courteously, perfunctorily, or abruptly.

Bureaucratic complications abound in Russia. When arriving in the Moscow airport and going through passport control, each visitor is subject to a stony stare by an immigration official that can last up to five minutes, the official supposedly comparing the real face with the passport photo. Also, any gold that is being brought into the country must be declared. Peter S. Goldburg, a travel writer, declares that the body of a British tourist who died while touring the Soviet Union was delivered to the British Embassy in Moscow, minus the gold fillings in the man's teeth. The Soviet explanation was that the man had not declared the gold when he entered the country.

Moscow

Red Square, meaning "beautiful square," lies in the center of Moscow. One-half mile long and paved with cobblestones, it is situated on a hill overlooking the Moskva River, which winds through the city.

The most colorful of the buildings facing the Square is the ancient St. Basil's Cathedral, which is now a museum. The cathedral has nine towers that are topped by onion shaped domes. Designs composed of brilliant shades of red, yellow, green, and gold decorate the domes. At the northwestern side of the Square stands the Historical Museum. On the eastern side is located the largest department store in the country, called GUM. The two most famous structures in the Soviet Union are located on the western side of the Square. The first is the tomb of Lenin, which is made of polished dark-red granite and resembles a flat-topped pyramid. The other structure is the Kremlin, the

Center of the Soviet Union's government. The high wall of the Kremlin is about 1½ miles around. Watchtowers rise high on top of the wall, five of which are topped with huge red stars that glow in the night. Within the wall are several pale-yellow palaces and four cathedrals with golden domes. Over 800 years ago a prince built a wooden fortress on the spot where the Kremlin is located, and later the town of Moscow grew around it.

THE CARIBBEAN

Winter playground and cruising waters for the eastern seaboard of the United States and Canada, the Caribbean Basin offers a subtropical climate in winter, an exotic culture, and a choice of sandy beaches and an unpolluted sea. After Europe, the Caribbean region attracts the most American visitors. Its waters are the most popular for cruising in the world. In 1987, the Caribbean Research Center in Barbados reported that the Caribbean attracted more than nine million visitors, including those on cruise ships.

Technically, the Caribbean Sea is an arm of the Atlantic Ocean, bounded on the north and east by the West Indies, on the south by South America, and on the west by Central America. The Gulf of Mexico merges with the Caribbean. The West Indies form an arc of islands stretching south from Cuba. Also included in the region are the Bahamas because they are so similar in culture and climate to the rest of the area.

Named for the Carib Indians who dominated the region until the coming of the Spaniards, the area once generated sugar fortunes based on slavery. Today, tourism is the big business.

Climate and topography favor tourism in most of the Caribbean. A general pattern of sunshine, easterly breezes, and puffy clouds prevails. The rainy season brings brief daily rain but does not really interrupt tourist activity. The hurricane season in the fall mars the otherwise equable climate. Because of the constant wind direction, most islands have a windward and a leeward side.

The windward side is more likely to be lush, while the leeward side is drier, especially if mountains are present to force the air up and cool it, precipitating rain.

Although the Caribbean is often seen as all of a piece, this view is only partly true. Geographically and climatically, the Caribbean islands can be tied together; politically, culturally, and economically, the Caribbean is more collage than community. The area is most notably divided between the British Commonwealth states and territories and those that are historically Hispanic, French, or Dutch. In much of the area the dichotomy between blacks and whites, with their roots in slavery, permeates and complicates the differences. Three-fourths of the Caribbean people are at least partially descended from African slaves. The other quarter includes direct descendants of European colonists and of East Indians and Chinese who came as indentured laborers after slavery was abolished in the nineteenth century. Three independent Caribbean countries—Cuba, Haiti, and the Dominican Republic—contain three-fourths of the region's population.

Travel to and within the Caribbean Basin is relatively easy by air. Major airlines fly nonstop from Miami and other Eastern cities to San Juan's international airport. The large Puerto Rican population of New York City supports high density traffic between that city and San Juan. Numerous other direct flights come into the Basin from Europe. Smaller planes provide service between islands. The flight schedules change seasonally, with the heaviest traffic being scheduled for the high winter.

The Bahamas, about 1,100 miles from New York City, can be reached in a little over three hours. Flying time to Puerto Rico and Jamaica, 1,600 miles away, is a little over three hours.

The Caribbean waters are the most popular in the world for cruising. Most cruises begin in Miami or Port Everglades, Florida. A typical cruise sails first to Nassau in the Bahamas where the passengers visit the straw market near the docks, have their names embroidered on a straw basket or hat, and walk around the small downtown section of town. The may take in the police band that marches during the changing of the guard at Government House or visit the casinos on Paradise Island, reached by bridge from Nassau.

San Juan, Puerto Rico, is one of the layover ports. Old San Juan has two gigantic forts, El Morro and San Cristóbal, that are well preserved. Both are national monuments. St. Thomas is another favorite cruise stop; its capital, Charlotte Amalie, is mostly a giant shopping arcade featuring cameras, jewelry, watches, linens, and liquor.

Kingston in Jamaica, Curaçao, and Aruba may be on the itinerary. On shipboard the passengers enjoy a cocoon-like existence, clustered around a small pool, playing games that elsewhere would be considered juvenile, gambling, drinking, and eating— breakfasts, luncheons, buffets, teas, dinners, and midnight snacks. Women usually outnumber men, sometimes two to one. The longer the cruise, the older the passenger group.

Grenada and its string of neighboring islands, the Grenadines, is one of the finest of boating centers. Sailors are always within sight of another small island. The same is true for the Virgin Islands. Many yachts are available for rent in St. Thomas and Grenada. By renting, the owner can write off costs as a business expense. Smaller boats can be rented "bare-boat," stocked only with food and liquor and sailed by the people renting the boat.

Cuba

Cuba is the largest Caribbean island, containing more land than all of the other Caribbean islands combined. Only ninety miles from Florida, it was the destination of the first "overseas" commercial flights from the United States. Havana, the capital of Cuba, was the big Caribbean tourist destination until the corrupt government was overthrown by Fidel Castro. Once Castro proclaimed a communist state there, most of the managerial and wealthy class left for the United States. The ten million who stayed seem satisfied with their communist government, especially since they receive millions in aid from Russia and a guaranteed market for their sugar. The island now is of

little tourist interest, for U.S. residents must have special permission from the government to go there.

The Bahamas

The Bahamas receives 70 percent of its income from tourism and gets more visitors than any of the Caribbean islands. The soil supports few crops, and most of the islands have limited fresh water. What the Bahamas has is some of the most beautiful beaches anywhere, a mostly benign climate, proximity to Florida, and good air connections to the major cities of the East Coast.

Though there are said to be a hundred islands in the Bahamas, only a few are inhabited. Nassau, the country's capital, has a majority of the population. Eleuthera and Grand Bahama are the other islands with substantial populations. A big attraction to visitors are the casinos on Paradise Island, Nassau, and Grand Bahama.

Some of the Bahamian cays are known transit points for drugs, especially cocaine produced in Bolivia, processed in Colombia and smuggled into the United States. At least one, Norman Cay, was at one time an armed camp with machine-gun armed guards employed by the smugglers.

Spanish Wells, once the watering spot for Spanish Galleons, is a community of 1,300 people who live in a Lilliputian world of their own just off north Eleuthera. About half the town is old New England, the other half, South Florida masonry. The old part of town could be lifted from Martha's Vineyard in New England; its architectural style was probably brought by loyalists who migrated to the island during the Revolutionary War.

Jamaica

About eighty-five miles south of Cuba lies Jamaica, with two million people, the large majority being black. Jamaica is a sovereign nation and a member of the British Commonwealth. Kingston, the capital, with a population of 570,000, is hot and humid. Most of the island is a mountainous plateau. The Blue Mountains, which rise to a height of seventy-four hundred feet, produce one of the world's most distinctive coffees. Montego Bay, with its own international airport, is one of the most popular resorts in the Caribbean. Other tourist centers with a number of first-class hotels are at Ocho Rios, Negril, and Port Antonio. Jamaica's potential as a travel destination has been marred by political disputes.

Cayman Islands

The Cayman Islands, a British Crown Colony of 17,000 people, lie 470 miles south of Miami. The Caymans offer one of the best models for tourist development found worldwide. The three islands that make up the colony (the total area is less than the borough of Brooklyn, New York) have several historical and geographical advantages. Beautiful beaches, one seven miles long, quiet bays, and year-round water temperatures of between eighty and eighty-five degrees have helped keep annual room occupancy close to 85 percent. The Caymans barely stick their heads above the water. A large number of the accommodations are condominiums that have proved excellent investments to the Americans who own them.

The islands were never bedeviled by slavery because most early arrivals were shipwrecked English, Irish, and Scots, deserters from Cromwell's army in Jamaica, or buccaneers hiding from the Royal Navy. Today about 40 percent of the residents are black. Subsistence farming, fishing, and catching turtles were the principal occupations until after 1960, when tourism and tax-haven banking came along. Hundreds of banks and corporations have offices in Georgetown and, emulating the Swiss, arrange for secret bank accounts to avoid and evade national taxes.

Haiti and the Dominican Republic

Hispaniola, to the east and slightly south of Cuba, contains two nations—Haiti, which occupies the western third of the island, and the Dominican Republic, which has 4.5 million people. Haiti's capital is Port-au-Prince, and the language is French. The capital of the Dominican Republic is Santo Domingo, and the language is Spanish. Haiti's people are almost all blacks; the Dominican Republic's are 73 percent mulatto, with white and black minorities. Haiti is mountainous, dominated by three mountain ranges; the Dominican Republic has Pico Duarte, at 10,407 feet, the highest in the Caribbean.

Puerto Rico

Puerto Rico, just east of Hispaniola, is a major Caribbean destination and the international airport in San Juan, the capital, is an air transit point for the Caribbean. Miles of beautiful beaches, comfortable swimming temperatures, and easterly tradewinds attract tourists; however, ambivalence toward tourists and tourism by many residents make Puerto Rico less attractive.

San Juan, a city of 435,000, has first-class hotels and stores. In addition to its historical sites it entertains visitors with revues and casinos like those in Las Vegas.

Although Puerto Rico is among the wealthiest of the Caribbean islands, its per capita income is about half that of the poorest in the United States. Unemployment is at least 20 percent; half the population is eligible for food stamps. Sugar cane, once the main source of income, is now subsidized by the government and is produced at a net loss.

The government has had some success in spreading tourism to other parts of the island. Small family-operated inns can be found in various places around the island and are government protected. An hour and forty-five minutes by ferry from the village of Fajardo is Culebra, a dependent island. It is being promoted as a haven for snorkelers, scuba divers, and sailors.

U.S. Virgin Islands

The U.S. Virgin Islands, numbering about fifty, lie east of Puerto Rico, and 1,000 miles southeast of Miami. The major islands—St. Thomas, St. Croix, St. John—are mountainous with many beaches and bays. Charlotte Amalie on St. Thomas (population about 100,000), the capital, is the most frequent cruise ship stop-over. St. Thomas is a vibrant, relatively prosperous island known for its night life. The former Dutch proprietorship is still evident in the architecture.

A boat trip away from Charlotte Amalie is St. John, location for the beautiful Rock resort, Caneel Bay Plantation. About half of the island is the Virgin Islands National Park, donated to the U.S. government by Lawrence Rockefeller. Included in the park are breathtaking underwater acres, considered by many the region's best snorkeling and scuba grounds. Cinnamon Bay, a highly regarded campground in the national park, has concrete cabins and tent sites.

British Virgin Islands

Not far away are the British Virgin Islands with Roadtown, the capital, on Tortola Island. Of the thirty-six islands only sixteen are inhabited; they comprise a long chain of coral and volcanic islands. Robert Louis Stevenson took the name of one of the islands, Treasure Island, for his classic novel. On Virgin Gorda is the beautiful and luxurious Rock resort of Little Dix Bay. The island is also known for the Baths, mammoth boulder formations creating caves and grottos, pools and coves at the edge of the sea.

St. Kitts, Nevis, Antigua, and Montserrat

Stringing southeast in an arc from the Virgin Islands are St. Kitts, Nevis, Antigua, and Montserrat. All are connected with the British government and receive aid from Britain. Antigua is known for its beautiful little Nelson's harbor, headquarters for Lord Nelson when he commanded the fleet in that part of the world. Tourism is its major source of income. Montserrat is at a disadvantage touristically because of its rugged mountains and lack of white sand beaches.

Guadeloupe and Martinique

The largest of the French-related islands in the Caribbean are Guadeloupe in the Leeward Islands and Martinique in the Windward Islands. The people, most of whom are blacks, are French citizens. Shaped like a butterfly in flight, Guadeloupe is made up of the two larger islands, Gran-Terre and Basse-Terre, and smaller islands. The former is relatively flat with a few rolling hills; Basse-Terre is mountainous with volcanoes rising to a height of 4,812 feet. Around the island are beautiful sandy beaches, three of which are set aside for nude bathing. Administratively, Guadeloupe is a department of France, and the French language, cuisine, currency, and customs are in use. Like Guadeloupe, Martinique is a rugged volcanic island. It also is a department of France.

St. Maarten/St. Martin, St. Barthélemy, and Saba

North of Guadeloupe are St. Maarten/St. Martin and St. Barthélemy. The island of St. Martin is spelled two ways for a reason. Half is Dutch controlled; the other half is a dependency of Guadeloupe and its people are French-speaking. Philipsburg, the Dutch capital, is a shopper's haven where international goods can be purchased at duty-free prices. The French capital, Marigot, is smaller and quainter.

A charming little island, St. Barthélemy is reachable from St. Martin by plane. The plane lands in a sheep pasture with only feet to spare before the runway gives way to the ocean. The harbor of its tiny town is picture-postcard beautiful where the visitor may tire of eating clawless lobsters because they are so abundant.

Not far away and reachable by a little plane is Saba, five square miles of nearly vertical landscape that offers lots of scenery and no beaches. A Dutch island, the language is English. Activities offered are horseback riding, burro riding, and hiking tours. Saba is dominated by a 3,000-foot extinct volcano. It is almost completely populated by women, children, and old men, because the young men must go abroad to earn a living.

St. Lucia and St. Vincent

Farther southward are the islands of St. Lucia and St. Vincent. St. Lucia is a mountainous island,

and Soufrière, the world's only drive-in volcano, has sulphuric fumes bubbling in its crater. Three of its peaks attract tourists: the two Pitons, 2,400 feet and 2,600 feet respectively, are landmarks for sailors and afford mountain climbing to the visitor. St. Vincent is the arrowroot capital of the world, the starchy root that has made a comeback in world trade since it is now used in making computer paper. In the capital, Kingstown, arcaded buildings line the streets and local crafts are sold. The Botanical Gardens are the oldest in the hemisphere and contain the famous breadfruit tree brought there from Tahiti by Captain Bligh, famous in the mutiny on the *Bounty*. Other sights are the ruins of Fort Charlotte overlooking the harbor, the fertile Marriaque Valley, and sixty-foot Baleine Falls.

Grenada

Swinging west, Grenada and the Grenadines continue the West Indian arc of islands. St. George, capital of Grenada, is a major yachting center for the Caribbean. The Grenadines form a chain of low-lying islands, perfect for the yachtsman to sail from one to another. The land grows cloves, nutmeg, mace, and cinnamon. Grenada is one of the loveliest of the Windwards; its Grand Anse Beach is two miles of pristine sand, while inland are dense forests and steep mountains.

Barbados

Barbados, about 200 miles north and east of Trinidad, is quite British. Its population of 300,000 crowds the 166 square-mile island, which depends upon sugar and tourism for its livelihood. Mostly flat, the Caribbean side has some beautiful, calm beaches.

Trinidad and Tobago

Sixteen miles north of the South American country of Venezuela are Trinidad and Tobago, completing the West Indian arc of islands. The two islands are separated by a twenty-one-mile channel. Tobago is sleepy if compared to lively Trin-idad. Both islands invite birdwatchers; Trinidad's bird sanctuary in the Saroni Swamp is well known. Those who go to Tobago also want tropical beaches without people. Trinidad gets its income from oil and industry as well as tourism; its Pitch Lake is made of tar that has been used for roads in all parts of the world. Port-of-Spain, with a multiracial population of 200,000, is the noisy, bustling capital of Trinidad. Trinidad is one of the Caribbean countries with a sizable East Indian population—about one-third of the people.

Netherlands Antilles

The Netherlands Antilles are an odd assortment of little Caribbean islands, two groups of three islands each. The two groups are 550 miles apart. The ABC Group—Aruba, Bonaire, and Curaçao—lies off the northwest coast of Venezuela. The other three—Saint Martin, Saint Eustatius, and Saba—are about 220 miles east of Puerto Rico. All have a maritime tropical climate blessed with constant northeast tradewinds. The islands have no agricultural value and so were largely spared the horrors of slavery.

Aruba is a dry, sandy strip of golden beaches, more desertlike than tropical. Its duty-free capital of Oranjestad invites shoppers, modern resorts offer night life and gambling. All hotels are government-owned.

Curaçao, the largest of the Netherlands Antilles, is a desertlike island with limited swimming beaches. Its capital, Willemstad, is very "Dutch" in architectural style.

Bonaire is a bird island, home to 145 species. The salt beds at the southern tip of the island, with one of the world's largest flamingo colonies, are a major tourist attraction. There are several resorts as well as rich scuba and snorkeling reefs. Part of Bonaire's income comes from Holland.

Bermuda

Bermuda is a special travel destination for several reasons. Its seven main interconnected islands have remarkable natural beauty with Caribbean characteristics and are located 650 miles east of North Carolina. The land area is small; greater New York City is fifteen times larger. New York City is 774 miles to the northeast; London more than 3,000 miles away.

Because it can be easily reached by air from the northeastern United States, Bermuda is highly popular with vacationers; it receives close to a half million of them annually. Tourism is the principal business. A self-governing colony of about 60,000 people, Bermuda has a governor appointed by the Queen of England. Blacks constitute about two-thirds of the population.

Bermuda's government seeks to attract affluent visitors, those with an income over $50,000 a year. The tourist office says, "We are not interested in the Coca-Cola and hamburger market." The islands have attracted a number of permanent residents from Britain, partly because of being a tax haven.

Unlike the Caribbean region, Bermuda has little or no evidence of poverty.

The tourist industry has cleverly promoted springtime in Bermuda in the form of a series of college weeks. Consequently, spring weekends are jammed with college students from the eastern seaboard of the United States. College weeks are scheduled anywhere from mid-March to the end of April, depending upon the date of the Easter weekend. Other promotional events are a Goodwill Golf Tournament and activities related to fishing, tennis, dog shows, bridge, amateur radio competitions, and yachting.

Familiarization trips for travel agents, begun in 1973, place agents in groups of thirty. They stay at different hotels, moving to a different hotel every four days.

Hamilton, Paget, and St. Georges are the only villages, all quaintly English. More than a hundred resorts offer a variety of accommodation: large and small hotels, cottage colonies, housekeeping apartments, and guest houses. Hotel rates are comparatively high, but most hotels offer the American plan—three meals a day included in the room rate. A Bermuda plan, similar to the Bed and Breakfast format, is more comprehensive than the Continental plan.

Tourists can travel around Bermuda's 150 miles of roadway by rental scooter, motor bike, or moped. A government-operated ferry service connects the islands, and travel by boat is also popular.

Cruise ships have long made Bermuda a favorite port of call. The tourist board, however, limits the number of cruise ships in port at any one time to assure that the island tourist facilities are not overwhelmed.

Bermuda weather is not exactly as portrayed in the promotion brochures. Winter temperatures are likely to be in the fifties; summers can be unpleasantly hot and muggy. High winds are common from December through April.

ASIA

Asia is defined differently by various geographers. Some include the island of Cyprus in the Mediterranean and the countries of the Middle East, including parts of North Africa. For our purpose, Asia is defined as seen in Figure 8-15, which includes eleven countries and at least 40 percent of the world's population. Of the eleven countries shown we concentrate on East Asia: Japan, Korea, China, Taiwan, and Hong Kong. Singapore, Indonesia, Thailand, and India are treated separately. All of the Asian countries offer thousands of years of history, culture, and art. A major incentive for Asian travel is the urge to shop for bargains and to experience exotic cultures, which vary significantly among the countries.

Lodging accommodations range from a scarcity of first-class rooms to a plethora, as in Manila and Singapore. Service may be primitive or reluctant, as in some Chinese hotels, to lavish in the luxury hotels of Seoul and Hong Kong. In the Sheraton Towers of Singapore the guest has a personal butler only a buzzer away.

Much has been said about the economic miracle of East Asia, the spectacular growth in industrialization and per capita income. Although industrial growth lags in the People's Republic of China, it too is showing remarkable increases in

8-15. The countries of Asia.

world, having bought about a third of the hotels in Hawaii and several large properties in California. Guam, Saipan, and Palau also have several Japanese-owned hotels.

Most of the population live on four main islands: Honshu, Hokkaido, Shikoku, and Kyushu. A continuing concern for all of the islands is the probability of earthquakes. The big cities—Tokyo, Yokohama, Osaka, and Kobe—are on Honshu. So too is Kyoto, the shrine city that is generally believed to be the most beautiful. In 1989 because of the strong yen and weak dollar, Japan had another distinction: it was the most expensive modern country to visit.

Americans traveling to Japan and beyond are likely to land first at Narita airport, forty miles north of Tokyo. Transportation is efficient, fast, and crowded.

Tokyo is a megalopolis whose suburbs stretch for miles. Some commuters travel two hours in and two hours home. The trains are so crowded that some commuters never get a seat and learn to sleep standing up. There's no danger of falling; there's no room to fall.

Tokyo's ten subway lines are close to most of the hotels, museums, temples, and shopping areas. The subway system is clean, efficient, and crime free. The station names are written in English on the subway platform walls and at street-level entrances and exits. Gates are also marked in English. Tickets are punched at entrance gates and taken up when getting off. Nevertheless, subway travel during the crunch hours between 7 and 9 A.M. and 4:30 to 6 P.M. is to be avoided.

Tokyo's prominent tourist sites are the Imperial Palace and the Meiji Shrine. The modern pulse of Tokyo is felt in the Ginza, the major shopping center and number-one nightspot. If lost in Tokyo—which is easy to do—the tourist can go to a phone, put in a ten yen coin, and when an operator comes on say, "Collect call for TIC." An English-speaking operator will answer and give directions.

The Shinkansen (bullet) trains astonish American riders with their speed and quietness. Computer-controlled, the average speed on some runs is 120 m.p.h. Trains on the major Shinkansen

its economy. With industrialization comes business travel, and discretionary travel is not far behind. Most of the travel in Asia is intra-regional but visitors from America, Europe, and Australia are increasing as travel becomes easier, more first-class hotels are built, and more package tours are marketed.

Japan

Japan forms a chain of volcanic islands in a two-thousand-mile arc off the east coast of mainland Asia. Japan is home to some 120 million people who by prodigious effort and zeal have amazed the world by becoming one of the wealthiest and most productive of nations in less than fifty years. Japan now dominates much of world banking and manufacturing.

Japan has been likened to a giant beehive with every inhabitant doing his or her best, programmed to run (not walk) to work, so eager to perform that many refuse vacations, work overtime, respect their seniors, and never complain. Japan has become a major player in the hotel routes run every four to six minutes. Getting off can be a problem since stops are only forty-five seconds long.

Kyoto, southwest of Tokyo, is the favored destination for tourists interested in temples, shrines, and multitiered castles. Shintoism, a kind of ancestor and nature worship, shares the religious scene with Buddhism. Buddhists build temples; the shrines are for Shintoists.

Japan has a number of first-class hotels. Japanese-style hotels offer *futons*, mattresses for sleeping on the floor rather than in Western-style beds. The ryokan (or country inn) is an experience in courtesy and a different lifestyle. The owners of these 80,000 inns greet guests personally and are on hand to wish them well on leaving. *Minshuku* are a type of inn often managed by farming or fishing families and serving native meals of rice, fried fish, pickled vegetables, dried seaweed, green tea, and a local delicacy such as candied crickets. Restaurants in office buildings, shopping arcades, and department stores offer meals at what are, for Japan, bargain prices. Plastic models of the menu items are displayed; diners point to what they want. Public baths are a part of Japanese life, as are hot tubs at traditional inns. The hot tubs are not for bathing. The bather washes first, then soaks in the tub.

Sumo wrestling (behemoths in breech clouts trying to throw each other to the floor or out of the ring) and Kabuki theater are uniquely Japanese. Elegantly costumed actors perform traditional tales in the Kabuki theater. Also uniquely Japanese is the tea ceremony. It is a ritual, a spiritual experience — The Way of Tea — connected to harmony, respect, purity, and tranquility. How the tea is prepared and drunk, what the subjects of conversation are, and what the cups for drinking tea are like are all part of the ritual. The Grand Tea Master is one of the most respected persons in Japan.

Another kind of spiritual experience is a walking trip up Mount Fujiyama (Fuji), Japan's highest and best-known mountain. Some 23 million people trudge up this 12,389-foot mountain each year, many stopping off at way stations rather than reaching the summit. It is hard to imagine 25 million Americans walking up a 12,000-foot mountain.

Visitors to Japan are struck by the sharp dichotomies in the culture, the beauty and serenity of the Zen Temples as found in Kyoto in contrast to the frenetic life of Tokyo. The hectic pace of industrialized Japan contrasts with the serene beauty of a Japanese garden, with the stones arranged to represent islands and sand raked to represent the movement of water. Some gardens contain a small tree or two, a stone lantern, or a small wooden bridge and stream or pool. The Japanese seek an idealized world of perfect order. Their search for perfection extends to perfect hospitality and cordiality.

The Japanese have tasted travel and like it. They are big spenders and from custom must bring expensive gifts home to friends, co-workers, and family. In 1987 Japan sent more visitors to the United States than to any other overseas country, including the United Kingdom, the traditional number-one source of international travelers.

People's Republic of China

Slightly larger than the United States with a population about a fifth of that of the entire world, China has decided to welcome tourists on a limited basis. Independent travelers are few, and must brave bureaucrats and other difficulties to travel on their own.

Until 1987 most visitors were part of tours that entered China by the eighty-nine miles of track linking the Hong Kong border to Canton. From Canton an express train runs north to Shanghai, an hour trip. Tour groups receive special treatment. For example, tourists travel "soft sleep." Chinese trains offer three classes of service: "soft sleep" (luxury with compartments and made-up beds); "hard sleep" (six berths in a compartment, open to the aisle), and "hard seat," 12 people squeezed into facing seats. Generally, transportation has three price levels, one for foreigners, one for Hong Kong Chinese, and one — the least expensive — for China's nationals. China is the world's major builder of railroads.

It is now possible to obtain tourist visas upon arrival at any one of China's five international airports. The mass of visitors to China are ethnic Chinese, called compatriots, mostly residents of Hong Kong, Macao, and Taiwan. In special stores foreigners can buy silks, rugs, jewelry, embroidery, lacquer ware, jade, and the like.

Since about 1985 China, with the help of foreigners, has built several luxury hotels. It is not surprising to see a Holiday Inn but the service may not be first class. Foreign management teams operating in China tell stories of disgruntled waitresses who walk off during peak meal periods to call for political meetings and of supervisors who will not give orders because of fear the employees under them will turn on them when the political pendulum swings in the other direction.

The overwhelming impression the visitor receives when visiting the cities of China is of millions of people, a sea of humanity, walking or slowly riding identical black-and-white, single-speed bicycles, at least a quarter of a billion bicycles in all. Roads are clogged with trucks carrying both produce and people. Air pollution in the cities is often high, which raises the chances of respiratory illness.

Made a monochromatic culture after the communist takeover, China is now trying to tolerate some diversity. Decentralization of China's economy has introduced new fleets of air-conditioned buses for tour operators and has placed twelve luxury cruise ships on the Yangtze River. Thousands of young people are being trained as interpreters and guides.

China was thought of as the cosmic center of the world, the Middle Kingdom between heaven and earth. Its major tourist cities in addition to Beijing, the capital, are Shanghai, Guilin, Hangzhow, Xian, and Suzhow. With a civilization thousands of years old, China has many tourist attractions, among them the Forbidden Palace in Beijing; the Great Wall that was built to keep out invaders (it now attracts them); the Qin Army Vault museum in Xian, where thousands of life-size clay soldiers and horses were fashioned to guard the burial of the emperor who built the Great Wall; the Grand Canal, a hand-built 1,000-mile waterway connecting Beijing with Hangzhow (115 miles from Shanghai). The Great Wall of China is the only thing people have made that is large enough to be easily identified from space. It stretches at least 3,700 miles through north China. Most visitors see part of it on a day trip from Beijing at Ba Da Ling.

Emperor Qin Shi Huang, first to bring the peoples of China together under one ruler, caused 1,800 miles of the Great Wall to be built. The 8,000 terra-cotta soldiers at Xian were part of his mausoleum; they constitute an underground army drawn up in columns to protect him after death. Torsos and legs of the figures are solid and heads hollow. Each head is individually modeled. It took 700,000 workmen 36 years to build the mausoleum.

The number-one tourist attraction is the Forbidden City, the palace of Chinese emperors until the National Revolution of 1911. Now a museum and public park, it is enclosed by 35-foot-high walls, themselves enclosed in the Imperial City which in turn is enclosed within the walls of Beijing (formerly called Peking).

For the Chinese, the single biggest attraction is the Mao Tse-tung mausoleum. They line up four-abreast and may wait several hours to walk through the mausoleum.

China has a variety of dialects, some so different that a Cantonese cannot understand the news broadcast from Beijing, different culinary styles, and fifty-five "national minorities."

The Yangtze River (the Chinese call it Chang Jiang) is the great north-south division, something like east/west of the Mississippi in the United States. The Chinese say it is much more than a geographical divide. The Chinese in the north, say the southern Chinese, are imperious, quarrelsome, rather aloof, proud noodle-eaters; south of the river they are talkative, complacent, dark, sloppy, commercial-minded and materialistic rice-eaters.[3]

Chinese food is considered by many to surpass that of the French in subtlety and taste. A tourist

---

3. See Paul Theroux, *Riding the Iron Rooster by Train Through China*. New York: G.P. Putnam's Sons, 1988, p. 109.

invited by a Chinese to a meal at a restaurant should not offer to pay or go Dutch. That would be taken to mean the host cannot afford the meal, an insult. A Chinese meal is not a talk fest as in many parts of the world. A meal is for eating food, eating a lot, and giving forth sounds of satisfaction, like belching.

At a banquet a guest who requests more rice is considered rude. The implication is that there is not enough other food. At a Chinese home the reverse is true. A guest shows appreciation of the food by asking for a second bowl of rice. A basic rule at a banquet: everyone shares; appropriating one of the numerous dishes served for oneself is definitely barbarous. Don't linger over dessert and tea. When the meal is finished it's time to go.

Good table manners in China include slurping one's soup, raising the rice bowl to the mouth to avoid spilling the rice, putting bones from soup on the table, and in some places spitting on the floor. Chopstick etiquette is precise:

Wield them gracefully. This means holding each about two-thirds of the way up the stick and keeping the lower end pointed downward.

If your chopsticks touch a piece of food, the rule is it's yours.

Don't point with chopsticks, or worse, touch anyone with them.

Using a chopstick as a spear is a gaffe.

Sticking chopsticks upright in a bowl of rice is taboo: it is done only with the rice placed on a Buddhist grave or at the family altar.

The communist party, however, is urging people to give up chopsticks in favor of Western-style knives and forks. Doing so, a communisty party chief claims, will help to avoid contagious diseases, such as hepatitis, that can be caused by eating from a common platter.

Recent political events in China have had a drastic effect on tourism. In mid-1989, student and worker demonstrations against corruption and government policy involved thousands of people in Beijing and other major Chinese cities. After thousands of demonstrators were struck down by bullets, an act that was observed by TV viewers around the world, pleasure travel to China came to an abrupt halt, a situation which could exist for months, or even years, to come.

Taiwan

Officially the Republic of China, Taiwan is a little country about the size of Holland, with a population of 19 million. The largest number of visitors originate in Japan. Americans traveling to Taiwan come primarily for business or are ethnic Chinese visiting friends and relatives. The country is fairly prosperous and tourism, incoming and outgoing, is increasing rapidly.

There are excellent hotels and hordes of motorcycles and little cars in Taipei, the major city and capital of the nation. Temples and shrines are numerous. The biggest tourist attraction is the National Palace Museum where thousands of Chinese paintings, sculpture, porcelain, and other treasures are stored in air-conditioned caves located behind the museum. Some of the treasures are on display, and English-language tours of the palace are conducted daily. The treasures were brought from mainland China by Chiang Kai-shek and his troops when they were forced from the mainland in 1949. The memorial to Chiang in downtown Taipei is impressive as is the Grand Hotel, built by the retired soldiers of Chiang after the exodus from China.

Relations between mainland China (People's Republic of China) and Taiwan (Republic of China) have relaxed considerably since Taiwan stopped pushing its claim that mainland China, with its huge size and a billion plus population, was really a part of Taiwan.

Hong Kong

Long a transit point in travel to China and a thriving commercial/financial center, Hong Kong faces transfer of political allegiance from Britain to China in 1997. Now a Crown Colony of Britain, the country is an enclave on the southeastern coast of China. Summers are hot, rainy and humid, winters warm and relatively dry. Densely crowded, Hong Kong has a population of about 6 million. The Japanese provide the largest number of visitors. The colony has several top-notch hotels, including The Peninsula and The Mandarin. The Peninsula, an old favorite, is known for its huge lobby and fleet of Rolls Royces.

Most American visitors stay in Kowloon on the mainland. Many of the best hotels are on or near the "Golden Mile" of Nathan Road. A few blocks away is an air-conditioned shopping mall whose walkways extend three miles. About a twenty-minute taxi ride away is Aberdeen, known for its floating restaurants.

The Portuguese Overseas Province of Macau is on a peninsula reached by hydrofoil. Hong Kong Chinese visit Macau by the thousands to gamble.

Thailand

The Kingdom of Thailand with its population of 5 million is fast becoming a tourist center. Bangkok, the capital, is an air transit point for other parts of Asia. The city is hot and humid and known for its silks and precious stones.

Devotedly Buddhist, Thailand has many beautiful temples and shrines. In the hilly country to the north is Chung Mai, Thailand's second largest city. Called the "Rose of the North," it is somewhat cooler than Bangkok. Thailand's best beaches are south; its most interesting ruins, north.

Indonesia

A chain of 13,000 islands stretching across an area that could reach from Oregon to Bermuda constitutes the country of Indonesia. Indonesia also occupies part of Borneo and New Guinea and has a total population of 160 million people. It is by far the largest Islamic nation in the world, with twice as many Muslims as Iran, Iraq, Syria, and Saudi Arabia combined. About the only part of the country that has a touristic reputation is tropical Bali, which to many is a kind of paradise whose people welcome sun worshippers, antique collectors, seekers after the truth, and just plain people from Peoria. The Balinese capital of Denpasar has direct flights from Sidney and Singapore. Visitors to Bali long remember the sounds of the gamelan orchestra and the beauty of young girls gracefully twisting and turning in the highly stylized Balinese dance. Bali has some 30,000 temples in an area about the size of Delaware. Unlike most of Muslim Indonesia, the Balinese are animist Hindus who regard life as a battle between the spirits of light and darkness. Their dancing is a display of this relentless struggle, a form of celebration or an exorcism.

Another attraction of Bali is the native theater where the actors wear beautifully ornate costumes usually representing the good spirit "Barong" (a mythological animal) and the evil spirit "Rangdda" (a mythological monster), to depict the eternal fight between the forces of good and evil.

Because of the heat, the humidity, the crowds, and the poverty, the rest of Indonesia attracts few pleasure travelers. More than 75 percent of the Indonesians live in Java. A few travelers visit Borobudur on Java, the world's largest Buddhist monument, eight tiers rising for a total of 105 feet, covered with 460 carved panels depicting the World of Desire.

Singapore

A sovereign island state, Singapore is considered the crossroads of the Orient and a major money market. Changi airport is modern, efficient, and handles millions of passengers yearly.

Singapore consists of one main island with fifty-seven islets, the total covering an area smaller than Long Island. The main island is connected to the continent of Asia by a mile-long causeway. Singapore's total population is 2½ million, made up of 77 percent Chinese, 15 percent Malaysians, and 6 percent Indians.

Singapore must be considered one of the cleanest nations; littering carries a heavy fine.

Singapore has the distinction, albeit contested, of having the tallest hotel, the seventy-three story Westin Stamford Hotel. The traveler can get real junk food, served on Sunset Dinner Cruises aboard a bona fide Chinese junk.

India

Like a big kite, India spans over 2,200 miles north to south, and is divided into three major zones: northern mountains, central plains, and the Deccan Plateau that lies to the south. Most of India's heartland is warm and dry in the winter, hot and wet during the summer monsoon. Overpopulated, with 800 million people, it is second only in population to China, and gaining. Relatively few Americans go to India (about 200,000 a year) because of distance, climate, and the possibility of becoming ill. Over 60 percent of the people are illiterate. Crowded Indian cities are not generally attractive as cities.

India is said to be a paradise for the railway enthusiast; the rail system begun during the days of the British Raj goes everywhere on the subcontinent. It is also possible to ride elephants, hunt tigers with a camera, and live at modest cost in a former maharajah's palace. India's Hindu temples, Buddhist shrines, and Muslim mosques and forts reflect its different rulers. For most tourists, a visit to the Taj Mahal in Agra is a must. Built as the tomb for Shah Jahan's wife, many regard it as one of the world's most beautiful buildings. A new express train makes the trip from New Delhi, the capital, to Agra in two hours. The Buddhist paintings in Ajanta caves are another attraction, as are the many Hindu temples within their sometimes erotic carvings.

Nepal

Nepal, a separate kingdom, lies between India and Tibet (now a province of China). The land of the Himalayas, Nepal attracts the mountain trekker and climber. About 6,000 of the 200,000 tourists who visit Nepal each year are trekkers who come to test themselves against the mountains and share the unsophisticated life of the Sherpas, the Nepalis who hire on as guides and workers for the trekkers. Visitors have a choice of altitude in Nepal, from near sea level to fabled Mount Everest, at 29,028 feet.

Katmandu, the capital, is home of the king and center for religious festivities for both Hindus and Buddhists. Nepal is Buddha's birthplace. Durbar Square in the center of Katmandu has the old Royal Palace, temples, vendors, and beggars. Katmandu satisfies a range of pocketbooks, from inexpensive guest houses to first-class hotels.

SOUTH AMERICA

A map of the Western Hemisphere shows that most of South America lies to the east of the United States. Lima, capital of Peru, on the west coast of South America, is farther east than Miami, Florida. Physically, South America is dominated by the Andes, the mountain range that runs north and south along the west coast, and by the Amazon Basin, in the north-central region. The Amazon River, mightiest of rivers, supplies almost a quarter of the world's fresh water. Portuguese-speaking Brazil occupies half of the continent and contains half of the continent's population.

The capital cities are the major air transit points for the continent. Air transport is most important because of the great distances between major cities and the few roads connecting them to other parts of each country. The Pan American Highway, designed to reach down through Mexico, Central America, and along the west coast of South America, then cross Argentina, and swing north into Brazil, remains to be completed in South America.

Most North Americans travel to and within South America on business or government-related matters. Caracas is the capital and gateway to Venezuela. Bogotá, high on the mountains, is Colombia's capital and major city. Quito is Ecuador's capital; Guayaquil is its major port. Lima is the center of power and capital of Peru. Peru, once the center of the Inca empire, has many sites that recall its past. Cuzco, the Inca capital, is seventy miles from the mountaintop fortress of Macchu Pichu, built by the last ruler as an impregnable refuge. Both Cuzco and Macchu Pichu have long been tourist attractions. In recent years, however, political unrest has kept most visitors out of Peru.

Chile, a long narrow country, lies on the southwest coast of the continent; Santiago is its capital. Buenos Aires, Argentina, is the most urbane of Latin capitals. Montevideo is the capital of Uruguay. Asunción is the only real city in Paraguay.

Brazilia is Brazil's capital carved out of the wilderness. Its modernistic design attracts some tourists, but most still go to the former capital, lively Rio de Janeiro, famous for its beaches and Carnival. São Paulo, Brazil's largest city, is an industrial center.

Because so much of South America is in the tropics, altitude determines climate. Caracas has a continuous springlike climate even though the nearby coast is hot and muggy. Bogotá, higher than Caracas, is also cooler.

The Spanish language and the Catholic Church form the common bonds of Latin America—South America, Central America, and Mexico. Brazil's Portuguese heritage is heavily spiced with the African culture of former slaves.

South America is a continent rich in resources but filled with poor people. Economic problems, many with historical bases, beset the continent. Latin America's population is nearly twice that of the United States, yet production is less than a seventh of the U.S. GNP. All of the countries are classified as developing and probably will remain that way until there is more political stability and less economic disparity. In some countries dependence upon one resource—for example, tin in Bolivia, coffee in Colombia, and phosphate in Chile—means prosperity when prices are high and economic disaster when prices are low or when a cheaper substitute product becomes available. Another problem is cocaine, which has become a major source of revenue for Bolivia, Peru, and Colombia.

AFRICA

The second largest continent, Africa, covers 20 percent of the world's land surface and is larger than Europe, the United States, and China combined.

North Americans traveling to Africa are most likely to go by air with changes in London, Paris, or Rome. Travel within Africa is often difficult. Egypt (often considered a Middle Eastern country because of its Moslem heritage) is a popular destination because of its antiquities. Kenya, to the south, attracts tourists to its game parks. Morocco, an easy ferry trip from Spain, is also popular, and Europeans like the beaches of Tunisia.

Africa can be divided into those parts that have plenty of water and those that lack it. The great Sahara—a desert 3.5 million square miles across Africa, is briefly interrupted by the Nile River that forms an elongated oasis. Along the southern border of the Sahara is the Sahel, a semidesert that grows larger each year. Southeastern Africa extending almost to the Cape of Good Hope is generally dry with seasonal rains, while West and Central Africa receive year-round tropical rains. Altitude is also a factor in climate. Several thousand feet of altitude can mean a pleasant climate in the tropical zone.

Africa is a patchwork of nations, most of which, until after World War II, were colonies administered by Britain, France, Portugal, or Belgium. Those European powers left behind their languages and some of their customs and political ideas.

Africa is also divided by religion. Half of the people are Moslems; most of the rest are Christians or follow a native religion.

The French African Community (CFA) includes countries whose territory was controlled by France: Gabon, Congo, Cameroon, Central African Republic, Chad, Niger, Burkina Faso, Ivory Coast, Senegal, Togo, and Benin. These countries are linked in a customs union with a shared currency tied to the French franc. The English influence is seen in Sierra Leone, Gambia, Ghana, Nigeria, Uganda, Kenya, Tanzania, Zambia, and Zimbabwe. Portugal controlled Angola and Mozambique. Belgium controlled the Congo, today known as Zaire.

In North Africa, Algeria was ruled by the French until 1962. Egypt was under British influence.

Since 1960 more than forty African countries have become sovereign nations. Although many countries are rich in resources, few have done well economically; most depend on aid from the industrialized world. According to the *Wall Street*

Journal,[4] twenty-two of the thirty poorest countries in the world are in Africa. Health hazards abound in many of them. In 1985 only one in four of Africa's 530 million people had access to clean water. Life expectancy for most people is fifty years. Malaria is widespread, and other tropical diseases may prevail in different countries. AIDS is growing at an alarming rate.

Egypt

Egypt is Africa's number-one tourist attraction because part of it is a museum of the past along the Nile River. Although Egypt is a large country—674 miles long by 770 miles wide—virtually everyone lives in the 3 percent of the country where the Nile flows. This fertile area is a 600-mile strip of land about eighteen miles wide on each side of the Nile. If its length is measured from its remote sources in Burundi, the Nile is the longest river in the world, 4,160 miles. The Nile flows north into the Mediterranean. The Upper Nile is therefore south of Cairo, and the Lower Nile is north. This enables the Egyptians to float down the Nile and be carried back to the south by the prevailing winds. Just north of Cairo the Nile opens up to form 70 miles of river delta that spreads to 150 miles wide when the river reaches the Mediterranean.

The Great Pyramid of Giza, just outside of Cairo, is 451 feet tall. Its base covers an area large enough to contain the cathedrals of Florence and Milan, St. Peter's in Rome, and Westminster Abbey and St. Paul's Cathedral in London. Luxor, Egypt's number-one tourist attraction, is the location of the Valley of the Kings, 422 miles south of Cairo. Sixty-four pharaohs' tombs have been found there, including that of Hatshepsut, Egypt's only female pharaoh. There are also many nobles' tombs decorated with scenes of ancient Egyptian life. The Temple of Luxor is right in town and the Temple of Karnak nearby. Aswan Dam and its early tombs and temples are 534 miles south.

Egypt is well equipped with hotels and has good train service and boats to cruise the Nile.

4. *Wall Street Journal,* March 21, 1983.

Visitors are generally impressed with the good nature of Egyptians although they may deplore the practice of demanding *baksheesh,* a tip (which sometimes seems more of a bribe than a reward for good service).

On Safari

Many North Americans and Europeans travel to East Africa to take part in safaris. A word that originated in East Africa, *safari* is a combination of the Arabic *safariyah,* "trip," and the Swahili verb "to travel." The traditional safari was a walking trek with a string of porters, gunbearers, and a European or sometimes an American heading the column. There are still foot safaris, but water safaris, railroad safaris, and safaris by horseback are also popular.

In Tanzania hunting quotas are set for the purpose of animal cropping and are strictly controlled. These quotas allow a hunter to bag a lion—for a stiff price. The hunter must sign up for a minimum of 30 days, for which the basic cost is $8,000 to $17,000, plus several thousand more for the license.

To many travelers, Kenya is synonymous with safari. Only eight miles from Nairobi, Kenya's capital and bustling city, the visitor can watch lions, cheetahs, hippos, and several species of antelope eating and being eaten in Nairobi National Park within sight of the city's skyline.

Kenya's Masai Mara National Reserve is 692 square miles where all of the big game of Africa can be viewed from a car. Masai Mara is considered the finest reserve in Kenya. Mount Kenya National Park is home to the Mount Kenya Safari Club, East Africa's most famous lodge. Mount Kenya itself reaches into the sky for over 17,000 feet. Mt. Kilimanjaro, Africa's highest peak, is backdrop for the Amboseli National Park. Water from the peak's melting snow feeds two swamps in the Amboseli. Even though the surrounding area dries up, the animals can drink in the swamps.

In the Volcano National Park of Rwanda the tourist can face a big silverback gorilla. It is important to learn appropriate behavior first. Making eye contact with a dominant male should be avoided. If he acts aggressive, one should look down immediately and take a submissive posture by squatting or sitting down. The gorilla may react to staring as a challenge and may charge.

For chimpanzees there is Burundi, in Central Africa, which is difficult to reach.

Kruger National Park in South Africa which is about the size of Massachusetts, is well managed, with a range of comfortable accommodations. It is a five- to six-hour drive from Johannesburg, South Africa's principal city, or an hour by air.

Many people are probably unaware that Africa's animals are being killed off rapidly, mainly by poachers. A 1980 study of elephants in thirty-five African countries showed that there were 1.3 million left. They were being killed at the rate of 50,000 to 150,000 a year. Some countries have none left. Elephants are high on the poacher's list because of the value of their tusks. A poacher can make as much at selling a pair of tusks as he might make in a year of work.

Despite widespread poaching and shrinking habitat for wild animals because of the growth of human population, Africa still has tens of thousands of square miles of protected animal parks and reserves. Selous Game Reserve in Tanzania is the largest, about half the size of Ohio. Serengeti National Park, also in Tanzania, has the largest concentration of migratory animals and a huge lion population. Tanzania Ngorongora Crater (44.5 square miles), the largest intact crater in the world, contains possibly the largest permanent concentration of wildlife in Africa, just about all of the large game animals except giraffes, whose legs will not let them negotiate the steep slopes into the crater. Tanzania is also thought to be the home of earliest humans. Humanoid footprints found by Dr. Mary Leaky in 1979 are believed to be 3–5 million years old.

Game parks and reserves occupy about a third of the total land area of Zambia. Zimbabwe borders on Victoria Falls, twice the height of Niagara Falls and one and a half times as wide. Dr. David Livingstone, the first white man to view the falls, wrote in his journal, "on sights as beautiful as this, Angels in their flight must have gazed." Hwange National Park in Zimbabwe is famous for its large herds of elephants.

Travelers on safari need to keep some safety precautions in mind.

- Don't jump in freshwater lakes or streams. They may be home to the parasitic worms responsible for the dreaded bilharzia (snail fever).
- Resist the urge to jog in a game reserve. A person on the run looks to a wild animal like "meat on the hoof." (It does very little good to climb a tree for safety in the Queen Elizabeth Park in Uganda, which is famous for its tree-climbing lions.)
- Never drive at night in a game park. A breakdown could result in a funeral minus the body.

South Africa

If it were not for its racial problems, South Africa would be one of the great tourist destinations, with a mostly pleasant climate, wild animal parks, and great natural beauty. Johannesburg is a business center and nearby Pretoria a political center. Cape Town, at the southern tip of Africa, resembles California in climate and topography. Durban, on the Indian Ocean is a popular vacation spot.

South African Airways is an efficient airline, and the Blue Trains, running between Pretoria in the north and Cape Town in the south, are believed by many to be the *ne plus ultra* of travel. Seven-course lunches and dinners are elegantly served. Each all-compartment train carries only 106 passengers at an average speed of 50 mph. The trip takes a little over twenty-four hours, as compared to two hours by plane.

LANDS "DOWN UNDER"

Australia

Smallest of those land masses called continents, Australia is still a huge country, about the size of the continental United States. Three-fourths of Australia is a low-lying plateau, and one-third of the country is desert. Australia's interior can be blisteringly hot, up to 140°F. Its 15.3 million people live mostly around the eastern and southern rims. The exception to the dry climate is the northeast and north coast, which is semitropical with heavy rainfall. Only 15 percent of the people live in rural areas. Sydney, with a population of three million, is the largest city. Its best-known landmark is its wing-shaped opera house, magnificently sited on a promontory. Melbourne, the nation's financial center, has two million people. Brisbane, north of Sydney, has a little over a million residents. Adelaide with its Mediterranean climate has about 600,000; Perth, 500,000.

Canberra is like Washington, D.C., a planned capital; in Canberra's case, the location was a compromise because of rivalry between Sydney and Melbourne.

In the center of the country is Alice Springs, one of the few towns for thousands of miles in all directions. Ayers Rock is an hour away by air, the world's largest monolith (single rock). It sticks up in the middle of nowhere. A shrine for the Aborigines, Australia's original inhabitants, it is now a major tourist attraction.

One of Australia's claims to fame is its Great Barrier Reef that extends nearly 1,300 miles just off the east coast. The reef, which allows snorkeling and underwater photography for miles, is home to a multitude of fish. Several islands on the reef have been made into destination resorts. One resort, the Four Seasons Barrier Reef Resort Hotel, floats forty-four miles offshore. Like Florida, Queensland, Australia has a gold coast with dozens of hotels spaced along the ocean.

Another attraction is Australia's koala bears, kangaroos, and wallabies, animals which exist nowhere else in the world.

Distances in Australia are tremendous. With a few exceptions, the roads are minimal. Rail buffs can enjoy a 2,500-mile ride between Sydney and Perth. Outdoor sports are abundant—sailing and fishing off good beaches, horse racing, rugby, and the slowest of sporting events, cricket. "Aussies" themselves are frequent travelers, domestically and internationally. Tourists to Australia are increasing. The rank order of visitors by country of origin is New Zealand, the United States, the United Kingdom, and Japan. The flight from the west coast of the United States to Australia is long and is best broken by a stopover in Hawaii or Fiji, or both.

New Zealand

About the size of California, New Zealand has several similar characteristics. The tip of its North Island is suitable for citrus, kiwi fruit, and avocados. The climate is moderated by the ocean. Like California, the likelihood of an earthquake is omnipresent. The geography is similar; the culture widely different. New Zealand has about 3 million people; California approaches ten times that number. New Zealand has 70 million sheep, the maximum that can be grazed on the land even after the application of fertilizer (applied from the air).

New Zealanders are largely ethnic English, Welsh, Scottish, and Irish, their politics semisocialistic. New Zealanders call themselves *kiwis*, after the rare flightless bird of the islands. Highly literate, the New Zealander is very keen on sports and travel. About 15 percent of the population are Polynesian, most being descendants of the Maoris who first settled the land, probably migrants from the Cook Islands or the Marquesas. Immigration of Polynesians from the South Pacific continues, but the country provides so many entitlements that immigration must be carefully limited.

New Zealand weekends are quiet times, little work, only a few stores open. Life for the most part is lived in the slow lane, a welcome change of pace for most American visitors. An airport shuttle-bus driver taking visitors to the airport repeats one of the standard jokes about the country, "Leaving New Zealand, are you? You can set your watches forward twenty years now."

Many of the resort hotels are both government-owned and government-operated, usually at a profit. The economy rests on the sheep and exports of seafood and of fruit.

New Zealand is composed of two islands, North Island, which has a few mountains in its center; and South Island, the cooler island, which has the Southern Alps that provide scenery rivaling or excelling Lake Tahoe and Yosemite in northern California. The two islands are separated by straits that can be crossed by plane, or by government ferry in three hours and twenty minutes.

Nelson, on South Island, sits on a cove surrounded on three sides by mountains; this creates a microclimate with more days of sunshine than anywhere else in the country. The Bay of Isles in the northeast of North Island also has a subtropical climate. Wellington, the capital, is windy. Auckland is by far the largest city. Lakes, fiords, glaciers, thermal attractions, and glowworm caves packaged in a relatively small country make New Zealand a multifaceted attraction for nature lovers.

WORLD CRUISING MAPS

The maps that follow (Figures 8-16 through 8-20)[5] show the ports of call of the world, and therefore provide excellent map reference for travel geography as well as other parts of this book. The maps can be imprinted on the reader's mind, to provide information regarding the locations of countries and oceans and other important geographical details.

North Americans are likely to choose first a local cruise, one to the Caribbean, Mexico, or Alaska. Europeans are likely first to cruise the Mediterranean, the Baltic, or the west coast of Norway. The areas of Africa and Asia call for longer cruises, but the fly/cruise arrangement makes almost any cruise area accessible.

Cruising is an industry almost certain to grow, not only for passengers wishing for change and a hassle-free vacation but also for those who wish to take advantage of the excursions possible from ports of call. Cruise ships usually sail at night. Passengers can explore ports and their environs during the day and then return to their ship for lavish food and the evening's entertainment.

5. Source: Courtesy of the *Official Steamship Guide International*, March 1988.

CULTURAL GEOGRAPHY AND TRAVEL

Travel geography deals with maps, places and things, transportation and useful information about how to get from here to there. The really fascinating information to a tourist is that about the people, their habits and beliefs and how their culture causes them to relate to others. Places, vistas, cathedrals, and palaces are a part of travel, but only a beginning. The inquisitive traveler is a questioner of cultures.

When international travelers come in contact with hosts or residents in another country, the experience can be more than people in proximity with each other, more than a business relationship or a host serving a visitor. Two cultures are brushing against each other—in some instances interacting, in others, colliding. Culture is a composite of language, belief systems, attitudes, ideology, and values. Culture contains spoken and unspoken rules of conduct and behavior roles, not the least of which are the rules of courtesy relating to visitors.

In many cultures, hospitality is mandated by custom. Americans hiking in the back country of Greece may be pleasantly surprised when a poor shepherd insists on sharing his wine, bread, and cheese with them. What they do not know is that they are expected to reciprocate in some way.

The things and the acts a society deems desirable or worthy are manifestations of its values. Manners, dress, and social forms are external expressions of culture; expectations, beliefs, and moral imperatives represent the internalized forms of culture. Cultural conflict occurs when an element acceptable to one culture counters or is distasteful to another culture.

People travel with their cultural baggage of biases, prejudices, likes, and dislikes; they see through cultural lenses. Their perceptions of people and their behavior are distorted by those cultural lenses. What one culture views as appropriate, another sees as gauche. Consider the simple act of shaking hands. A strong, forceful grip is considered an expression of confidence and warmth in the United States; in other countries, especially parts of southern Europe, it may be

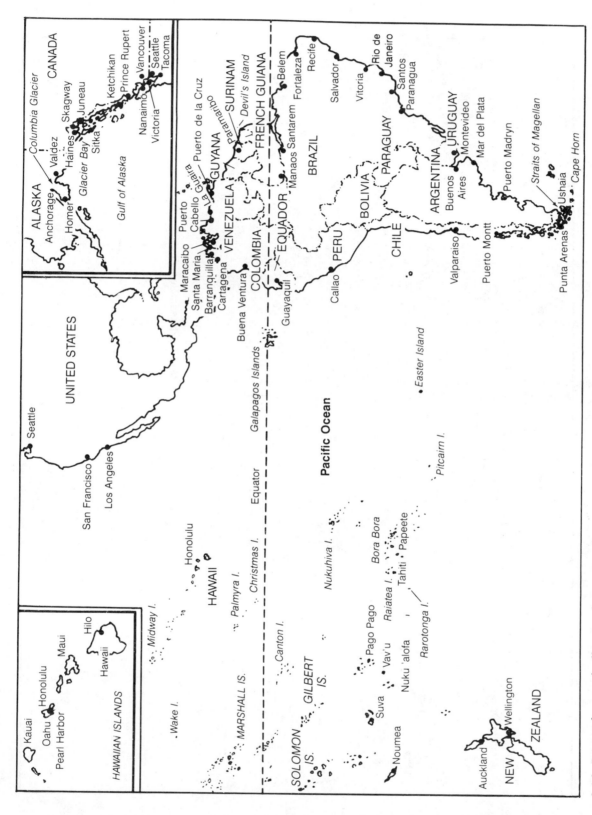

8-16. Principal ports of call in South America, the Trans-Pacific, and Alaska.

221

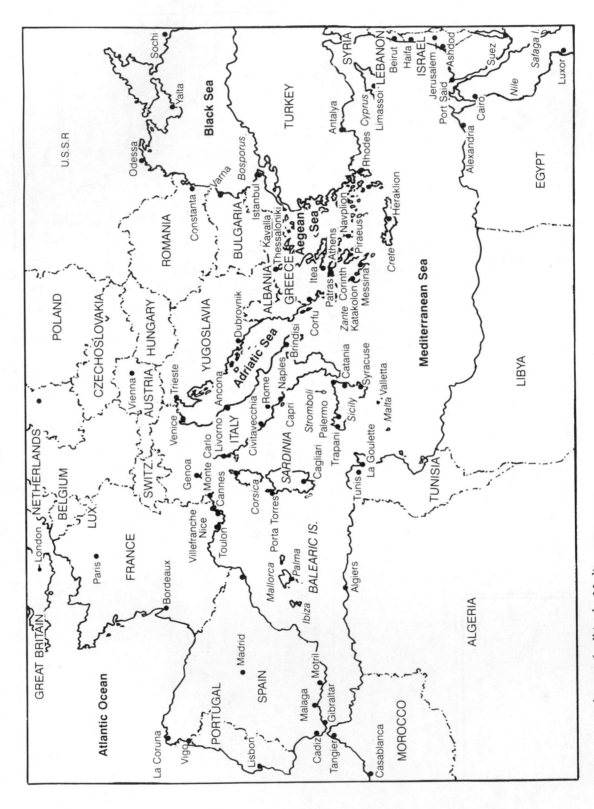

8-17. Principal ports of call in the Mediterranean area.

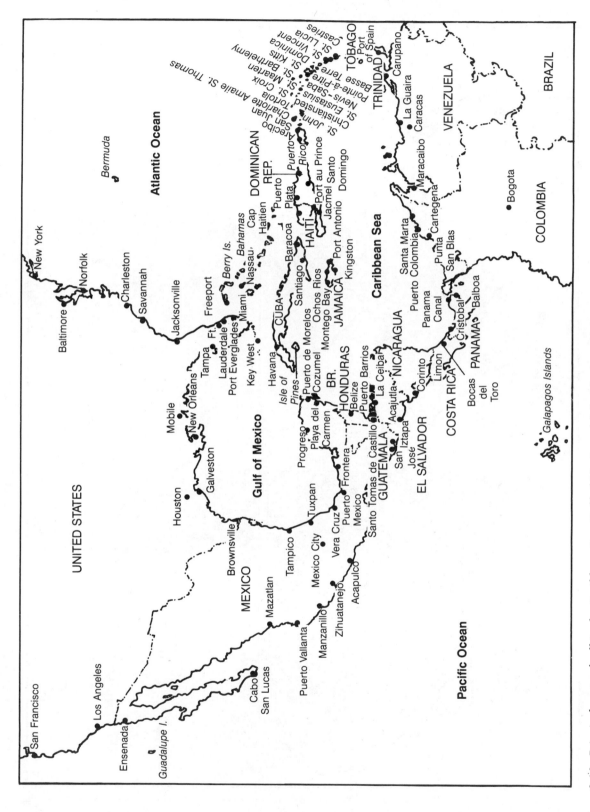

8-18. Principal ports of call in the Caribbean Sea, Gulf of Mexico, and the Mexican Riviera.

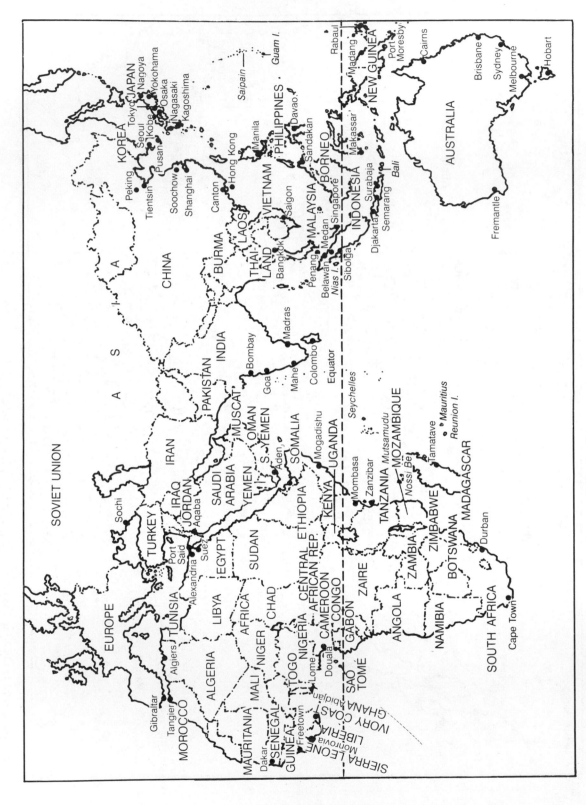

8-19. Principal ports of call in Africa, Australasia, and the Far East.

224

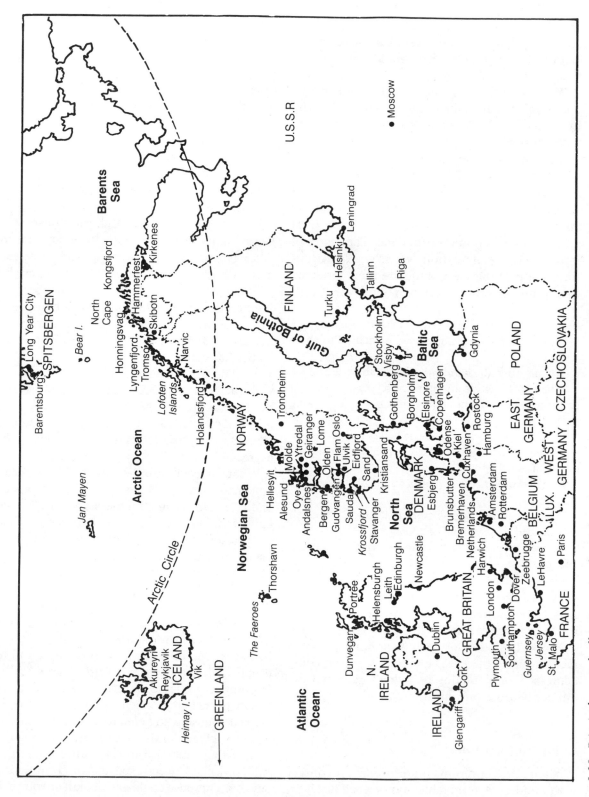

8-20. Principal ports of call in Europe and Scandinavia.

225

considered an expression of aggression. Orientals are not really comfortable with handshaking and can be visibly embarrassed should someone pat them on the back.

What is acceptable, what is rude, or downright offensive? When shaking hands, who makes the first move? Should women offer to shake hands with women?

In Australia women do not usually shake hands with other women. Men in the Philippines wait for the women to extend their hands. In Japan and Korea women do not expect to shake hands during an introduction. The Japanese bows for a formal greeting, nods for an informal one. The degree of formality in social relations varies widely. Argentines, for example, take etiquette more seriously than people in other nations in South America:

Titles (Mr. or Ms.) are used when addressing anyone.

When shaking hands, the head is inclined to show respect.

When eating, the hands are always above the table.

When approaching an official, such as a policeman or customs official, one should greet him before asking a question.

Use of a toothpick in public is bad manners.

For women to cross their legs in public is considered unladylike.

Hands should never be placed on the hips in a public situation.

When greeting a person from a distance, never call out (instead, raise a hand or smile).

Women do not speak to strangers without an introduction.

Handshakes in Taiwan are customary only for males who are acquaintances or close friends. On first acquaintance a nod or slight bow is appropriate.

Nonverbal behavior such as smiling, eye contact, lowering the eyes, touching a person being addressed, or slouching in a chair are seen quite differently from one culture to another.

Comparing Customs

What are the conditions under which eye contact with another is acceptable and in good taste? In the United States direct eye contact between server and guest is deemed important, but it may be contrary to custom in other cultures. Eye contact, Americans think, signifies honesty. In the Orient averting the eyes can be taken as a sign of respect. In Japan when two people meet, the one whose eyes are lowered acknowledges the other as senior or more honorable or more respected.

How does a particular culture condition its members for speaking with the boss, or a person of higher status? To whom may one initiate conversation, when, and about what?

Japanese society is hierarchical. "Respect language" is used in speaking with a superior. Another language, more brusque and directed, is used by a superior to a junior. The Japanese have one language for women and one for men. Women do not call their husbands by their first names. Rather, husbands are referred to as "my master," quite a far cry from feminist-style in North America.

How personal does the employee expect to be with the boss? In Mexican culture, for example, the boss assumes a paternal image, with strong personal concern for the employee. The employee expects to be protected and in return gives a high degree of loyalty.

What about smiling? Does it always mean a person is pleased? Not at all. When a Japanese smiles, it can mean, "I understand," or "I'm embarrassed." When the Japanese batter strikes out at a baseball game, he smiles instead of throwing his bat down in disgust or walking disconsolately away. Laughter is also interpreted differently in some cultures. In many West African countries laughter indicates discomfort, embarrassment, or surprise.

Courtesy in Japan is better described as manners, inculcated from birth as the way social behavior should be done. Who bows first and how deeply is defined by the culture. Status and face (reputation) was once valued more than life itself. In Japan's feudal past behavior was explicitly prescribed. Those who failed to live up to their obligations or were remiss in their manners lost face and, if they belonged to the samurai (privileged military) class, were expected to commit ritual suicide. They also could and did kill anyone below them who showed a lack of respect. It was considered an insult, for example, to touch a superior person or sit in any but a prescribed way in his presence.

The preservation of face permeates social relations in Japan today. The Japanese Golden Rule: "Do or say nothing to lose face or to cause others to lose it." It is better to ignore a problem or say nothing if it may lead to loss of face. Sometimes it is better to say *yes* when *no* is the correct answer.

This code leads to what many regard as strange behavior. The Japanese believe it egregiously vulgar to openly state unpleasant truths. Critical statements are acceptable but must be done indirectly or through an intermediary. The Japanese remain extremely sensitive to criticism and insults, no matter how slight.[6]

It helps to recognize that the Japanese are a decorous people, who are rigorously taught to be correct, hard-working, obedient, and always to seek purity. They are trained to be discreet, not to embarrass others, to present a flawless face to the world, and to be part of the team, whether it be baseball or corporation. Social behavior is prescribed in detail, and society is critical of anyone who deviates.

Visitors to Japan are struck by the ambivalence of the Japanese toward Westerners. They manifest a great desire to show enterprise, determination, and perfection while at the same time are suspicious and unwilling to allow any real intimacy with a foreigner. History partly explains the ambivalence. Until the middle 1800s Japan was a totally closed society that did not allow contact with foreigners. Once that policy changed, Japan's leaders decided the country needed to adopt Western technology if it were to progress. At the same time, respect for tradition continued. This created a cultural ambivalence.

Concurrent with the suspicion of the *gaigin* is the fascination with things American: rock music, jeans, fast food, baseball, and Disneyland— Tokyo Disneyland. California Disneyland is

clean; Tokyo's is more so. A group of Japanese were asked what had given them the most happiness in life. Half replied: "Disneyland."[7]

In a poll conducted in 1980, 64 percent of the Japanese respondents claimed that they did not wish to have anything to do with foreigners. Yet almost every American visiting Japan comes home praising the impeccable courtesy, hospitality, and politeness of the Japanese.

As in most places, things may not always be as they appear. In Japan women are second-class citizens. Or are they? Women hold few business management jobs. The only women on Japanese golf courses are the caddies. The only women in nightclubs are the hostesses. True enough, but who is the chancellor of the exchequer in the home? From the paycheck that is dutifully handed over to the wife, the husband receives enough to buy lunches, drink with the boys, and perhaps money for the race track. Mama-san holds the family together, the iron hand in a silken glove.

Few if any cultures mold the individual to serve the nation as does Japan. The individual submerges the self into the society. The national code of honor and work that starts in the home is "do your utmost, strive, and work; your performance reflects on the entire family."

The traveler who wants to do business in Japan will need a third-party introduction; it is unacceptable to make contact directly; moreover, the third party intermediary must be of the appropriate rank. Business cards are viewed as an extension of the person. A person's position should be clearly stated on the card to let the Japanese know where he or she stands in the hierarchy of the business or profession. The cards are treated with the same respect accorded to the person. The business card of a business person has English on one side, Japanese on the other. The card is presented by holding it out with both hands, with the translation side face up. Cards are presented to each individual, as the traveler says his or her name. Americans doing business in Japan are surprised

6. Boye De Mente, Charles E., *The Tourist and the Real Japan*. Rutland, Vermont: Tuttle Co., Publishers, 1967.

7. Pico Gyer, *Video Night in Kathinandu*. New York: Alfred A. Knopf, 1988, p. 334.

and often annoyed at how slowly business negotiations move. First meetings are largely ceremonial and it may take months, even years, to be accepted in a business relationship.

Shoes are removed when entering private homes and some restaurants. It is helpful to wear shoes without laces and socks without holes in the toes.

Often statisticians divide the world by religion. How people eat, the methods they use to get food from the plate (or other utensil) to the mouth, says something about cultural variation as well. The Japanese Restaurant Association divided the world's population into four categories as seen in Figure 8-21.

Sitting erect in Japan is a mark of a person in physical and mental control. Tilting back in one's chair or crossing the legs is a sign of disrespect.

1.2 billion
eat with chopsticks.

1.5 billion
eat with a fork, knife,
and spoon.

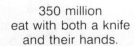

350 million
eat with both a knife
and their hands.

250 million
eat only with
their hands.

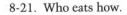

8-21. Who eats how.

Deeply implanted in the Japanese psychology is an overpowering need to maintain harmony in personal relations, so much so that personal desire is often suppressed in favor of the family and by extension the company and the nation. The emphasis on maintaining harmony with others has infiltrated into the language itself, which uses indirection. Words are not precise or concrete as in the English language. In communication direct statements are avoided and final commitments are hard to make. Business decisions occur only after long and drawn-out discussion.[8]

Americans generally converse while sitting face to face; the Chinese prefer to sit side by side. They do not touch in public. Touching another's head is a major social insult because the head is thought to be sacred.

Business in the Orient requires much patience. In India it is a violation of custom to discuss business in the home or on social occasions. In the People's Republic of China the family is all important, and decisions result from group discussion. Decision making and negotiations may last a year, and *Yes* can mean a number of things other than "yes."

Emotional Differences

Are there real differences in the way cultural groups control their emotions? The answer is definitely yes. A Swede visiting Italy might be a little surprised to see all of the handwaving, body movement, and exclamations expressed by two Italians in routine conversation. Swedes are known for their concern about appearing calm and cool. Adult Swedes are not supposed to cry openly. Rational argument is given more weight in Sweden than in many other countries. There is no Swedish equivalent of the French "crime of passion."

Research suggests that Swedes go to greater lengths than many other cultural groups to avoid conflict. When conducting a seminar in Stockholm, the writer offered a prize of a bottle of gin for the highest score on a test. The Swedish winner

8. Boye De Mente, *Made in Japan*. Lincolnwood, Ill.: Passport Books, 1987.

was reluctant and embarrassed to accept the prize because it is not considered good manners to appear superior to others!

Gift Giving

Gift giving is a ritual in several parts of the world. In much of Asia gifts are given privately to avoid embarrassment; in the Middle East they are given publicly to avoid the possible impression that bribery is involved. In the Orient a gift has more significance if both hands are used in the presentation. Cash as a gift or as a tip in several countries, including Japan, is presented in an envelope. Most gifts made by Oriental and Middle Easterners are not given without strings attached. Reciprocity in some way— a recommendation, preferment, or a gift in return—is expected. Tips, however, are not expected and may be seen as degrading in such countries as New Zealand, Japan, and China. This attitude seems to be changing around the world, including the socialist countries.[9]

Cultural Color Consciousness

Travel sophisticates are aware of the symbolics of color. White, symbolic of purity and virginity in the Western world, is associated with death in Japan. The white-and-black menus United Airlines used looked smart to the Western eye but are the colors used at Japanese funerals. The menus were changed once the cultural *faux pas* was pointed out.

A person who takes red roses to the hostess of a dinner party in Germany is being romantically aggressive. Red is considered manly in Britain and France, but dark red is a mourning color along the Ivory Coast and is blasphemous in other African countries. A red circle is unpopular in some parts of Asia; it reminds people of the Japanese flag during World War II.

People in the United States think of pink as a feminine color; most of the rest of the world considers yellow more feminine. In America the white lily is often seen at funerals, while yellow flowers represent death or disrespect in Mexico.

Adapting to Different Customs

Visitors to foreign countries are urged to adopt, or to keep a stiff upper lip when confronted by customs that make them uncomfortable. A prominent American was the honored guest of a Middle Eastern sheik. Numerous cups of tea were served, the same cup being used by several people (without washing). The group sat down on a carpet to dine. As pleasantries were exchanged, the sheik was preoccupied with rubbing the bunions on his feet. The food was brought on a huge tray, half a lamb sitting on a mound of rice. As the honored guest, the American was supposed to reach in (right hand only) to pick out a choice piece of lamb. The sheik, quick to observe the Arabic custom of hospitality, grasped a large piece of lamb and handed it to the American. The American spent the rest of the meal trying to avoid the part of the meat handled by the sheik, a clash of customs that produced mixed feelings.

Awareness of the hosts' customs can avoid embarassment and the impression of rudeness. Had President Lyndon Johnson known that Thais never cross their legs so that the sole of a foot is pointed even indirectly toward a person of high esteem, he would have not inadvertently made such a gesture during his visit to the King of Thailand in the 1960s.[10]

A U.S. businessman wanted to build a chain of motels in Mexico and scheduled an appointment with a leading lawyer to discuss the project. The appointment was for 10:00 A.M. The lawyer, a patrician in appearance and manner, arrived at his office at 11:00 A.M. and offered no apology for being late. Then he demanded 10 percent of the cost of the project, off the top, for his services. The American left in a huff.

---

9. See Chapter 3, "Intercultural Business Communication," in *Communication for Management and Business*, Sigband and Bell: Glenview, Ill.: Scott, Foresman, 1986; and David A. Ricks, *Big Business Blunders, Mistakes In International Marketing*. Homewood, Ill.: Dow Jones-Irwin, 1983.

---

10. *International Business*, Schnitxe, Liebrenz, Kubin, South-Western Publishing Co., 1985, p. 139.

THE TOURIST BUSINESS

The fact that the Mexican lawyer was late, however, only illustrated the customarily relaxed attitude toward punctuality that prevails in most Latin American countries. The lawyer probably did not intend any discourtesy in being an hour late for the appointment. Americans, invited to a dinner party scheduled for 8:00 P.M. might ask, "Mexican or American time?" Mexican guests may well show up at 9:00 P.M. "If you're on time in Mexico, you're early."

Observing the casual attitude toward punctuality and the custom of taking a siesta in the afternoon, U.S. visitors to Latin America may get the idea that the residents are lazy. What they do not usually see is the Latin business person back at the office, working until eight or so in the evening.

In Spain it is said that the only time punctuality is taken seriously is when attending a bullfight. Italy is in the Latin tradition, at least for social events. On the other hand, the Germans, British, Scandinavians, Swiss, and French take punctuality very seriously and when invited to a social event will wait outside until the exact time of the invitation. Being early is considered discourteous in many cultures.

Tourism provides a setting for change. Host and visitor interact, one observes the other, sometimes both change in their attitudes, sometimes there is revulsion; other times envy; sometimes admiration and understanding. Among the factors that play on the interchange are beliefs and value systems, comparative status and wealth, race and age differences, religious differences, and differences in customs and dress.

When the differences are great or the belief systems firmly fixed, the differences may only strengthen firmly held prejudices. British snobs who travel abroad may see differences as support for their prejudices. The anthropologist may be fascinated by such differences, while the average tourist may see them as a curiosity or material for a trip talk back home.

Motivation for travel varies considerably and colors the perception of the traveler. The adventurer who tours Tibet expects some discomfort during the trip but may be enthralled to learn first-hand about the Tibetans and their lifestyles.

The cruise passenger probably wants as little stress as possible and concentrates on the food and beverage and the entertainment provided. A stopover at a Caribbean straw market may be about as close as such a person wants to get to the native peoples.

The people who sign up for Lindblad tours want to experience the exotic and the unknown. One of the tours takes a group to Easter Island, home of about 1,000 Polynesians, far off the coast of Chile. Lars Lindblad tells of going to much trouble and expense in setting up an elaborate dinner complete with caviar and smoked salmon for a group of VIPs. As the group sat down to dine, shadowy figures were seen moving outside the dining pavilion. Lindblad, knowing the natives' propensity to invite themselves to any meal, quietly passed the word to begin eating when he clapped his hands. The moment he did, however, the Polynesians leapfrogged the guests and completely devoured the food. The invited guests ate canned pork and beans.

Such behavior can be taken humorously. There was no humor involved when a Lindblad tour leader on a trip to Burma pointed her camera to take a picture of the Rangoon airport. A Burmese soldier shot her dead.[11]

Most tourist/host contacts are superficial, basically economic exchanges. The fact that 40 million tourists descend upon Spain each year probably has had little effect on the basic personality of the Spaniard. The Swiss hotelier is probably not concerned with the Muslim beliefs of his rich Saudi guests. Other contacts are more meaningful. The young Mormon missionaries in white shirts and black pants who appear on bicycles around the world are active proselytes for a way of life and have effected dramatic change in the lives of the people they convert. In a way, the Mormon missionaries are tourists, tourists who come for a two-year stay, learn the language of their hosts, and strive to become deeply involved in the lives of the hosts.

11. Lars-Eric Lindblad, *Passport to Anywhere*. New York: Time-Life Books, 1983.

Legal Differences

Ignorance of cultural attitudes as expressed in law can have serious consequences. Buying hashish in Morocco is easy. Taking it into Spain, a short ferry trip away, can land the offender in jail. A person who smokes marijuana in Singapore may receive a caning that leaves welts for days.

In some countries laws are very flexible; the powerful flout them, the visitor can be abused by them. At a reception given by the American ambassador in Mexico a man was observed who looked very much like a walking cadaver. A friend observed that only six months previously the man was the picture of health. What had happened? While driving in Mexico City the man had accidentally hit a local boy. The driver immediately stopped to see what he could do to help. That act of common decency proved his undoing. An unscrupulous lawyer took on the accident victim's case and over a period of six months had managed to siphon away almost all of the American's life savings. The American was not allowed to leave the country. The advice given to the observer was that if involved in an accident, "Don't stop. Drive like hell."

Each ethnic group carries an image of itself that determines to a large extent how individuals in the group feel about themselves and their group. The Japanese, for example, are proud and highly sensitive to what others feel about them; this attitude carries over to always doing their best. This view in turn accounts in part for their pride in workmanship and their great concern with maintaining face. Knowing this, the visitor is not surprised that the taxi driver or the waitress neither expects nor wants tips.

The author once sat in the Malaga, Spain, airport all day waiting for two seats on a plane, this after being assured that seats would be available. What was exasperating was that other travelers arrived without reserved seats, and after a brief discussion with the airport manager, were on the next available flights. Bribery had gotten them seats. In many countries bribery for plane and train seats or for hotel room assignments is a reluctantly accepted custom. The United States is no exception.

THE TOURIST BUSINESS

DISCUSSION QUESTIONS

1. Although the average annual per capita income of most Third World countries is less than $1,000 a year, a country like India is still a huge travel market. Why?

2. The Pacific Rim countries are thought to represent travel markets that will grow at a higher rate in the next decade than will most of the rest of the world. Is this likely to be valid in light of the instability evidenced in the Peoples Republic of China and South Korea in 1989?

3. Some observers of the travel scene state that South America will never be a prominent pleasure travel destination. Take a position, pro or con, on this statement. What is your opinion?

4. Over the next twenty years, will there be another pleasure attraction built to equal Disney World in Florida? On what do you base your conclusion?

5. How would you compare the U.S. in the number and variety of pleasure travel attractions with those of Europe?

6. Can we expect the number of visitors to Russia to increase dramatically over the next ten years? Give your reasons.

7. Mexico City is called a primary city for Mexico in that it is the epicenter of business, government, and culture in the country. What other cities of the world have similar stature in their countries?

8. Rail travel has dropped off in Europe in the 1980s. Will it increase in the future? Why or why not?

9. Most of the less developed countries are not tourist meccas. Why is Mexico an exception?

10. What value is there in being able to locate all of the nations of Europe on a map? Is it important to be able to do that for Africa or Asia?

11. Which of the Caribbean islands have French as the official language? Which have Dutch?

12. Why is it that the Bahamas, a foreign country, receives more American visitors than Puerto Rico, a commonwealth of the U.S.? Are there reasons other than geographical ones?

LOCATION QUESTIONS

1. Name two countries that border on West Germany.

2. Name two countries that border Brazil.

3. Name two countries that border Sweden.

4. Name three of the five New England states.

5. Name four of the Pacific Rim countries.

NINE

ECONOMIC AND SOCIAL IMPACTS OF TOURISM

The following prayer was read from Greek Orthodox pulpits throughout Greece:[1]

Lord Jesus Christ, Son of God, have mercy on the cities, the islands, and the villages of our Orthodox Fatherland, as well as the Holy Monasteries, which are scourged by the worldly touristic way. Grace us with a solution to this dramatic problem and protect our brethren who are sorely tried by the modernistic spirit of these contemporary western invaders.

(a) That tourism affects the economy of a destination area cannot be questioned; however, the extent of its effect, its implications, and its repercussions are debatable. Much of the research in tourism is concerned with tourism's economic impact on a state, nation, island, or community. But since countervailing forces are at play within an economy, the costs and benefits accruing from tourism are not immediately quantifiable. Cost-benefit studies involve the collection of masses of data and the use of highly sophisticated analytical techniques. The statistical analyses are sometimes complicated, and results are often disputed among the experts.

It is indisputable that income from travel/tourism is huge for most states in the United States and other free industrialized nations. The amounts, however, are subject to definitions and to the reliability and interpretation of the data collected. One of the higher spending estimates, which defines tourism as any trip that is made over twenty-five miles from home, is shown as Figure 9-1. Even these huge estimated expenditures must be raised significantly in order to be current.

TAXES AS TANGIBLE BENEFITS

Travel/tourism generates tax income, some of which is directly applied and some of which is computed indirectly. Many countries have a departure tax on travelers; other countries have what amounts to an admission tax. Cities and other tax authorities impose a hotel room tax on anyone who is stopping at a hotel or motel and sometimes other lodging such as a bed-and-breakfast facility. New York City, which has the world's largest hotel room inventory, adds a 15 percent hotel room tax: a 5 percent tax on the room in addition to an 8.25 percent sales tax and a $2-a-day room charge.

---

1. David Ogilvy, *Blood, Brains and Beer: An Autobiography.* New York: Atheneum, 1978, p. 155.

9-1. 1986 Tourism Expenditures in the U.S. for Trips over 25 Miles from Home

Expenditures Category	Expenditures (Billions of $)	% of U.S. Total
Public transportation	$60	13%
Personal transportation	171	37
Lodging	44	9
Food	64	14
Entertainment and recreation	28	6
Purchases	100 / 467	21 / 100
Foreign visitor spending	$13	
Grand total*	$480 billion in 1986	

*Preliminary estimates for 1987 indicate the Grand Total reached $537 billion.
Source: Travel Industry World Yearbook—The Big Picture.

Most taxes on visitors come in the form of a sales tax on expenditures such as gasoline, cigarette, liquor, and other taxes paid by visitors and residents alike.

The State of Florida collects nearly 20 percent of its total sales tax from visitors. Tourists pay the regular state sales tax of 5 percent on goods and services. In addition, twenty-four localities have a bed tax of up to 3 percent that is used to fund local tourism development.

Foreign visitors generate large tax revenues for the United States. The U.S. Travel and Tourism Administration (of the U.S. Department of Commerce) estimated that income for 1986 totaled $1,636 million—$750 million of it in federal taxes, $604 million in state taxes, and $282 million from local taxes.[2]

Many governments raise most of their tax income from import duties, which are much easier to collect than income taxes. The traveler pays the taxes indirectly by buying food, beverages, and other goods that have been imported and by staying in hotels and other facilities that have imported building materials and many of the goods used in their operations.

States, of course, benefit to different extents from international tourism. Of all the states, California benefits the most, followed by Florida, New York, and Texas. Figure 9-2 shows the tourism receipts for the top ten states in 1986.

Hospitality businesses also benefit differentially from visitors' expenditures. The U.S. Travel and Tourism Administration estimated that foreign visitors divided their spending into the following percentages in 1986:

Purchases and incidentals	30%
Lodging	26%
Food and beverages	21%
Domestic transportation	15%
Entertainment	9%

9-2. International Tourism Receipts, Top Ten States—1986

States	Receipts (billions of $)	% of Total
California	$3.56	22%
Florida	2.36	14
New York	1.91	12
Texas	1.59	10
Hawaii	1.56	9
Illinois	.44	3
Washington, D.C.	.41	2
Massachusetts	.39	2
Arizona	.37	2
Nevada	.33	2

Source: U.S. Travel & Tourism Administration, U.S. Department of Commerce.

2. Somerset R. Waters, *Travel Industry World Yearbook. The Big Picture—1988*. New York: Child and Waters, 1988.

IMPACT ON QUALITY OF LIFE

Does tourism introduce costs in the form of reduced quality of life at a destination? The answer is obviously affirmative when a destination is not prepared for a large number of visitors. Some of the negatives are obvious: traffic congestion, increased crime, noise and air pollution, vandalism, excessive demand on public facilities and water supplies, and overcrowding of beaches, forests, and parks that results in the destruction of plants and wildlife and reduces visitor and resident enjoyment alike.

Yet quality of life is a highly subjective matter. It can be viewed from many perspectives—number of entertainment options available to residents, ease of movement in and around the area, presence or absence of smog and advertising signs, availability and crowding of public transportation, road congestion, and so on. Great differences exist in what people like and dislike. Many New Yorkers' eyes light up when they think of returning home; others cringe at the thought of going to New York. Some visitors to Waikiki may enjoy the crowds, while others rage at the congestion they perceive. Greece badly needs the tourist dollar; yet the conflict reflected in the prayer quoted at the beginning of this chapter is real.

OPPORTUNITY COST AND TOURISM

Does tourism give the economy more than it takes? Are the benefits evenly distributed, or do they go to a relatively small minority? Do the increases in government revenue generated by tourism pay for the added cost of government services?

Dollars brought into an economy by tourism stimulate that economy, causing costs of goods and services to increase and the price of land to skyrocket. In some areas the economy becomes overheated. Landowners and developers may become rich, but the cost to the average citizen usually multiplies because of the increased cost of housing.

Within a community the costs and benefits of tourism are not evenly distributed. What may benefit one group may cost another group. Hotel and restaurant operators may benefit from tourism, but permanent residents may suffer in terms of crowding, pollution, noise, and in some cases, a changed way of life.

Most communities would probably prefer a "smokeless," nonindustrial economic base such as that provided by tourism or service industries. But in many areas whether tourism is beneficial or not is academic; the area may have no other options. Tourism development may be a necessary choice for areas that have natural beauty, a pleasant climate, and yet are remote from skilled labor markets and the raw materials needed for manufacturing. Bermuda, situated 600 miles from any other land mass, was once a small agricultural producer. Tourism was an obvious choice to improve the island's economy. Today it is by far the major industry, comprising about 70 percent of the total income.

Economists point out that every resource has an *opportunity cost*—the cost of not using a resource to its maximum. In tourism, are the human resources—that is, the residents of a destination area—fully employed? Would they produce more for the economy in jobs other than those connected with tourism?

In many destination areas other means of employment have been attempted and proved unsuccessful. For example, the Bahamas have tried producing pineapples and cotton, fishing—even rum running—and none proved economically feasible over time. The opportunity cost for tourism employment under present conditions in the Bahamas is very small, but few other opportunities for employment exist.

The Bahamas and most of the smaller Caribbean islands can barely subsist as agricultural economies. Per-capita income on some of the islands is less than $800 a year. They are too remote from industrial centers to be competitive as small manufacturers. They have little choice but to consider tourism for future development; yet some of the leaders and many of the people resent tourism because they feel the work is degrading.

The Mixed Economy

Tourism is not necessarily an "either-or" proposition. It often blends well with other businesses. Puerto Rico is an example of a mixed economy in which tourism is combined with agriculture. The economic mix of a country shifts with time. A few years ago, Barbados was dependent upon sugar; tourism now shares the economic limelight.

Cape Cod is an example of an area forced to rely to a large extent on tourism. Originally an agricultural and fishing community, by the 1930s these industries were no longer competitive and the gap was filled by tourism. Nantucket Island and Martha's Vineyard were once whaling centers; now tourism and construction are the principal industries.

The largest concentration of hotel rooms in the world is in New York; tourism forms a sizable part of the city's economy but only a part. London can be thought of as a huge financial and industrial center, but also a major tourist center; nearly 95 percent of all American visitors to England spend some time in London. Chicago, San Francisco, Los Angeles, Houston, and Boston also combine various industries with tourism. Florida's mixed economy rests upon four legs—tourism, government spending, agriculture, and industry. Though Spain has some 40 million visitors each year, tourism there does not interfere with agriculture and industry.

WHO BENEFITS FROM TOURISM AND BY HOW MUCH?

Should tourism be encouraged and expanded? What amount of public funds should be used to market and advertise tourism? What is the power per dollar of advertising?

Nations and communities in today's interdependent world must import. Tourism can bring in substantial amounts of money that offset the cost of a country's imports. Some nations are largely self-sufficient or could be but need the foreign exchange brought by tourism. Mexico, Ireland, Greece, Austria, Spain, Portugal, and many small agricultural countries are examples.

The first beneficiaries of tourism are likely to be the land developers, the landowners, and those entrepreneurs who provide transport, accommodations, food and drink, sight-seeing, and other entertainment for the traveler.

What benefits accrue to the rest of the population of the tourist destination area? Do the 40-million-plus travelers to Florida each year benefit areas other than south Florida and Orlando? Does the citizen living in Jacksonville benefit from the tourist industry 200 or 300 miles south of it? What good is the tourist industry to the retired person living in Florida? In what way does tourism affect the schoolteacher who lives in Honolulu?

The critics of tourism are quick to point out that in most of the less developed countries, capital goods such as those needed to build a hotel or restaurant—cement, steel, fixtures, air-conditioning units—are not available locally and must be imported. Much of the food consumed by the visitor, such as steaks, hamburgers, white flour, and the like, must also be imported. The country involved therefore does not reap as many benefits from the tourist dollar as it might seem. Tiny Gambia in West Africa is a case in point. The government borrowed heavily to build tourist facilities, gave foreign investors years of income-tax exemptions, exempted them from local excise taxes, and gave them the freedom to export capital and profits. Once in operation the tourist facilities were found to import 85 percent of their supplies.[3]

One thing that is not usually imported is the staff. Locals in tourism work at jobs that are usually more desirable and more enriching than work in basic agriculture, typically the other alternative. Evidence that the governments of developing countries know the importance of tourism for employment is the alacrity with which they take over failing hotels. The hotels are too important to employment to allow them to sit empty.

COST-BENEFIT RATIO

Those concerned with developing a visitor industry—whether a government or private person—want to know the likely extent of potential benefits and their costs. For every tourist dollar, how

---

3. *Los Angeles Times*, November 22, 1981, p. 9.

many dollars can be expected to be returned to the private sector and to the public sector? Benefits divided by costs equals the cost-benefit ratio.

The Multiplier Effect

When a "fresh" dollar enters an economy, it affects that economy in various ways. Some of the dollar immediately leaves the economy as profit, savings not loaned to another spender, and in various purchases of imports. Technically, these are lumped together as "leaks."

The part of the dollar that remains in the economy may be saved and loaned to another spender, invested, or used for purchases. This process is referred to as the first round of spending. Part of what is spent is respent for a second round of spending. As the money that stays within the economy is spent and respent, it stimulates the economy, causing further spending.

In economic terms, the tourist dollar is an export that brings in new money. The part that remains in the economy, being spent and respent, sets a Tourist Income Multiplier. The greater the percentage of the tourist dollar that remains in the economy and the faster it is respent, the greater its effect in "heating" the economy of an area.

When a visitor arrives at a destination, a sizable amount of money has already been spent in the area for his or her transportation. Suppose the traveler came by plane. The airlines will spend a certain amount of the traveler's money in the destination area. Airplane mechanics are needed there. Some of the pilots and flight attendants may live there. The fuel for the planes may have been purchased through a local supplier who makes a profit on the fuel and also employs local people. The multiplier effect has already started. The airline employees and the suppliers spend a certain amount of money they receive within the local economy; they may deposit some of it in the bank to be loaned out at interest. The bank profits, and at the same time, the money may be used to build a home or start a business in the destination area.

If the visitor stays at a hotel, between 20 and 40 percent of the hotel bill will go to local employees of the hotel. They are likely to spend a large proportion of what they earn within the destination area. This spending expands the multiplier effect—each time the money is spent, it stimulates the economy.

The tourist pays twenty dollars to take a tour. The tour operator buys gasoline, and most of the purchase price goes out of the economy. But the tour operator also pays local drivers, makes a personal profit, and will spend some or most of that profit within the economy.

The tourist rents a boat to go sailing. If the boat was built within the destination area, much of the purchase price will remain in that economy. The boat owner's profit remains in the economy, and the owner in turn spends most of that profit.

The illustrations can go on, but it is plain to see that rounds of spending are kicked off by the injection of the tourist dollar into a destination economy.

Leaks of dollars occur when money leaves the economy for purchases of imported goods and services from outside the community. Other leaks occur when profits leave an area.

In economic terms the various sectors of an economy are linked together, each part affecting the others. When the links increase in number and strength, the impact of the tourist dollar on the economy also increases and less money leaves the area. In other words, the more money that remains in the economy, the fewer the leaks and the higher the multiplier effect.

Figure 9-3 graphically illustrates what happens to a tourist dollar spent for accommodations and what happens to a tourist dollar spent for food and beverages. At each round of spending, leaks occur and money leaves the economy of the area. The charts were drawn by H. Zender and Associates, Washington, D.C., and form part of a study done for the Agency for International Development, Washington, D.C.[4]

4. Figure 9-3 is presented only as an illustration of how rounds of spending take place in a destination area. The multiplier effect as developed in the Zender report has been sharply criticized in the article, "Income Effect on Tourist Spending: Mystification Multiplied," Kari Kivett and Iqbal Gulati, *Social and Economic Studies*, Institute of Social and Economic Research, University of the West Indies, Jamaica, vol. 19, no. 3, September 1970, pp. 326–43.

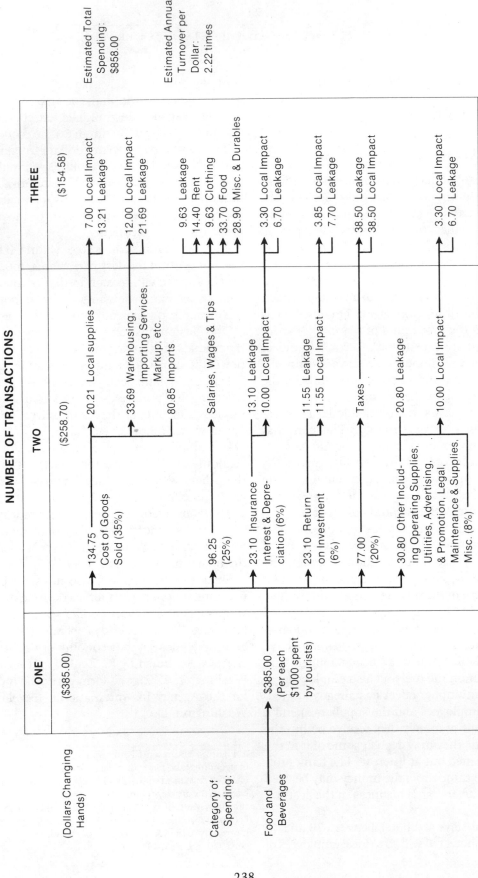

(Note: Arrows Point to Dollars Changing Hands.)

NUMBER OF TRANSACTIONS

	ONE	TWO	THREE
(Dollars Changing Hands)	($385.00)	($258.70)	($154.58)

Category of Spending:

Food and Beverages — $385.00 (Per each $1000 spent by tourists)

134.75 Cost of Goods Sold (35%) → 20.21 Local supplies → 7.00 Local Impact / 13.21 Leakage
33.69 Warehousing, Importing Services, Markup, etc. → 12.00 Local Impact / 21.69 Leakage
80.85 Imports

96.25 Salaries, Wages & Tips (25%) → 9.63 Leakage / 14.40 Rent / 9.63 Clothing / 33.70 Food / 28.90 Misc. & Durables

23.10 Insurance Interest & Depreciation (6%) → 13.10 Leakage / 10.00 Local Impact → 3.30 Local Impact / 6.70 Leakage

23.10 Return on Investment (6%) → 11.55 Leakage / 11.55 Local Impact → 3.85 Local Impact / 7.70 Leakage

77.00 Taxes (20%) → 38.50 Leakage / 38.50 Local Impact

30.80 Other Including Operating Supplies, Utilities, Advertising, & Promotion, Legal, Maintenance & Supplies, Misc. (8%) → 20.80 Leakage / 10.00 Local Impact → 3.30 Local Impact / 6.70 Leakage

Estimated Total Spending: $858.00

Estimated Annual Turnover per Dollar: 2.22 times

Source: H. Zender and Associates, Washington, D.C.

9-3. Model of estimated tourist expenditures for food and beverages.

238

Import Propensities

To establish what part of the tourist dollar remains at the destination, it is necessary to findout where it is spent and how much of it is sent out of the destination area. The *import propensity* of the tourist dollar is the percentage that is sent to another area for purchases or other purposes. It represents a leak from a destination area.

Figure 9-4 shows import propensities of tourist dollars spent in Hawaii. (The figure is presented only as an illustration of the general effect. The particular amounts may not be accurate. The effect of the dollars spent in travel to Hawaii was not considered.) The tourist dollar is broken down by where it was spent—hotel, restaurant, store, and so on. The percentage of that expenditure that leaves Hawaii is figured as its import propensity. Import propensities are necessarily estimates, but they are needed to arrive at a multiplier effect for either the private or public sector. These estimates would not necessarily hold true for a different destination area.

From an economic viewpoint, services performed in tourism are exports. This concept may be somewhat difficult to grasp, because services are not tangible like machinery or wheat. Nevertheless, offering services to tourists produces income for the tourist destination area in the same way as tangible goods shipped from the area.

Items that must be imported to support tourism are, indeed, imports and are charged against the benefits of tourism to the economy.

If a tourist spends $100 in an American hotel, about $40 of that goes to the hotel employees. That $40 would be considered economically as resulting from export. If food for the tourists was brought into the hotel from outside the community, its cost is an import. The more of the tourism dollar that qualifies as an export, the better it is for the economy.

Expressed mathematically, the tourism multiplier is

$$TIM = \frac{1 - TPI}{MPS + MPI}$$

where:

9-4. Apportionments of Hawaii Visitor Expenditures by Types of Business and Impact Propensities Associated with Each Type of Establishment

Type of Business Establishment	Apportionment of Visitor Expenditures	Import Propensity
Hotels	24.6%	38%
Hotel apartments and apartments	4.1	39
Restaurants	31.4	41
Food stores	0.6	49
Liquor stores	6.0	66
Clothing and accessory stores	9.3	44
Jewelry, gift and souvenir stores	5.2	60
Department and variety stores	1.7	54
Drug stores	0.3	65
Photography stores	1.1	57
Interisland transportation	4.5	39
Ground transportation	4.9	37
Tour agents	1.8	29
Miscellaneous	4.8	45
Totals	100.0%	—

Note: Figures do not necessarily add to totals because of rounding.

SOURCE: First National Bank of Hawaii, *The Impact of Exports on Income in Hawaii*, 1964, p. 38.

TIM = Tourism Income Multiplier, or factor by which tourist expenditures should be multiplied to determine the tourist income generated by these expenditures.
TPI = Tourists' Propensity to Import, or buy imported goods and services that do not create income for the area.
MPS = Marginal Propensity to Save, or the resident's decision not to spend an extra dollar of income.
MPI = Marginal Propensity to Import, or the resident's decision to buy imported goods or spend money abroad.

A large-scale study of the effect of tourist spending on the economy of the Bahamas was carried out by the Checchi Company of Washington, D.C.[5] In this study, the multiplier effect derived was 0.894. It was estimated that of the dollar spent by the tourist about thirty-four cents went to import goods and services that created no income for the Bahamas. It was also estimated that forty-six cents of every dollar spent by Bahamian-based companies and individuals was spent on imported goods and services. Another twenty-eight cents went for savings and investment. Stated in economic terms, the economy's marginal propensity to import was 0.456, its marginal propensity to save was 0.281, and the tourist propensity to import was 0.341. Using the Tourist Income Multiplier formula, the arithmetic is

$$\text{TIM} = \frac{1 - 0.341}{0.281 + 0.456} = \frac{0.659}{0.737} = 0.8942$$

Thus, the Bahamas study estimated that, of each tourist dollar spent in the Bahamas, eighty-nine cents was spent within the Bahamian economy. (It should be pointed out that arriving at the propensity to import may be extremely difficult. Two researchers may well come up with two different estimates.)

The multiplier effect found as a result of tourist spending varies widely in different areas:

New Hampshire—1.6 to 1.7
Hawaii—0.9 to 1.3
Greece—1.2 to 1.4
Ireland—2.7
Canada—2.43[6]

The estimate of the economic impact of tourist spending on the destination area, of course, is greatly influenced by the size of the multiplier effect that applies. The larger the multiplier, the greater the economic impact of a tourist dollar on an area.

The key to understanding the size of the multiplier effect is the amount of the tourist dollar that leaves the economy as compared with the percentage that remains in the economy to be spent over and over again. The more that leaves, the lower the multiplier effect; the higher the amount that remains in the economy, the greater the multiplier effect.

Another factor in cost-benefit analyses is how many times the tourist dollar is respent within the economy. Studies vary in assuming turnover of the tourist dollar from once or twice to as many as twelve times.

To be more precise, multipliers should be computed for different effects of visitor spending. For example, the U.S. Travel Data Center estimated in 1980 that the multiplier of visitor spending on the U.S. economy as a whole was 2.96. A separate multiplier of 2.23, however, was computed for the effect of visitor spending on employment.

Distribution of Tourist Spending

If the benefits from tourism can be personalized and expressed in simple terms, residents of the area are more likely to favor the development of tourism. In the previously mentioned study for the Bahamas, the consultant explained how tourist income could be translated into tangible benefits for the residents. The construction of two condominiums in the islands was used as an example. The customs duties on materials and furnishings and income from spending by tourists who would stay in the condominiums would generate enough government revenues to pay for one new schoolroom. For every two hotel rooms built 200 tourists could come to the islands each year, leaving enough in taxes to pay one teacher's salary.

Another way of expressing the multiplier effect is to talk in terms of the effect of direct impact and indirect impact of tourist spending on an area. The Kentucky Department of Travel Development showed direct and indirect impact in Figure 9-5.

---

5. *A Plan for Managing the Growth of Tourism in the Commonwealth of the Bahama Islands.* Washington, D.C.: Checchi Company, 1969. The particular data may have changed since then, but the proportions remain the same and the procedure is unchanged. This source is cited hereafter as Checchi Company study, 1969.
6. Lawrence G. Ecroyd, "What's New in Canadian Travel Research," *Proceedings of the First Annual Conference of the Travel Research Association,* 1980, p. 39.

ECONOMIC AND SOCIAL IMPACTS OF TOURISM

9-5. Annual Impact of 100 Additional Tourists per Day on the Average Kentucky Community, 1986*	
Direct Impact	**Indirect Impact**
$1,006,670 in retail and service industry sales	$1,778,786 in business receipts
$299,668 in wage income	$529,513 in wage income
39 new travel industry jobs	56 new jobs
$70,898 in state and local tax receipts, enough to support 37 school children	$125,276 in state and local tax receipts, enough to support 66 school children
Increase in population of 65	Increase in population of 102
24 new households	27 new households
$84,000 increase in bank deposits	$149,000 increase in bank deposits
Two more retail and service establishments	Four more business establishments

*Includes direct, indirect, and induced impact (impact as money moves through the economy).
Source: Kentucky Department of Travel Development.

COSTS OF PUBLIC SERVICES

Tourists increase the costs of various public services. These vary widely from an underdeveloped area like the island of Grenada to a highly sophisticated city like Honolulu. Tourism can increase public service costs for such services as highways, airports, police and fire protection, sewerage, natural resources, and local parks and recreation.

Public Costs of Immigrant Workers

Some tourist areas already have full employment or the residents do not choose to work in some tourist-related jobs, as is the case in the Bahamas and the U.S. Virgin Islands. If workers must be brought in, the initial cost to the community is high. Additional public services of all kinds are needed. The U.S. Chamber of Commerce estimates that for every 350 additional residents, a city needs to hire one more policeman, one more fireman, and four more teachers.

Much hotel employment is of an unskilled or semiskilled nature, work that requires a minimum of education or training. Such unskilled or semiskilled employees are usually paid at the bottom of the wage scale and make the smallest tax contributions, not always enough to offset costs of the increase in public services required.

Social Costs

These costs are relatively observable; other social costs are not. At what point does crowding of an area become so pronounced as to make the area intolerable for the permanent residents? What is the social cost of attracting an undesirable group of people to an area? What about the cost of inflation to permanent residents whose incomes are insufficient to maintain a high standard of living? Social cost in terms of psychological tensions produced by tourism were mentioned earlier in the chapter.

Mass tourism is built upon middle-class income and values. Where wide disparities exist between the cultural background of the visitor and the resident, dissonance is greater. The affluence of the visitor as compared with the living standard of the resident may be a more important problem that other cultural differences.

Real social costs and real psychological costs are often impossible to separate. Congestion brought on by tourism is often cited as a social cost. Yet cities like Paris, New York, and San Francisco are highly congested in and out of the tourist seasons, and little is said about the added congestion brought on by visitors in these areas. New York, Chicago, and Paris are trade centers as well as tourist centers and are geared for high-density populations. But to an area that had a slow pace of life before tourism emerged as a force, the increased numbers of visitors produces changed attitudes and lifestyles in residents.

An increase in visitors is said to increase criminal activity. Affluent tourists present tempting targets. A tourist may be carrying several hundred dollars, the equivalent of a month's labor or more to the poor resident. Whether or not increased tourism increases criminality is open to debate. Places like Singapore, where there is rigid law enforcement, do not seem to have a problem with protecting visitors. Other places do experience more robberies, muggings, and the like when visitor populations increase. A study of tourism and crime in Mexico, for example, reported a strong relationship between the volume of foreign tourism and the rate of fraud, larceny, robbery, kidnapping, and other unclassified crimes.[7]

The economic gap between visitors and residents may amplify grievances by the local population. Where a resident population is made to feel inferior or has a history of being exploited, these feelings could well be intensified.

In less developed areas, enclaves of tourism may be a source of frustration and resentment when only the limited tourist-visited areas receive good roads, an adequate water supply, and up-to-date utilities, while the rest of the community remains as it was.

A jet airport on a Caribbean island is fine, yet the natives who earn a marginal income can only observe; they cannot participate. They cannot afford to fly, nor can they afford to eat in the new restaurants or buy at the new boutiques. Their position vis-à-vis the tourist accentuates their poverty and may lead to unrest.

It is apparent to some visitors to some areas that all is not right between visitor and resident, especially the poor resident. Travelers complain about indifference or even insolence on the part of waiters, taxi drivers, and others. When a local government excludes the poor sections of the population from the good beaches of the area or gives preference to visitors, there is little wonder that the residents develop grievances.

Destination development also brings new roads, airports, hospitals, restaurants, and attractions that provide previously unavailable options in lifestyle. The highway running the length of Baja California is a good example. It probably would not have been built except for expected tourist use; yet it has facilitated access to markets and reduced the isolation of the residents.

When Tourist Meets Host

For many observers, tourism is a bridge between peoples, fostering communication, mutual understanding, and a desirable redistribution of wealth. To others, tourism is a negative factor, destroying traditions, the environment, customs, and manners. They see tourism as cultural imperialism, a cause of envy and enmity. Both views have some elements of truth (see Figure 9-6).

Consider, for example, how visitors are viewed by many of the residents of the U.S. Virgin Islands. Ethnically, about 65 percent of the islanders are of African descent, 25 percent come from neighboring islands and Puerto Rico. The rest are white. Tourism in the Virgin Islands has produced economic growth and is responsible for about one-third of the jobs and gross income for the three islands of St. Thomas, St. Croix, and St. John. Yet many of the islanders are anything but friendly to the visitors. Violence is also reported periodically. The governor points out that "tourism is the wheel that drives our public services . . . but a lot of our young people don't understand the relationship between the dollars generated by tourism and the number of police—and teachers and nurses—we can hire." Racial tension, said the governor, increased between 1977 and 1987.[8]

Critics of tourism claim that tourism does not provide meaningful jobs, that hotel owners and contractors who build condominiums do not contribute enough to government coffers, and that the differing values of urban tourists and rural islanders may create unrest.

7. G. D. Jud, "Tourism and Crime in Mexico," *Social Science Quarterly*, September 1975.

8. Ed McCullough, "Tensions Between Virgin Islanders, Mainland Continentals, Simmer," Associated Press, June 21, 1987.

Interestingly, the hue and cry against tourism has not occurred in countries where the power elite are large owners of hotels and resorts. In Mexico, for example, two past presidents of the country are major owners of resort properties in Cancún and Acapulco. Little is said in these countries about tourism being destructive of traditional values or the environment, or that serving people of a different race or culture demeans service personnel.

Tourism critics usually concentrate on what happens to Third World countries when tourists arrive in large numbers. Tourism, they say, is nothing but a new form of colonialism, controlled by profit-seeking corporations from the industrialized nations. The inhabitants are relegated to inferior, menial positions—the unskilled, low-paying jobs. Tourism, say these critics, is divisive, pitting the rich against the poor, and possibly disrupting long-term development. Tourism is involved in nothing less than rewriting the economic and political geography of the world.

Advocates of tourism counter this argument by pointing out that most tourism takes place within and between the industrialized world—North America, Europe, and more recently Japan and those parts of Asia that are rapidly industrializing. With the exception of Mexico and Thailand, relatively few tourists visit Africa, South America, and the poor countries of Asia. Tourism advocates agree that tourism changes the economies of the host countries. They argue that it usually offers better opportunities for the residents than their other choices, which are often limited. These advocates claim that tourism causes social change that comes about through choice. They argue that, given the option of cutting cane at $2 a day in a hot, humid climate or working for $4 a day as a chambermaid in an air-conditioned hotel, the choice is easy.

IMPACT OF TOURISM ON CULTURE

The effects of tourism on the arts of developing regions has been debated, pro and con. The impacts have been favorable in a number of places. Pottery making, weaving, embroidery, jewelry

9-6. Some Costs and Benefits of Tourism to a Community

Costs	Benefits
• Additional sewage treatment, police and fire protection, schools, possibly airports • Possible increase in crime of all sorts • Greater pollution: air, noise, water • Increased congestion • Possible limits on access to beaches, ocean views • Increased divorce and social dislocation • Increase in cost of living: food, rent, transportation, labor	• More employment options • Rise in property values • Increased tax revenues • Added entertainment options • Possible beautification of area • Greater ease of travel for residents—more roads, airports, possibly public transportation • Greater educational opportunities through additional schools or colleges • Greater choice of cars, food, clothing, etc.

making, and other crafts were revived in Tunisia and Cyprus. In Malta tourism encouraged craft work in knitwear, textiles, and glass making; peasant music and folk dancing were revitalized, and new dances were developed. West African carving, originally closely related to ritual, was gradually disappearing until tourist purchases gave it new stimulus; African artisans responded by developing new forms and styles based on traditional models. In the Bahamas a couple on the out island of Andros developed a style of batik printing on cotton, labeled it Androsia, and made it into a profitable business that sold largely to tourists.

In Fiji wood carving was a lost art. An artist from Hawaii reintroduced wood-carving techniques so that indigenous carvers could create the works needed for a new hotel. The carvers then set up a shop on the hotel grounds where they sell their products to visitors.

Tahitians prepared the Lauhala thatch for the Bora Bora Hotel in Tahiti, and Tahitian carved bowls are used for ceremonial banquets in a new hotel on that island. A Thai umbrella maker was commissioned to create an entire ceiling and the light fixtures for a hotel on the island of Bali. In Indonesia local weavers made the decorative wall hangings for a hotel. Thai silver workers produced the servingware for a hotel buffet. The visitor can thus experience a touch of the cultural heritage of the host country in a hotel with modern luxuries and service.[9]

In general, placing local arts and crafts in hotel lobbies, guest rooms, and restaurants increases the demand for them and at the same time creates a desirable local ambience in the hotels.

Plastic Art Appears

Inevitably, pseudo art objects appear in the form, say, of shell beads made in Manila or Hong Kong and sold in Hawaii. Machinery replaces the hand in making cheap imitations, and plastic copies of art substitute for the authentic. Markets exist, however, for both the authentic and the copy, much to the regret of the self-appointed arbiter of taste who disdains the copy much as the connoisseur deplores the dime-store diamond. Both have their place.

Several anthropologists take the view that Third World artists have consciously responded to the souvenir market and in doing so have actually improved indigenous art. New art forms have evolved and can continue to evolve. So-called primitive people can be just as creative when they have ceased to be entirely "primitive." For example, Eskimo art that uses ivory from Arctic animals has changed drastically in many cases from its earlier form. Although some Eskimo artists market their products just as any other business people do, by ascertaining what will and will not sell, their works are exquisite by any standard.[10]

A number of developing nations have established state-run craft shops that tend to "authen-ticate" the produce and ensure its quality. The range in quality, however, is great. In Apia, Western Samoa, the state-operated craft shop displays all sizes and designs of tapa cloth (made from tree bark), kava bowls, eating utensils, and the like. Some have quality workmanship, others do not. The state-operated crafts shop in the Acapulco Convention Center enhances the objects for sale with dramatic displays and its prestigious setting. Other craft centers, however, seem to do little but provide jobs for middle-income functionaries.

The tour group that insists on a Maori dance in New Zealand probably commercializes the dance to a degree but also encourages an art form that had been fading. Tourist purchases of Maori wood carvings have actually revived that art form among the native peoples.

There is small doubt that tourism can sustain or create new interest in history, particularly in the folk arts of the past. Villages near Oslo, Norway, and in Stockholm, Sweden, are examples. Such interest creates new craft opportunities. Tourists to Norway, for example, are fascinated by the troll figurines based on Norwegian folktales.

On balance, it seems safe to say that tourism enhances the arts and crafts of a destination by providing new markets for artisans, often reviving a fading art or craft and fostering the development of traditional forms. In a number of instances tourism has encouraged new art forms or adaptations of traditional ones.

Cultural Symbiosis

Dr. Philip McKean, an anthropologist who studied the impact of tourism on cultural patterns in Bali, concluded that the culture change brought about by tourism actually strengthened several of the folk traditions.[11] Beginning in 1969, when a jet port was opened in Bali, tens of thousands of

9. Gerald L. Allison, "The Impact of Tourism on Developing Countries — Heritage Preservation and Tourism," in *Tourism: Principles, Practices, Philosophies*, ed. Robert W. McIntosh and Charles Goeldner. New York: John Wiley and Sons, 1984, pp. 361–69.
10. Nelson H. H. Graburn, ed., *Cultural Expressions from the Fourth World*. Berkeley: University of California Press, 1979.

11. Philip McKean, "Tourism, Culture Change, and Culture Conservation in Bali." Paper delivered at the Seventy-first Annual Meeting of the American Anthropological Association, Toronto, 1972.

tourists arrived to enjoy the island and to be entertained by Balinese temple performances of dancing and religious rites.

They purchased handicrafts, paintings, and carvings. They enjoyed the scenery, the accommodations, and the people of the island. Interactions between tourists and the Balinese were, for the most part, formalized and well structured via the staffs of hotels and tour agencies, who essentially served as "culture brokers."

In exchange for their money, the tourists were allowed to enter the mythic realm of the Balinese cosmos. They were welcomed as spectators at well-staged aesthetic events. Rather than diluting the island's culture and fostering the development of pseudo-cultural events, which would have destroyed the indigenous tradition or would have "homogenized" the cultures, the Balinese culture suffered not at all. The people welcomed outside participants in their ritual performances which, in the Balinese tradition, enhanced their ceremonial value. The income from tourist tickets to such temple performances was welcomed and used to improve both the performances and the equipment needed for them.

TOURISM AND SOCIAL CHANGE

Tourism is certain to bring change—change welcomed by some segments of society and arousing contention among other segments of the population.

In a small, close-knit society, the effects of tourism are pronounced and obvious. Visitors bring change just as the Peace Corps, missionaries, or new businesses bring change. Visitors, usually cloaked in personal and middle-class values, unconsciously spread those values as they travel. The tourist in Rarotonga, the Cook Islands, continues to tip as if in New York or Keokuk, Iowa. The resident does not know whether to be pleased or resentful. The resident who traditionally gives hospitality freely may feel that tipping is demeaning and that it creates an inequity in compensation among hospitality employees.

The elders of some societies are concerned that their young people of both sexes, tempted by big money, may turn to prostitution. Indeed this has happened to an unfortunate degree in several nations.

Some societies resent change more than others. While the Danes arrange for visitors to "Meet the Danes," other societies would just as soon keep tourists away from the residents. In Bali the taxi driver may take the tourist into a private home unannounced, a visit no more welcome than it would be in the United States or elsewhere. Some of the Pacific island nations encourage tourists to stay in villages, others do not.

Dress codes, of course, vary around the world, and many societies resent outsiders violating such codes. In Mexico City, for example, women appearing in public wearing shorts are looked upon with disfavor. Visitors to Micronesia have been known to wander into private buildings to take pictures of women weaving, who are traditionally topless as they work. Obviously, tourists' behavior can create cultural dissonance; so too can education, new religions, television, and movies.

The same tourist attraction may be seen differently by different observers. Some believe tourism commercializes history, ethnic identity, and the cultures of the peoples of the world. It packages the cultural soul of the people for sale along with their other resources, forcing unprecedented cultural change on people already reeling from the body blows of industrialization, urbanization, and inflation.

An example of such commercialization is a public ritual in Fuenterrabia, a Spanish walled town near the French border. The ritual celebrates the Alarde, Fuenterrabia's victory over the French in a famous siege in 1638, which lasted sixty-nine days. The Alarde is a re-creation of the event by large numbers of citizenry, a parade with martial music, and endless drumming. The ceremony was originally a statement of collective valor and of equality of all peoples of the town, an affirmation of their existence and identity even though most of the people earned money outside of Fuenterrabia; it was an event that closed the wounds of gossip and bad faith opened during the preceding year.

When the Spanish Tourism Ministry promoted the event as a tourist-attracting festival, few Spaniards wanted to participate in it. Merchandizing caused the Alarde to lose its authenticity and its meaning for the people.

Government policy can be critical in stimulating or depressing tourism. Under Franco, wages and prices were tightly controlled in Spain. There were no strikes. (When a group of hotel employees in Majorca did attempt a strike some years back, it lasted only a half day. All striking employees were drafted into the army; the first order: return to work.) After Franco, strikes became more common. In 1979 visitor numbers dropped; this decline was due to strikes, rising prices, a general depression, and political uncertainties.

The "demonstration effect" on host peoples is well-known in tourism writing. The visitor, especially the visitor from the industrialized world to a less developed country, is seen as someone to emulate. The visitor wears blue jeans, and blue jeans are suddenly popular among the young people of the host country. The visitor prefers Scotch whisky; Scotch whisky becomes the premium drink to serve at home or order at a bar. The visitor displays a laid-back manner; laid-back behavior becomes popular.

While it is common to castigate tourism as a diluter of culture and a source of tension among the residents of a destination area, such a view must be carefully qualified. Cosmopolitan centers such as New York and London and countries such as Switzerland, Denmark, and France have cultures that seem to suffer little as a consequence of a large influx of tourists.

Where the visitor and the resident are of a similar economic, educational, and cultural level, social change is less. Where there are sharp differences in culture and economics between visitor and resident, more social change can be expected.

Tourists Also Change

It is fairly obvious that visitors to foreign cultures are affected differently by what they experience.

The visitor seeking relaxation or pleasure is only minimally interested in the history, folkways, and psychology of the host peoples. Bars and swimming pools are pretty much the same the world over. Other visitors actively search for and examine the host culture, compare it with their own, and perhaps experience change in their attitudes about the host people and themselves.

A study assessing tourist attitude changes toward a host people was conducted among British tourists to Greece and others visiting Morocco. The visitors were there for recreation and pleasure; yet their attitudes toward the host peoples changed as a result of the two- to three-week tours of those countries.

To the tourists to Greece, the Greeks seemed less suave, more religious, and less affluent than they had been before. Attitudes toward Moroccans also changed. Moroccans came to be seen as poorer, more conservative, more talkative, more musical, more tense, and more mercenary than before the trip. Fellow countrymen were seen, post-trip, as more affluent and less tense.[12]

Generalizations about attitudinal and other changes brought on by travel, of course, cannot be made. People with strong prejudices about ethnic groups may only strengthen their prejudices as a result of travel. They selectively see what they feel is important for them to see. The basically generous and open person sees the good. The person who needs to protect a certain view perceives what is needed to maintain that self-image. The British aristocrat taking the Grand Tour in the eighteenth century probably came back feeling just as arrogant as when he left. Tour people traveling together to Fiji today may come home with two widely different views of the Fijians: as lovable, warm, and friendly, or as lazy and irresponsible.

SOCIAL TOURISM

Social tourism, though not well defined, implies at least a partial subsidy of travel itself or of the

12. Stephen Bocher, ed., *Cultures in Contact*. New York: Pergamon Press, 1982, pp. 210–12.

destination experience. The most obvious examples of social tourism are the government-owned and -operated tourist businesses in communist countries. In these countries tourism is a government monopoly; trains, airlines, and destination facilities are all owned and operated by the state or by agencies of the state, including state-run unions. The entire apparatus of tourism may be heavily subsidized for the resident of the country and in many cases for those from abroad.

The government of Yugoslavia, for example, can decree the construction of a number of resort hotels and operate them at a loss with the justification that foreign exchange is needed. A Soviet citizen may be assigned to vacation in a Black Sea resort for health reasons or as a reward; the real cost of the vacation is borne by the state.

In Europe subsidized vacations take a number of forms. Employees may draw upon holiday funds set up jointly by a trade union and the employer. In the Netherlands and the United Kingdom, holiday bonuses may be provided by an employer, as they often are in Germany. In Belgium employers sometimes grant cash benefits for travel. In New Zealand state employees receive price reductions in hotels.

A number of European governments subsidize and otherwise encourage tourism in several ways. Germany, Belgium, Spain, France, Ireland, Norway, the Netherlands, Sweden, and Switzerland all invest heavily in tourism. The range of aid or subsidy is great. Belgium grants subsidies for the modernization and construction of family hotels. Spain has provided money for water tourism, winter sports, camping sites, and rural and mountain recreational facilities. The state owns the chain of approximately eighty inns, the *paradores*. In France assistance is provided for holiday villages and camping grounds: loans and grants are made for rural lodgings rented to tourists for at least three months a year for a minimum of ten years. Inland cruising has been encouraged in Ireland by subsidy. In Norway loans and grants are made for the less expensive accommodations and campsites. The Swedish state subsidizes and makes loans for investments by the private sector for lower-cost accommodations in the mountain areas of northern Sweden.

Social Tourism in the United States

In the United States, social tourism exists in fact, if not in name. The camper in a state or federal park may be charged less than 10 percent of the true cost of camping. The remaining cost is borne by the government. Church camps, YMCA and YWCA camps, Boy Scout and Girl Scout camps, and various fresh-air camps would have to be included under the label of social tourism if it is defined as subsidized vacationing.

Social tourism usually implies that a government or other organization subsidizes a vacation or a vacation facility for someone, usually a person of the working class. Many of the lodging facilities built in American state parks since 1965 have, however, been first class, and the rates charged are such that they are not likely to be used by a low-income family or individual—social tourism with a twist. The high room rates and first-class hotel facilities of the new tourism might be called social tourism for the middle class. Nevertheless, it is subsidized tourism.

In addition to federally subsidized tourist areas, state-subsidized attractions are also being developed. Funded either by bond issue or massive support by the federal government, several states have moved into the resort business in a big way. Some of the resort facilities are spectacularly beautiful and economically successful.

The state of Kentucky led the way in constructing lodge and restaurant facilities that compete favorably with the best of private enterprise. The lodge structures are indeed first class. Kentucky's resort parks represent a new concept for state parks. They are complete resorts that include a range of facilities: lodges (hotels), beaches, pools, and tennis courts.

The Desirability of Social Tourism

Is social tourism desirable? The answer, of course, depends upon one's political philosophy. Can it not be said, however, that swimming in a beautiful lake, tramping through a well-kept forest, staying at an attractive lodge, or eating in a fine restaurant overlooking natural beauty is desirable and should be encouraged by the government? Are not such experiences helpful and recreational?

Wilderness advocates might object to the building of resort parks, believing that any intrusion on nature is desecration. Some extreme "forever wilders" would not even allow access to wilderness areas by hikers or for the removal of fallen timber. Such an argument is hard to swallow when it is possible for such areas to be used by thousands of people enjoyably, healthfully, and nondestructively. The alternative is to crowd people into urban areas, saving the wilderness areas for a few backpackers or for "the future."

Certainly, with increased population and increased leisure, the day may come when the state parks are as crowded as some of the federal parks. Steps will have to be taken to ration their use and to control the environment to avoid pollution. It may be necessary to ban automobiles from sections of such parks, as is being done already in some of the federal parks. It may be necessary to spread parks throughout a state to avoid congestion. These observations suggest the need for the planning and building of a number of additional such parks spread throughout the United States, particularly near population centers.

Most of the federal parks are located in western states, removed from the great population centers of the east. They represent social tourism—but social tourism primarily for those who can afford to travel considerable distances. State resort parks can make recreational experiences available to vast new numbers of people, presumably at prices they can afford. For the very poor, the facilities and accommodations in such state parks could be made available at reduced rates or at no charge at all.

Because of differences in capabilities and circumstances, some individuals and their families achieve more benefits from society than others. Among these preferred benefits have been the wherewithal to travel, the ownership of sites of natural beauty, and the time to enjoy nature. Social tourism is an attempt to redress the disparities in distribution of goods, making it possible for large segments of society to enjoy many of the pleasures hitherto experienced by a few. State and federal lands are owned by the people as a whole. Why should they not be "facilitated" to be enjoyed by all or most of the people?

GOVERNMENTS MAKE TOURISM CHOICES

The costs and benefits of tourism should be considered for everyone concerned, including the residents of the tourist area. Spain's eighty-some *paradores* and other government inns enrich the lives of the middle-class Spaniards who vacation in them, as well as bring cash into the country via the foreign visitor.

Some governments avowedly want nothing but the so-called "quality market"—the affluent who are usually in the fifty-plus age bracket. Puerto Rico, for example, has encouraged the development of hotels to appeal to that market. Campers are not allowed on any of the island's beaches. Most Caribbean island governments also do not welcome campers. Some governments are not interested in attracting travel clubs such as Club Med because they believe that such clubs do little to improve the economy of an area. Other governments welcome them.

Some governments prefer a mix of tourists ranging from the low-spending student to the rich retiree. They have discovered that catering only to the quality market is labor-intensive and ignores other potential markets. Several governments are now pursuing a policy of developing second-line hotels, one step below the deluxe or luxury standard. By doing so, they tap vast new tourist markets.

Some tourist development projects can be viewed as demonstration models that encourage others to build and develop. Club Med villages might be considered pump primers for tourism. The villages are enclaves that leave little income for the local economy. Much of the food is imported and much of the work is done by "working members." But the clubs stimulate tourist interest in an area and encourage further tourist development.

ECONOMIC AND SOCIAL IMPACTS OF TOURISM

While tourism admittedly brings in money and stimulates an economy, uncontrolled or too rapid growth of tourism often results in second thoughts by residents of the area. Route 28 and other parts of Cape Cod are disastrously clogged during the height of the summer season, and the Cape Cod Planning and Economic Development Commission recommends a limit on the number of hotels and restaurants on the cape. At one point, Oregon's governor and its Department of Economic Development wanted to keep Oregon for Oregonians. The governor invited people to "come and visit us again and again. But for heaven's sake, don't come here to live."

The effect on tourist development of rising nationalism, of pride in self and country, has not been studied in any depth. New nations often complicate and extend customs clearance. It can be viewed as a ritual, which in effect announces to the visitor, "Look how important we are. Look how difficult it is for you to get into our country." The "busy" customs inspector takes on greater importance if the visitor is made to stand in line and is asked a series of questions (usually of little importance). The official stamping of the passport adds to the ritual.

The effect of political leadership on tourism is always important. In developing nations it may be overriding. A nation's leader can trigger feelings of hostility or welcome, encourage pride or resentment in workers, exacerbate feelings of inferiority, or inspire confidence. The leader can encourage law and order or permissiveness and hooliganism. He or she can urge planned growth or participate in quick profits from tourism. The political climate of a destination can do much to help or hurt tourism.

Toward Controlled Tourism

Determining which industry is most important to a state is fraught with problems of definition. Defining tourism very broadly, the U.S. Travel Data Center reports that travel and tourism rank number one in employment in seventeen states and the District of Columbia. This may be stretching the tourism/travel definition too far, but the rankings assigned by the data center as seen in Figure 9-7 are interesting nonetheless.

Several states have begun questioning the value of tourism and the wisdom of advertising and promoting tourism to their states. A few have cut the budgets of their tourism departments; others have tried to decide on the economic impact of tourism or have conducted cost-benefit analyses. Two states decided to rate the value of tourism in terms of expenditures per day, taxes generated, and jobs created as opposed to environmental and

9-7. State Travel and Tourism Employment Ranking as Compared with Other State Industries

State	Rank	State	Rank
Alabama	6	Montana	1
Alaska	1	Nebraska	2
Arizona	1	Nevada	1
Arkansas	1	New Hampshire	1
California	2	New Jersey	5
Colorado	1	New Mexico	1
Connecticut	9	New York	4
Delaware	2	North Carolina	2
Florida	1	Ohio	8
Georgia	2	Oklahoma	1
Hawaii	1	Oregon	2
Idaho	1	Pennsylvania	3
Illinois	9	Rhode Island	6
Indiana	7	South Carolina	2
Iowa	4	South Dakota	2
Kansas	4	Tennessee	2
Kentucky	2	Texas	2
Louisiana	1	Utah	1
Maine	1	Vermont	1
Maryland	3	Virginia	2
Massachusetts	4	Washington	3
Michigan	5	West Virginia	3
Minnesota	2	Wisconsin	3
Mississippi	3	Wyoming	1
Missouri	2	Dist. of Columbia	1

SOURCE: U.S. Travel Data Center, 1982.

social costs—a twist to the old comparison of quality market versus mass market. Should the big spenders be encouraged to come to an area, and those who spend very little (for example, campers) be discouraged?

In 1975 the governments of the states of Maine and Maryland employed the Arthur D. Little Company of Boston to study the social and environmental impact of various types of tourists on their states. The Little Company rated visitors in terms of average daily expenditures and environmental–social effects. Conventioneers and business visitors got the higher ratings; campers, the lowest. Skiers and sightseers rated higher than snowmobilers and salt-water boaters.

The researchers found that visitors who stayed in hotels or motels on the eastern shore of Maryland spent four times as much as campers, generated six times as many jobs, seven times more income for the area, and more than five times as much tax revenue.

The government of Puerto Rico attempted to disperse tourism from around the downtown San Juan area to other parts of the island. In the middle 1970s, Puerto Rico pushed the development of *paradores*, privately owned modest inns that are located around the island and are promoted by the tourist office. In Hawaii one faction feels that tourism has already been overdone and has changed the quality of life unfavorably for the permanent residents.

Economic impact studies, of course, cannot quantify such variables as lifestyle, the effect of tourism on the psychology of the serving personnel, or the cost of air pollution and noise. The quantifiable benefits of tourism usually, but not always, justify its development, especially in less developed areas. Most tourist experts favor controlled development and, for some destinations, a leveling off of plans for future expansion.

In cities where tourism is only a part of the economy, albeit a major part, visitors are not always seen as beneficent beings bringing money. London, Honolulu, San Juan, Cape Cod, and the state of Vermont have thousands of residents who wish there were fewer visitors and want to put a lid on tourism development. Why, say they, should we suffer because of tourists crowding our roads and driving up the prices of nearly everything, but especially of land and labor? Why should there be tourists coming to see what is beautiful and destroying what is beautiful in the process?

ECONOMIC AND SOCIAL IMPACTS OF TOURISM

DISCUSSION QUESTIONS

1. Some observers take a strong position against tourism development, saying that it reduces the quality of life of the residents. Argue against this position.

2. Advanced industrialized nations often experience a travel deficit. Should governments of such nations be concerned about this situation? Defend your answer.

3. Tourism development in an area brings advantages to some residents, disadvantages to others. Which groups may be favored, which hurt?

4. Less developed countries often rely heavily on import duties rather than income taxes for revenue. Take a position for or against import duties as they affect tourism development.

5. In less developed countries leaks in the economy occur when money is sent out of the country. How can these leaks be stopped?

6. Is tourism a blessing or a blight to destinations with a high population density?

7. Overall, has tourism helped or hindered in the development of arts and crafts in less developed destinations?

8. How do you feel about the U.S. government funding social tourism?

9. Suppose you were a resident of a Caribbean island that has experienced rapid growth in tourism. What are some benefits you probably would have gained from tourism? What are some disadvantages that have resulted?

10. What does the import propensity of a good have to do with the multiplier effect brought about by tourism in an area?

11. Does money sent out of an area reduce or increase the multiplier effect? Give examples.

12. Are the bulk of hotel and restaurant employees likely to pay relatively large or small taxes to the community? Why?

13. Give some examples of social dissonance that results from visitors from a sophisticated society coming to one less sophisticated.

14. According to some anthropologists, tourism commercializes history and culture. Explain.

15. Does tourism necessarily induce change? What conditions accelerate change as a result of tourism?

16. Does increased tourism necessarily bring increased crime? Why or why not?

17. Define social tourism and provide five examples of it.

TEN

TOURIST DESTINATION DEVELOPMENT

Every tourist destination has to be developed in one way or another. A Grand Canyon, natural wonder that it is, cannot attract visitors unless there is access by road, air, or water. Relatively few visitors will make the trip unless there are hotels or motels or overnight accommodations for RV's and tents. Other services and amenities "develop" the destination. The problem in tourist destination development lies in determining what groups or markets will want to visit the destination and providing those things that will prove enjoyable to them. A camper wants safe water for drinking and other personal use, but may not expect much in the way of luxury. The visitor paying $300 a day at a resort or hotel expects a great deal more, perhaps a sandy beach, a golf course, a sauna, elegant meals, and so on. The expectations of the visitor (the market) largely determine the design and components of the destination. Other determining factors are the expectations of the resident population and government policies and restrictions.

DEVELOPING A MASTER PLAN

Large-scale development that occurs as part of building tourist destinations requires comprehensive planning by a number of experts; it is not unusual for fifty to one hundred people to be involved in creating the master plan. The costs may range from $100,000 to several million dollars for such a plan and its presentation.

The master plan usually includes something of the history of the land holdings involved and a description of the ownership and of the zoning regulations that apply. Also included are data on the original cost of the land, the development costs such as construction costs per square foot and per hotel room, cash flow expected year by year, and the final capital gains expected from the entire project. A market and feasibility study is done separately, and parts of it are abstracted into the master plan. Drawings, usually in color, illustrate the entire area and include amenities such as hotel, golf course, and beach club. The management organization that will operate the project, both as it is being built and when it is finished, is also described, and organizational charts, details of financial controls, compensation methods, performance incentives, and budgets are included.

Most projects call for multiple use of the land — resorts, apartments, condominiums, vacation estates (free-standing residences), and worker housing. Tourist attractions, accommodations, and other service facilities should blend together, a matter of esthetics and planning. Uluru National

Park in Central Australia is an example of what can be done. Originally hotels and commercial facilities were situated at the base of Ayers Rock, the principal natural attraction in the park, and the historic location for aboriginal ceremonies. These buildings were relocated between Ayers Rock and Mt. Olga, affording good distant views of both attractions.

In planning parks and the use of other natural areas, roads, hiking and riding trails, and viewpoints are sited so as to capitalize on views. Botanical gardens, zoos, and landscaping are integrated into the tourist attractions.

Accommodating the Market

One of the problems resort developers must solve is determining the number of hotel rooms. Enough rooms must be available to accommodate the projected number of tourists arriving but not so many that rooms are left empty. It may be difficult to arrive at a balance. Current occupancy figures are sometimes hard to find. Neighboring owners are not eager for more hotel construction because of increased competition. Private capital may be reluctant to pioneer development in an area, preferring to let the government or someone else test the waters first. On the other hand, once an area shows high occupancy, more rooms than can be filled are likely to be built. Waikiki, Orlando, and Las Vegas are examples of destinations that were overbuilt at various times and had to wait for the market to catch up with the rooms.

Government agencies and consultants are often called upon to produce a projection of rooms needed in the upcoming year and for other intervals in the future. These projections are extremely difficult to make because of factors that cannot be controlled. Just because a destination area has been growing at a 20 percent rate in the past does not mean that it will continue to do so in the future.

It makes no sense to say that any destination area will grow indefinitely at a fixed rate. Business recessions can play havoc with forecasts of tourist growth. Instead of increases of 10 to 20 percent as predicted, many areas may experience declines.

Forecasts of growth are more reliable in some destination areas than others. Some destination areas are highly dependent upon inexpensive air fares, which cannot be taken for granted, for continued growth. Still others cater only to a luxury market, the size of which may change with the economy.

Forecasters, of course, cannot foresee the atypical occurrences, the so-called discontinuities that cannot be predicted. A study of Hawaiian tourism from 1969–1978 showed no fewer than ten such discontinuities. Forecasters could not factor in an island-wide strike in 1970 nor the fact that pollution on Waikiki Beach would receive national attention. Nor could it be predicted that the mainland would experience such bad weather during the winter of 1979 that many January flights were canceled.

One factor in determining the number of guest rooms needed for a particular area is the average number of days a guest stays in an area. This period varies from one or two days up to thirteen days or more. Other factors to consider are occupancy rate and patterns of occupancy. For example, at an island destination, many of the visitors may be from cruise ships—shoppers who spend a few hours ashore and require no hotel rooms. Destination areas that show wide variations in their occupancy rates must plan for the high-occupancy season. Such areas as Scandinavia need a large inventory of rooms for summer visitors; the same rooms stay mostly unoccupied during the rest of the year.

Forecasting Employment Needs

Forecasting manpower needs is also a requirement of destination area development. Direct hotel employment depends partly on the degree of luxury and the occupancy rate available in the hotel. In some areas as many as three employees are on the payroll for each guest room. The Savoy of London is an example of such a high employee/guest ratio. Luxury resorts, as represented by Rockresorts, have an employee/guest ratio of 1.5 employees or higher per guest.

In commercial hotels the ratio of employees to guests is likely to be less than one employee for each guest room. Where minimum service is offered, the ratio may be as low as four rooms for every employee. In large commercial hotels, the ratio is likely to be about eight employees per ten guest rooms. Hotel-related employment includes persons employed in nonhotel restaurants, bars, entertainment spots, retail stores, beauty and barber shops, visitor attractions, taxi service, auto rentals, tour buses, and more.

Professors James E. Jonish and Richard E. Peterson of the University of Hawaii correlated projected future growth in hotel rooms in Hawaii with occupancy rates and came up with a rather alarming conclusion. In the period from 1952 to 1972, the average duration of stay fell from twenty-five days to nine days, an average of eleven hours a year. The professors assumed that even though more visitors would go to Hawaii, the length of stay would continue to decline. They predicted that even with no hotel room growth, occupancy rates would fall below 70 percent by 1982. Such occupancy, said the authors, can be interpreted to mean failure for a number of hotels, since likely rate cutting will make costs exceed income. Indeed, rate cutting did occur in 1970, and the minimum average price of a room in almost any Waikiki hotel dropped from $20 to $15; in 1971 airline-affiliated hotel rooms were selling for $8, $10, and $12.

The cost of zero tourism growth in Hawaii, according to the authors, would be high; hotel employment could drop by over 6,000. The salary income of the private sector would fall by $404 million, and unemployment would rise by 48 percent. Since about 20 percent of visitor expenditures go into tax revenue collections, the average revenue loss would be $81 million. The authors found that, during the period 1954 to 1971, an increase of 1,000 hotel rooms in Hawaii lowered the occupancy rate by three percentage points. When visitor days were increased by 1 million during the same period, occupancy rates jumped five percentage points.[1]

1. James E. Jonish and Richard E. Peterson, "The Impact of Tourism in Hawaii." University of Hawaii, College of Business Administration, 1972.

As it turned out, the concerns roused by the study were gainsaid by history, a booming American economy, and a plethora of inexpensive package tours. More than 4 million visitors went to Hawaii by 1983, overflowing the hotel space available and reinforcing the fact that occupancy forecasts are subject to many variables.

INVESTMENT MODELS

The paperwork involved in arriving at a rate of return on investment for a resort project is tremendous. Computer programs that calculate rate of return have been developed by some consulting firms. Built into the programs are provisions for discounting the investment money over a period of years, reflecting various rates of depreciation for buildings, furnishings, and equipment, and arriving at an estimated sale price after a specified period of time.

The models reflect all taxes that will be paid year after year: federal tax, excise, and other types of taxes may apply. Allowance is made for time elapsed before an income stream begins, usually at least two years in the case of a major project. Maximum depreciation is taken according to the depreciation regulations in effect.

Sophisticated real estate investors are well aware of two key advantages not available for most other investments. The principal advantage is leverage: If they own the land, investors can borrow a large amount of the equity money—up to 90 percent in some cases in the past—needed for investment in hotel or land development. The relationship of debt to equity is described as the leverage of that project. For example, a $20 million project with $16 million debt and $4 million of equity financing is referred to as being 80 percent leveraged. Lenders have good collateral in the land and in real estate improvements and are therefore willing to loan a higher percentage of the value than they would on other types of investment. The other advantage is the tax shelter offered by anything that is depreciable, such as the buildings, furnishings, and equipment of a resort hotel.

The analysis of a particular resort development is extremely detailed and is usually turned over to specialized consultants. A consultant's analysis may be used for comparison with the developer's own analysis. A company may have complete confidence in its own analysis, but it will usually pay for an independent analysis as well. The analyses are then used as supporting documents in making a loan request from a lending institution. The lending institution almost invariably insists upon an independent market and feasibility study.

From the late 1960s to the early 1980s, the cost of money increased to a historic high in the United States. In addition to charging high interest rates, lenders were also demanding and getting "points," premium interest or a percentage of gross revenue. These extras can be amortized and also reflected in the program for the model. By projecting all income, cost, depreciation, and taxes over a definite period of time, such as ten years, entrepreneurs are able to arrive at a more accurate guess as to their return on investment.

As with all models, the resort model is built using assumptions that may or may not approximate reality. No one can predict the future in the business world with any high degree of certainty. But, by using the model, potential investors take into account factors that may be otherwise overlooked.

The model can be used for investment projections on hotels, golf courses, marinas, condominiums, restaurants, or any tourist attraction. The model reflects a long-term income stream that varies from year to year, depending upon depreciation policy, the effect of various taxes, and the cost of capital at the moment.

Thomas L. Sandor, of Peat, Marwick, Mitchell and Company, has given special permission to include the following detailed explanation of how his firm performs an economic analysis of a proposed resort development. It may be considered representative of the kind of analysis usually required.

Figure 10-1 describes one approach that encompasses the role of different functional or technical specialists during the resort development cycle. Typical participants in the planning phase of a resort are:

- market and financial analysts
- architects
- engineers and/or potential contractors
- urban planners

These groups normally work together closely during the planning cycle. Emphasis during particular phases may be on one or another of the participants, but all become involved at some stage.

A newcomer to the interdisciplinary approach is the sociologist/psychologist team. Only very recently have developers, rather than academicians, undertaken the responsibility for analyses of such subjects as the impact of resort developments on social patterns. Even today only the most enlightened developer engages sociologists or psychologists to study such issues as environment and social patterns. In many cases the economic benefits of such studies are not clear to a developer, although they may aid in getting a favorable rezoning decision.

Typical of the interdisciplinary approach are the heavy inputs from both urban planners and architects at early stages of the analysis. They set the tone for the resort development by devising a conceptual master plan (for example, see Figure 10-2), and set the stage for the type of input that market analysts can provide. They define the physical development potential of the resort in planning terms.

It then becomes the responsibility of market and economic analysts to determine if the size and timing of the conceptual development plan can be justified in economic terms. Figure 10-3 shows a conceptual resort master plan indicating two resort hotels, a golf course, a racquet club, and some resort condominiums. The market analysts must respond to the nature, sizing, and timing of this scheme in terms of market support. The preliminary plan may be modified to account for their input.

Role of the Market Analyst

Market analysts ask a series of questions to determine the marketing feasibility of a project.

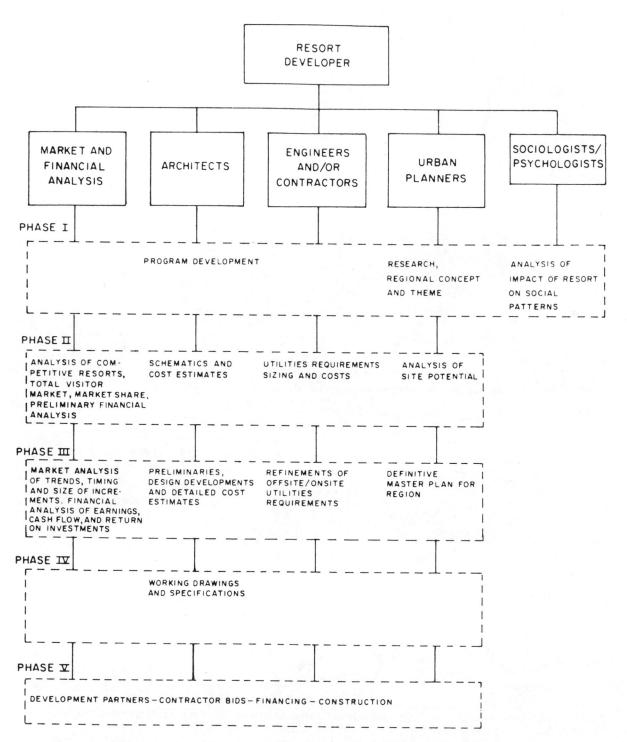

10-1. The resort development cycle — an interdisciplinary approach. Courtesy Thomas Sandor; National Practice Director; Real Estate and Hospitality; Peat, Marwick, Mitchell & Company.

10-2. Conceptual master plan for hypothetical resort region. Courtesy Thomas Sandor; National Practice Director; Real Estate and Hospitality; Peat, Marwick, Mitchell & Company.

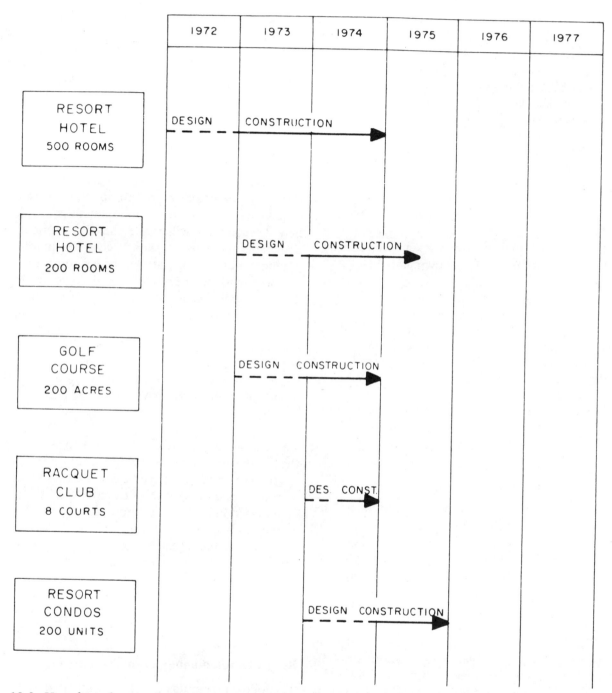

10-3. Hypothetical resort development schedule. Courtesy Thomas Sandor; National Practice Director; Real Estate and Hospitality; Peat, Marwick, Mitchell & Company.

THE TOURIST BUSINESS

- Is the cost of travel to the area rising or falling?
- What is the total visitor market to this region? Is it growing?
- What airlines and highways serve the area?
- Which resorts compete for this market?
- What drawing cards does this resort have, as compared with those of the competition?
- How successful are comparable resorts in terms of hotel occupancy, golf course and racquet club utilization, swimming pool use, and other revenue-producing concerns?
- Has the sales velocity of resort condominiums been good? In what quality and price range?

In their final analysis, the market specialists address such issues as the following:

- What year should the hotel come into being?
- How many rooms should it have?
- What is the appropriate room rate?
- What occupancy level can the hotel achieve?
- How fast can resort condominiums be absorbed?
- What types of condominiums can readily be absorbed?
- What should the price range of the condominiums be?

Role of the Economic Analyst

Economic analysts check with engineers and architects to learn the expected land improvement and construction costs and then determine how these costs fit with the pricing structure determined by the market analysts. For example, how does the indicated room rate or condominium selling price fit with estimated construction costs?

If the construction costs and market pricing trends are incompatible, then the market analyst, architect, and/or engineer will meet with the developer and pose questions that will allow pursuit of alternate strategies, such as

- How much quality has to be sacrificed in order to lower the construction costs?
- Can a unique product be created to justify the higher pricing?

- How will lower quality or unique products affect the marketability of the product?
- Should the recreation facilities be reduced to minimize cost?
- Can the golf course, possibly a $4 million investment (often a "loss leader" in a resort), be justified in economic terms by its enhancement of the resort environment?

After these discussions, the basic development plan may be downgraded to lower costs and meet the requirements of a highly competitive market, or it may be decided that the uniqueness of this new development will make the higher pricing acceptable to the consumer. If cost and market pricing trends are compatible, the economic analyst will work with architects and engineers to develop detailed cost data for the project. These data will be broken down in the following ways:

- gross project investment
- construction cost by depreciation basis
- quarterly capital requirement schedule
- quarterly cash equity requirements and maximum cash exposure for the project

These schedules allow the developer to estimate the total investment expected for the project, how much of that amount must be covered by interim financing, and how much of the cost will have to be provided in cash equity funds during the construction phase of the project.

When the market parameters of the resort are defined and the cost factors involved detailed, it remains only to identify other financial inputs before moving to the computerized projection of project profitability.

Resort Development Computer Model

The following inputs are defined in preparing the computer model:

- relationship and number of hotel departments and other revenues and expenses
- debt structure (interest rate, loan-to-value ratio, amortization period)

- tax rate of investor
- depreciation method
- other operating expenses

Once these inputs are detailed, the first computer run can be undertaken. The computer run shown in Figure 10-4 is an investment model developed some years ago by Peat, Marwick, Mitchell and Company in response to the needs of the real-estate industry and is reproduced here with their permission. It provides the developer with the key indicators of real-estate development profitability, namely after-tax cash flow and return on equity investment.

In the case of a corporation whose stock is publicly traded, potential earnings is a key criterion; however, cash flow still remains the major indicator by which real-esate investments are evaluated. Cash flow takes into account leverage and accelerated depreciation, the two major advantages of real estate over other investment opportunities.

The computer run shown in Figure 10-4 is for the Honokaa Beach Hotel (a 500-room resort hotel). It shows a ten-year *pro forma* profit-and-loss statement, an after-tax cash flow and other outputs, the calculation of discounted cash flow and return on investment, and diagnostic data with regard to depreciation. The computer run assumes that the hotel will operate at 70 percent occupancy. The analysis shows that the hotel will produce an 18 percent return on the investment.

Other computer runs are made for the other income-producing recreation attractions, such as the golf course, racquet club, and the condominiums for sale. The total cash flows for all of these projects are shown in graph form (Figure 10-5).

This exhibit details an optimistic and conservative range of results for cash flow and return on investment based on a range of occupancy, utilization, and condominium sales assumptions.

Destination development often involves sizable investment, running into tens of millions of dollars. In large part they are real estate investments for which traditional measures of profit and loss are obscured by depreciation and tax-shelter factors. They represent heavy debt, high capital investment, and low "book profit" in the early years.

Provided that the land on which a project will stand is subordinated to the loan, as much as 100 percent of the development cost has been available. Generally, a project is financed by a combination of debt and equity. Developers usually leverage their investments by borrowing as much as possible. Most of the debt financing from major destination developments comes from insurance companies, real estate investment trusts, and pension funds.

THE DISNEY PHENOMENA

The destination of development phenomena of all time are the Disney attractions: Disneyland in Anaheim, California; Disney World near Orlando, Florida; the Disneyland in Tokyo, Japan; and a Disney theme park being built outside Paris. These theme parks attract more than 40 million visitors each year and have been responsible for reshaping the nearby communities. They have resulted in the construction of thousands of guest rooms, restaurants, and travel-related facilities. All of this happened within about thirty-five years, a testament to the appeal of fantasy and fun and to the imagination and daring of Walt Disney and his associates. The Disney attractions have fueled the expenditure of billions of travel-related dollars and helped bring millions of foreign visitors to the United States.

Disneyland in Anaheim, California, was the dreamchild of one man, Walt Disney, who was shocked by the dreary appearance of the usual amusement park, the less-than-clean facilities, unimaginative rules, and sometimes surly employees. His idea was to build a family-oriented amusement park, a combination of entertainment, education, and music, all within a wholesome atmosphere.

At Disneyland visitors can step back into time in Main Street, U.S.A., a replica of small-town America at the turn of the century. They can go to Tomorrowland, Adventureland, Frontierland, and Fantasyland. They can see a New Orleans square or visit Bear Country, where mannequins in the form of bears sing and dance. Disneyland is

Number of Years = 10   Income Tax Rate = 0.5400
Initial Equity Investment = $2587800.

Year	Total Revenue	Operating Expense Excluding Depreciation and Interest	Depreciation Expense	Interest Expense	Amortization Expense	Before Tax Net Income
1	3957188.	3012276.	659714.	983459.	0.	−698262.
2	5033700.	3809972.	601400.	976889.	0.	−354560.
3	5335470.	4033583.	550309.	969695.	0.	−218117.
4	5655825.	4270966.	505414.	961817.	0.	−82373.
5	5995080.	4522354.	483152.	953191.	0.	36383.
6	6354810.	4788914.	471525.	943745.	0.	150625.
7	6735960.	5071346.	460334.	933402.	0.	270877.
8	7140105.	5370818.	449563.	922077.	0.	397647.
9	7568505.	5688262.	439195.	909676.	0.	531372.
10	8022735.	6024847.	429217.	896096.	0.	672575.

Accumulated Values at End of Year 10

Year	Total Revenue	Operating Expense Excluding Depreciation and Interest	Depreciation Expense	Interest Expense	Amortization Expense	Before Tax Net Income
10	61799378.	4653339.	5049823.	9450047.	0.	11318991.

Investment Tax Credit in First Year = 0.00

Profit (Loss) After Taxes (Before Available Tax Losses)	Tax Shelter Available	Principal Amortilization	Before Tax Cash Flow	After Tax Cash Flow	Cumulative After Tax Cash Flow	After Tax Debt Service Coverage Ratio
−698261.	698262.	69159.	−107706.	−107706.	−107706.	0.8977
−354559.	1052822.	75729.	171111.	171111.	63404.	1.1626
−218116.	1270939.	82923.	249269.	249269.	312673.	1.2368
−82372.	1353311.	90801.	332241.	332241.	644914.	1.3158
16736.	1316928.	99427.	420108.	420108.	1065022.	1.3991
69288.	1166303.	108872.	513278.	513278.	1578300.	1.4876
124603.	384173.	119215.	611996.	611996.	2190296.	1.5814
182918.	0.	130541.	716669.	664204.	2854500.	1.6310
2443.				540684.	3395184.	1.5137
244431.	0.	142942.	827625.	582080.	2977264.	1.5530
309385.	0.	156522.	945271.			

Cumulated Values at End of Year 10

Profit (Loss) After Taxes (Before Available Tax Losses)	Tax Shelter Available	Principal Amortilization	Before Tax Cash Flow	After Tax Cash Flow	Cumulative After Tax Cash Flow	After Tax Debt Service Coverage Ratio
−405950.		1076130.	4679861.			

10-4. Computer run based on an investment model for a 500-room hotel operating at 70 percent occupancy. Courtesy Thomas Sandor; National Practice Director; Real Estate and Hospitality; Peat, Marwick, Mitchell & Company.

	Annual Discounted After Tax Cash Flows	Accumulated Annual Discounted After Tax Cash Flows	After Tax Earnings Per Share
1	−2687065.	−2687065.	—
2	133844.	−2553421.	—
3	164990.	−2388430.	—
4	186364.	−2202066.	—
5	199704.	−2002362.	—
6	206775.	−1795588.	—
7	208935.	−1586653.	—
8	192168.	−1394484.	—
9	132569.	−1261915.	—
10	120948.	−1140967.	—

	Discounted Value of After Tax Cash From Sale	Final Present Value of All After Tax Cash Flows, Discounted at 18.0%
10	1181483.	40516.

Annual Debt Service For—	
First Mortgage	1052618.
Second Mortgage	0.
Third Mortgage	0.
Fourth Mortgage	0.
Sale Price of Investment	19978884.
Sale Price Less Debt Outstanding Less Closing Expense	9878659.
Capital Gain	11264551.
Recapture Amount	651729.
Actual Capital Gain	10612822.
Federal and State Capital Gain Tax	3343039.
Recapture Tax	351934.
After Tax Cash From Sale in Year 10	6183685.

Year	DEPN1	DEPN2	DEPN3	FPRINS	FINIRS	SPRINS	SINIRS
1	361270.	0.	298444.	69159.	983459.	0.	0.
2	347723.	0.	253677.	75729.	976889.	0.	0.
3	334683.	0.	215626.	82923.	969695.	0.	0.
4	322132.	0.	183282.	90801.	961817.	0.	0.
5	310052.	0.	173099.	99427.	953191.	0.	0.
6	298426.	0.	173099.	108872.	943745.	0.	0.
7	287235.	0.	173099.	119215.	933402.	0.	0.
8	276463.	0.	173099.	130541.	922077.	0.	0.
9	266096.	0.	173099.	142942.	909676.	0.	0.
10	256117.	0.	173099.	156522.	896096.	0.	0.

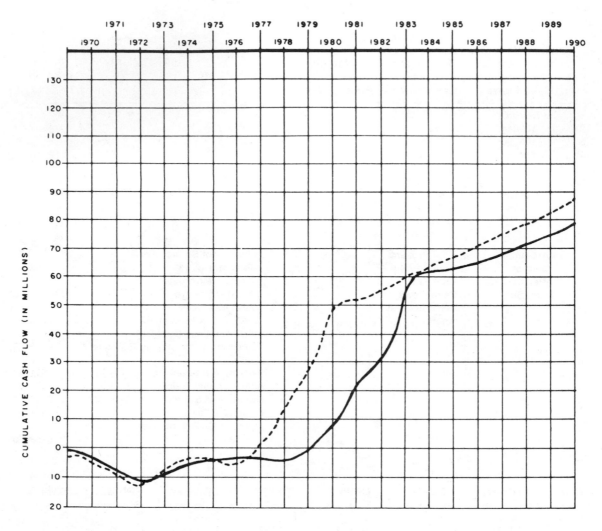

OPTIMISTIC ─ ─ ─ ─ ─ ─ ─ ─ RETURN ON EQUITY INVESTMENT OF 29.5%
CONSERVATIVE ───────── RETURN ON EQUITY INVESTMENT OF 23.5%

10-5. Consolidated and resort development after tax cash flows and returns on investment. Courtesy Thomas Sandor; National Practice Director; Real Estate and Hospitality; Peat, Marwick, Mitchell & Company.

always changing, adding rides, name bands, special celebrations, parades, and big-name entertainers. Remarkably, the original Disneyland was put together in *one* year on what was 65 acres of orange groves.

With the development of Disneyland, the old amusement park, exciting enough in its day, has had to move to a new plane to become entertainment mixed with education, with a dollop of titillation. Art Linkletter is reported to have said to

Walt Disney when the place opened, "Walt, you're making a bum out of Barnum today."

By 1980 more than 187 million guests had experienced "leaving behind today and entering the world of yesterday, tomorrow, and fantasy." In 1983 alone, attendance was 13 million. And not just children enjoy Disneyland — adults outnumber children four to one.

Disneyland provided impetus for the construction of a convention center, a sports stadium, and over 10,000 hotel/motel rooms in Anaheim. About 40 percent of all people who visit California visit Disneyland. It employs 3,000 permanent employees and adds 3,000 more during peak seasons.

Tokyo Disneyland opened in 1983. Constructed on what was 600 acres of barren land near Tokyo Bay, it has the capacity to serve between 10 to 12 million visitors annually. So far its business forecasts have been realized.

The development of Walt Disney World represented one of the most complicated, comprehensive, and costly land developments ever undertaken. In scope and imagination, it deserves to be called fabulous.

Located fifteen miles southwest of Orlando, near the middle of Florida, Disney World covers forty-three square miles, an area twice the size of Manhattan, about the same size as San Francisco. It dwarfs Disneyland. Its latest addition, EPCOT (Experimental Prototype Community of Tomorrow) Center, required a billion-dollar investment.

Planning and development of the first phase of Disney World involved dozens of consultants and the expenditure of about $300 million. The land acquisition for this tremendous project constituted a real-estate coup. Disney acquired 27,433 acres in the Orlando area in 1964 and 1965 for about $200 an acre. Much of the land was swamp, covered with snake-infested palmetto. The swamps fit with the Disney plan of building the Magic Kingdom around water. About $12 million had to be spent for flood and water control, which included some forty miles of winding canals and fifteen miles of levees. The cost of land in and around the project quite naturally skyrocketed so that, by 1970, surrounding land sold for $10,000 an acre. The company does not even conceal plans to sell some of its holdings later and reap a financial harvest on land appreciation.

Disney World's Magic Kingdom of entertainment was patterned after Disneyland in Anaheim. It differs from Disneyland in that it offers theme resorts linked with the entertainment complex by monorail, water craft, and land vehicles.

The lakes surrounding Disney World have 4½ miles of beaches, traversed by more than 150 water craft that range from submarines to paddle-wheel steamers. There are golf courses, stables with riding trails, and nature tours. Recreational activities include swimming, tennis, archery, bicycling, and camping. Walt Disney had appointed five leading conservationists to Disney World's planning board. Consequently, 7,500 acres of Disney property are designated as conservation areas where biologists and wildlife enthusiasts can study nature.

The theme resorts are large hotels, each offering a different style of living and architecture. The Contemporary Resort features an open-mall lobby longer than a football field, with an eighty-foot ceiling. A monorail train connecting all parts of the park travels directly through the lobby to the station located inside. An Asian hotel features a Thai motif; a Polynesian-style hotel carries out the islander theme, with all rooms facing the water. A Venetian hotel, reminiscent of St. Mark's Square in Venice, has its own 120-foot campanile.

The Florida State Road Department has constructed highway interchanges off major highways and has widened local public roads to afford easy access to the project. A central energy plant supplies power, air conditioning, hot water, and compressed air to the entire complex. The system is driven by two 6,000-kilowatt gas-turbine generators. Waste heat from these generators passes to large boilers, which provide high-temperature hot water. The water in turn energizes four 1,500-ton absorption chillers to 40°F, which are used to air-condition the park and building complex. Most of the utilities of the project are underground, including conduits, warehousing, refrigeration, employee wardrobe and lounge areas, and space for the delivery of food, merchandise, and supplies.

Waste collection and removal for such a large development are necessarily extensive, state-of-the-art operations. Sewage is chlorinated, solids are removed, and the nitrate- and phosphate-rich effluent is used to irrigate the golf courses and a 600-acre experimental farm. The collection and removal of trash is automated, using underground pneumatic tubes to transfer trash from collection stations to a central disposal site quickly, economically, and hygienically. A twenty-inch pipe carries the receptacles that transport the waste at sixty miles per hour. It is a system based on the AVAC system of vacuum collection of solid waste that has been used in Sweden for years.

Linking and controlling the entire project is a comprehensive information/communication system encompassing computer systems, telephone systems, automatic monitoring and control systems, mobile communications, television, and wideband systems. Guests can make reservations for hotel rooms, entertainment, and recreation before and during their stay. A special Walt Disney World credit card is provided to hotel guests for use throughout their stay.

The hotels are designed to handle convention business, especially during the off-season. A closed-circuit television system makes it possible for conventions to be held simultaneously in two or more locations.

Evidence of the thought and planning that have gone into Walt Disney World was the establishment of a forty-acre flora research center near the site. Because Florida's indigenous flora do not offer much visual variety, the center was established to experiment with scores of new plants and trees to see if they would adapt to the ecology of central Florida. Thousands of bushes and trees not native to the area were planted; many of them were then used in the Walt Disney World project.

By 1976 Disney World was attracting 12 million visitors a year. It was also attracting its share of criticism. The Orlando area was generally considered overbuilt in hotel/motel rooms, mushrooming from 5,000 rooms in 1965 to over 28,000 in 1975. By 1974 a number of properties were in financial trouble. Editorials appeared denouncing the whole destination development as benefiting only specific groups. The chairperson of the Orange County Commission was quoted as saying, "Unless he is a land speculator, owns a bank, or sells insurance, the average taxpayer around here not only has had zero profit from this tremendous growth — he is paying for it. And I don't mean in our new bumper-to-bumper style of driving, increase in crime and all that. I mean in

cash, for new roads, additional law enforcement, welfare and the rest. No hard feelings, but I wish the mouse had stayed in California."[2] Since then, however, criticism has been muted because of the economic boom created by Disney World.

EPCOT Center, the Experimental Prototype Community of Tomorrow, opened at Disney World in 1982. It is a far cry from what was originally envisioned by Walt Disney: a community of 20,000 people living under a glass dome, the entire area air-conditioned. This concept has quietly disappeared. EPCOT instead consists of two sections—Future World and World Showcase—linked by a fifteen-mile monorail to the Magic Kingdom and several of the resort hotels.

Future World is a series of corporate-sponsored attractions: Spaceship Earth, Universe of Energy, Journey into Imagination, and Land and World of Motion. Visitors enter EPCOT through Future World and ride up through the Spaceship Earth where animated scenes show human progress via communications — all sponsored by American Telephone & Telegraph Company. The General Motors pavilion, shaped like a giant wheel, features the automobile. Exxon Corporation sponsors the Universe of Energy. Kraft Inc. shows innovative ways to grow crops. Eastman Kodak explores creativity in their Journey into Imagination attraction.

The World Showcase features the cultures, traditions, and accomplishments of nations from around the world, including Canada, France, China, Mexico, Britain, Germany, Italy, and Japan. Other countries are expected to add pavilions. Each country offers a film or other attraction, as well as a number of shops and restaurants.

On balance, the Disney attractions have recast theme parks by "imagineering" and building on people's love of nostalgia and fantasy. Beginning in the 1930s, Disney movies transported audiences around the world into a Technicolored dream with anthropomorphic animals and fairy tales set to music, all with happy endings. The

2. Leonard E. Zehnder, *Florida's Disney World: Promises and Problems.* Tallahassee: Peninsular Publishing Co., 1975.

Disney parks move the visitor one step further into a see-and-feel world of scary pirates, talking and singing bears, and Mickey Mouse, all safe, sanitary, and fun. Technical backup has been excellent. Marketing has been superb; Disney targets fifty major markets. Besides being the most extensive and expensive tourist attraction ever built, Disney World was the most widely publicized business venture in history. The Disney ventures attract more foreign visitors than do most nations.

Disney World has played the major role in changing Orlando from a city of 99,000 in 1970 to one of 150,000 in 1985. The area has become an aggregate of hotel rooms, numbering close to 60,000.

THE CRITICAL MASS CONCEPT

Just as an atomic explosion requires a critical mass to explode, a destination needs a minimum number of accommodations, attractions, shopping options, and entertainment offerings to compete successfully. In other words, visitors must have enough things to do to remain interested if their stay is to extend for more than a day or so. Solitary mountain cabins or isolated beaches appeal to relatively few people. The majority of tourists favor places like Las Vegas, Miami Beach, the French and Italian Rivieras, Paris, London, San Francisco, and New York, all of which offer a variety of restaurants and stores for shopping, plus entertainment galore. The isolated resort, no matter how great its initial appeal to guests, loses its luster after a few days. People, being social creatures, want to be around other people; the sophisticated traveler is interested in cultural attractions as well as restaurants, theater, history, and scenic beauty or uniqueness.

The critical mass for an area depends on the particular market to which that area is addressed. The destination developer must put together an assemblage of facilities that will keep visitors interested for several days. This is the problem faced by those who would develop an island in Polynesia, a mountain resort, a Spanish village, or a remote area of Puerto Rico as a new destination.

Places that are remote, such as the Grand Canyon or Yosemite Park, need shops, restaurants, sight-seeing tours, and "created" events as well as their spectacular scenery. Otherwise, the guests stay only a day or two. The more remote the destination, the more likely it will attract only the adventuresome — and the adventuresome want adventure. They quickly exploit what there is to do and move on.

New destinations may not be able to afford the facilities necessary to create the critical mass required to make the destination successful. The destination may limp along for years, losing money until the critical mass is reached. Like so many businesses that lack the necessary initial capital to get off the ground, the smaller destination may ultimately fail even though it seemed to have a promising future.

Initial investments may require considerable capital for infrastructure, including roads, utilities, airports, shopping centers, public transportation, vacation homes, and condominiums. Planners must consider what visitors are going to do besides swim, eat, drink, and sleep. Will visitors be permitted to rent motorized bicycles, as in Bermuda? Can trails be made available for trail bikes, and can trail bikes be rented? Is the area suitable for horseback riding, and who will provide the horses? How can visitors be transported to a historical castle, an ancient temple, or a wildlife park? Can rental cars be made available at convenient points? Will the residents of the area really welcome tourists? What is the supply of local handicrafts? Should the government operate a crafts store? Will sophisticated gamblers be interested in a small casino if the area lacks name entertainment? How many condominiums are necessary to make potential buyers feel as though they are in a viable community, one that will not fail because of its small size? The area's planner catalogues all of the attractions of the destination and then decides at which point the critical mass will be reached.

Overbuilding a destination can be not only costly but self-defeating. The destination with too many rooms and facilities may spread the visitors so thinly that it always looks like off-season, too few people for too many facilities. The developer then must bring in large numbers of people to fill the space. For example, what is now the Sheraton Macuto in Venezuela, not far from the Caracas International Airport, was once an officers' club, very expensive and very exclusive. When the dictator Jimenez was overthrown, the officers' club was made into a luxury resort, but the costs of transportation and accommodations were excessive for any mass market in the United States. The hotel was taken over by the Sheraton International Corporation, and they and the Venezuelan government put together an inexpensive group inclusive tour (GIT), originating in New York City. The hotel then came alive and began to enjoy success. The GIT tapped a new market for the hotel and brought its occupancy to the critical mass necessary to make it attractive.

The Dominican Republic offers another example. About 1975, the island decided to develop tourism. Several first-class hotels were built—but in widely separated places. Critical mass of visitors was attempted by a plan similar to that offered by Venezuela for the Macuto—an inexpensive, all-inclusive package tour lasting one week—not so long that the visitor becomes bored. The number of visitors to the island increased sharply.

LANGUEDOC-ROUSSILLON DEVELOPMENT

The French government has been active in developing the Languedoc-Roussillon coast as a major tourist destination on a scale that more than satisfies the critical mass theory. The area covers some twenty miles of the Mediterranean coast, stretching from the Rhone delta to the Pyrenees (Figure 10-6). When finished, the tourist zone will have the same capacity as the Côte d'Azur.

Before 1963 the Languedoc-Roussillon coastline supported only a sprinkling of fishing villages.

10-6. A general view of La Grande Motte in the Herault area of the French Mediterranean. The French government has actively encouraged tourism there under the Languedoc-Roussillon Tourist Project. The architecture is unique in tourist hotel construction; the Ziggurat-shaped apartment complexes are intended to modify the effects of winds on the village.

Brackish lagoons proved ideal for millions of mosquitoes, and fresh water was lacking. An antiquated road system made access to the coast time-consuming.

That changed beginning in 1963, when the government started building a toll superhighway, the A–9, parallel to the coast but away from the beaches. The road passes through Montpelier, which is about six hours by high-speed train, the TGV, from Paris. Lagoons were dredged, pure water provided, some conservation areas established, and several "super" resorts built.

When complete, the region will be divided into five tourist units, each unit a complete resort containing up to 50,000 beds. Green belts will separate the five clusters. The government is responsible for all of the infrastructure—the roads, airports, services, car parks, car ports, marinas, and country parks, as well as for the eradication of pollution and mosquitoes. Private investors will take over the development of hotels, camping, apartments, trailer sites, activity centers, and other tourist facilities.

SPECIALLY DEVELOPED DESTINATIONS

Rockresorts—Isolation for the Rich

Imagine yourself to be a very rich person with a fine sensibility for natural beauty and an urge to preserve and cultivate that beauty and share it with others. Your name might be Rockefeller, with access to one of the great fortunes of the world and a sense of stewardship inherited from the family.

What better way to share and conserve natural beauty than to create a resort in the midst of that beauty? This is what Laurance Rockefeller has done on the island of Hawaii, in the Virgin Islands, Puerto Rico, Wyoming, and Vermont. The resorts created are among the most beautiful in the world; many people believe they are the ultimate in blending resort facilities into a natural environment in such a way as to enhance the quality of that environment.

Rockresorts have been described as a view with a room, a haven for the governmental, monied, and intellectual elite, a vehicle for developing depressed economies. They are of such a scale, quality, and remoteness from the usual markets that only a Rockefeller would undertake them. The Aga Khan, with his resort complex on the island of Sardinia, is the only resort operator who can claim membership in the same league.

The idea for these resorts was gestating in Rockefeller's mind in the late 1940s when he explored the Caribbean, island by island. In 1952 he bought Caneel Bay Plantation on the island of St. John in the U.S. Virgin Islands (Figure 10-7). St. John, nine miles long and no more than five miles wide, had almost no industry or agriculture. It had no electricity, no water system, and a small, unskilled population. Everything for the resort had to be brought in or developed from scratch. Submarine power cables from St. Thomas were laid; tanks and the water to fill them were barged in. Vocational education programs for future employees were put into effect.

Rockefeller donated a good part of the island to the U.S. government, to become the Virgin Islands National Park. Caneel Bay Plantation comprises some 400 acres, seven beaches, and a number of cottages hidden behind sea grape hedges. It is not for the swinger or the tourist who wants a little bit of Manhattan in a tropical setting.

The guest eats at one of two al fresco dining rooms. Playing on beautiful tennis courts, snorkeling, and lying on the beach constitute the day's effort. Guests may attend talks by park rangers in the evening, or they may rent a jeep for a day and explore the island. A dozen or so Sunfish are used, mainly by the employees. (There are about 300 employees for the 130 guest rooms, more than one employee for each guest.)

Although only a small percentage of the world's population can afford the rates at Caneel Bay Plantation, a few miles down the road the same sort of natural beauty can be enjoyed for a modest cost. Cinnamon Bay was opened in 1964 by the National Park Service; in 1969, it was taken over by Rockresort management, who invested $1 million to improve its facilities.

THE TOURIST BUSINESS

10-7. Caneel Bay Plantation, St. John, U.S. Virgin Islands, one of the most beautiful resorts in the world. Spread over 200 acres of a former Danish sugar plantation, the resort has only 130 guest rooms. Its occupancy rate is unusually high.

Rockefeller's next venture took him to Puerto Rico, where the government felt that tourism needed to be encouraged in locations other than San Juan. Dorado Beach, built on a swamp on the grounds of a former grapefruit and coconut plantation, was the result (Figure 10-8). More than a million tons of earth were removed to reclaim much of the area used for the guest units and the two eighteen-hole golf courses. The swamps were either drained or turned into lagoons, streams, and other water hazards for the golf course. As at Caneel Bay, it was necessary to teach waiters and others to serve clientele with gourmet tastes skillfully. Guest rooms in beach houses and cabanas make up the 306 rooms spread on either side of a central building. Twenty miles west of San Juan, the 1,500-acre estate includes two miles of the Atlantic coast and two Robert Trent Jones golf courses.

Cerromar Beach, completed in 1971, became a sister resort. It too has two eighteen-hole golf courses, plus a casino, supper club, shopping arcade, sauna, and 508 guest rooms and suites. Condominiums are a part of both Dorado Beach and Cerromar Beach. The two resorts, with a total of 800 rooms, can cater to large conventions. (Both resorts are now managed by Hyatt Hotels.)

Little Dix Bay, a resort hideaway resembling St. John in its relative inaccessibility, was built on British Virgin Gordo, only eight square miles in size. Work started in 1958. The kind of problems encountered at Little Dix Bay help to explain why only a person of perseverance and great wealth can succeed with a resort in such a location. A dirt airstrip had to be built. An experimental solar plant to distill sea water failed, an electric desalting plant proved inadequate, and now water is barged from Puerto Rico, sixty miles to the west. All food must be imported, as well as most of the employees.

Little Dix Bay has no telephones and no air conditioning. It is thought by many to be the perfect escape resort. At the thatched huts on the beach are little flags, which guests hoist any time they want food or drink. The dining room is an open-sided pavilion under vaulted roofs that angle down close to the floor. The tablecloths are clamped to the tables to prevent the breezes from blowing them away.

Mauna Kea Beach Hotel, on just about everybody's list of great hotels, was built in 1965 following a request from the governor of Hawaii to develop the island of Hawaii as a tourist area. Like all Rockresorts, it is aesthetically integrated with the land and water (Figure 10-9). Mauna Kea was sold to United Airlines for about $51 million and is now operated by Japanese-owned Westin International Hotels.

Rockresorts' next venture was the stately Kapalua Bay Hotel and Club near Kaanapoli Beach on the island of Maui. The site offers a magnificent view of the ocean and the island of Molokai. It too was part of a land development scheme and is no longer managed by Rockresorts.

In 1985 Laurance Rockefeller unveiled The Boulders at Carefree, Arizona. Just twenty miles from Scottsdale, the new resort has nearly one hundred adobelike *casitas* (little homes) that are a rich man's version of a Pueblo Indian village. Built at a cost of $200 million, the resort includes lakes and a golf course.

The Carambola Beach and Golf Club on St. Croix, U.S. Virgin Islands, is the most recent of the Rockresorts. It has 156 guest accommodations and is a centerpiece for a low-density community of some 4,000 acres that will include residential units, a conference center, and several golf courses.

Rockresorts cannot be judged using the usual financial frame of reference. The payoff period is not the usual resort's two or three or even five years, but rather seven years. It is well known, however, that a successful resort multiplies the value of the land around it. Condominium developments built on adjacent property can be highly profitable and can also provide customers for the food and beverage operations of the hotels. Rockresorts represent, as one writer put it, *noblesse oblige*. They also represent one man's vision of beauty and a desire to share that vision.

Rockresort management has a style, a polish, and a grace found in few places. It is not precision service, as stressed by the luxury resorts of Europe. It is informal, open, but nonetheless impeccable.

10-8. The Dorado Beach Hotel in Puerto Rico caters to both the golf lover and the person who appreciates a tropical beach.

10-9. One of the great hotels in the world, the Mauna Kea Beach Hotel was built at Kamuela, Hawaii. As is true with most of the Rockresorts, the hotel was built both as a fine resort and as a means of bringing life to an economically depressed area. The hotel sits on the dry side of the large island of Hawaii. Though the area gets less than 20 inches of rainfall a year, plenty of water is available by pipeline from the nearby mountains. The resort is assured of almost year-round sunshine without the usual concomitant water shortage.

That the Mauna Kea acted as a seeding operation for destination development is evident. By 1988 three other large resorts had been built in the same general area of Hawaii: the Moana Lani, the Sheraton Waikaloa, and the Hyatt Waikaloa.

In 1987 Rockresorts were purchased by CSX, a transportation and natural resource company that also owns the Greenbrier resort, one of the classic resorts in the United States.

Nantucket: Master Planning by an Individual

Visitors to Nantucket may feel they are stepping into a mid-nineteenth-century whaling town. Indeed they are, or at least the town looks like one man's view of what Nantucket was like in 1850. The island, thirty miles off Cape Cod, has been largely redesigned by one man, Walter Beinecke, who has spent millions in buying property on the island and razing rundown buildings. By buying up large parcels of the downtown area and virtually all of the wharf, Beinecke was able to raise rents and prescribe the design and operation of businesses. His holdings include 155 buildings. Beinecke says he is determined to protect the island from the developers who have taken over much of Cape Cod and turned it into honky-tonk strips of motels, gas stations, and fast-food stands.

In place of the buildings he has torn down, he has put in a marina, a string of narrow one- and two-story gray-shingle shops, and a bandstand. To most visitors the island is authentic; others say it is not. One of his companies, the Nantucket Historical Trust, is owner of the Jared Coffin House, a fine restaurant and inn that must, according to its lease, remain open year-round even though it loses money during the winter.

TOURIST DESTINATION DEVELOPMENT

Conservation forces and government bodies have preserved a third of the island's 31,000 acres as open space and maintain that, to protect the character of the island, one-half of it must be kept undeveloped. The Nantucket Conservation Foundation has accumulated 6,300 acres of land, most of it gifts from wealthy landowners. A public counterpart, the Land Bank, raises money for land purchase by a 2 percent tax on real estate transfers.

Not everyone agrees with the need to conserve. Two-thirds of the 6,000 year-round residents, it is said, live off real estate, prices for which have soared.

Sea Pines Plantation: Practical Idealism

Sea Pines Plantation on Hilton Head Island just off the coast of South Carolina is another well-planned self-contained destination, an example of "practical idealism." A resort catering to tennis, golf, and ocean lovers, Sea Pines Plantation is one of the tightest, most completely controlled resort developments anywhere. Charles Fraser, its developer, believed strongly that the only way to have aesthetic control was through ownership. Some forty pages of restrictions are attached to every deed issued to purchasers of the hundreds of individually owned properties in the plantation. Fraser retained the legal power to negate any building or landscaping plan proposed by an owner. The Plantation includes condominium villas, a small town, and a series of apartments. Most of the houses have cedar-shake roofs and bleached-cypress siding.

Fraser had definite ideas about the seashore and the location of housing in relationship to the shore. No homes line the beach, for Fraser felt that the beach would be limited to those houses that front the ocean. Instead, dozens of public swaths are interspersed between arterial roads. Walkways through the swaths to the ocean allow everyone easy acess to the sea. Neither the beach nor the line of primary dunes behind it has been built upon. Although there is an unusual density of homes, the landscaping is such that each appears well-separated from the others and individual. Some houses are set back in the woods along the numerous fairways; others have been built along narrow drives that lead toward the beach from the principal roads.

Considerable effort was made to save the trees, with roads being built around the trees to avoid cutting them down. Fraser, it was said, would not remove a tree until at least two automobiles had crashed into it. Twenty-five percent of the Plantation has been left in its natural state, to the point where alligators were kept in the ponds and streams until they were 6 feet long. Fraser also saved 75 percent of the marshlands.

The real-estate operation style of Hilton Head — providing the house or condo owner with a second home plus the opportunity for equity appreciation — has spread south to Amelia Island near Jacksonville and north to Fripp Island, Kiawek Island, and Seabrook Island.

The ups and downs of land development were felt by Sea Pines Company when the 1973–1975 recession hit. Fraser had pushed ahead with the development of Palmas del Mar, similar to Sea Pines Plantation, in Puerto Rico near San Juan. The highly leveraged company had run up a debt of $300 million and a negative worth of $42 million. Luckily the banks did not foreclose, and over time Sea Pines became profitable. Later Fraser sold his interest in Sea Pines Plantation but left as his legacy a model for destination development.[3]

SKI AREAS

Selection of a site for a ski area is critical since weather and availability of snow cover during the ski season are overriding considerations. According to Ted A. Farwell, a vacation-oriented ski resort must possess seven factors.[4]

1. A vertical drop of 1,500 feet in the northeastern United States or a 3,000 to 4,000 foot vertical drop in the west. Base areas must be large enough to accommodate 3,000 to 5,000 skiers.

3. Fred Mark, "The High Stakes At Hilton Head." *State Newspaper*, Columbia, S.C., December 7, 1986.
4. Ted A. Farwell, "Resort Planning and Development." Cornell Hotel and Restaurant Administration Quarterly, May 1980.

2. A location where prevailing winds will not whip away snow, usually a north or northeast exposure.
3. An annual snowfall of 200 inches, coming at frequent intervals. Less snow calls for snowmaking equipment, which is expensive.
4. Slopes for both beginners and for experts, ranging from grades of 25 to 75 percent.
5. A climate cold enough to maintain the snow, preferably with lots of sunshine.
6. An adequate source of water if snowmaking equipment is to be used.
7. A base area large enough to accommodate lift terminals, base buildings, parking, lodges, and other amenities.

It also helps to be within driving distance of a metropolitan area with tens of thousands of ski enthusiasts, as is the case of Mammoth Mountain. The busiest of all ski resorts, Mammoth hosts as many as 21,000 skiers a day, most of them from the Los Angeles Basin, several driving hours south.

Though not usually associated with the South, skiing has developed rapidly there. Southern resort skiing is believed to have begun in 1959 at the Homestead, near Hot Springs, Virginia, when that well-known hotel converted part of its golf course to a ski slope. North Carolina has a number of ski resorts. All rely on machine-made snow for a good part of the winter and are plagued with winter rains that undo much of what the snowmakers have done.

Vail Village in Colorado is a particularly successful ski resort. At an altitude of 8,200 to 11,200 feet above sea level, it is 110 miles west of Denver, a drive of about two and a half hours. Once a relatively remote sheep pasture in the heart of the Rockies, commercial property values in Vail Village increased from the original value of about $150 an acre to about $6 per square foot after the town was transformed into a ski resort.

Because the village core area totals only about 140 acres, it has been kept primarily for pedestrians by placing parking lots underground. The initial cost of underground parking is offset to some extent by the savings that result because snow removal is not necessary. One side effect of this decision, not originally planned, has been that the one-day skier is being replaced by the person who stays for a longer period because the day-skier has no place to park.

It took Vail Village four years to become profitable. Once that happened, the commercial land was leased rather than sold. Leases run for a period of forty-nine years, with options to extend an additional forty-nine years. An unusual feature of the lease arrangement is that the lessee pays 8 percent of the value of the property, with the property being revalued at the ends of the fifth and tenth years. Thereafter, it is revalued every ten years for the life of the lease.

MASTER PLANNING: PREREQUISITE FOR SUCCESS

This chapter shows that, by casting the most critical eye possible upon a proposed land or resort development, planners can better anticipate what will happen to sales and profits. If they are government planners, they can better forecast cost and benefits to the area. Developers can call for inputs to their plans from a variety of experts. Based upon certain assumptions, they can project cost and return on the investment well into the future.

A master plan allows planners to stage their investments by increments. Foreseeing the future is not possible, but by staging investments, they can modify their plans according to what really happens. If projection of visitors or buyers exceeds their forecasts, they can bring in the second stage more quickly. If the forecasts prove to be overly optimistic, the development can be slowed or halted. In this sense a master plan is a hedge against the future.

With a master plan, the developer is more likely to be able to borrow money from institutional lenders. If the project is sizable, a master plan is mandatory in order to interest the decision makers from the lending institutions. The master plan does not provide prescience, but it does force planners to examine contingencies that otherwise might be overlooked.

Figure 10-10 shows the proposed master development site plan for the Mauna Lani Resort on what was 3,000 acres of stark lava on the south Kohala coast of the big island of Hawaii. Belt Collins and Associates were involved in the planning process for this major resort/recreation community and support-employee community since 1974. The master plan included development strategy, detailed design and infrastructure requirements, the design and construction supervision of an award-winning golf course, and the preservation of major historical sites. Civil and landscape design services were provided for the Mauna Lani Point residential area, Mauna Lani Bay Hotel, the first championship 18-hole golf course, and the first phase infrastructure systems. Currently Belt Collins and Associates are working on the design of a second resort, the Ritz-Carlton

at Mauna Lani, and related infrastructure systems. The estimated construction cost is $500,000,000.

Figure 10-11 is the landscape development plan for the Mauna Lani Bay Hotel and its environs, and Figure 10-12 is an aerial view of the completed hotel. The master staircase of the hotel is shown in Figure 10-13.

Destination planning is a matter of evolution, one planner building on designs and materials used by predecessors. Once in a while a planner and/or architect comes along who takes what has gone before and uses it so dramatically and on such a scale that the finished product can be called a breakthrough. In resort planning, Christopher B. Hemmeter raised the size, scope, and investment of the destination resort to a new level.

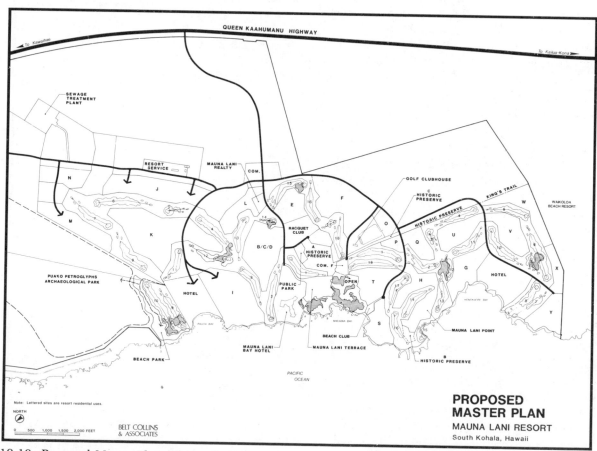

10-10. Proposed Master Plan, Mauna Lani Resort, South Kohala, Hawaii. Courtesy of Sheila Donnelly and Associates, Honolulu, Hawaii

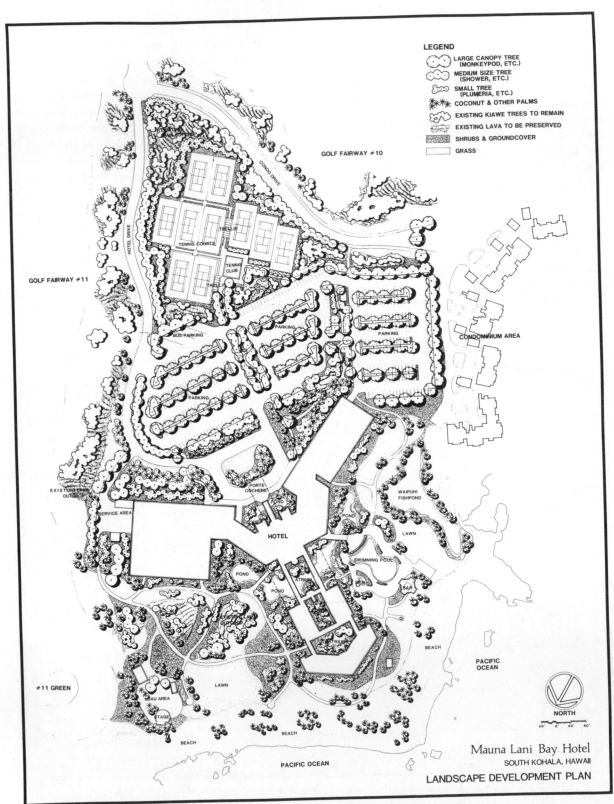

LEGEND

- LARGE CANOPY TREE (MONKEYPOD, ETC.)
- MEDIUM SIZE TREE (SHOWER, ETC.)
- SMALL TREE (PLUMERIA, ETC.)
- COCONUT & OTHER PALMS
- EXISTING KIAWE TREES TO REMAIN
- EXISTING LAVA TO BE PRESERVED
- SHRUBS & GROUNDCOVER
- GRASS

GOLF FAIRWAY #10

GOLF FAIRWAY #11

TENNIS COURTS

TRELLIS

TENNIS CLUB

TRELLIS

BUS PARKING

PARKING

PARKING

PARKING

PARKING

CONDO DRIVE

HOTEL DRIVE

CONDOMINIUM AREA

EXISTING LAVA OUTCROP

SERVICE AREA

PORTE COCHERE

POND

POND

POND

WAIPUHI FISHPOND

LAWN

HOTEL

POND

ATRIUM

POND

SWIMMING POOL

BAR

BEACH

PACIFIC OCEAN

#11 GREEN

LUAU AREA

STAGE

LAWN

ATRIUM

BEACH

BEACH

PACIFIC OCEAN

NORTH

40' 0' 40' 80'

Mauna Lani Bay Hotel
SOUTH KOHALA, HAWAII
LANDSCAPE DEVELOPMENT PLAN

10-11. Mauna Lani Bay Hotel, South Kohala, Hawaii: Landscape Development Plan.

The Westin Kauai, which is now owned by the Bass brothers of Texas and a Japanese construction company, illustrates Hemmeter's architectural eloquence. Everything is on a grand scale. From the port cochere the guest descends three levels by escalator, encountering a breathtaking reflecting pool with an island in the center, on which eight marble stallions cavort in mist from three fountains rising six stories high. The swimming pool is three-fourths the size of a football field (see Figure 10-14). Oriental art is placed in the lobby, all corridors, around the pools, on the grounds, even on the beach, which is situated on a protected cove. Huge horses, all Percherons, Belgians, and Clydesdales, are used to pull the guest carriages around the property.

When completed, the resort will have ten restaurants and lounges and 200 acres of lawns and botanical gardens, all on 520 acres along a half-mile expanse of white sand bay. Also, ten miles of waterways will be negotiated by gondola.

Other even larger resorts are being planned in Southern California which will call for sophisticated financial analysis, market forecasts, and ecological impact studies and planning to recruit the needed personnel numbers and skills to operate the resorts.

10-12. An aerial view of the Mauna Lani Bay Hotel as it is today.
SOURCE: Courtesy of Sheila Donnelly and Associates, Honolulu, Hawaii.

10-13. This is the master staircase of the Mauna Lani Bay Hotel, on the big island of Hawaii. The hotel is one of several Japanese-owned resort hotels on Hawaii. These properties are unusual in the huge investments involved and in the owners' willingness to build a complete resort, along with tennis courts and golf courses, on land that was almost completely covered with lava and that was until recently considered impractical because of the cost of development.
SOURCE: Photo courtesy of Sheila Donnelly and Associates, Honolulu, Hawaii.

10-14. The pool of the Westin Kauai, which is three-quarters the size of a football field, suggests the glamor and lavishness of the resort.
SOURCE: Photo by Media Systems, Hawaii.

TOURIST DESTINATION DEVELOPMENT

DISCUSSION QUESTIONS

1. Feasibility studies necessarily make economic forecasts and predict the numbers of visitors to the location or area being considered. Suppose you were doing a market study for a proposed resort hotel on the island of Tahiti. What are some of the factors you would have to consider?

2. Condominium and resort hotels must have local planning board approval before they can be built. Environmental impact studies are usually required. Can you see any economic justification for such studies?

3. Discuss the relationship of the federal tax structure to investments in hotels and in resorts.

4. As owner of five acres of valuable beach property, would you sit on it and let it appreciate over the years or would you be willing to participate in a beach resort development? Give your reasons.

5. In your opinion, can Disneyland and Disney World expect a decline in visitors over the next twenty years? Give reasons for your conclusion.

6. Are there places or conditions where the critical mass concept of destination development does not apply? Explain.

7. If you were developing a beach resort, would you include a number of condominium apartments to be sold to individual owners? Why or why not?

8. Why is it so difficult to project accurately the number of guest rooms that will be needed in the future for a particular destination area?

9. Aside from the number of visitors to an area, what factors influence the number of hotel employees that are needed for a destination area?

10. A destination that receives large numbers of cruise ship visitors often incorporates these numbers into total visitors reported for the destination. Why is this misleading?

11. Merely publishing the number of guest rooms available in a country can also be misleading with regard to the extent of tourism. Why?

12. When developing a destination area, why does the development company usually go outside of the company for independent market and feasibility studies?

13. Name some of the risks to an investor in a destination development.

14. Where does the sociologist/psychologist fit into a group planning a destination development?

15. Most resort developments today involve condominium development as well. Why?

16. Golf courses, often included in resort developments, are really loss leaders. Why?

17. When a resort development is called highly leveraged, what is meant?

18. Why is it so important in projecting hotel development to compute the tax shelter available at the end of each year?

ELEVEN

DESTINATION DEVELOPMENT: PROBLEMS AND CHALLENGES

In recent years vast stretches of land have been studied and improved to create new tourist destinations. Most of these developments have taken place in areas where mild or subtropical weather prevails – the Mediterranean, the Caribbean, Hawaii, the American Southwest. Other developments have occurred in ski country – Vermont, New Hampshire, Maine, and Colorado.

By scrutinizing an entire area and the interrelationships taking place within the environment, planners have been able to recommend total community development with all elements in harmony. At the same time, the communities are planned to be economically viable and attractive as tourist destinations. They are more than just real-estate developments, which are usually undertaken for the profit of a few individuals or a corporation and then may prove less than satisfactory for the good of the larger community.

LAND DEVELOPMENT

Motivation for the development of new tourist destinations has sometimes come from philanthropic-minded individuals or from state or national governments interested in improving the economy and way of life of a large group of people. Ideally, the results are beneficial to everyone con-cerned. *Land development* is one term often used for this broader type of planning. Unlike real-estate development, land development is likely to deal with unused or agricultural land rather than already existing residential, business, or industrial sections. The proposal may include a resort as part of the total plan, or the resort may be the central feature. The plan is likely to include a town or village made up of permanent residents and employees of the resort. Villages for retirees may be included.

"The highest and best possible use" of the real estate has usually meant the best profit for the developer. Land-development planning in its best sense is intended to be beneficial not only for the developer but also the user and the community at large. It takes into consideration the welfare of the people who will be employed in the new facilities – their lifestyle and economic welfare – as well as the satisfaction of the visitor and the owner.

Development of a Destination

Land development may include long-range plans for all facilities needed for a tourist destination: water supply, roads, police protection, health care, tourist reception and accommodations, tourist attractions, and other entertainment. It also will include short-term and long-term urban planning — shopping facilities, recreational facilities, provisions for schools and churches, sewers and sewerage treatment, and flood control. Some plans include community clubs and green belts as well. Recommendations may be made concerning the management of golf courses, hotels, gift shops, and tourist attractions. Plans may include marinas, aerial tramways, and other facilities having tourist value.

Cities such as Edmonton, Alberta, and San Francisco have enacted controls on cityscapes, large areas of the city where guidelines are placed on maximum volume for a building and the avoidance of large boxlike buildings. Cincinnati, Ohio, has a hillside ordinance that encourages mixing land use on a hillside to balance social, economic, historic, aesthetic, and ecological concerns. Toronto designates public views as landmarks and does not allow new construction to obstruct those views.

Wisconsin has designated thirty-two roads totaling over 150 miles as "rustic" roads and mandates that they are to retain these unique qualities by means of upkeep standards and zoning.

Tourist areas are developed for a number of reasons, among them the following:

1. For immediate gain to the developer. The developer assembles a package and sells pieces of it to other entrepreneurs, acquiring a profit in the process.
2. For long-term appreciation of the land. Over a period of time, land almost always appreciates. Profits from the land sale are taxed as a capital gain at less than the maximum rate that is charged for ordinary income.
3. To increase the value of property around a development. A hotel, for example, may be the "frosting on the cake," the lever for appreciating surrounding land. Its value as an operating hotel may be small.
4. To increase employment in an economically stunted section.
5. For political reasons. An area may be built up as a means of granting aid to a region, paying political debts, and redistributing income within a region or country.

6. To create a lasting tribute. A resort may be viewed as a monument to someone's ability or pride, an opportunity to build something beautiful and enduring.
7. To express national pride. In some of the smaller countries, a new hotel is a showplace, perhaps the most imposing building in the country, a place for government entertainment and an official government facility to house distinguished visitors.
8. To meet a challenge. Some areas have been developed, at least partially, because an individual or group thinks of a resort as a challenging business. Several resorts in the Caribbean were built by persons or families for the joy of doing it.
9. To obtain foreign capital. A government, such as Spain or Bulgaria, needs foreign exchange with which to buy technology and manufactured products abroad. Tourism development is viewed as a means of attracting visitors and acquiring the needed foreign exchange.

Failure of Tourist Areas

Tourist areas fail, aesthetically and financially, for three principal reasons: lack of market research, lack of area planning, and lack of sufficient long-range funding. A hotel or other tourist facility cannot survive without a market. Many facilities have been built with little or no thought given to market feasibility. Established resorts fail because of changing tastes, obsolescence, changes in transportation, new competition, and poor management.

Tourist facilities that have not been controlled or planned carefully can become part of an unappealing jungle of buildings. The "motel rows" found off highways leading to many American cities are examples of this. Each motel owner is forced to erect a larger sign and to forgo landscaping or other amenities in order to compete. Nobody profits, least of all the traveler. When an area grows without controls or planning, each entrepreneur shifts for himself or herself, with little regard for the area as a whole. The area suffers and in the long pull, the entrepreneur does not do well, or does less well than if planning and controls had been instituted.

Ecological Considerations

Ecology, the science of the relationships between organisms and their environment, plays a definite role in destination development. One of the organisms is the human being, the great change agent in the environment, the instrument in making deserts bloom or rivers change course, constructing buildings that shut out the sun, and making arrangements for people to live thousands to the square mile.

Ecologists and others are rightfully concerned that though there are believed to be more than 1.5 million species of life, humans are responsible for wiping out at least one species each day, some say one per hour. The gene pool these extinct species represent is lost forever. To save a species, however, can sometimes be very costly in terms of human well-being. Destination development considers the ecological effects of a development and the factors that will least upset the ecological balance in the destination area.

What is ecologically desirable has a range of answers. Should we spend millions of dollars to save a small species of fish as was done to save the snail darter in the Tennessee Valley project? What kind of urban environment is best? There are people who cannot stand crowds; others are unhappy without them. Millions of people opt for New York City, the most exciting place in the world, they say. Others feel differently: "Fence it off and evacuate."

Many ecological controls are of obvious value: protection of a water supply, prevention of erosion, protection of unique natural beauty, elimination of malarial mosquitoes, and so on. When it comes to the question of overcrowding, the answers are less clear. Holland is one of the most crowded environments on earth, yet many consider it one of the most beautiful and desirable countries.

Ecology has cost/benefits, and often the most vocal ecologists bear none of the costs. A white-river rafter who opposes the construction of a dam that removes rapids may have little concern for the benefits a dam may bring. The homeowner in a low density area may oppose a resort development that could provide hundreds of jobs for less affluent people. The resident may be pleased, however, to patronize the new restaurants and shops a resort development may bring.[1]

Around the world beachfront development has been largely unplanned. The result is that, by accident or wealth, relatively few people live in accommodations fronting on many of the beauty spots of the world. Long stretches of coastline are completely blocked from view by contiguous residences and hotels/motels. On the island of Maui, one condominium after another, each accommodating only a limited number of people, effectively blocks from view some of the loveliest beaches in the world. The Costa del Sol of Spain is another example of lack of planning, resulting in a jumble of buildings and lack of open space. Parts of Cape Cod have developed into what might be called "resort slums."

In some less developed countries, choice views may be acquired by foreigners to the exclusion of the nationals. To forestall this, Mexico for many years has banned non-Mexicans from owning land within thirty-one miles of the ocean and mandated that all beaches are open to the public.

In the past the elite and the rich usually acquired the choice land sites of an area and lived in enclaves of affluence. Current regional planning theories consider all of the people, or at least the middle class, as well. Regional planners suggest that open spaces be provided along oceanfront areas. They also require that all beachfront be public property and accessible to everyone. As one planner put it, to do otherwise is like inviting 100,000 people to a football game and allowing only the tallest and the strongest to force their way to the front row, where only they are able to see the game.

Overuse of an area may affect not only the people involved, but also the actual climate. Parts of Greece illustrate this effect, although tourists did not cause it. During World War II, the Greeks cut down huge tracts of forests for use as firewood to

1. For further reading on tourism and the physical environment, see the special issue of *Annals of Tourism Research* (Volume 14, Number 1), Program Press, New York, 1987.

keep from freezing. With the forests gone, water ran off quickly from the land, eroding it. Moreover, the lack of trees, which produce moisture in the atmosphere, actually reduced the amount of rainfall in certain areas. If large tracts of forest are cleared to allow the development of tracts for tourism, the same kind of problem could well emerge.

On Zakinthos, which lies between the Greek mainland and Italy, the Greek government banned development of a seven-mile stretch of beach on the Ionian Sea, in order to protect the breeding ground of the loggerhead turtle. Every summer about 800 females of this species drag themselves onto the shore of a cove to lay their eggs in the sand. Tourism had halved the number of loggerhead nests in the decade prior to 1986 when the ban was put into effect. The decree set aside 1,100 acres as a "zone of complete protection" that runs the length of the bay and stretches inland for 220 to 250 yards. It also limited building activity adjacent to the protected beaches.

Swamps, once thought of as wasted land, are now valued as wetlands where fish and wildlife live and as nature's way of controlling floods and filtering polluted water. A policy called *mitigation* allows landowners to build on a marsh in some jurisdictions, but only if they replace the marsh elsewhere.

Planning tourism for islands presents special climate problems. Because of prevailing winds, most islands have a windward side and a leeward side. The windward side is usually warm, wet and cool; the leeward side is comparatively dry and warm. Some planners suggest that dramatic resort accommodations, services, and entertainment facilities be built on the favored leeward side, holding the windward side development to low-rise buildings and expanses of agricultural and forest lands. Valleys can be used for green space, recreational sites, camping, and wildlife refuges. The planners would permit the dry and sunny leeward side to have high-rise hotels, but only if they were interspersed with open spaces, gardens, parks, and corridors to the sea.

One way to ensure open spaces and corridors in concentrated tourist centers is to zone for parks and historical preservation sites. Each area should have an upper limit placed on the number of rooms that can be built—a set number that will not permit crowding and the consequent erosion of the environment. Planners of the Aspen, Colorado, ski area have done this. They estimate that between 28,000 and 30,000 skiers can be accommodated on the slopes without undue stress. Working back, they suggest that the number of hotel rooms be limited to the maximum number of skiers that can enjoy the area.

GOVERNMENT PARTICIPATION IN AREA DEVELOPMENT

Local, state, and federal governments participate in every tourist development in one way or another. The degree of participation or intervention covers a wide range.

The necessity for government planning is seen clearly along oceanfronts and offshore islands. Sand dunes are necessary to maintain the ecology of coastal islands; the dunes protect the islands from wind and wave force. The prevailing winds coming in from the sea tend to move sand dunes inland. To prevent such movement, some plant growth, for example, sea oats, is necessary to disrupt the flow of air and allow the sand to settle out on the top or front of the dunes rather than behind them. The dune grows taller until a critical point is reached where the energy of the wind is no longer sufficient to move the sands to the top. When this happens, a new dune is formed to the windward side of the existing dune and the island begins to build seaward rather than inland.

If dune buggies and animal grazing disturb the growth of plant life, the dunes will be swept inland and the beach destroyed. Construction of beachfront cottages, motels, and parking lots occasion the same result. A study by the University of Georgia recommends that at least one-third of any island used for recreation and residence be retained in its natural state, with no more than access trails in the reserve area. The building of beachfront property should be government-controlled to ensure it is at least 100 yards back from highwater lines. Bulldozing of sand dunes should be prohibited.

Islands need a forest canopy to act as an airfoil, lifting the wind up and over the island. If clearings are made in the forest, the bordering trees are subjected to abnormal wind pressures that may uproot them. Pine trees, because of their great height, are particularly vulnerable to this danger.

Offshore islands continue to expand and contract because of wave action. Mild summer waves generally add sand to the border or berm of the islands, while heavy winter waves more frequently remove sand. In the summer the islands grow as prevailing on-shore winds move dry sand from the berm to the dunes. In winter, the process is reversed. The border or berm helps to moderate such changes by providing a reservoir of sand available to the dunes and the beach. Where the dune movement is not understood and dunes are destroyed by construction or overuse, large parts of the island may be claimed by the sea and become unavailable for anyone's use or enjoyment.

Government has participated in tourist development in several ways. The state of Vermont owns no ski developments but has built access roads to new developments. The state of New Hampshire, alongside Vermont, has built several ski developments as a state enterprise. Florida has built interchanges from state highways to link them with Disney World.

The federal government had made expensive studies and provided large loans for tourist development in the Ozark region. Federal and state parks encourage tourists to come into their areas. The American states spend many millions in advertising and promotion to attract tourists each year.

Most tourist developments require that state and local public money be used to extend sewerage systems, water lines, roads, and other public utilities. The establishment of state and federal monuments and historic sites is a public cost.

Government Planning Abroad

Abroad, participation in tourist development is almost completely controlled by the government. In Spain and Portugal, for example, where private enterprise was reluctant to invest in tourism, the governments have stepped in to prime the pump to get tourism started. The Spanish *paradores* — government-owned and -operated hostelries — are beautifully located, maintained, and operated. Portugal has about twenty government-owned *pousadas*, many historically interesting, as well as some small government-owned hotels. The Greek government has built hotels that are transferred either to the private sector or a mixed company as soon as they are operating well.

A large number of national governments encourage tourism by providing specific incentives for private investment. Credit for tourism investment is usually given only to developments approved by the government. Such credits take the form of long-term loans at lower than market rates of interest. In most countries loans for hotel construction are for about twenty-five years; reconstruction and equipment loans, either ten or fifteen years. Other aids may include reduced customs duties on imported construction materials and equipment needed for tourist services.

At Cancún, Mexico's government built a model resort development from scratch on a largely deserted beach. Separately, on the mainland, a town was constructed to accommodate the people who built the development; it now houses the development's employees.

In Puerto Vallarta the government's tourism development agency, Fonatur, tried to accommodate the varied interests of the village while moving ahead with the acquisition of land and the construction of hotels, building the infrastructure to support them.

Fonatur works closely with the El Presidente chain of hotels. Both report to the minister of tourism. When the government decided to develop Ixtapa, north of Acapulco, the Ixtapa El Presidente was built. The same thing happened in Cancún. The El Presidente, one of the first hotels there, was built to seed the hotel business on that peninsula. The same process happened at Loreto, about halfway down Baja California and at the Bahia de Huatulco, on the coast 335 miles south of Acapulco. Fonatur provides large sums to foment the growth of tourism.

Need for Government Aid

Without government aid, tourism in some regions cannot grow substantially. For example, in the Caribbean, a jet airport is an absolute necessity if large numbers of tourists are to be attracted to the islands. No independent developer is likely to build such an airport. Similarly, inaccessible mountain areas are not likely to be opened for tourist development without access roads being built by the state. The U.S. government, wanting to "showcase" the results of its invasion of the Caribbean island of Grenada, has poured millions of dollars into the island, building roads and encouraging the development of a duty-free shopping mall for tourists.

Venture capital is notably reluctant to build hotels in developing countries. Almost invariably, the national government finances at least one luxury hotel and hopes that visitors will come as tourists but leave as investors. It also hopes that private capital will build other tourist facilities.

Governments have other good reasons for financing at least one or two hotels. Such hotels bring in expert technical advice on construction and operation. Outside management is used to train large numbers of nationals, offering training that would otherwise be unavailable. Precisely this process has happened in Jamaica, Trinidad, Barbados, and the Ivory Coast.

Need for Government Control

Land speculation produces a major problem in nearly every tourist development. As soon as a hotel goes up on a property, adjoining land jumps in value. One device used by a government is to price the land at its value over a long period previous to the classification of the zone for tourism development. Another is to impose a progressive tax on nonutilization of land in tourist development areas or to place a tax on added value. In some cases, the government may buy up the land secretly in advance. The Languedoc-Roussillon project in southern France is an example.

PUBLIC PARTICIPATION

It is often urged that a wide spectrum of the resident population take part in development planning and that divergent interests be considered in an attempt to avoid growth at one group's expense and to spread the benefits of development equitably.

This approach, which tries to serve everyone's interest, is certainly admirable, but unfortunately it all too often results in long delays, even stalemates. Even professional planners disagree among themselves. No one denies, however, that there is need for planning experts, ecologists, and a master plan that considers not only the residents and resources of the particular village or beach but also relates the parts to the region—in other words, regional planning.

SIX-PHASE DEVELOPMENT SCENARIO

In the past an economic pattern seemed to be developing as the result of experience with new hotels in some developing countries, especially some of the island nations in the Caribbean. Typically, in phase 1 the country, eager for tourist dollars, grants extensive tax advantages to hotel entrepreneurs. Import duties are waived, and a tax holiday on profits may be given for ten or more years. Nearly everyone welcomes the new hotel as a boon to the economy. Landowners do not expect huge profits on the sale of their land. Land speculation has not yet set in. Labor is cheap. The nationals, who may be unemployed or receiving only a few dollars a day, are delighted to work in the hotels at low wages. Tourists are seen as benefactors bringing economic blessings.

Phase 2 is a halcyon period for all concerned, and it may last five or ten years. The hotel owners who had reasonable land construction and operation costs did extremely well financially. Their labor costs may be only 20 percent or less of the gross sales, as compared with 25 to 40 percent of the sales in the United States. Local produce and seafood are available at reasonable cost. Taxes are low, and profits can be repatriated without interference from the government. The entrepreneurs may have only small properties, twenty to fifty rooms, but because

DESTINATION DEVELOPMENT: PROBLEMS AND CHALLENGES

they can get good rates, they make handsome returns on their investments and efforts.

Storm clouds begin to appear in phase 3. The natives start to resent the tourist, who is immeasurably rich by their standards. They also see that relatively few of the locals are benefiting very much from tourism. Land speculators are getting rich. Perhaps a demagogue appears to stir latent feelings of inferiority.

The government begins to take a hard line on tourism. Perhaps 80 percent of the tourist dollar almost immediately goes out of the country. The economy changes character. Tourism may have been pushed at the expense of agriculture, which has been allowed to decline by default.

Phase 4 signifies trouble for the hotel operators and perhaps for the economy generally. The end of the tax holiday period has come. Hotel operators face high or rising fixed costs over which they have no control. The local union may insist on wages equivalent to those received in a large American city. Labor efficiency, which was never high, drops off even further. The tourists may be insulted or, at best, treated lackadaisically. Quite naturally, the tourists decide not to return and also to tell their friends of their poor treatment.

The government, seeing that there are few repeat visitors, becomes alarmed and increases its tourist promotion budget. It may place political constituencies over the already established areas of tourism. The government, which formerly permitted the entry of skilled personnel, now refuses immigration permits. Local produce and seafood prices continue to rise.

Being realistic, the government recognizes that the nationals are not prepared by training or inclination to be effective in resort management. Yet national pride insists that locals hold management positions. Reacting to such pressure, the government opens a hotel training school on the vocational level. The nationals resent this and again national pride calls for a hotel school on the management level. The school is opened, but few applicants appear. Tourism has reached a plateau, and an economic recession in the tourist market may cause a precipitous drop in tourism to the country.

Phase 5 brings hard times for the resort operators. During the ten-year period when tourism was on the rise, too many hotel rooms were built. Some hotels have been built on very expensive land, too highly priced because of land speculation uncontrolled by the government. Little regional planning has been done, or the planning has not been implemented. A hodgepodge clutter of buildings has closed off the beauty spots from the general public and keeps much natural beauty hidden from the general view. The new hotel operators have had to erect high-rise buildings at high cost, often side by side with other high-rises.

The investors in the new hotels see that they themselves cannot operate them, so they attach their operations to international chains, with worldwide marketing facilities. These have a tremendous advantage over the independent operator who has relied almost exclusively on travel agents and word-of-mouth advertising for business. Smaller properties may look relatively unattractive compared to the huge neighboring multimillion-dollar resort. They must lower their rates to stay in business and are beset by a number of problems that did not exist when they first arrived.

Phase 6 completes the developmental pattern of the resort in the newly developed country. The area has matured, and maturity has brought a number of unexpected political and psychological problems. With higher labor and other costs, some hotels cannot be operated profitably, and the government may step in with financial aid or completely take over. There may even be riots.

Of course, this scenario need not materialize and has been avoided in a number of developing nations, perhaps most of them. However, the scenario is based on what has happened in such places as Puerto Rico, Jamaica, and in modified form in Guam and several other developing areas. Many of these problems could have been avoided if regional governmental planning had been done initially and enforced as the area developed.

Costa Smeralda as an Example

Giving further credence to the theory that destination development goes through a cycle beginning with high optimism and passing through stages that include rejection by residents is the experience of Costa Smeralda.

Costa Smeralda (Emerald Coast), on the Italian island of Sardinia, is one of the world's largest resort developments. Begun in 1962 by a consortium headed by the Aga Khan IV, the original plan called for thirty-five to forty hotels, yacht marinas, and more than 8,000 villas and apartments, shops, restaurants, and support services.

The Italian government helped build the infrastructure for the resort and eventually subsidized the resort itself to the tune of $30 million. Some of the founding members of the consortium built the first hotels, shopping centers, houses, and apartments as private investors. They also started Alisarda, an airline that connects Costa Smeralda with the Italian mainland and southern France. At the center of Costa Smeralda is the village of Porto Cervo, which among other amenities includes a marina that can dock seventy yachts at one time, each with hookups for water, electricity, and telephone.

By the 1970s the Sardinians were vocally dissatisfied. Though tourism had produced about 15,000 jobs, only half were filled by locals. The contrast between the well-do-do who frequented Costa Smeralda and the peasants nearby was resented. Moreover, the status of the tourists coming to the resort was changing; the wealthy visitors who originally flocked to Costa Smeralda were being replaced by middle-class tourists on package tours. A once-a-week flight began from London's Gatwick airport bringing mostly package-tour visitors. The planning agency for the Costa Smeralda was taking years to complete a master plan, and politicians began questioning the value of tourism. The locals were being prohibited from building huts on the beach for their own use and for ice-cream stands.

In January 1983 the Aga Khan threatened to sell out his majority interest. Apparently this was enough to give the Sardinian authorities second thoughts and to quiet their criticisms. By July 1983 the Sardinian authorities had endorsed a master plan that would see $700 million invested, resulting in four times the number of accommodations over the next twenty years.

COMPONENTS OF DESTINATION DEVELOPMENT

Transportation

Vital to the success of any resort destination area is the available means of transportation. The three critical factors in transportation — cost, convenience, and speed — affect the success of every resort, even if it is intended to be highly exclusive. The closer a development is to population centers containing people of some affluence, the greater the likelihood of success for the development. If several modes of transportation are available for travel to the area, so much the better.

As distance increases between market and destination, the potential number of visitors decreases. Also as distance increases, the affluence of the potential market must increase for the traveler to be able to afford the cost and time of the longer trip. As previously pointed out, however, absolute distance may not be as important as travel time and convenience.

As advances are made within a mode of transportation and changes in modes come about, the travel flow changes. In the case of Hawaii, the introduction of long-flight planes and of new routes that bypass the islands change the travel flow map drastically. When major airlines overfly a destination, tourism suffers. This has happened in the past when some airlines began overflying Hawaii between the West Coast and Japan. Fiji has suffered similarly.

The airlines and destination development in some areas are inextricably bound together. The airlines cannot promote ticket sales without accommodations at the other end; certain destinations cannot develop unless airline schedules and promotion support the development. Familiarization trips for travel agents, largely financed by the airlines, are a major means of promoting a destination. Hong Kong travel agents are taken to Paris and Europe, agents from Chicago go to Spain and the Orient, and so on. The promotion of air travel must keep in step with destination development.

A problem arises when highly competitive carriers create demand for destinations. In some places the hotels may be saturated and raise rates to a level beyond the reach of the average traveler. On the other hand, highly competitive routes can bring the air fare down to less than five cents a mile, whereas in other parts of the world the rates may go as high as forty cents a mile. Government policy may prevent competitive transportation in favor of the nation's flag carrier, which runs at extremely high load factors and charges high fares. Manila exemplifies how the airlines and the hotel business can get out of step. Within a two-year period, some 12,000 first-class hotel rooms were built in Manila. The government protected its national carrier, however, so that charter flights were largely eliminated. Moreover, the airport could not handle the number of flights necessary to fill the rooms.

The Hotel

An integral part of any resort development, of course, is the hotel. The hotel may be the principal reason that the traveler comes to the area, be it for business, pleasure, or convention purposes. If well planned, the hotel adds to the general appearance of the area and can be a major source of employment.

When the hotel is viewed as a necessary part of the total resort development, the investment per room is subject to different standards than if the hotel were to stand on its own. Developers have built hotels costing $200,000 and more per room. If judged by the rule of thumb that the hotel room rate should be based on $1.00 per $1,000 invested, such hotels clearly may not be profitable as independent ventures. Yet the hotel may be highly profitable when viewed as a part of a total complex. The developer recaptures the hotel cost in the sale of surrounding land and other facilities. Seen in the perspective of the total development, the cost of which may run as high as $500 million to $1 billion, the cost of the hotel is minimal.

Tourism and Shopping

For many people a significant part of the travel experience is shopping, the opportunity to buy opals in Australia, silks in Thailand, leather goods in Mexico, woolens in Scotland, loose diamonds in Holland—the list goes on and on. Few resort areas can succeed without providing space for resort shops, restaurants, evening entertainment, and travel services. Shop facilities offer a diversity of wearing apparel and items ordinarily not stocked in the usual store. There is a relatively uniform relationship between hotel revenue in a resort area and volume of sales in shops within the resort hotel and near it.

Some countries have developed duty-free shopping as a part of destination development. The tiny sheikdom of Dubai, United Arab Emirates, has a 22,000 square-foot emporium where a liter of Scotch sells for less than $3, more of a bargain there because alcohol is completely banned in most Moslem countries. Four million people pass through the airport each year. The government deeply discounts merchandise at the airport as a way to make Dubai more of a destination than a stopover. The Irish government set up Shannon airport and duty-free shopping as a way of helping the economically depressed western part of Ireland.

Condominium Sales

In the 1960s inclusion of the condominium plan in resort hotel financing became fairly common. Selling guest rooms—studios, suites, or individual dwelling units and apartments—as condominiums within a resort, generated large cash flows for the developer. In some cases the condominiums were sold before the resort was built.

The big appeal of condominiums is that developers may need only 10 percent front-end money to build them. This capital may be raised through a limited partnership syndicate. If all goes well, within two to five years the total project cost and developer's profits can be regained by selling the condominiums.

Condominium buyers usually put 20 to 35 percent down in cash and get a mortgage on the balance of their debt. In other cases the developer holds the mortgage and receives the prevailing rate of interest for it. In some developments the condominium owners are required to pool their condominiums with the resort complex for rental when they are not occupying the space.

The advantage to the developers is that they get their profits out of the building much sooner than if they attempted to operate it. The space buyers get a tax advantage: interest that they pay on their mortgage is tax deductible. Although they are charged for the maintenance of their space, they expect to have the charges at least partially offset by earnings from the rental of their spaces.

In the strange way that income taxes are computed in the United States, condominium owners who make their unit available for rental when they are not occupying it are allowed the cost of their trip to their condominium as a business expense. In other words the condominium owners get several tax advantages and, in addition, can write off part of their vacation expenses for income tax purposes. Little wonder that condominiums have been exceedingly popular in Hawaii, Florida, and the Virgin Islands!

Condominium and other real estate ventures are also a popular means of increasing equity as the property appreciates in value. Thousands of small investors have bought condominiums, and many have experienced appreciation of 100 percent or more over a ten-year period.

The tax shelter advantages condo ownership offers assume that the equity value of the apartment remains at its purchase price or appreciates. Yet from 1980 to 1983, many condos lost as much as 50 percent of their market value.

The prospective condo buyer is well advised to read the fine print. Maintenance fees can run as high as $500 a month on two-bedroom units. Assessments may be made against owners by the management company to cover unforeseen costs. As in any business venture, costly construction delays can occur, markets for renters can be saturated, and the character of a destination can change for the worse.

Some of the more common arrangements in condominium agreements are:

1. *The standard resort condominium.* Each unit is individually owned. It is lived in or rented to others by the owner, subject to the purchase agreement. The owner usually participates in common taxes and common maintenance of the property.

2. *An active rental pool arrangement.* The condominium management rents units according to the desires of the owners. Management receives a percentage of up to 60 percent of the income for its services, which may include maid service and maintenance.

   By agreement, condominium units may be rented according to the choice of the renter or on a rotating basis, so that all owners receive equal renting opportunity. Usually owners must furnish and maintain their units according to preset standards. Rooms must be painted or papered and furnished according to a particular style and standard.

3. *Right to use.* A partnership or corporation holds title to the real estate of the condominium with individual investors being granted rights to use facilities. The purchaser buys not real estate but a long-term right to use it. The Miami-Caribbean National Corporation, for example, sells a "vacation license" entitling the buyer to a one-week occupancy of a specific unit or of a unit in several properties for the life of the project, between forty and sixty years. While in residence, the buyer pays a reasonable daily charge to cover current expenses.

4. *Time sharing ownership (TSO).* This arrangement is similar to the right-to-use plan, except that the owner is a tenant in common with other owners and actually owns a share of the property that he or she can sell, transfer, or bequeath. The difference between it and the standard condo ownership is that the owner, under TSO, is limited to certain time periods for personal use. Other owners use it for other periods, or it can be rented to the general public. TSO as a plan for financing and operation is spreading rapidly. Because the owner really owns the unit for personal use for a few weeks each year, his or her cost is much lower than for a full ownership. Typically an entrepreneur purchases all of a condominium or several apartments in a number of condominiums. Time-share units are sold for a period of forty years, the buyer also agreeing to pay monthly maintenance costs. The enterpriser may operate a management company that schedules and maintains the apartments.

5. *Recreation club.* The buyer gets an individual title to the land and its improvements instead of ownership of a specific unit or lot. The plan is similar to membership in a private club.

DISCUSSION QUESTIONS

1. Put yourself in the place of a schoolteacher who has lived on the island of Oahu for thirty years. What would be your feelings about the phenomenal growth of tourism on that island?

2. Land developers and real estate operators use the phrase, "the highest and best possible use" as related to their business. Take a position for or against this guideline.

3. Discuss the concept, "Tourism is a change agent."

4. Suppose you were an influential resident of a Caribbean island. Would you favor welcoming campers to the island? Give reasons for or against.

5. As president of a small, less developed country lacking first-class hotels, would you favor building a luxury hotel or would you promote the construction of several modest hotels? Give your reasons.

6. As a member of the local government of a small island, would you try to keep hotels and condominiums from being built directly on the beachfront? Give reasons.

7. Less developed islands or countries may go through six phases of development. Is such a scenario inevitable? What can be done to avoid some of the problems suggested by the scenario?

8. In some ways Hawaii has been a model of tourism development with tourism becoming the island's leading income producer. What conditions might arise in the future that could cause the visitor count to decline sharply?

9. In planning a resort hotel, would you include a number of condominiums and condo sites to be sold to the public in the plan? Why or why not?

TWELVE

HEALTH AND TRAVEL

HEALTH PROBLEMS ENCOUNTERED IN TRAVELING

International travel has its drawbacks. Food poisoning and adaptation to strange foods, respiratory ailments, motion sickness, mountain sickness, and stress in general are some of the more common problems. Everyone, but everyone, airline crews included, suffers jet lag when traveling long distances by air. After a trans-Atlantic flight the biological clock, built into the body, says it's three in the morning. The stomach demands a complete meal. The traveler succumbs and feels dopey for the next few days. Veteran fliers say, "Don't give in and go to bed. Stay awake. Walk. Then go to bed at, say, eight o'clock."

When "under the influence" of jet lag, the mind slips a cog and you're back to something like being the village idiot. The locals are well aware of your descent from normalcy and are ready and waiting to overcharge and to accept large-denomination money for small. International corporations warn their traveling people not to make decisions during the first twenty-four hours after landing.

Travel to mountain destinations comes close to providing the same symptoms as jet lag. A person's capacity to work, say scientists, declines about 3 percent for every 1,000 feet of altitude. At 16,000 feet a visitor can do about half the work done at sea level. Less oxygen impairs thought and judgment. One accountant in Leadville, Colorado (altitude 10,500 feet), said he had to go down to mile-high Denver to balance his books. A British businessman living in La Paz, Bolivia (altitude 12,000 feet), reported that frequently after he had called a cab, he could not remember the destination when the cabbie arrived fifteen minutes later. Alcohol hits the newcomer harder at high altitudes. Dr. Robert Grover of the University of Colorado Health Sciences, puts it like this, "The adage is that the three-martini person at sea level is a two-martini person in Denver (or Mexico City) and a one-martini person at Leadville (Colorado)."

After adapting somewhat to living at a high altitude, the return to sea level is accompanied by headaches and other symptoms.

The real amount of illness contracted abroad or health problems exacerbated by travel is not likely to be known for some time. Of the 28 million Americans traveling abroad in 1986, 900,000 were sick enough to require medical care while away from home.[1] About 40 percent of all tourists

---

1. "What if you break your leg in Karachi?" *U.S. News & World Report*, June 15, 1987. p. 52.

293

in developing countries experience symptoms of traveler's diarrhea.

Dr. Robert Steffan of the University of Zurich has studied reports of illness involving tens of thousands of travelers.[2] He divides the world into three zones according to incidence of intestinal upset: The low-risk zone includes the United States, Northern and Central Europe, Australia, and New Zealand. The intermediate-risk zone covers Southern Europe, the Caribbean (except for Haiti and the Dominican Republic), the South Pacific, Singapore, Hong Kong, Israel, Japan, and South Africa. Mexico, Central and South America, Haiti, the Dominican Republic, the rest of Africa, and Asia are in the high-risk zone.

From 20 percent to 55 percent of travelers to the high-risk zone become ill. More than half of those who visit Tunisia, for example, become ill. That's not a very good prospect for the visitor.

According to Dr. Karl Neumann, a travel health expert, travelers going to the intermediate zone should get an injection of gamma globulin to prevent infectious hepatitis, a danger if one is an adventurous eater, goes camping, or ventures outside the usual tourist areas. The traveler should also forgo nonemergency dental treatment, shaving by a barber, manicures, or other activities that may puncture the skin.

The high-risk zone may require protection against malaria, yellow fever, cholera, dengue fever, and other diseases, according to the area and health conditions at the time of travel. One should drink carbonated beverages because carbonation kills germs. Watermelon should be avoided because it is often injected with unsafe water to increase its weight before it is sold. Milk is almost always a bad bet, and hot dogs are a no-no.

More than two-thirds of the travelers studied failed to heed such good advice: they ate salads, uncooked vegetables, and fruits that were peeled by a native. More than half used ice cubes, many of which could be counted on to be made from polluted water. Raw oysters, beefsteak tartar (raw,

ground beef), sandwiches with fillings, and puddings are all good hosts for bacteria.

Somewhat surprisingly, younger travelers experienced a higher incidence of illness, probably because of being more adventurous, eating in less expensive restaurants, and being less careful about suspect food. Marijuana smoking, says Dr. Steffan, seems to increase vulnerability.

Surveys of travelers have found that heading the list of factors considered in traveling to a particular destination is the assurance of finding safe drinking water and sanitary facilities. Health and cleanliness concern the traveler more than safety, scenic beauty, or even the cost of the journey.

Emporiatics (from the Greek *emporos*, "traveler") is a branch of medicine that is gaining prominence as more people travel abroad. Common traveler's diarrhea, for example, afflicts one-third of the people who travel to less developed countries — more than 1 million Americans and 4 million people worldwide each year.[3]

Eighty percent of traveler's diarrhea is caused by bacteria. Being ill anywhere is no fun, but being ill in a foreign country can be particularly frightening, psychologically as well as physically. Language problems, strange food, and difficulty in finding a physician make travelers feel frightened and helpless. The travelers who are ill and alone in a foreign country — even in a first-class hotel whose staff have the best intentions — may wish they had never left home.

Food Poisoning

The most common "travel illness" is dysentery or traveler's diarrhea, variously known as "turista," Delhi Belly, the Aztec Two-Step, and other appellations, some with overtones of black humor. Food poisoning can be caused by several bacteria, prominent among them are the bacteria shigella, salmonella, staphylococcus, and certain strains of the bacteria Escherichia coli, commonly called E. coli. In one study, E. coli were found to be responsible for 70 percent of the illnesses studied.

---

2. Karl Neumann, "Problems With a Tropical Climate." *Los Angeles Times*, Part IV, February 24, 1985.

3. "New Medical Specialty Emerging to Cope with Travelers' Illnesses." *Wall Street Journal*, January 18, 1985, p. 19.

La Turista as traveler's diarrhea is called in Spanish-speaking areas, is probably responsible for hundreds of thousands of fewer visits to Latin America by Americans.

Usually, symptoms of food poisoning come on abruptly and include vomiting, sometimes bloody with mucus, and diarrhea. They last from a day to a week. Symptoms may also include fever, abdominal cramping, and if severe, dehydration. Amoebic dysentery is not a self-limiting diarrhea, and can last for months, long after the traveler has returned home.

Staph

A common cause of food-borne disease is staphylococcus bacteria, commonly known as staph. Normally present on the hands and skin, it is transferred to food from infected cuts, abrasions, burns, boils, and pimples. Staph will multiply in almost any food that is not an acid medium, is moist, and is not kept either below 40°F or above about 140°F.

Salmonella

Salmonella bacteria grow well in poultry, meat, egg products, puddings, shellfish, soups, gravies, and sauces that have not been refrigerated properly or are not heated to a high enough temperature to destroy the germs.

Bacillary Dysentery

Bacillary dysentery (shigellosis) may have an onset period of about two days and is a self-limiting diarrhea lasting about six days. The disease is very contagious, for only ten shigella organisms are enough to cause the disease. Widespread in the tropics, it is spread by direct transmission or by consumption of food, milk, or water contaminated by people, flies, or other insects.

Cholera

Cholera is spread by ingesting food and liquids contaminated by sewage that contains vibrio comma. Cases of cholera have been reported in Africa, Asia, and the Middle East. Although cholera-infected countries are supposed to report cases immediately to the World Health Organization, many do not because of concern over potential economic losses from drops in tourism. For political reasons some countries officially refer to cholera as "diarrheal illness" to prevent identification of this specific disease. Cholera immunization is not required of people arriving in the United States from cholera-infected areas. Some other countries require proof of immunization, which incidentally is only partially effective and can offer a false sense of security. Cholera symptoms are similar to other food poisoning symptoms but more severe. Mucus and blood in the stool are telltale signs. Vomiting and diarrhea cause dehydration, which can be serious.

Cooking kills the cholera bacteria. Of course, contamination can occur again after the cooking takes place. In cholera-infected areas, travelers should drink only carbonated bottled water, carbonated soft drinks, boiled water, or treated water.

Giardiasis

The next time you are on a camping trip and are tempted to drink from that sparkling mountain stream, don't do it. It could well contain *Giardia lambia*, the most commonly encountered parasite in the United States and Great Britain. Giardiasis has been identified in nearly 100 nations. Beaver, elk, sheep and deer have been implicated as carriers.[4] When swallowed, the parasite moves down the intestinal tract to the colon. The disease manifests itself from one to four weeks after ingestion. Symptoms include a bloated stomach and foul taste in the mouth, chills, and vomiting.

Travelers should boil suspect water; Giardia cysts are killed almost instantly when heated to 176°F. The explorer Livingstone took pride in drinking water "swarming with insects, thick with mud, putrid with rhinoceroses' urine and

---

4. Ted Kerasote, "Drops to Drink." *Audubon*, July 1986, pp. 28–29.

buffalo dung." He came down only with dysentery. The modern traveler could be less lucky.

Infectious Hepatitis

More Americans return home from abroad with infectious hepatitis than any other serious disease. Unlike food poisoning, which usually runs its course in a few days, infectious hepatitis has a long incubation period, ten to fifty days, before the symptoms of yellow discoloration, severe loss of appetite, weight loss, fever, and extreme tiredness set in. The disease can be fatal.

Risk varies with the part of the world visited. It is about ten times greater in southern Europe than in the United States and Canada, in northern and central Europe, and in Israel. The highest risk comes in central Africa, followed by Central and South America, where chances of picking up the culpable virus is 100 times greater than in North America. Precautions against hepatitis should be taken in parts of Mexico and countries bordering the polluted Mediterranean—Spain, France, Italy, and Greece.

In Southeast Asia or sub-Saharan Africa the traveler should be concerned about the possibility of contracting hepatitis B, which is caused by a virus different from hepatitis A, but has similar symptoms; both forms attack the liver. The A variety has an even longer incubation period than the B type, several weeks or months from the time of infection. While infectious hepatitis is passed along through food or liquid, the B type is carried by blood or substances contaminated by blood. Unsterile needles are the big culprits. Tattoos, acupuncture in Hong Kong, being shaved by a barber, ear piercing, being manicured, and having dental treatment are ways of becoming infected. Insist on disposable needles. Other vectors may be involved.

A vaccine is recommended when travel to a suspect area is planned. The vaccination requires three injections over a 6-month period.

AVOIDING FOOD-BORNE DISEASES

Travelers in places where food and water are suspect can take a number of precautions:

1. Eat only food that has been thoroughly cooked. Avoid any uncooked food, such as pork, which may harbor the trichinosis worm that gets into the bloodstream and fastens onto muscle tissue. Incompletely cooked pork may also harbor a tapeworm, whose larvae can migrate through the bloodstream and lodge in the brain. There is no known cure. Not all cooked food is safe. Also consider how long it has stood since being cooked.

2. Drink only pasteurized mild and/or well-accepted bottled drinks such as Coca-Cola. Drink beer or wine, which are self-purifying because of acidity or alcohol present.

3. If the water supply is unsafe, so too are the ice cubes made from the water.

4. Do not forget that water condensation on the outside of the cans or bottles can be contaminated by the ice in which it has been packed. Dry containers before opening and pouring.

5. To purify suspect water, use ten drops of 1 percent bleach per quart of water if the water looks clear, twenty drops if it is cloudy. Let stand for thirty minutes. If you do not detect a slight chlorine odor, repeat the process. Iodine can be used for water purification: five drops of iodine or 2 percent iodine per quart of clear water, ten drops per cloudy. You can also boil the water for at least fifteen minutes. Many veteran travelers follow this rule: when outside your own country, drink only bottled water, or carbonated drinks. The carbonation in these drinks is supposed to kill any germs present.

6. Eat no fruit or vegetables that have been contaminated on their surfaces when growing, or that have been contaminated by water used in cleaning. To be safe, eat only fruits that can be peeled. Avoid salads.

7. Avoid those foods in which bacteria easily thrive, foods such as milk products, eggs, or any protein food not in an acid condition.

8. Wash your own hands frequently and thoroughly. A study in Mexico revealed that 15 percent of the coins and paper money had diarrhea-causing microorganisms on them. It makes little sense to insist on peeling your own oranges if your hands are contaminated. The hands you shake may pass along diarrhea-causing germs. Contamination can also come from touching contaminated objects such as doorknobs, handrails, and souvenirs in shops and absentmindedly putting contaminated

fingers into one's mouth and nose or rubbing one's eyes. The hands that infect you may be your own.

9. Campers may think that melted snow and ice are always safe. They are no better or worse than the purity of water that went into making them. Freezing only preserves germs; it does not destroy them.

10. Water gurgling directly out of the ground or running out from between rocks may not be safe. Contaminated water may have entered the ground farther up a hill or on the other side of a hill or mountain. Rapidly moving water is no safer than water from a stagnant pool.

11. Avoid "hot" sauces left on the table from meal to meal. Research has found them to be heavily contaminated.

12. Follow the Peace Corps motto: "If you can't peel it, cook it, or boil it, forget it."

WHEN DIARRHEA STRIKES

When symptoms such as diarrhea or vomiting appear, travelers should eat only bland foods such as boiled rice, toast, or tea. In Turkey physicians recommend peach juice for the same reason. Some herbal drinks seem to settle the stomach. One remedy widely used in Europe and the Middle East is the aperitif Fernet Branca. Other recommended drinks are blackberry cordial, bitters in soda water, and ginger ale. Whether these remedies help has never been proven in a scientific study. Recent studies show that bismuth (Pepto-Bismol) is effective as a preventive measure and as a treatment.[5] Taking 4 tablets a day reduces the chances of illness by more than 50 percent. If symptoms appear, take one tablet with each three meals and continue until a day after the symptoms stop, generally in three or four days. The most important treatment, say some physicians, is to replace lost liquids. A diet of tea, boiled rice, and applesauce is recommended, but milk or other dairy products should be avoided.

The Federal Center for Disease Control suggests the following for diarrhea: one 8-ounce glass of orange, apple, or other fruit juice rich in potassium and pectin; ½ teaspoon of honey, corn syrup, or table sugar; a pinch of table salt. In another glass mix eight ounces of carbonated or boiled water with ¼ teaspoon baking soda. Drink alternately from each glass. Supplement with carbonated beverages or water and tea made with boiled or carbonated water as desired. Avoid solid foods and milk until recovery occurs.

Certain drugs seem to be effective against food poisoning—drugs such as Mexaforma or Enterovioform. The U.S. Public Health Service recommends against using these particular drugs because they are suspected of causing damage to the central nervous system. In any event, some physicians say that diarrhea is nature's way of ridding the body of dangerous poisons and that any drugs that slow down the process are not indicated.

A quick way to stop agonizing diarrhea is to take opium in the form of Lomotil or Paregoric, available without prescription in many countries but potentially highly addictive. These drugs work by drastically slowing down the action of the large intestine. No child under the age of five should receive these potent drugs because the bowel stasis can cause severe dehydration.

Though seldom fatal, dysentery can kill the very young, the very old, and the debilitated because of the dehydration that results from it. Many veteran travelers routinely carry a prescribed antibiotic such as tetracycline on all trips, thus avoiding the necessity of searching out a doctor overseas.

VACCINATIONS AND OTHER PRECAUTIONS

International travelers to many countries should be inoculated for typhoid, paratyphoid fever, and tetanus. Many of these provide only limited protection. For example, the typhoid fever vaccine provides immunity using a low-dose inoculation of the live disease. (A large dose would give the traveler the full-blown disease.) Receiving this vaccine may help, but the traveler must still exercise caution in terms of avoiding contaminated food and water.

Often, physicians warn, persons planning trips take a series of shots against typhoid and other diseases, then become careless, believing the

5. Karl Neumann, "Ounces of Prevention," Los Angeles Times, November 6, 1988.

shots will prevent the diseases. Many such shots serve only to attenuate a disease if it strikes, not prevent it completely. These people are in more danger than if they had not taken the shots.

The Centers for Disease Control of the Federal Public Health Service frequently update information on disease problem areas around the world. The Centers suggest taking vaccinations far enough in advance of a trip to a danger area to allow for the incubation period for quarantinable diseases. For example, it takes five days before a vaccination against cholera is considered effective, and six days before a shot for yellow fever.

An idea of the kinds of hazards involved in a trip to Zaire, for example, can be seen in the recommended precautions for traveling to that country. The medicine kit should include something for malaria, intestinal troubles, migraines, skin disease, neuralgia, and creams that will nullify insect bites. It also should include such items as mercurochrome and antiseptic powder. The shot record for the wise visitor is extensive: yellow fever, polio, cholera, tetanus, typhoid, typhus, smallpox, and gamma globulin to ward off hepatitis. For combating malaria, it is wise to start a pill-taking regime two weeks prior to the trip and continue six weeks after arriving back home. Of course, drugs to be taken before traveling should be planned and prescribed by a physician.

Compared to Zaire, Senegal is modern and up to date, yet the U.S. Public Health Service recommends shots for yellow fever, typhoid, and cholera, as well as gamma globulin. Club Med, which has a village outside Dakar, the capital, places malaria pills on the table along with salt and pepper.

OTHER DISEASES

Malaria

IAMAT, the International Association for Medical Assistance to Travelers, states that the incidence of malaria is increasing. In tropical Africa (south of the Sahara but not including South Africa), there were 150 million cases of it in 1980. Malaria exists in Central America and Haiti, large areas of South America and Africa, parts of the Middle East, Southeast Asia, India, and some islands in the South Pacific. A major reason for the increase is the developing resistance to traditional insecticides by forty-five of the sixty species of anopheles mosquitoes that carry the disease.

Malaria is endemic in part of Africa. Just about everybody has it or will get it. The risk factor involving the fatal form varies widely. In Turkey, for example, the risk of any malaria contracted being fatal is 1 percent. The malaria contracted in Haiti is 100 percent certain to be fatal. Protection consists of taking oral medication and minimizing mosquito bites.[6]

Since the mosquito usually strikes at night, use a bed net in risk areas. Avoid perfumes, cologne, and aftershave lotion since perfumes and dark clothing attract the mosquito. A mosquito repellent helps. Wear long-sleeved blouses or shirts. Avoid evening cocktail parties or swimming after sundown. Twilight is good mosquito feeding-time.

Get the malaria medication appropriate for the area of travel from your physicians, and get enough to last the entire trip plus enough for four to six weeks after return. Malaria usually manifests itself within a week or two of exposure, but relapses can occur as many as twenty years later.

Mosquitoes in rural parts of Southeast Asia and Japan transmit Japanese encephalitis. The Asian flying tiger is another airborne pest to avoid; it can carry dengue and yellow fever.

Hikers and campers in rural South America may be unfortunate enough to be bitten by the "kissing bug," so called because it bites the face. It passes a parasite into the bloodstream and this attacks the heart muscle and can cause death.

Snail Fever

After malaria, the most widespread disease in the world is schistosomiasis, also called snail fever or bilharzia. The worm is found in a wide area and affects an estimated 200 million people in about seventy countries in Asia, Africa, South America,

---

6. Karl Neumann, "Avoiding Malaria Bug." *Los Angeles Times*, January 24, 1988, p. 11.

and the Caribbean. In Egypt it is believed 85 percent of the rural population is infected.

Part of the worm's life cycle must occur within a water-dwelling snail. The mobile larvae can penetrate the skin of a person in the water and develop into a worm up to an inch long within the blood vessels of the host. The worm's eggs lodge in various tissue. Unless treated before the disease reaches an advanced stage, death may occur from internal bleeding. A newly discovered drug, proziquentel, is effective against the disease.

The best advice is to stay out of any water — lakes, ponds, or streams — that may harbor the snails and their parasite, the worms. Take no chances, since the worm larvae are so small they are almost invisible.

SWIMMING IN POLLUTED WATERS

Another hazard, often overlooked, is risked by bathing or swimming in polluted water. In one part of the bay on which Puerto Vallarta, Mexico, is situated, swimmers noted how murky the water was as compared with another part of the same bay. On questioning, it was learned that a number of hotels dumped their sewage directly into the bay.

In the past a common sight on Acapulco Bay in Mexico was an accumulation of garbage floating in the water. The same is true of the waters around the hotels on the island of Madeira. Much of the Mediterranean is similarly polluted. Obviously, swimming in such waters exposes the swimmer to a variety of harmful bacteria.

MEDICAL CARE AWAY FROM HOME

Physicians advise against treating oneself by buying unknown medicines from a pharmacist. The drug regulations in developing countries can be very lax. Many medicines banned by the Federal Drug Administration in the United States are sold over the counter in some countries outside the United States. Not a few of them can cause severe side effects.

Persons with chronic health problems who have to travel abroad should carry plenty of any medications routinely needed. They might also take out a separate travel policy covering health insurance if their current health insurance policy does not cover travel away from home. Hospital costs in the United States are staggering but may be higher in some foreign countries. Medicare provides no medical coverage whatsoever in any foreign country, except in limited circumstances in Mexico and Canada.

If a health problem occurs, the first-class hotels can usually get a doctor who speaks English, and do so fairly quickly. American consuls abroad have lists that include qualified physicians and, sometimes, dentists, veterinarians, hospitals, clinics, and fee information. After hours, a duty officer at American consulates will give the names of three or four doctors, either generalists or specialists, over the phone. If emergency transportation is needed to get home from a foreign country, the nearest American consul can arrange it on a commercial or other airline.

If a really serious illness strikes, the best thing to do, according to experts, is to get to the emergency room of the closest hospital or clinic. If the patient is ambulatory, a taxi may be faster and much cheaper than an ambulance. The majority of ambulances throughout Western Europe are for transportation only, but in France, Germany, and Israel, special ambulances are available for cardiac problems. A few are also available in Switzerland and Britain.

In Russia, Intourist, the government travel agency, handles everything including dispatching doctors to tourist hotels and providing polyclinics and hospitals especially designated for foreigners.

JET LAG

As travelers quickly change from one time zone to another, the body's natural clock, its circadian rhythm, is upset. In addition to adjusting to time changes, the body must cope with the added stress of travel itself. Anticipating the trip, travel to and from airports that may involve traffic tie-ups, parking problems, and a dozen other unexpected difficulties no doubt add to jet lag. The excitement in making a trip stimulates the flow of adrenalin, which suppresses the feeling of fatigue but builds a debt to be repaid later.

Circadian rhythms are present in all animals. Internal clocks, not yet well identified, control body temperature, the flow of adrenalin, the digestive process, and sex hormones in humans. Body temperature varies throughout the twenty-four-hour period, reaching a low point about three A.M. The body's ability to cope with external factors also varies. Alcohol affects a person more at midday than at night. Blood pressure and sensitivity to pain vary throughout the cycle. Some rhythms are "cued" by external signals, such as the dark/light cycle; others are cued internally.

Usually adrenalin begins to pump through the veins at about six A.M., preparing a person to awaken, even though he or she may be experiencing a real-world clock time of midnight. The body clock tells the traveler to sleep; the real clock says it is time to get up. Later, the body clock turns up the adrenalin and other hormones, yet the real world says, "time to sleep." Changing time desynchronizes the body systems. For some people resynchronization may take several days. In experiments conducted on rats, continued desynchronization shortened their life spans by 10 percent.

Apparently no one can completely avoid jet lag. There are, however, ways to reduce jet lag. Doctors who have studied the problem and veteran travelers make these recommendations:

1. Be in good condition before starting a long trip. Get plenty of rest before the trip and along the way. Rest and relaxation should be scheduled as a regular part of travel.
2. Travelers who hop back and forth between time zones should stay on their home time. Flight personnel and those on short business trips between time zones should keep meal and sleep schedules on home time.
3. Plan to break up long trips by taking a one- or two-day stopover to reset the biological clock along the way. For example, a New York–Tokyo trip can be broken up with a short stopover in San Francisco. When a trip involves eight or more time zones or if travel exceeds fifteen hours, some companies ask their employees to split the trip by taking a one-night stopover or to schedule a full day of rest after arrival.
4. Get ready for a biological clock change by pushing bedtime up or back a few days before the trip, in effect resetting the biological clock.
5. Do not overeat or overdrink. Alcohol seems to have a greater effect on the body at high altitudes. Carbonated drinks, including beer and champagne, are more noticeable in their effects than noncarbonated alcoholic beverages. Some travelers mistakenly try to overcome jet lag by drinking alcohol during the flight, then upon arrival in their hotel room, take a sleeping pill. According to some pharmacologists, this can lead to brain damage, even death.
6. Simply being in an airplane can be tiring. Veteran travelers carry a sweater, earplugs, and an eye mask. Do not be reticent about stretching out if there is room on the plane. It also helps to get up and move around to keep the circulation flowing in the legs. Remove shoes and then slip on flight slippers or heavy socks. United Airlines recommends that pilots do deep knee bends to fend off the tendency of the blood to settle in the legs while sitting. Light isometric exercises or just walking around the plane can help.
7. At high altitudes the body dehydrates rapidly because of the very low humidity in the plane. Drinking alcohol also dehydrates the body by hastening the excretion of water. Drink water every hour to replace that loss.
8. Try to arrive at a destination in the late afternoon or evening, never in the morning. Hotel rooms are seldom available in the morning, and the weary travelers find themselves sitting in the lobby exasperated and resentful. Take a walk, eat lightly, and go to bed. Try to plan the travel schedule so that the day following arrival is free.

Body clocks follow a rhythm that changes slowly. When we change from one time zone to another, the stomach is on the old system, and we tend to want to sleep according to the established time on which the biological clock is set. Elimination systems are also confused. For most travelers, adjusting to a new time zone seems to take place at about one hour per day. If a person flies across the United States, coast to coast, the body clock is desynchronized by three hours, or by three time zones, and it will take three or four days to resynchronize. A trans-Atlantic crossing covering five or six time zones may take five or six days for complete readjustment to occur. Many people, especially senior citizens, take much longer. For some reason flights from east to west are more debilitating than travel in the opposite direction.

Adjustment to jet lag varies widely among individuals. It may be easier to readjust to a home scene than to a foreign destination. People traveling in groups seem to adjust better than those traveling alone.

An anti-jet lag diet developed at the Argonne National Laboratory is being used by the army's 82nd Airborne Division to reduce the effects of jet lag under rapid-deployment conditions. The diet, also called the World Traveler Diet, recommends the following:

Eat lightly the day before a long flight. The foods to eat are eggs, cottage cheese, fish, salads consommé, fruit—all relatively low in calories and carbohydrates. On arrival eat big high-protein breakfasts and lunches. For a day or two have high-carbohydrate dinners. Get to bed early.

OZONE SICKNESS

Ozone sickness, believed to be brought on by breathing excessive ozone at higher altitudes, can be a serious problem. At ten parts per million, ozone can cause swelling in the lungs, bleeding, and death. FAA regulations call for not more than one part per million of ozone in long-range flights.

In 1976 the problem began to appear on long flights of the Boeing 747-SP, flights that at the time flew farther and higher than most others. (In the SST, which cruises at up to 60,000 feet, excess ozone had not been a problem because outside air is brought into the cabin from a very hot part of the engine's compressors, and the heat breaks down the ozone.)

Ozone is closer to the earth at the North Pole than it is farther south, and fingers of ozone extend from high altitudes into the lower altitudes, especially during the January–May period.

Oddly enough, ozone affects nonsmokers more than smokers and affects the young more than the old. Alcohol increases its effects. Symptoms include a hacking cough like bronchitis, shortness of breath, gasping, mild chest pains, and dry nasal passages. Symptoms can be alleviated by breathing pure oxygen or breathing through a wet cloth or paper towel held firmly over the nose and mouth.

EAR AND SINUS BLOCKAGE

On the way down from high altitudes, some people suffer excruciating pain resulting from the difference between the pressure in the inner ears and the surrounding air pressure in the plane. Severe cases of earblock deafness and dizziness can last for days or weeks. Blocked ears can occasionally become infected.

Jaw movement, which keeps the eustachian tubes open, can help to prevent this problem. Air is allowed to enter the inner ear and equalizes the external pressure that builds up as the plane descends. Chewing gum, yawning a lot, and holding the nose and mouth shut while forcing air up into the ears from the throat helps. Cold and sinusitis victims are urged to use decongestants before or during flights and nose sprays shortly before descent. Avoiding alcohol helps, since alcohol constricts sinus and throat passages and increases the chances of a block. Trapped gas in diseased teeth can also cause pain.

MOTION SICKNESS

Getting there may be half the fun, but it can also be exhausting. Depending on the conditions of travel, it can be downright nauseating, the nausea and other symptoms caused by motions with which the passive and helpless traveler is unfamiliar.

Seasickness can be much more painful and extensive than airsickness. There are also those who get carsick and some who even get sick just thinking about plane or ship travel. Motion sickness is not confined to sissies. Lord Nelson, the most famous British admiral and one known for being not much afraid of anything, had a chronic problem with seasickness.

The first symptoms of motion sickness are likely to include feelings of anxiety, excitement, dizziness, and blurring of vision. These occur when the organs of balance, the vestibular canals in the ears, are disturbed and are at variance with what is experienced by other senses. Sensory confusion results.

A faint pallor, the beginnings of a cold sweat, and queasiness in the stomach follow. If the symptoms continue, vomiting or acute nausea is almost inevitable. The act of vomiting relieves the symptoms temporarily, only to be followed by more of the same. Over a period of time there can be a serious loss of body fluid.

Just getting off a ship or plane does not always relieve the symptoms. There is a peculiar phenomenon of landsickness, caused by the after-effects of a rolling or pitching ship, which makes the person who has gotten off the ship feel that the land itself is moving. The effect may last for hours following disembarkment.

Age does not bring many benefits physiologically, but it does appear to help in motion sickness. Susceptibility to the sickness begins around the age of two and increases to a maximum at about the age of ten or twelve. Thereafter some kind of adaptation occurs that makes motion sickness less frequent among the middle-aged and elderly. Women, for some reason, are more susceptible than men.

Motion sickness is rooted in the vestibular system in the ear, which has nothing to do with hearing, only the sense of balance and movement. The receptors responsible for motion sickness in the ear are three semicircular canals, fluid-filled tubes lying at right angles to each other. When activated, they tell us about changes in the rate of speed with which the head is turning.

Also within the ear are some flat blobs of jelly covered with dense crystals called otoliths. When acted upon, they tell us how far the head is deflected from the upright. When walking or running, the otoliths send messages to the brain telling us in what plane we are located, and then they set off reflex eye movements that help stabilize the visual field while we are moving. When we are sitting or standing, the same impulses are sent to the brain—tending to confuse the whole system. Fortunately, after a period of time, depending upon the individual, the brain adapts to these confusing signals and there is adaptation to the motion, whether it be bouncing in the sky, rolling on the waves, or riding in a car on a bumpy road. People vary tremendously in how they respond to this misinformation and how long it takes to adapt to it. Some never adapt.

To combat motion sickness, try to get as horizontal as possible, face up. It has been found that the incidence of sickness in the supine position is as little as 20 percent of that experienced by the person who is sitting or standing. Regardless of your position, do not let the head wobble back and forth. Hold the head against a high back seat or use the neck muscles to keep the head steady.

On a ship, movements can be minimized by lying flat on a bunk, preferably midship where the motion of the vessel is least severe. Concentrate on something other than the state of the stomach. Read if it does not aggravate the symptoms. Apparently the brain has a limited capacity for processing information from the body or from the outside. Keeping the mind active preempts the nervous receptors that initiate the sickness.

Most drugstores carry nonprescription dimenhydrinate (Dramamine) tablets, as do airlines, to ease motion sickness. L-Hyoscine Hydrobromide is thought to be the most effective among the drugs in use. Antihistamines are also used.

A prescription drug, scopolamine, is available under the trade name Transderm-V. Applied behind the ear, the drug is slowly absorbed through the skin to reduce the nerve activities in the inner ear, hence motion sickness. A disk containing the drug can be left on and remains effective for as long as seventy-two hours. Side effects may include dryness of the mouth, drowsiness, and temporary blurring of vision.

Remember not to travel on an empty stomach, as this aggravates motion sickness.

TOO MUCH SUN

A most common annoyance for vacationers is sunburn, brought on by the temptation to accelerate the most visible evidence of the vacation, the tan. Because the sun's rays are most potent during midday, between about ten A.M. and two P.M., physicians suggest starting a tan with less than an hour of direct sunning during these hours.

Exposure to the sun's rays is known to increase the incidence of skin cancer. Tanning lotions are available that screen out the harmful ultraviolet spectrum. They are graduated in strength, numbered one to thirty. Start with the strongest, gradually decreasing as a tan develops. Fair-skinned people and those susceptible to burning should be exceptionally careful. This is not only protection against the discomfort of a burn; it is also protection against serious illness such as skin cancer later.

A sunburn is just as much a burn as one sustained in a fire, and is not to be treated lightly. Like other burns, sunburn can be treated by soaking in cold water or by application of cold wet compresses. Drinking liquids helps dilute the toxic substances that the burn releases into the bloodstream.

TOO MUCH HEAT

Heat exhaustion, heat cramps, and heat stroke are serious reactions to excessive sun and heat. Symptoms of heat exhaustion include sweating, dehydration, weakness, dizziness, and finally collapse. Heat cramps are a further progression of heat exhaustion. The muscles, deprived of salt, go into spasms. Most serious of all is heat stroke. The body can no longer maintain normal temperature. Heat stroke can force body temperatures up to 107°F, with possible brain damage. Reduce body temperature with ice packs on the forehead or with damp towels or sheets wrapped around the body. Dousing the body with cold water can cause too much of a shock. Seek medical assistance.

TOO MUCH HUMIDITY

Air temperature obviously influences a person's sense of well-being and comfort. High temperature can be dangerous, even traumatic. Just as important is the humidity and its relationship to the "apparent" temperature—how hot the weather feels and how we react to it.

Humidity has a dramatic effect on apparent temperature. The National Weather Service chart in Figure 12-1 shows that a 90°F temperature with an 80 percent humidity produces an apparent temperature of 113°F. Should the humidity rise to 90 percent, the apparent temperature jumps to 122°F. Humidity of 90 percent is not uncommon in many parts of the tropics and subtropics.

The National Weather Service warns that an apparent temperature above 130°F is extremely dangerous. Heat strokes or sunstrokes may be imminent. Between 105°F, and 130°F, sunstroke, heat cramps, and heat exhaustion are possible. Between 90°F and 105°F, sunstroke, heat cramps, and heat exhaustion become more likely in the event of lengthy exposure and activity.

Heat stress susceptibility varies with age, health, and body characteristics. Elderly travelers should be especially careful.

HOMESICKNESS

Though not a disease in the usual sense, homesickness can be painful and ultimately lead to organic illness. Even veteran travelers experience the yearning for the security and support of home.

Under ideal conditions travel can be exhilarating: new faces, new challenges, the experience of beautiful scenery, fine accommodations, excellent meals. Bring on the rain, travel delays, jet lag, unfriendly people, and boredom, and it is quite normal to wish to be with family and old friends in a predictable, comfortable environment where one is accepted and liked.

Anyone who gets ill in a foreign country, cannot speak the language, and knows no one in the place may experience an acute attack of homesickness. "Boy, what I'd give to be home in my own bed.

12-1. The Effects of Relative Humidity on Perceived Temperature										
Air Temperature										
70	75	80	85	90	95	100	105	110	115	120
Relative Humidity / **Apparent Temperature***										

Relative Humidity	70	75	80	85	90	95	100	105	110	115	120
0%	64	69	73	78	83	87	91	95	99	103	107
10%	65	70	75	80	85	90	95	100	105	111	116
20%	66	72	77	82	87	93	99	105	112	120	130
30%	67	73	78	84	90	96	104	113	123	135	148
40%	68	74	79	86	93	101	110	123	137	151	
50%	69	75	81	88	96	107	120	135	150		
60%	70	76	82	90	100	114	132	149			
70%	70	77	85	93	106	124	144				
80%	71	78	86	97	113	136					
90%	71	79	88	102	122						
100%	72	80	91	108							

*Degrees Fahrenheit
SOURCE: National Weather Service.

Where can a bona fide doctor be had? How long will it take him to get to my hotel room? Will the doctor be able to understand what's wrong with me?"

Couples traveling alone may get more than they want of each other and are delighted when another American pops up in a restaurant, a hotel lobby, a tour bus, or the next seat on a plane. The couple may be more than a little homesick. The other American reassures them that America is still there, and that yes, there are still people who speak English. College students backpacking around Europe in the summer are supposed to be so thrilled by it all that home never enters their mind. Watch them rush to the nearest American Express office for the mail from home, devouring what they get, crushed at getting none.

Even at its best, travel is tiring, and when it becomes exhausting, or when problems without apparent solutions arise (such as being stranded in a foreign city with little or no money), homesickness is a natural consequence. The traveler yearns for someone from back home, would like to eat in an American restaurant, wishes to be instantly transported back to the magic healing balm of home.

INTERNATIONAL ASSOCIATION FOR MEDICAL ASSISTANCE TO TRAVELERS (IAMAT)

Two million travelers, mostly from the United States and Canada, hold membership in the International Association for Medical Assistance to Travelers (IAMAT), an organization in which some 3,000 physicians participate. All of the doctors speak English. They are supposed to be familiar with North American medical techniques because most took at least part of their training in North America.

Membership in IAMAT is free, and the participating physicians have agreed on a set schedule of fees. The organization is financed mostly by members' donations, which are tax deductible.

IAMAT, headquartered at 350 Fifth Avenue, Suite 5620, New York, New York will make available on request a traveler clinical record, designed to record medical condition and treatment received on a trip. The organization also provides a world immunization and malaria risk chart, and a series of world climate charts covering 1,440 cities around the world with advice on clothing to be worn and sanitary conditions (including the quality of water, milk, and food) in a designated city.

HEALTH AND TRAVEL

DISCUSSION QUESTIONS

1. What is the most common ailment experienced by travelers to countries where sanitation is substandard?

2. Name the bacteria most prominently connected with *turista*, the food poisoning commonly experienced in Mexico and other tropical countries.

3. Most of the food poisoning caused by the E. coli bacteria could be prevented by a simple precaution. What is it?

4. Skin infections are likely to be contaminated with what bacteria that can be transmitted via food?

5. A type of bacteria commonly found in poultry causes what well-known kind of food poisoning?

6. Can ice spread disease? Explain.

7. Insufficiently cooked pork may harbor which parasites?

8. Many travelers abroad drink only beer or wine. Why are these beverages likely to be free from bacteria?

9. Why is it safe to eat a banana but possibly hazardous to eat an apple while traveling in the tropics?

10. Generally speaking, which types of food are most subject to food contamination?

11. Campers often drink water directly from running streams. Why is this not advisable to do?

12. Why should a traveler to Africa, the Caribbean, or parts of Central America be wary of swimming in freshwater streams or lakes?

13. If a traveler should become ill in a foreign country where he or she does not speak the language, what should be done?

14. Jet lag hits almost every air traveler when changing time zones. What are the symptoms? What causes jet lag? Describe at least three ways that the effects of jet lag can be minimized.

15. Suppose you visited the Inca fortress Machu Picchu, which is high in the Andes Mountains. What kind of symptoms might you expect to experience?

16. What do the vestibular canals in the ears have to do with motion sickness?

17. Suppose you have been on an ocean voyage for five days. What kind of adjustment might be necessary upon debarking?

18. Suppose you are flying and begin to experience motion sickness. What are some of the things you can do to avoid it?

THIRTEEN

WEATHER AND TRAVEL

The song "April in Paris"—lilting and spritely—suggests flowers and sunshine. In fact, April in Paris brings a high temperature of about 60°F, a low of 40°F, and it rains half the month. Umbrellas and overcoats are abundant. As seen in Figure 13-2 at the end of this chapter, Paris in April has an average daily temperature between 42°F and 59°F, sometimes dropping as low as 29°F. Fourteen days of the month have rain.

The Algarve in spring? Maybe. But occasionally the Algarve is cold and rainy even into May, with an ocean temperature much too low for swimming. And those "heated swimming pools" are only for the polar bear members.

When the first tourists of the modern period, the wealthy British, took the Grand Tour of the Continent, they might have lived in various cities of Europe for as long as three years. They expected to stay through the seasons—the wet and the cold as well as the sunny and warm weather. Today's pleasure travelers have different expectations. They usually hope for unlimited balmy, dry weather. (The skiers want unlimited snow.) Often time and money limitations make it imperative that travelers select a time when the weather at their destination is at least acceptable.

Most destinations have definite wet and dry seasons. During the wet season, rain may be continuous and prodigious. Who wants to travel to those parts of Asia experiencing the monsoon rains, periods when the skies open and it rains day after day? In a little country like Costa Rica, the rainy season—from about the middle of June through September—brings copious downpours that start nearly every day around three o'clock in the afternoon and last well into the night. Summer is the wet season for much of the plateau of central Mexico, when rains can flood roads and imprison visitors in their hotel rooms. Acapulco is hot and wet from June through September. The hurricane season, late summer and early fall, is not the most pleasant time to visit the Caribbean. Northern Spain has snow and is usually cold through the middle of April.

Misconceptions about weather easily develop. From travel literature one might expect the Mediterranean coasts to be dry and sunny during the winter, warm enough to enjoy bathing in the sea. Wrong. Visitors should not expect to swim on the French Riviera in January or in the waters of Costa del Sol in February (unless they like 50°F water). The Greek islands may be sunny, but during winter they are raw and cold. Even though Bermuda is at the same latitude as North Carolina and is warmed by the Gulf Stream, it does not present much more than sunning opportunities during

January. Wet suits are called for by California swimmers during the winter, with water temperatures at 55°F or lower in the Pacific. In summer ocean temperatures in southern California seldom exceed 70°F. Water temperatures in south Florida and the Bahamas can be more than chilly at times in the winter, too warm for many people in the summer.

Weather is primarily determined by certain natural constants — the great ocean currents, the prevailing winds, the jet streams high in the sky, and the angle at which a particular location faces the sun at a particular time. Altitude also is involved; the higher one goes, the colder it gets (it snows at the equator at high altitudes). A great deal of misinformation abounds concerning the weather in various parts of the world, and as anyone who has traveled in the rain knows, scarcely any place is pleasant when it is cloudy, rainy, or bitterly cold.

The South Sea islands sound like a paradise, but they can be beastly hot and muggy, whereas Iceland and Scandinavia can be very pleasant places in midsummer. Parts of Italy can be much too hot for comfort in the summer, but Nairobi, near the equator in Africa, can be very pleasant. West Africa tends to be hot and muggy most of the year, yet parts of South Africa can be balmy and dry. Indonesia tends to be hot and muggy year-round, as does Singapore, and during the summer Hong Kong can be most unpleasant.

OCEAN CURRENTS AND WEATHER

Latitude alone tells us little about climate. Sunny Naples is farther north of the equator than New York. London is on the same latitude as the middle of Newfoundland, and Scotland is as far north as Ketchikan, Alaska. Combined with the effect of being far or near from the equator are the massive weather-tempering effects of ocean currents and altitude.

Large bodies of water moderate climate, reducing the cold and ameliorating the heat. Although farther north, the Mediterranean basin has a climate similar to Jacksonville in northern Florida because of the moderating effect of the Mediterranean Sea.

The Japan Current moves eastward into the Pacific and becomes the North Pacific Drift. As it approaches the United States, one branch heads north, tempering Alaska's climate. Moisture, warmth, and long summer days make for big strawberries and huge cabbages in parts of Alaska. Part of the North Atlantic Drift turns southward, a current responsible for the equable climate of southern California. The North Pacific Drift also makes the residents of Washington state feel at home on the southwestern shores of England and Ireland.

The Gulf Stream emanating from the Caribbean produces a great warming influence as it flows northward. As the Gulf Stream approaches the Azores far out in the Atlantic Ocean, part of it bends southward and the rest becomes the North Atlantic Drift, warming Iceland, the British Isles, and northern Europe. The soothing effect of the North Atlantic Drift produces palm trees in some locations along the southwest coasts of England and Ireland, and even as far north as Scotland. Because of this warm water, the southern part of Portugal enjoys an almost subtropical climate even though it is as far north as Philadelphia. Warm-water currents give Las Palmas in the Canary Islands the same weather conditions as San Diego, California.

The Humboldt Current affects the whole west coast of South America, cooling Lima in Peru and bringing spooky fogs over the arid lands of Chile's coast.

The Benguela Current moves up the west coast of Africa, but it is prevented from penetrating far into the land mass by prevailing winds and mountains.

THE EFFECT OF ALTITUDE

Adiabatic cooling (cooling because of the air's reduced density at high altitudes) is something to be reckoned with wherever there are mountains. The normal adiabatic rate is 3.5°F per thousand feet, meaning that for every thousand feet up from sea level, the temperature drops about 3.5°F. Altitude also brings drier air, especially important for the comfort of the traveler in the tropics. While Britain ruled India, the British took to the hills during the hot summers. Delhi swelters in the summer, but Kashmir in northern India is comparatively cool.

Large sections of east Africa offer delightful climate because of the altitude. A visitor to Kenya can be uncomfortably hot in Mombasa, on the coast, but will need long underwear in the mountains.

The two factors that influence the climate in any tropical area are prevailing winds and altitude. Much of South America is mountainous, and there is snow at the equator at the higher altitudes. In Ecuador, for example, the coastal port of Guayaquil is hot and muggy year-round, while Quito, the capital, sitting 9,348 feet above sea level, is never very warm.

Many people have great difficulty adjusting to altitude. Travelers to places like Quito are sometimes hospitalized with altitude sickness. Symptoms of altitude sickness include listlessness, drowsiness, or anxiety. Some of the trains traveling around the Andes carry oxygen for the passengers. Travelers can get sick going up to La Paz, the capital of Bolivia, 12,000 feet above sea level, and get sick again when coming down. Even Mexico City, with an altitude of 7,400 feet, presents altitude problems for some visitors.

Bogotá, the capital of Colombia, and its environs present a sharp illustration of the effect of altitude on climate. Visitors find perennial fall weather in Bogotá, but driving down from Bogotá toward the coast, they experience spring and finally hot, muggy summer within a few hours of the city. Bogotá residents can pick their own climate within a few hours of the city.

Think also of the relation between sun, mountains, and valleys, especially in beach and lake destinations with mountains in the background. In the mountains the valleys heat with the first rays of the sun. The warm air creeps up the natural corridors to the heights, causing clouds and sometimes strong winds around the mountaintops. As the day progresses, the rays of the sun lengthen, the valleys cool, and the clouds may dissipate. When a valley cools, the mountain breezes reverse themselves, sending cold, some- times strong, winds down the mountain to sweep the valley. Because of these facts, a room with a mountain view will be warmer than one with an ocean view during the day but naturally cool and comfortable all night.

WEATHER AND JET STREAM

High in the sky, usually between 30,000 and 40,000 feet, the tremendous force of jet streams that travel west to east streaks around much of the globe. The jet streams can push eastbound airlines across the United States so hard that transcontinental flight time can be reduced by two hours. Planes flying westward may be slowed appreciably.

Oddly, little was known about the jet stream until near the end of World War II when B-29 Superfortresses, flying at higher altitudes, were slowed down by as much as 200 miles per hour. Meteorologists plotted jet stream paths and found these winds traveling as fast as 400 miles per hour, faster in winter and slower in summer. Pilots can search out the jet streams and ride them when traveling eastward. Sometimes the winds are widespread and unavoidable. At times, jet streams across the United States move north and south with the seasons. Just how much the jet streams affect weather conditions is not completely known, but their effect is significant.

WEATHER MISCONCEPTIONS

Few people have occasion to know in detail the climatic conditions around the world. Looking at the map, it would be easy to assume that Baja California and the area around Guaymas, Mexico, would be swimmable during the winter. The weather is warm enough for fishing. The water temperature and the air temperature, however, are far from warm beginning around the middle of November. To be assured of warm weather and warm water, the traveler must go as far south as Mazatlán.

Summer would seem to be a fine time to visit Mexico City and the central plateau on which it sits. The rainy season in June and July, however, can mean days of steady downpour and even flooded roads.

The travel posters suggest that Queensland, Australia, and the Great Barrier Reef that parallels its coast present fine swimming and fishing during the Australian winter (our summer). The weather is certainly warm enough, but some of the towns on the coast get as much as 200 inches of rain each year, and hours of rain each day are not uncommon throughout the year. Queensland lies within the tropics. Moving south into Sydney and toward the lower coast of Australia means winter weather during our summer months, not snow but cold. During our summer months one should not expect to swim at all in the ocean.

A South Seas dream—gorgeous days spent lying under the palms—can be misleading. Most of the smaller islands, including Samoa and Western Samoa, get much more rain than most visitors like. The humidity is high. Sitting in a hotel with few other options available while rain beats down outside can be quite boring. The South Sea islands are not known for their fine restaurants, and the native dances lose their fascination after a few performances. Rain and humidity are bugaboos in most tropical areas.

THE MEDITERRANEAN CLIMATE

Climates of the world have been classified in various ways, but most climatologists classify the Mediterranean climate as one of the loveliest and most appealing to visitors. The Mediterranean climate occurs in those lands bordering the Mediterranean Sea, of course, but curiously, it is the same sort of weather experienced on the coasts of California and central Chile, at the tip of South Africa, and in much of south Australia.

This climate is characterized as being hot and dry in the summer and mild and somewhat wet in the winter. It includes foggy periods because these lands border water. In California spring seems to be foggiest. Rain comes in the winter.

ISLAND WEATHER

Rain, which kills the tourist's spirit, plagues the tropics. The amount of rainfall is largely determined by the topography and the prevailing winds. Most islands with mountains have a wet side and a dry side. On the island of Oahu in Hawaii, Waikiki is dry; the other side of the island is wet. On the big island of Hawaii, rain is very scarce on the leeward (western) side. But Hilo, on the windward (eastern) side, gets more than 100 inches of rain, making it delightful for orchids but not necessarily for visitors. The Kohala coast area, on the dry side, usually gets less than ten inches a year.

Most islands receive less rain on the leeward side, away from the approaching wind. Clouds blown by prevailing winds onto an island are lifted by the mountains and dump their rain on the windward side, leaving the leeward side relatively dry. The size of the island also has something to do with the amount of rainfall. Small islands get less rain than large ones. For example, the little islands of Bonaire and Aruba in the Caribbean get almost no rain. Curaçao, a little larger, gets so little rain that sea water must be distilled to meet its fresh water needs.

LENGTH OF DAYLIGHT

Length of daylight is a consideration for the traveler. In the Northern Hemisphere, the farther north one is, the longer the hours of light in June. Below the equator the opposite is true. A visitor to Iceland, Alaska, or northern Norway can expect around-the-clock light on June 21, "the midnight sun." Conversely, the sun will shine only a few hours a day in these places during December and January. At the equator the hours of daylight vary little from season to season. The seasons also reverse at the equator; visitors to Australia enjoy summer in December and winter in June.

The length of daylight is twelve hours everywhere on earth at the time of the equinoxes, about March 21 and September 21. It is always twelve hours at the equator, but daylight increases toward each pole as summer approaches, reaching a maximum at the time of the solstices, about June 22 and December 22.

The average hours of bright sunlight vary greatly from one place to another. London gets about 1,480 hours of bright sunshine during the whole year; Paris gets 1,740; Washington, D.C., 2,200. The Florida Keys and southern California both get about 2,700. Madrid gets 2,910, while Cape Town, South Africa, is the sunshine winner with 3,096 hours.

Sunshine is one thing, temperature another. The French Riviera does well in the sunshine department—2,700 hours a year—but the winter temperature drops to an average of 47°F. Honolulu has plenty of rain, so that it receives less sunshine than the French Riviera, 2,450 hours a year. The temperature, however, drops only to an average of 71°F during the winter.

PLACES TO AVOID IN CERTAIN SEASONS

Egypt is unbearably hot during the summer, especially along the Red Sea—in Aswan and Luxor in Upper Egypt, the temperature in the shade usually is between 105°F and 110°F. The healthiest time to visit Egypt is between October and May when the weather is surprisingly cool.

People who dislike hot, muggy climates should avoid areas at sea level in the tropics, especially those surrounded by water. Bangkok, Thailand, for example, is nearly always hot and muggy, with temperatures in the 80s. The parts of tropical islands that are on the windward side of mountains are hot and muggy. Nandi, on the main island of Fiji, is dry compared to the capital city Suva, on the windward side of the island.

June, July, and August are the hot and wet months (the monsoon period) in India. Temperatures in New Delhi commonly climb above 100°F from mid-April to July.

Avoid Taiwan during the typhoon season, August to mid-October. The typhoon season hits Japan between June and September. Hurricanes are likely in parts of the Caribbean in August and September.

Springtime and early fall are good seasons for visiting South Korea. The country is likely to be hot in midsummer and quite cold in winter.

The best time to visit Mexico and most of Central America is between November and April, avoiding the wet season.

Visit Argentina between October and December, their summer. During June, July, and August (their winter), the temperature is in the 50s. Uruguay is pleasant most of the year, but it can get cold during their winter (June through August). Rio de Janeiro is pleasant during our summer period but hot and muggy during our winter. June through August is the time to visit the ski resorts in Chile.

Around the world, in tropical latitudes climate largely depends upon altitude. Nairobi, Kenya, is pleasant. Because of altitude, Caracas, Venezuela, enjoys a perpetual springlike climate.

The Caribbean coast of South America is hot in areas where no trade winds blow.

WEATHER FOR POPULAR DESTINATIONS ABROAD

Algarve Coast. Continuous sandy beaches with clear water, but chilly. Winter water temperatures remain around 66°F and maximize during June to October at about 70°F. It can get hot during July and August.

Amsterdam. Lots of sprinkles and mist but not a heavy total rainfall. January, February, and March temperatures range from about 34°F to 46°F. June through September temperatures range from about 55°F to 69°F.

Azores. Delightful in the summer, but the climate cannot compare with that of Madeira and the Canary Islands farther south. Sea temperatures range from 60°F to 71°F. Because of prevailing winds, there are more cloudy days than clear ones. A temperate marine climate—cool, dry, and moderately sunny summers; gray and wet winters. Average monthly temperatures vary only twenty degrees from the hottest to the coolest.

Bavaria. Summers are cool by American standards, with winters fairly pleasant except during heavy storms. Short, heavy showers make summer the wettest period of the year. Few days have temperatures over 90°F. December, January, and February are overcast and gloomy; spring and autumn are quite dry and sunny. The mercury drops below freezing during more than 100 nights. There are also heavy foggy spells during the winter. Munich gets about ten snowfalls a year, totaling about 44 inches.

Berlin. Mild winters, damp and gray, about half the time between December through February, with little freezing weather. May through September is generally pleasant with considerable sunshine.

Cairo. Very dry, less than 1.5 inches of rain a year, and almost guaranteed sunshine. About 135 days have temperatures of over 90°F; 100°F summer readings are not unknown.

Copenhagen. The perfect "walking city." May and June are tops for good weather, with little rainfall, maximum sunshine, and cool but comfortable temperatures. August gets more rain, and autumn has light rainfall persistently. Temperatures at that time are between 50°F and 60°F. October averages only three hours of sunshine a day. During November, December, and January, the sun appears only about one hour a day.

Dublin. The best time to visit is April through June, when the city gets the most sunshine. Though the total rainfall is only about 30 inches a year, very low for Ireland, light misty showers are very frequent during the gray winter days. Winters are surprisingly mild, but expect only about two or three hours of sunshine each day.

Edinburgh. August is the wettest month of the year. The city gets approximately 197 days of heavy mist. Winter temperatures range between 24°F and 58°F. It never gets very warm in all of Scotland, the daily average in August varying between 53°F and 63°F.

French Riviera. October, November, and sometimes December can get considerable rain. Travelers should not expect to jump into a warm, balmy Mediterranean during the winter. The average sea water temperature in Monaco in January through April does not usually exceed 57°F.

Grand Canary Island. Usually about a twenty-degree spread throughout the summer; winter brings a high of about 79°F and a low of 58°F. Less than 10 inches of rain falls all year, very little during the summer months. The island averages six hours of sunshine. (Compare this with an average eight hours in Phoenix, Arizona, seven hours in Miami and Los Angeles.)

Greece. April, May, and June have plenty of sunshine everywhere, with only light showers. July and August are very dry, sunny, and clear—almost no rain. Most precipitation occurs in the winter. The islands can get hot during the summer, above 100°F, with plenty of sunshine. Athens experiences an average winter temperature range of 45°F to 60°F.

Helsinki. Oddly enough, it averages more sunshine than London in the summer months of June, July, and August. Water temperatures are low, about 55°F to 60°F in June, and rising to 62°F to 66°F in July. Average hours of daylight in June are seventeen. Winter is a long, gray season.

Lisbon. Usually has fewer than seventy days a year with more than 0.10 inch of rain. Temperatures are equable, very similar to San Diego, California. The high and low averages of Lisbon are 67°F and 55°F, while those of San Diego are 68°F and 55°F. Both cities have about the same amount of sunshine each year.

London. Gets about 24 inches of rain annually, lower than Montreal, Chicago, Boston, or New York. Though not really wet, London is damp because 70 days a year the city gets 0.10 inch or more of rain, and 164 days get some rain. Some wet snow about a dozen times each winter. January, February, and March get fewer than two hours of sunshine per day; June, July, and August get over six hours per day of sun.

Madeira. Sea water temperatures vary from 60°F in March to 70°F in September. The temperature range from summer to winter is seldom over ten degrees, with the average annual high being 70°F degrees and the average low about 60°F, dropping as one goes up into the mountains, which reach to 5,000 feet. May, June, July, and August are almost completely free of rain. The island gets about 22 inches of rainfall a year.

13-1. Reid's, a hotel located on the island of Madeira, off the coast of North Africa, is a stunning resort. In the high season some 70 percent of the guests dress for dinner here. The original hotel, at the top of the hill, ⌐ates from 1891. The new wing, tennis courts, pool, and various sunning plazas are terraced down the cliff to the sea, where intrepid guests who can brave the chilly water jump into the Atlantic for a swim.

Madrid. The best weather occurs during spring and autumn. Winters can be quite chilly, and during January, February, and March, the city gets six or fewer hours of sunshine a day. December only gets a little over four hours of sunshine daily. Summers can be hot with forty to fifty days over 90°F. High humidity makes November and February uncomfortable. The mercury drops below 42°F about forty to fifty days during the winter. Many Madrid residents leave the city during the hot summer months.

Malta. At about the same latitude as Las Vegas and Norfolk, Virginia, the island is sunny year-round. It is subtropical, with no snow or freezing weather. There are about nineteen days of 90°F or warmer weather. Precipitation is about 20 inches. The swimming season is generally considered May to October because the winter water temperatures are 60°F to 64°F.

Oslo. Has 27 inches of rainfall with about a dozen thunderstorms during the summer. The months of May, June, July, and August normally average about seven hours of sunshine per day, with June 21 getting almost nineteen hours of daylight. Winter temperatures range from about 20°F to 32°F. July has the highest temperatures, about 73°F, with a few days in the upper 80s.

Paris. Autumn is short and most often is quite wet, though September and October can provide good weather.

Reykjavik. The capital of Iceland has a surprisingly mild climate because of the North Atlantic Drift that moves right around Iceland. The thermometer seldom drops below freezing. On the

THE TOURIST BUSINESS

other hand, it seldom gets to 70°F. It is dark and gloomy in Reykjavik during the winter. From October to March, the place gets fewer than three hours of sunshine a day and only one hour during November and January.

Rome. Can be very hot in the summer at times. Normal winter range is 35°F to 50°F, summer is 55°F to the low 90s. The description "sunny Italy" does not apply from November through February.

Stockholm. Midsummer days normally register 65°F to 70°F, with nights in the mid-50s. In winter the mercury hangs between 25°F and 35°F. Rainfall is 23 inches, about half that of New York; it is usually greatest in July, August, and October. Stockholm gets only about 40 totally clear days as against 180 cloudy ones. Snow can start in October and continue through early April.

Tel Aviv. Rarely experiences a day over 90°F. The lowest temperature recorded is around 34°F. The city is usually warm and dry, with about 30 inches of rain a year.

Vienna. Has only 26 inches of rain, which is distributed uniformly throughout the year. (Compare with New York, which gets 43 inches, Chicago, which gets 32, and Washington, D.C., with 41.) Winter temperatures are brisk and snappy, between 26°F and 50°F. October is fairly cool, ranging between 50°F and 75°F.

Zurich. Temperatures seldom reach 90°F but drop to about freezing 100 nights a year. Rainfall ranges from 39 to 46 inches and is over twice as heavy from May through October as during the other months. Zurich gets only about 1,700 total hours of sunshine a year, mainly during the summer.

TEMPERATURES—IN °F **PRECIPITATION**

Month	Daily Average Max.	Daily Average Min.	Extreme Max.	Extreme Min.	No. of Days Over 90°	No. of Days Under 32°	No. of Days 0°	Rel. Hum. A.M. 7:00	Rel. Hum. P.M. 1:00	Inches Total Prec.	Inches Snow Only	No. of Days Total Prec. 0.004"	No. of Days Total Prec. 0.1"	No. of Days Snow Only 1.5"	No. of Days Thun. Stms.	Max. Inches in 24 Hrs.	Wind Velocity 18 M.P.H.	Wind Velocity 30 M.P.H.	Visibility ½ Mile
Jan.	43	33	58	9	0.0	19	0	90	77	2.2	0.0	15	7	0.0	0.0	0.9	7.0	0.2	7
Feb.	45	34	63	5	0.0	14	0	90	69	1.8	3.5	13	6	1.0	0.2	1.0	14.0	1.2	4
March	53	37	76	23	0.0	9	0	88	59	1.4	11.0	15	5	2.0	0.7	1.1	5.0	0.2	3
April	59	42	86	29	0.0	1	0	80	50	1.7	0.0	14	5	0.0	1.1	1.1	8.0	0.3	—
May	66	48	89	32	0.0	—	0	79	52	2.1	0.0	13	6	0.0	1.1	1.6	4.0	0.1	—
June	72	53	99	39	0.8	0	0	79	55	2.2	0.0	11	6	0.0	3.3	1.5	2.0	0.0	—
July	76	57	103	46	2.4	0	0	81	55	2.2	0.0	12	6	0.0	3.1	1.4	3.0	0.0	—
Aug.	75	56	98	45	1.1	0	0	84	54	2.6	0.0	12	7	0.0	3.7	1.3	4.0	0.0	—
Sept.	69	52	91	38	0.3	0	0	91	59	2.2	0.0	11	6	0.0	3.2	1.2	4.0	0.2	1
Oct.	60	46	82	25	0.0	1	0	94	68	2.0	0.0	14	6	0.0	1.7	2.0	5.0	0.3	4
Nov.	48	39	68	21	0.0	7	0	93	76	2.1	0.0	15	7	0.0	0.2	1.1	5.0	0.1	7
Dec.	42	34	61	9	0.0	9	0	92	80	2.0	0.0	17	6	0.0	0.0	1.3	6.0	0.2	7
Year	59	44	103	5	4.6	59	0	87	63	24.0	15.0	162	73	3.0	17.0	2.0	5.5	0.2	33

Elevation 292 Feet
Latitude 48° 43′ N   Longitude 2° 24′ E
Total precipitation means the total of rain, snow, hail, etc. expressed as inches of rain.
Ten inches of snow equals approx. 1 inch of rain.
Temperatures are as °F.

Wind velocity is the percentage of observations greater than 18 and 30 M.P.H. Number of observations varies from one per day to several per hour.
Visibility means number of days with less than ½-mile visibility.
Note: "—" indicates slight trace or possibility blank indicates no statistics available

13-2. Climate: Paris, France.

13-3. Climate, Dublin, Ireland.

Month	TEMPERATURES—IN °F Daily Average Max.	Min.	Extreme Max.	Min.	No. of Days Over 90°	Under 32°	Under 0°	RELATIVE HUMIDITY A.M. 9:00	P.M. 2:00	PRECIPITATION Inches Total Prec.	Snow Only	No. of Days Total Prec. 0.04"	0.1"	Snow Only 1.5"	Thun. Stms.	Max. Inches in 24 Hrs.	WIND VELOCITY 18 M.P.H.	30 M.P.H.	VISIBILITY ½ MILE
Jan.	46	35	62	4	0	—	0	87	80	2.7	—	13	8	—	0.3	1.9			
Feb.	47	34	65	8	0	—	0	85	76	2.2	—	11	7	—	0.3	1.8			
March	49	35	72	15	0	—	0	84	72	2.0	—	10	6	—	0.3	1.5			
April	53	37	72	19	0	—	0	78	67	1.9	—	11	6	—	0.3	1.1			
May	58	42	80	22	0	—	0	77	69	2.3	—	11	7	—	1.0	1.5			
June	64	47	84	31	0	—	0	76	69	2.0	0	11	6	0	1.0	1.1			
July	66	51	86	35	0	0	0	79	70	2.8	0	13	7	0	2.0	1.8			
Aug.	65	50	85	33	0	0	0	83	72	3.0	0	13	7	0	1.0	1.5			
Sept.	62	46	82	29	0	—	0	85	73	2.8	0	12	7	0	1.0	2.7			
Oct.	55	41	73	22	0	—	0	86	75	2.7	—	12	7	—	0.3	2.2			
Nov.	50	38	67	15	0	—	0	87	79	2.7	—	12	7	—	0.3	1.5			
Dec.	47	35	63	7	0	—	0	87	81	2.6	—	13	8	—	0.0	1.9			
Year	55	41	86	4	0	0 +	0	83	74	29.6	0 +	142	83	0 +	7.8	2.7			

Elevation 155 Feet

Latitude 53° 22' N   **Longitude 6° 21' E**

Total precipitation means the total of rain, snow, hail, etc. expressed as inches of rain.

Ten inches of snow equals approx. 1 inch of rain.

Temperatures are as °F.

Wind velocity is the percentage of observations greater than 18 and 30 M.P.H. Number of observations varies from one per day to several per hour.

Visibility means number of days with less than ½-mile visibility.

Note: "—" indicates slight trace or possibility blank indicates no statistics available

TEMPERATURES—IN ° F   **RELATIVE HUMIDITY**   **PRECIPITATION**   **WIND VELOCITY**

Month	Daily Average Max.	Daily Average Min.	Extreme Max.	Extreme Min.	No. of Days Over 90°	No. of Days 32°	No. of Days Under 0°	R.H. A.M. 9:00	R.H. P.M. 3:00	Inches Total Prec.	Inches Snow Only	No. of Days Total Prec. 0.001"	No. of Days 0.1"	No. of Days Snow Only 1.5"	Thun. Stms.	Max. Inches in 24 Hrs.	Wind 18 M.P.H.	Wind 30 M.P.H.	VISIBILITY ½ MILE
Jan.	45	36	58	9	0.0	13	0	87	80	1.8	—	17	6	—	0.2	1.6	10.0	0.3	8.7
Feb.	46	36	63	11	0.0	12	0	84	72	1.5	—	13	5	—	0.1	0.8	11.0	0.4	6.7
March	49	37	70	17	0.0	8	0	79	63	1.7	—	11	5	—	0.8	1.1	8.0	0.2	5.7
April	55	40	82	26	0.0	3	0	72	58	1.5	—	14	5	—	1.0	0.7	7.0	0.1	0.9
May	63	46	89	30	0.0	—	0	69	57	1.7	0	13	5	0	3.0	1.0	7.0	0.1	1.3
June	68	51	94	37	0.1	0	0	68	57	2.1	0	11	6	0	2.0	1.6	4.0	0.0	1.2
July	71	55	93	42	0.3	0	0	68	55	2.2	0	13	6	0	3.0	1.4	6.0	0.1	0.7
Aug.	70	54	94	41	0.1	0	0	73	58	2.2	0	13	6	0	3.0	2.2	6.0	0.0	2.2
Sept.	65	50	92	31	—	—	0	78	63	1.9	0	13	6	0	1.0	1.3	8.0	0.1	3.5
Oct.	57	45	83	25	0.0	2	0	83	70	2.7	—	14	7	—	0.4	1.6	5.0	0.0	9.2
Nov.	49	39	63	20	0.0	5	0	87	79	2.2	—	16	6	—	0.2	1.4	8.0	0.3	8.6
Dec.	46	37	60	11	0.0	8	0	87	81	2.3	—	16	7	—	0.2	1.1	11.0	0.2	11.0
Year	57	44	94	9	0.5	51	0	78	66	24.0	0 +	164	70	0 +	15.0	2.2	7.4	0.2	59.0

Elevation 80 Feet

Latitude 51° 28′ N   **Longitude 0° 27′ E**

Total precipitation means the total of rain, snow, hail, etc. expressed as inches of rain.

Ten inches of snow equals approx. 1 inch of rain.

Temperatures are as °F.

Wind velocity is the percentage of observations greater than 18 and 30 M.P.H. Number of observations varies from one per day to several per hour.

Visibility means number of days with less than ½-mile visibility.

Note: "—" indicates slight trace or possibility blank indicates no statistics available

13-4. Climate: London, England.

TEMPERATURES—IN ° F

PRECIPITATION

Month	Daily Average Max.	Daily Average Min.	Extreme Max.	Extreme Min.	No. of Days Over 90°	No. of Days Under 32°	No. of Days Under 0°	RELATIVE HUMIDITY A.M. 8:00	RELATIVE HUMIDITY P.M. 2:00	Inches Total Prec.	Inches Snow Only	No. of Days Total Prec. 0.04"	No. of Days Total Prec. 0.1"	No. of Days Snow Only 1.5"	No. of Days Thun. Stms.	Max. Inches in 24 Hrs.	WIND VELOCITY 18 M.P.H.	WIND VELOCITY 30 M.P.H.	VISIBILITY ½ MILE
Jan.	35	28	49	-10	0	20	—	89	86	1.5	—	9	5	—	—	0.6	38	5	5
Feb.	36	27	54	-13	0	19	—	92	86	1.2	—	7	4	—	0	0.8	36	4	5
March	40	30	62	-1	0	21	—	87	77	1.5	—	8	5	—	0	0.7	31	4	4
April	50	36	79	20	0	6	0	80	66	1.6	—	9	5	—	1	0.8	21	1	1
May	61	44	85	26	0	—	0	73	60	1.6	—	8	5	—	1	1.1	19	—	1
June	69	51	90	31	—	—	0	73	61	1.9	0	8	5	0	2	1.2	16	—	1
July	72	54	91	39	—	0	0	77	63	2.4	0	9	6	0	4	1.6	15	—	—
Aug.	69	53	89	33	0	0	0	82	67	3.0	0	12	7	0	3	1.6	18	—	1
Sept.	63	48	86	26	0	—	0	87	70	2.0	—	8	6	—	1	1.3	24	—	2
Oct.	53	42	74	19	0	—	0	90	77	2.2	—	9	6	—	1	1.1	28	1	3
Nov.	43	35	57	5	0	5	0	89	83	1.9	—	10	5	—	—	1.1	36	3	2
Dec.	38	31	54	-1	0	12	—	89	87	2.1	—	11	7	—	—	0.9	40	4	4
Year	52	40	91	-13	0 +	84	0 +	84	74	23.0	—	108	67	—	13	1.6	27	2	29

Elevation 16 Feet
Latitude 55° 38' N   Longitude 12° 40' E
Total precipitation means the total of rain, snow, hail, etc. expressed as inches of rain.
Ten inches of snow equals approx. 1 inch of rain.
Temperatures are as °F.

Wind velocity is the percentage of observations greater than 18 and 30 M.P.H. Number of observations varies from one per day to several per hour.
Visibility means number of days with less than ½-mile visibility.
Note: "—" indicates slight trace or possibility blank indicates no statistics available

13-5. Climate: Copenhagen, Denmark.

TEMPERATURES—IN °F

PRECIPITATION

Month	Daily Average Max.	Min.	Extreme Max.	Min.	No. of Days Over 90°	Under 32°	Under 0°	Rel. Hum. A.M. 7:30	P.M. 1:30	Inches Total Prec.	Snow Only	No. of Days Total Prec. 0.1″	Snow Only 1.5″	Thun. Stms.	Max. Inches in 24 Hrs.	Wind Velocity 18 M.P.H.	30 M.P.H.	Visibility ½ Mile
Jan.	55	40	70	18	0.0	2	0	59	52	2.5	—	8	—	0.6				
Feb.	56	40	72	20	0.0	3	0	62	53	2.2	—	7	—	0.6				
March	59	44	72	23	0.0	—	0	64	58	2.7	—	7	—	1.3				
April	63	48	81	29	0.0	—	0	70	61	2.2	0	6	0	1.7				
May	69	54	87	36	0.0	0	0	72	63	2.4	0	7	0	3.0				
June	75	61	92	36	—	0	0	71	62	1.6	0	5	0	5.4				
July	80	65	100	49	2.1	0	0	70	64	1.0	0	2	0	3.8				
Aug.	80	64	97	50	2.0	0	0	70	61	1.0	0	3	0	3.6				
Sept.	77	61	92	40	—	0	0	73	63	2.4	0	6	0	4.0				
Oct.	69	54	82	34	0.0	0	0	72	61	5.8	0	10	0	3.1				
Nov.	62	46	77	28	0.0	—	0	70	62	4.4	—	9	—	1.7				
Dec.	56	41	68	18	0.0	1	0	66	59	3.1	—	9	—	0.8				
Year	67	53	100	18	4.0	6	0	68	60	31.0	0 +	79	0 +	30.0				

Elevation 13 Feet

Latitude 43° 39' N   Longitude 7° 12' E

Total precipitation means the total of rain, snow, hail, etc. expressed as inches of rain.

Ten inches of snow equals approx. 1 inch of rain.

Temperatures are as °F.

Wind velocity is the percentage of observations greater than 18 and 30 M.P.H. Number of observations varies from one per day to several per hour.

Visibility means number of days with less than ½-mile visibility.

Note: "—" indicates slight trace or possibility blank indicates no statistics available

13-6. Climate: Nice, France.

THE TOURIST BUSINESS

DISCUSSION QUESTIONS

1. Weatherwise, is summer the best time to visit Mexico City? Explain.
2. How is the weather in Acapulco during the summer?
3. Would you expect to swim in the Mediterranean in January? Why or why not?
4. How does Scotland compare in latitude with Alaska?
5. In what ways does the Japan Current affect the weather in the states of Oregon and Washington?
6. What would the climate of England be without the Gulf Stream?
7. What is adiabatic cooling? What is its relationship to the summer climate of Denver, Colorado?
8. Is it possible to become ill from moving too rapidly from sea level to high altitudes?
9. Should a resort that is located with a backdrop of mountains expect to be warmer or cooler at night because of the presence of mountains?
10. In what way does the jet stream affect continental United States flights?
11. During a visit to the northeast coast of Australia, what weather problems can be expected?
12. Besides being applied to the climate around the Mediterranean Sea, where else in the world is the Mediterranean climate found?
13. Which side of an island is almost certain to be the driest? Explain why this is true?
14. How many hours of daylight would you expect to experience on the equator? How many hours of daylight would you expect to experience on June 21 in north Alaska and northern Norway?
15. What are the summer months in Rio de Janeiro?
16. When would be a good time to avoid visiting Taiwan?
17. When would you go skiing in Chile?
18. Besides location north or south of the equator (latitude), what other major factors determine climate and weather?
19. What climate would you expect in Juneau, Alaska?
20. What factors give Caracas, Venezuela, a springlike climate year-round?

GLOSSARY

AIR TRAVEL

Air mile — International air mile, a measure of distance equaling approximately 6,076 feet.

Airport code — Three-letter code identifying airports nationally and worldwide. Examples are DEN — Denver, and LAX — Los Angeles International.

Airline Reporting Conference (ARC) — Division of the Air Transport Association that sets requirements for establishing a travel agency in order for the agency to qualify to sell tickets of major American airlines; it also collects payments for tickets sold and distributes monies from those sales to the appropriate airlines.

Air Transport Association (ATA) — Trade association formed in 1936 to promote business by serving as an information center for industry planning. Represents virtually all scheduled airlines in the United States.

City Terminal — Airline ticket office located elsewhere than at the airport, where passengers may check in, receive seat assignments, and get transportation to the airport.

Configuration — Arrangement of seats in a transport vehicle or aircraft cabin. The number of seats abreast in a row, the size of the seats, and the seat pitch are varied to provide different passenger densities for the classes of service available.

Deadhead flight — Transporting an aircraft for the purpose of moving or returning it to some location without carrying revenue-paying passengers or cargo. Also called a ferry flight.

Estimated time of arrival (ETA) — Time when a carrier (usually an aircraft), guest, or group is expected to reach a given location or destination.

Estimated time of departure (ETD) — Time when a carrier (usually an aircraft), guest, or group is expected to leave a location.

Federal Aviation Administration (FAA) — Governmental body, under the United States Department of Transportation, which exercises an overall control of airports, equipment, pilots, and routes, and issues mandatory requirements and standards to govern civil aviation.

Flight crew — Those responsible for operating an aircraft, including the pilots, flight engineer, and flight attendants.

Fly–drive package — Tour package that includes airline transport from one's point of origin to the point of destination and return, and the use of an automobile for local transport while at the destination.

Freedoms of the air — Basic traffic rights as bilaterally arranged between nations. Freedoms of commercial airlines include (1) the right to overfly, (2) the right to land for technical reasons, (3) the right to carry from home country to another country, (4) the right to carry from another country to home country, and (5) the right to carry between foreign countries. Also called the Five Freedoms.

Gateway city — City that functions as the first destination for visitors to an area because of its location and transportation patterns.

Ground time — (1) Time spent on the ground at intermediate stops. (2) The time spent in airports and in waiting for connecting flights.

International Air Charter Association (IACA) — Trade association of supplemental and charter airlines.

International Air Transport Association (IATA) — Worldwide trade association of international airlines. The IATA conference promotes a unified system of air transportation on international routes; sets fares, rates, safety standards, and conditions of service; and appoints and regulates travel agents to sell international tickets.

International Airlines Travel Agent Network (IATAN) — Owned by IATA, appoints U.S. travel agencies to represent international airlines serving the United States.

Passenger mile — One passenger carried one mile; computed by multiplying the number of vehicle miles traveled by the number of passengers transported.

Passenger service agent — Usually an airline employee who assists passengers at the airport by providing information and directions, assisting the elderly, arranging ground transportation, and so forth.

Positioning — Moving an aircraft, ship, bus, or other transport vehicle to a location where it will again begin revenue service.

Ramp agent — Airline employee who loads and unloads baggage, cargo, and food supplies onto an aircraft.

Revenue passenger mile — One paying passenger carried one mile in commercial transport service.

Scheduled airline — Any airline providing scheduled service for passengers or cargo.

Shuttle service — Provision of transportation from one point to another for both people and baggage, usually basic in nature and over short distances, as from aircraft to terminal.

Through passenger — Passenger scheduled to continue a journey on the same vehicle, although it makes intermediate stops.

Transit passenger — Person traveling with an itinerary that includes one or more stops in foreign countries that are not the person's destination. At each stop the person may leave the plane or even change planes or wait for the next scheduled flight without officially entering the country by going through customs.

RAIL TRAVEL

Amtrak — Name used by the National Railroad Passenger Corporation, a semipublic corporation formed in 1971, charged with managing U.S. intercity passenger-railroad service.

Bedroom — Accommodates two adults, contains two foldaway beds, enclosed washroom facilities with toilet.

Club car — Provides luxury seating and personal service at a surcharge.

Coach — In railroads, a car for ordinary travel at minimum rates. In airplanes, the tourist-class section.

Diner — A restaurant car on a train.

Dome car — Specially designed railway car with a glass roof for sightseeing. Also called a bubble car.

Eurocity Train — Intercity train in Europe; air conditioned, has catering service, and meets high standards of punctuality and cleanliness.

Eurail Pass — Railroad ticket providing unlimited rail travel throughout seventeen countries of Western Europe. A flat rate is charged for a specified number of days. Also available at special children's rates.

Metroliner — High-speed Amtrak trains operating between Boston and Washington, D.C. All seats are on a reserved basis. No sleeping accommodations. Meals available.

Pullman — Railroad sleeping and parlor car used in North America.

Roomette — Slightly larger than a single bedroom, has toilet facilities.

VIA — The Canadian equivalent of AMTRAK.

Wagon-Lits — Company-operated railroad sleeping cars in Europe. Similar to the Pullman Company in the United States.

SHIP TRAVEL

Air–sea — Travel programs or itineraries using some combination of both air and sea transportation.

Bareboat charter — Boat, yacht, or other vessel rented without supplies or crew.

Berth — Sleeping and sitting bed arrangement on a ship or train where upper and lower beds (berths) are attached to a wall. They may fold away when not in use.

Boat — Small open aircraft propelled by oars, sail, or engine, not ordinarily thought of as an ocean-going vessel. Ships, as opposed to boats, carry lifeboats.

Bon Voyage — French term of farewell. Bon voyage parties are often major celebrations held before departure when the trip covers a significant distance.

Cabin — Sleeping room on a ship, usually less luxurious than a stateroom.

Captain's table — Dining-room table hosted by the captain of a cruise or passenger ship. Other officers may also host tables.

Companionway — Stairway.

Crossing the line — Ceremony observed when a ship crosses the equator. Those who are crossing the equator for the first time are subjected to initiation ceremonies. Father Neptune comes aboard and holds court, interviewing the first-timers to see if they are worthy of being given a pass to cross the line. The passengers then go through the initiation ceremonies, which include dunking in the swimming pool and other lighthearted pranks.

Cruise Lines International Association (CLIA) — Trade association of cruise lines seeking to promote cruises by offering educational programs for travel agents.

Disembark — To leave a ship.

Free port — (1) Port or part of a port where cargo can be unloaded or loaded and shipped without payment of customs duty. (2) A port open under equal terms to all vessels.

Hydrofoil — Water transport vessel using fins or foils that raise the craft partly out of the water, thus reducing friction and drag and therefore making very high speeds possible for long periods of time.

International Passenger Ship Association (IPSA) — Trade association of companies that operate cruises marketed in North America. Supersedes the Trans-Atlantic Passenger Steamship Conference (TAPSC).

Keep alone if possible — Steamship or cruise booking in which a passenger traveling alone is willing to share a cabin to avoid paying the single rate but prefers single occupance. The initials "KIP" on the reservation request alerts the berthing department to try to assign a cabin where the passenger is the only occupant.

Knot — Measure of speed, equivalent to one nautical mile per hour.

Lido deck — Area around the swimming pool, as well as the deck of a ship on which the swimming pool is located.

Liner — Large, ocean-going passenger vessel or ship subject to maritime regulations.

Nautical mile — Used to measure sea and air navigation distances; approximately 6,076 feet.

Port — Left side of a ship, looking forward; originally called larboard.

Port of entry — Officially designated port where foreign passengers or goods may enter a country.

Promenade deck — On a passenger ship an upper deck enclosed by glass.

Purser — Person responsible for all hotel and financial functions of a passenger ship and for the service and care of the passengers.

Registry — Country in which a ship is registered. This often is not the country of ownership. For example, a ship may be British-owned but registered in a foreign country, such as Panama, Liberia, or the Bahamas. The certificate of registration does not attest to a vessel's quality, safety, or to the nationality or skill of its crew.

Sail permit — Income tax clearance certificate issued by the Internal Revenue Service. Required for all resident aliens before departure from the United States to a foreign country.

Sea legs — Ability to walk on the deck of a ship while it is pitching or rolling. More generally, ability to tolerate the movement of a ship or other vessel. Also resistance to seasickness.

Ship — Seagoing vessel of substantial size that navigates in deep water.

TRAVEL AGENCY TERMINOLOGY[1]

Agency appointment — Process whereby travel agencies are approved by conferences to represent

---

1. For a more comprehensive listing see Charles J. Metalka, *The Dictionary of Tourism*, Second Edition, Merton House Travel and Tourism Publishers, Wheaton, Ill. 1986; and Claudine Dervals, *The Travel Dictionary*, P.O. Box 14508, Tampa, FL, 1985.

a group of carriers, or by a company, hotel, or other supplier, to represent and sell its services.

Agency representative — Salesperson representing an airline, tour operator, hotel, and so forth, calling on travel agents.

Airline representative — Salesperson or account executive representing an airline and calling on travel agencies, commercial accounts, or other organizations that have the ability to produce substantial business for the airline.

Airport transfer — Service, sometimes complimentary, offered by hotels to guests that provides transportation to and/or from the area's airport either on demand or according to a schedule.

Airline Reporting Corporation (ARC) — An airline industry organization entrusted with the establishment of standards for appointing travel agencies and for the operation of the area settlement plan through which travel agents and approved suppliers report and remit payments for airline tickets.

HOTEL TERMINOLOGY

Agency representative — Salesperson representing an airline, tour operator, hotel, and so forth, calling on travel agents.

Airline representative — Salesperson or account executive representing an airline and calling on travel agencies, commercial accounts, or other organizations that have the ability to produce substantial business for the airline.

Airline transfer — Service, sometimes complimentary, offered by hotels to guests; provides transportation to and/or from the area's airport either on demand or according to a schedule.

American plan (AP) — Hotel accommodations with three meals daily included with the price of the room. In Europe, called full pension. *Modified American plan* — MAP (also called half pension) — includes a room, breakfast, and either lunch or dinner.

Back-to-back — Method of operating tour flights on a continuing basis. For example, a flight arriving with passengers would immediately board another group of passengers, either for a return trip or for a continuing flight. Also, the hectic situation in which some customers are departing at the same time as others arrive.

Best available — Supplier's promise to provide the best possible accommodations for a client. When part of a request for a reservation, it means that the client desires the best accommodations available in the property.

Certified Travel Counselor (CTC) — Certificate of professional competence attesting to travel agent's successful completion of a study program developed and administered by the Institute of Certified Travel Agents.

Charter flight — Scheduled or nonscheduled flight that meets specified charter conditions and is booked or contracted by one or more groups for their exclusive use. Such flights are usually less expensive than regularly scheduled ones because charters sell a larger percentage of their seats.

Check-in time — Time at which a hotel or motel room is ready for occupancy. Also, the time at which a passenger should register at a terminal prior to departure.

Check-out time — Time by which a guest of a lodging is required to vacate accommodations to avoid an additional charge.

Circle trip — A journey with stopovers that returns to the point of departure without retracing its route. Travel from point A with stops at points B and C and returning to A is a circle trip if point B is off the regular route between points A and C or point C is off the regular route between points A and B.

City Terminal — Airline ticket office, located somewhere other than the airport, where passengers may check in, receive seat assignments, and get transportation to the airport.

Closed dates — Periods when everything available at a facility or service has been booked.

Commercial rate — Special discounted rate offered by a hotel or other supplier to a company, individual, or other valued repeat customer.

Concierge — Employee in many major hotels in charge of guests' services, such as baggage handling, dinner reservations, letter mailing, and other personalized services.

Condominium hotel — Hotel partly or totally comprised of individually owned condominium units.

Conference—An association of carriers formed to establish rules for the mutual benefit of its members. Among other things, a conference may establish rates; allocate routes; formulate and enforce safety, service, and ethical standards; and establish rules, governing the conduct of others (for example, travel agents) who do business with its members.

Confirmation slip—Printed document certifying that the holder does in fact have a confirmed reservation for a room, seat, or some other space.

Confirmed reservation—Oral or written statement by a hotel, restaurant, airline, or other supplier that the request for a reservation has been received and will be honored. Reservations are confirmed within a context of binding limitations and obligations. For example, a hotel often requires that a guest arrive before 6:00 P.M. or chance the loss of the reservation.

Connecting flight—A flight that requires the passenger to change aircraft as part of the itinerary.

Continental breakfast—Light morning meal usually of a beverage and toast or rolls. See also English breakfast.

Continental plan—Hotel room rate that includes both the use of the room and a continental breakfast.

Deluxe—Declared to be of the highest standard; when part of a hotel rating system, a property wherein all rooms have a private bath and a variety of services are available.

Domestic escorted tour (DET)—Packaged, preplanned itinerary within the traveler's home country, including the services of a tour manager/escort.

Domestic independent tour (DIT)—Term used in the United States or Canada to describe a prepaid, unescorted itinerary within a country. Also known as a domestic inclusive tour.

Double—(1) Hotel or motel room designed to accommodate two persons. (2) Reservation for two persons. (3) Room provided with a double bed.

Double-double—(1) Room designed to accommodate two, three, or four persons. (2) A room with double beds.

Double-occupancy rate—Per person room rate contingent upon someone else also occupying the room as a paying customer.

Downgrade—To change to a lower-grade class of service.

Economy hotel—Hotel with no private bath facilities and limited services. Also referred to as a tourist or second-class hotel.

Elderhostel—Network of several hundred universities and colleges in the United States and Canada that offer persons over sixty years of age the opportunity to experience a combined program of education and adventure. Accommodations are provided in campus dormitories, and special courses are offered.

English breakfast—Hearty breakfast, usually served in Great Britain and Ireland, of cereals, meats, egg dishes, breads, and beverages. *See also* Continental breakfast.

European plan (EP)—Hotel accommodations with no meals included in the price of the room.

Familiarization trip/tour—Trips or tours offered to travel writers and agency personnel by airlines and other suppliers as a way of informing the customer-influencing segments of the industry. Often called a fam trip.

Family plan—Discount offered by hotels, airlines, and resorts to members of a family traveling together.

First-class hotel—Hotel offering a high standard and variety of service; most rooms have a private bath.

Foreign escorted tour (FET)—Preplanned all-inclusive tour outside the tourist's own country, including the services of a tour manager.

Foreign Independent Tour (FIT)—A foreign tour put together for someone not traveling as part of a group.

Fully appointed—Description of a travel agency that has been officially appointed by the major airlines, steamship, and cruise conferences to sell products and services and issue tickets.

Gateway city—City that functions as the first destination for visitors to the area because of its location and transportation patterns.

Ground arrangements—Land services provided to a client at each destination visited in an itinerary, which may include transfer to a hotel, car rental, entertainment tickets, and so forth.

Ground operator—Company that provides local transportation, sight-seeing, and other services to a client at a destination.

Group inclusive tour (GIT)—Prepaid tour allowing special air fares to a group and requiring that all the members travel on the same flight round trip and travel together during their entire time abroad.

Guaranteed reservation — Advance booking with payment guaranteed even if the guest does not arrive unless canceled in accordance with the accommodation's cancellation policy.

High season — Time of year at any destination when tourist traffic and therefore usually rates are highest.

Hotel representative — Person or company retained by one or more hotels to arrange hotel reservations for wholesalers, travel agents, and the public. Often simply referred to as a hotel rep.

Hotel voucher — Coupon used by a tour operator to cover payment for all specified prepaid tour features. Guests surrender the hotel voucher on check-in, and the hotel sends the voucher and billing statement to the tour operator for payment.

Incentive travel — (1) A trip offered as a prize, particularly to stimulate the productivity of employees or sales agents. (2) The business of operating such travel programs.

Inclusive tour — A tour in which specific elements — air fare, hotels, transfers, etc. — are offered for a flat rate. An inclusive tour does not necessarily cover all costs.

Institute of Certified Travel Agents (ICTA) — Industry organization offering a voluntary education accreditation program for retail travel agents.

International Association for Medical Assistance to Travelers (IAMAT) — Worldwide nonprofit membership association concerned with the health dangers associated with travel and the dissemination of information to reduce such dangers.

International Association of Tour Managers (IATM) — Professional organization of tour escorts.

International Passenger Ship Association (IPSA) — Trade association of companies that operate cruises marketed in North America. Supersedes the Trans-Atlantic Passenger Steamship Conference (TAPSC).

IT number — Code number identifying a tour that has been submitted and approved by the ATC or IATA and that allows travel agents to obtain override commissions for air transportation sold as part of such approved tours.

Land only — Provision in a travel brochure that the price stated includes only services to be provided once the client arrives on the scene. Costs of transportation to and from the location are not included.

Minimum connecting time — Officially specified minimum amount of time that should exist between a passenger's scheduled connecting flights.

Modified American plan (MAP) — Hotel accommodations including breakfast and either lunch or dinner with the price of the room. Same as demipension and half pension.

National Association of Travel Organizations (NATO) — Trade association headquartered in Washington, D.C.

National Passenger Traffic Association (NPTA) — Professional association of corporate travel managers.

National Tour Brokers Association (NTBA) — Membership association of motor coach tour operators licensed by the Interstate Commerce Commission.

Open jaw — Round-trip itinerary or ticket in which the departure point is different from the arrival point; a trip from Chicago to New York with a return from Boston to Chicago would be an open jaw.

Open ticket — Ticket that does not specify the date on which a certain service is to be performed, leaving the passenger to secure a reservation at a later date.

Overbooking — Deliberate or mistaken confirmation of more reservations that there are seats or rooms.

Override — Extra commission paid by carriers, wholesale tour operators, hotels, and so forth to travel agents as bonuses or incentives.

Pacific Area Travel Association (PATA) — Membership organization of government and private business representatives that seeks to promote and monitor travel to and within the Pacific area.

Point-to-point — Term for basic transportation only. A point-to-point fare is the basic rate from one city to another.

Pre/post convention tour — Extension of a convention tour whereby, for an additional charge, extra days or destinations may be added to the beginning or end of a basic convention itinerary.

Reconfirmation — Action attesting to one's intention to use a reservation. An international airline passenger is required to reconfirm a reserved seat on subsequent flights if a stopover exceeds a certain time limit. If no reconfirmation is made, the seat may be legally resold.

Revalidation sticker — Official notice that a change of the original reservation has been made; it is affixed to the flight coupon of an air ticket.

Run-of-the-house rate — Flat rate for which a hotel or motel agrees to offer any of its available rooms to a group.

Scheduled airline — Any airline providing scheduled service for passengers or cargo.

Shoulder period — Calendar period between a peak season and an off-season, for which the promotional fare or rate is lower than peak and higher than off-season.

Shuttle service — Provision of transportation from one point to another for both people and baggage. Usually basic in nature and over short distances, as from aircraft to terminal.

Space available — Literally, if the space is available. Often a reduced fare or charge category in which the service will be provided if space is available.

Special-interest tour — Prearranged and packaged itinerary designed to appeal to or respond to a request by a group of persons with a particular interest. Such a tour may focus on horticulture, birdwatching, law, gourmet dining, backpacking, music, dance, religious events, sports, and so on.

Studio — Hotel or motel room with one or more couches instead of beds for sleeping.

Suite — Accommodations that include two rooms, one for sleeping and another for sitting, as well as a private bath.

Supplier — The actual producer of a unit of travel merchandise such as a carrier hotel sight-seeing operator. Sometimes also called a purveyor.

Throwaway — Item in the land portion of a tour that is rarely used. It is included in the tour package merely to qualify the passenger for a tour-basing fare.

Ticket stock — Blank airline tickets of a carrier's own stock or standardized stock used to book passage on any U.S. or foreign airline that is a member of ATC or IATA. Blank tickets become valid only after they have been completed and validated with a travel agency's stamp.

Tour-basing fare — A reduced-rate excursion fare available only to those who buy prepaid tours or packages. Inclusive tour, group inclusive tour, incentive group, contract bulk inclusive tour-basing fares are all tour-basing fares.

Tour broker — Person or company licensed by the Interstate Commerce Commission to organize, market, and operate motor coach tours in the United States.

Tour desk — (1) Desk, table, or counter space, often located in the lobby of a hotel and staffed by a hotel employee for the purpose of answering questions, providing information on sights to see, and responding to a variety of guest requests. (2) Desk at an airline ticket office staffed by an airline employee who sells tours and packages to passengers.

Tourist class — Accommodations or other facilities or services that are below first class.

Tour package — Travel plan including most elements of a vacation, such as transportation, accommodations, and sight-seeing, at a price which is lower than if the traveler purchased each service separately.

Tour sales agent — Usually an airline employee who is responsible for selling tours and packages sponsored by the airline.

Tour shell — Brochure containing graphics or illustrations but no copy, to be overprinted by travel agents and tour wholesalers.

Travel Industry Association of America (TIAA) — Nonprofit association of government organizations and private companies formed to promote travel to and within the United States.

United States Tour Operators Association (USTOA) — Trade association of tour operators.

Wait List — List of passengers who are awaiting confirmation of a flight, ship, tour, and so forth that is sold out.

RECOMMENDED READING

BOOKS

Bosselman, Fred P. *In the Wake of the Tourist*. Washington, DC: The Conservation Foundation, 1978.

Daley, Robert. *An American Saga: Juan Trippe and His Pan Am Empire*. New York: Random House, 1980.

Gee, C. Y., Choy, D. J. L., and Makens, J. S. *The Travel Industry*, 2nd ed. New York: Van Nostrand Reinhold, 1989.

Gunn, Clare A. *Tourism Planning*. New York: Crane, Russak and Company, 1979.

Gunn, Clare A. *Vacationscape, Designing Tourist Regions*, 2nd ed. New York: Van Nostrand Reinhold, 1988.

Howell, David W. *Passport, An Introduction to the Travel and Tourism Industry*. Cincinnati: Southwestern Publishing Company, 1988.

Kane, Robert M., and Vose, Allen D. *Air Transportation*. 8th ed. Dubuque, IA: Kendall/Hunt Publishing Company, 1982.

Lundberg, Donald E. *The Hotel and Restaurant Business*. 5th ed. New York: Van Nostrand Reinhold Company, 1989.

Lundberg, Donald E. and Lundberg, Carolyn B. *International Travel and Tourism*. New York: John Wiley & Sons, 1985.

Mayo, Edward J. and Jarvis, Lance P. *The Psychology of Leisure Travel*. New York: Van Nostrand Reinhold, 1981.

McIntosh, R. W., and Goeldner, C. R. *Tourism: Principles, Practices, Philosophies*. 4th ed. New York: John Wiley and Sons, 1984.

Metelka, Charles J., ed. *The Dictionary of Tourism*. Wheaton, IL: Merton House Publishing Company, 1981.

Miller, Jeffrey. *Legal Aspects of Travel Agency Operation*. Wheaton, IL: Merton House Publishing Company, 1982.

Reilly, Robert T. *Travel and Tourism Marketing Techniques*. Wheaton, IL: Merton House Publishing Company, 1980.

Stevens, Laurence. *Guide to Starting and Operating a Successful Travel Agency*, 2nd ed. Wheaton, Illinois: Delmar Publishers, 1985.

Stevens, Laurence. *Your Career in Travel and Tourism*. Rev. ed. Wheaton, IL: Merton House Publishing Company, 1981.

Superintendent of Documents. *Health Information for International Travel*. Washington, DC: U. S. Government Printing Office.

Swinglehurst, Edmund. *Cook's Tour: The Story of Popular Travel*. New York: Sterling Publishing Company, 1982.

Travel Career Development, 3rd ed. Wellesley, MA: Institute of Certified Travel Agents, 1987.

Waters, Somerset R. *The Big Picture*. New York: The American Association of Travel Agents, published annually. (Order from ASTA, 488 Madison Avenue, New York, NY 10022.)

PERIODICALS

Cornell Hotel and Restaurant Administration Quarterly
Cornell University, School of Hotel Administration
Ithaca, NY 14853

Hotel and Motel Management
Harcourt, Brace and Jovanovich, Inc.
One East First Street
Duluth, MN 55802

Hotels and Restaurants International
Cahners Publishing Company
Division of Reed Holdings Company
270 St. Paul Street
Denver, CO 80206

The Travel Agent
American Traveler Inc.
Two West 46th Street
New York, NY 10036

Travel Trade
Travel Trade Publishing Company
Six East 46th Street
New York, NY 10017

Travel Weekly
Ziff-Davis Publishing Company
Public Transportation and Travel Division
One Park Avenue
New York, NY 10016

INDEX